# PROPERTY AND SOVEREIGNTY

*The chapters in* Property and Sovereignty *offer deep and scholarly examinations of this important topic. But they do so much more. They force the reader to expand his or her horizon about the meaning of property and its relationship to the State. The extraordinary breadth of the book takes us from property issues in fragile states to outer space; from state regulation of property to property rules in virtual worlds; and from issues of property and poverty to issues of property in the arts. The book is an excellent and expansive addition to the literature of property.*

Michael Diamond, Georgetown University Law Center, USA

# Law, Property and Society

Series Editor:
Robin Paul Malloy

The Law, Property and Society series examines property in terms of its ability to foster democratic forms of governance, and to advance social justice. The series explores the legal infrastructure of property in broad terms, encompassing concerns for real, personal, intangible, intellectual and cultural property, as well as looking at property related financial markets. The series is edited by Robin Paul Malloy, and book proposals are welcome from all interested authors.

**Robin Paul Malloy** is E.I. White Chair and Distinguished Professor of Law, and the Kauffman Professor of Entrepreneurship and Innovation at Syracuse University College of Law, USA. He is Director of the Center on Property, Citizenship, and Social Entrepreneurism. He is also Professor of Economics (by courtesy appointment) in the Maxwell School of Citizenship and Public Affairs, Syracuse University. Professor Malloy writes extensively on law and market theory and on real estate transactions and development. He has authored eight books (one now in its third edition and another in its second edition), and edited seven additional books. He has also written more than 30 scholarly articles, and contributed to 12 other books. His recent books include: *Law and Market Economy* (2000, in English and translated into Spanish and Chinese); *Law in a Market Context* (2004); and *Real Estate Transactions* 4th Edition (with James Charles Smith, 2013).

# Property and Sovereignty
## Legal and Cultural Perspectives

*Edited by*

JAMES CHARLES SMITH,
*University of Georgia, USA*

Routledge
Taylor & Francis Group
LONDON AND NEW YORK

First published 2013 by Ashgate Publishing

2 Park Square, Milton Park, Abingdon, Oxfordshire OX14 4RN
52 Vanderbilt Avenue, New York, NY 10017

*Routledge is an imprint of the Taylor & Francis Group, an informa business*

First issued in paperback 2020



**British Library Cataloguing in Publication Data**
A catalogue record for this book is available from the British Library

**The Library of Congress has cataloged the printed edition as follows:**
Property and sovereignty : legal and cultural perspectives / By James Charles Smith.
pages cm. -- (Law, property and society)
Includes bibliographical references and index.
ISBN 978-1-4094-4470-1 (hardback : alk. paper) 1. Property. 2. Real property.
3. Sovereignty. I. Smith, James Charles, 1952- editor of compilation.
K720.P755 2013
346.04--dc23

2013019354

ISBN 978-1-4094-4470-1 (hbk)
ISBN 978-0-367-60109-6 (pbk)

# Contents

## PART IV: REGULATORY PROPERTY



## PART V: THE SHAPING OF PRIVATE LAW

# List of Contributors

**Megan J. Ballard** is Professor at Gonzaga University School of Law. She joined the Gonzaga faculty in 2004 after having taught law for four years at Washburn University School of Law. She currently teaches property, comparative law, wills and trusts, among other courses. Ballard frequently writes and delivers presentations on legal protections for home. She earned her law degree from the University of Wisconsin-Madison, where she also earned a M.A. in Ibero-American Studies and an LL.M. as a Law and Globalization Fellow. Ballard practiced law with Perkins Coie in Seattle, as well as Foley and Lardner in Madison, Wisconsin. She also served as a law clerk for Justice Shirley S. Abrahamson, now Chief Justice of the Wisconsin Supreme Court.

**Alfred L. Brophy** is the Judge John J. Parker Distinguished Professor at the University of North Carolina School of Law. His most recent book is *A Companion to American Legal History* (co-edited with Sally E. Hadden, 2013) and his next book, *University, Court, and Slave: Proslavery Thought in and Jurisprudence in the Old South*, will be published by Oxford University Press in 2014.

**Wian Erlank** is Senior Lecturer on the Law Faculty at North-West University in South Africa. He graduated from Knysna High-school with university exemption and an A average in 1997. He obtained his LLB degree from the University of Stellenbosch in 2002, followed by an LLM in International Trade Law in 2004 and a doctorate in law (LLD) in 2012 for his dissertation entitled *Property in Virtual Worlds*. He was admitted as an advocate of the High Court of South Africa in 2008. After lecturing part time at the University of Stellenbosch in the faculty of Law as well as the Department of Ancient Studies, he was appointed as lecturer in law at North-West University in 2011 where he has taught subjects including land reform, research methodology, property law, and legal skills. Doctor Erlank spent three years as a permanent doctoral candidate and researcher at the South African Research Chair in Property Law and there obtained expert knowledge of national, international and comparative property law as well as the constitutional aspects thereof. His areas of expertise and publications include property law, IT law, cyberlaw, social media law, virtual property law, and space law. He has published in these areas and regularly presents papers at both national (South Africa) and international conferences.

**Daniel Fitzpatrick** is Professor of Law at the Australian National University and a member of the Global Faculty at New York University School of Law. He has written widely on property theory in a law and development context, with a particular focus on natural disasters and armed conflicts. He was the UN's land rights adviser in post-conflict East Timor (2000) and post-tsunami Indonesia (2005–2006). In 2007 he won the Hart Article Prize from the UK Socio-Legal Studies Association. He has published in the *Yale Law Journal*, the *Law and Society Review*, and the *Yale Journal of International Law*. Dr Fitzpatrick is the primary author of the UN's guidelines on addressing land issues after natural disasters. He has been a Visiting Professor at the University of Muenster (2002), a Visiting Professor at the National University of Singapore (2006–2009), and a Distinguished Visitor at the University of Toronto (2007).

**Steven Freeland** is Professor of International Law at the University of Western Sydney, "Marie Curie Visiting Professor" at the iCourts Centre of Excellence for International Courts, Denmark, Visiting Professor at the University of Copenhagen and the University of Vienna, and a Member of Faculty of the London Institute of Space Policy and Law. He has also been a Visiting Professional within the Appeals Chamber at the International Criminal Court. Among other appointments, he is a Member of the Space Law Committee of the International Law Association, and a Director of the International Institute of Space Law. He sits on the Editorial Board of the *Australian Journal of Human Rights*, the *Australian International Law Journal*, the *Annals of Air and Space Law* and the *Space Law Review*, and is a member of the Advisory Board of the *Asian Journal of Air and Space Law* and the *Journal of Philosophy of International Law*, as well as a series of books entitled *Studies in Space Law*. He is also Co-Editor of the book series *Annotated Leading Cases of the International Criminal Tribunals*. He has authored over 300 publications on various aspects of International Law, and has been invited to present conference papers and keynote speeches in over 35 countries.

**Daniel J.H. Greenwood** is Professor of Law at Hofstra University School of Law. He previously taught at the S.J. Quinney College of Law at the University of Utah, where he held the position of S.J. Quinney Professor of Law. He received his A.B. magna cum laude from Harvard College and pursued graduate studies in political science at the Hebrew University of Jerusalem for two years. He is a graduate of Yale Law School, where he was an editor of the *Yale Law Journal*. After graduating, Daniel Greenwood clerked for U.S. District Court Judge Richard Owen in New York and then joined the litigation section of Cleary, Gottlieb, Steen & Hamilton in New York City. Professor Greenwood's research interests lie in the structure and rights of business organizations and other artificial and natural groups; the intersection of democratic theory and corporate law; and problems of group rights in an individualist democracy. He has published numerous law review articles, book chapters and popular opinion pieces on corporate law, corporate speech rights, and the role of corporations in politics, as well as on minority religious rights and related topics.

**Alexandra R. Harrington** is Visiting Assistant Professor of Law at Albany Law School, where she teaches courses relating to public international law and legal profession. Her publications address a variety of fields relating to international law, including environmental law, climate change, natural resources regulation, international organizations, human rights, children's rights, international trade law, corporate social responsibility, and criminal law, as well as domestic fields such as constitutional law and military law. She routinely presents her works at domestic and international conferences, including a United Nations Academic Impact in Action panel. She also serves as a member of the Global Health Committee of the Global Health Center at the SUNY Albany School of Public Health. In addition, Professor Harrington is a Doctor of Civil Law Candidate at the McGill University Faculty of Law and is affiliated with the Center for International Sustainable Development Law, the Centre for Human Rights and Legal Pluralism and the Institute for Comparative Law at McGill University. She has served as a professor at the University of Montreal Centre d'Etudes et de Recherches Internationales summer programs and as a Consultant to the Commission for Environmental Cooperation of the North American Agreement on Environmental Cooperation.

**Larissa Katz** is Associate Professor of Law at University of Toronto. She has undergraduate degrees in philosophy and law from the University of Alberta and graduate degrees in law from the Yale Law School. After law school, Professor Katz clerked for the late Justice Charles D. Gonthier at the Supreme Court of Canada and worked at Sullivan & Cromwell LLP (NY) in the litigation department. Professor Katz teaches and writes about property law and theory. Her work is published in the *Yale Law Journal*, *University of Pennsylvania Law Review*, *Legal Theory*, *Jurisprudence*, *University of Toronto Law Journal*, *McGill Law Journal* and the *Canadian Journal of Law and Jurisprudence*.

**Michael B. Kent, Jr.** is Associate Professor of Law at Campbell University Law School. He previously served as Associate Professor at John Marshall Law School in Atlanta, Georgia and as a visiting faculty member at Stetson University College of Law. He teaches real property, environmental law, land use regulation, and state and local government law. He is the author of several articles, most of which deal with eminent domain, regulatory takings, and land use issues. Prior to his academic career, Professor Kent practiced with the law firm of Tisinger, Tisinger, Vance & Greer in Carrollton, Georgia, and served as law clerk to Judge Emmett Ripley Cox of the United States Court of Appeals for the Eleventh Circuit and to Judge J. Owen Forrester of the United States District Court for the Northern District of Georgia. He is a graduate of the University of Alabama and the University of Georgia School of Law.

**Anna Elizabeth Lineberger** is an associate attorney at Bryan Cave in Denver, Colorado, where she works in the Private Client practice group. She received a JD from the University of North Carolina in 2011 and served as a law clerk for the U.S. Bankruptcy Court in Raleigh, North Carolina.

**Lance McMillian** is Associate Professor at Atlanta's John Marshall Law School. His diverse array of work has appeared in publications such as the *North Carolina Law Review*, the *Wisconsin Law Review*, the *Washington and Lee Law Review*, and the *Wisconsin Law Review*. He has also been cited by a number of federal and state courts for his analysis of class action lawsuits. In his free time, he enjoys strumming the guitar, banging the drums, and reading Russian literature. Professor McMillian is married to Judge Carla Wong McMillian of the Georgia Court of Appeals, who finished two spots ahead of him in their law school class.

**David Ray Papke** earned his A.B. from Harvard College, J.D. from the Yale Law School, and Ph.D. in American Studies from the University of Michigan. He has held faculty positions at the University of Illinois, Indiana University-Purdue University at Indianapolis, and Yale University. In 1986–87, he was a Fulbright Professor at Tamkang University in Taiwan, and he has lectured in Denmark, Nevis-St. Kitts, South Korea, The Bahamas, Uganda, and Vietnam. Since 2002, he has been a Professor of Law at Marquette University, where he teaches American Legal History, Family Law, Property, and a range of interdisciplinary courses and seminars involving law and the humanities. Professor Papke has a special scholarly interest in the role of law in American culture, and he is the author of the following books: *Framing the Criminal: Crime, Cultural Work, and the Loss of Critical Perspective* (1987), *Narrative and the Legal Discourse: Storytelling and the Law* (1991), *Heretics in the Temple: Americans Who Reject the Nation's Legal Faith* (1998), and *The Pullman Case: The Clash of Labor and Capital in Industrial America* (1999). With Christine Corcos, et al., he has also published *Law and Popular Culture: Text, Notes, and Questions* (LexisNexis, 2007; second edition, 2012), the first comprehensive textbook concerning the relationship of law and popular culture.

**Malla Pollack** is an attorney and the co-author of *Callmann on Unfair Competition, Trademarks & Monopolies* (Thomson-Reuters 4th edition). Her numerous articles and amicus briefs have supported the public domain in all forms of intellectual property.

**David S. Rosettenstein** was Professor of Law at Quinnipiac University School of Law, where he taught courses in family law, labor law, and remedies. Beginning in 1981 he taught as Assistant Professor of Law at the University of Bridgeport, where he played a key role in helping that law school forge its affiliation with Quinnipiac, which went into effect in 1992. He was the author of more than

40 books and articles and books. Professor Rosettenstein passed away on February 19, 2013, after completing work on the chapter published in this volume.

**James Charles Smith** is the John Byrd Martin Professor of Law at the University of Georgia, where he has taught since 1984. He presently teaches property, real estate transactions, secured transactions, housing law, and other upper-level courses. Smith, a graduate of Saint Olaf College and the University of Texas School of Law, practiced law for four years with the law firm of Baker Botts in Houston, Texas. He is author of five books (*Property: Cases and Materials; Real Estate Transactions: Problems, Cases, and Materials; Federal Taxation of Real Estate; Neighboring Property Owners; and Contracts and Conveyances of Real Property*) and numerous articles dealing with commercial law, lending, property, and taxation. He has run the Boston Marathon five times.

# Introduction: Property and Sovereignty in the Twenty-First Century

James Charles Smith

This book explores the relationships between property and the concept of sovereignty from a number of different perspectives. In property discourse, sovereignty has a dual meaning. First, the term "sovereignty" has a political meaning, referring to the nature of state sovereignty and the controls developed and administered by a government or a governmental entity. The sovereign defines property rights, determines who owns property entitlements, decides how to protect such entitlements, and ultimately enforces its decisions by force. This conception of sovereignty, often identified as "political sovereignty," focuses attention on the roles played by government in establishing property regimes. Scholars dealing with the connections between property rights and sovereignty in this sense sometimes emphasize that property is simply whatever the state chooses to make it (a positive law view). Other scholars, however, address the authority of sovereign states to define and regulate property from other theoretical perspectives, including natural law, which posit limitations on the state's power to define, modify, and abolish property.

The second modern meaning of the term "sovereignty" goes beyond the nature of governments and the roles they play. It refers to the power and control held by the owners of private property, which they are able to exercise over other individuals. Property confers power. Private property structures relationships not only between individuals, but also between organizations and individuals. This concept is sometimes called "owner sovereignty." This idea is generally attributed to Morris Cohen, who explored the idea that property rights are delegations of sovereign authority in a famous essay, Cohen, *Property and Sovereignty*, 13 Cornell L.Q. 8 (1927).

The book begins in Part I with a set of chapters exploring the evolution of property rights in fragile and conflict-affected nation states. In Chapter 1, Megan Ballard explores the extent to which post-conflict restoration of property rights might require a sovereign to relax legal norms. Armed conflict causing widespread displacement often occurs where formal property registration systems, if they exist, are either incomplete or otherwise unreliable. Moreover, most people fleeing from their homes do not take records with them to prove rights to the properties they abandon. The lack of property documentation poses obstacles to implementing the remedies for forced eviction required under international law once the conflict is resolved. To provide restitution or compensation to victims, Ballard calls for the sovereign emerging after a conflict to adopt flexible standards for a claimant's proof of pre-conflict property interests. In particular, relaxed evidentiary standards to match homes and land with displaced persons are often appropriate.

The examination of the relationships between property and sovereignty in states and societies undergoing stress continues in Chapter 2 with Daniel Fitzpatrick's case study of East Timor, which became independent from Portugal in 1974 and subsequently suffered from persistent military conflict and famine. He reviews the body of literature asserting a normative preference for simple legal rules of property, to reduce transaction costs for owners, sellers, and buyers of property, and finds that it fails to account for the development of land law in East Timor. A paramount objective is the avoidance of violent conflicts over scarce resources. Fitzpatrick explains how the incentives for social and political ordering, in systems emerging from violent conflict, have led to the emergence of simple default rules of state title to land, and complex rules bearing higher information costs relating to private rights to land.

Alexandra Harrington's chapter concludes Part I by asking whether a sovereign state that loses its territory due to environmental catastrophes, such as rising sea levels, should have the right to acquire replacement territory elsewhere. The problem is particularly acute for small island developing states, such as Papua New Guinea. She explores the origins, parameters, and limitations of a right to territory and discusses its implications for states and for the international system as a whole. Based on the importance of territory, beginning with Roman law and continuing into modern international law, Harrington argues for the recognition of a limited right for states that are recognized as sovereign by the international community.

Part II of the book offers two views of sovereign regulation of property in new worlds. First, in Chapter 4, Steven Freeland considers property rights in outer space, explicating the international legal principles that regulate the exploration and use of outer space. The sources of law include treaties sponsored by the United Nations, national legislation, and customary law. A fundamental norm, known as the non-appropriation principle, puts outer space, including the moon and other celestial bodies, off limits to ownership rights and sovereign or territorial claims. The principle is well established with respect to sovereign claims. Freeland explores its application to claims made by private entities, which are likely to become increasingly important as space technology advances, concluding that private claims are also properly barred.

Like the discovery and exploration of physical worlds beyond planet Earth, the invention and occupation of virtual worlds raises new questions about the nature and scope of property rights, and their regulation by sovereigns. Virtual worlds, in which online environments are populated by players who interact and transact with one another, have become a highly popular type of video gaming. Wian Erlank, in Chapter 5, explores issues related to the control and governance of virtual worlds. Developers of virtual worlds function as sovereigns by imposing tight limits on players' acquisition of property rights. Sources of virtual world law include the program code for the virtual world, which serves as immutable law, the end user license agreement (EULA), and customary law that players create amongst themselves without the influence of the developer.

Part III of the book turns to the arts to illuminate the relationships between property, sovereignty, and culture. This part begins with a review by Michael Kent and Lance McMillian of the interconnections between property and sovereignty displayed the HBO television series *Deadwood*, which aired from 2004 to 2006. Deadwood began as a lawless South Dakota gold mining camp, with no established property laws or legal institutions. The wealth created by the gold, and represented by the gold claims, led to norms that protected the miners' gold claims and the right to assign those claims. Kent and McMillian note that the development of property-like expectations in turn fostered the development of political sovereignty reflected in a bona fide town government, supported by citizens and social institutions. *Deadwood* is a fictional rendition of the familiar story of the birth of property rights, leading to the rise and recognition of a state bearing the accoutrements of modern government.

Anna Lineberger and Alfred Brophy provide the second portrayal of property and sovereignty in the arts. In Chapter 7 they analyze the landscape art that appeared in two volumes, both titled *American Scenery* but prepared by different authors, in 1840 and 1852. The key elements of the artwork run from natural scenes and wilderness to rude huts, steamboats, bridges, railroads, manicured gardens, beautiful homes, and cities. They connect those elements to ideas about the progress of civilization, reflected in statements by lawyers and judges about how technological progress (including law) allowed Americans to take control of nature and improve open it. Lineberger and Brophy also illuminate the linkage between the theme of progress and rhetoric of sovereignty and dominion over the land. Art reflects ideas of pre-Civil War Americans about the ways that property law and other "technologies" allowed Americans to control and improve upon nature and thus fulfil the mission of empire.

In Part IV of the book, two chapters focus on regulatory property, for which the government as regulator asserts control over a resource to further its ends. In Chapter 8, David Papke addresses the relationship between ideology and the government regulation of housing through its zoning power. He explains the development of the term "underclass" during the 1970s as a label for the urban poor, connoting sympathy for those citizens and a commitment to welfare and job creation programs that might aid them. One avenue was reflected in judicial decisions ruling the suburban exclusion of the "underclass" through zoning was unlawful "exclusionary zoning." Papke then traces a dramatic change in the tide, with the notion of the "underclass" first turned against the urban poor and then dropped almost completely from policy-making and political discourses. Programs designed to provide the urban poor with entitlements and jobs fell by the wayside, and the courts concomitantly abandoned their efforts to stop exclusionary zoning by the suburbs.

In the second chapter dealing with regulatory property, Malla Pollack analyzes "governmental marks," which are trademark claims asserted by sovereign entities. Two examples she discusses at length are tourism marketing programs developed by New York City and Las Vegas, which seek to prevent private businesses from selling unlicensed souvenirs decorated with trademarks referring to their respective cities. Pollack argues against allowing trademark rights in governmental marks. She finds that most governmental marks lack a basic requirement for trademark-status; they do not signify one unique source. But even when commercial practice had induced a substantial percentage of the public to perceive a government to be the unique source, she contends that legal recognition of the government as the source is incompatible with liberal, representative government and decreases citizen-control of government.

The final part of the book, Part V, explores sovereign shaping of private property entitlements to achieve instrumental ends. It begins with Larissa Katz, who in Chapter 10 challenges the mainstream moral critique of the law of adverse possession that labels adverse possessors as undeserving "land thieves." Finding the analogy of adverse possessor to land thief misleading, she claims that there is a much closer analogy between adverse possession and revolution or, more precisely, a bloodless *coup d'état*. Just as recognizing an existing government's actual authority, regardless of its origin, solves moral problems that stem from the absence of a responsible regulator (this she calls an "agendaless object"), recognizing an adverse possessor's claim solves the problems stemming from an inability to identify a present, responsible owner. The morality of adverse possession rests on positivist strategy of ratifying the claims to authority of a squatter without regard to the substantive merits of her agenda or her personal virtue.

Next, Daniel Greenwood explains how the law enables corporations to yield sovereign-like power over employees and other citizens. Labelling modern corporations as "semi-sovereign," he criticizes our modern conception of corporations as private entities, which merit protection against the government, rather than as government-like entities, from whose excesses citizens need protection. In calling for a reversal of this ideology, Greenwood notes that the ancient conception of corporations was different. Prior to the Industrial Revolution, it was universally understood that corporations—such as the Knights Templar, the British East India Company, the Massachusetts Bay Company, and universities—were sovereign-like, having the authority to make law for their members, and therefore subject to extensive regulation to protect their members and other persons.

David Rosettenstein, in Chapter 12, considers the interplay between status, contract, and sovereign interests in the context of Roman family law. Modern law throughout the world has struggled with identifying an appropriate vision for dealing with the distribution of assets on divorce. Many jurisdictions have protocols that depart from the traditional approaches adopted by property lawyers for identifying proprietary interests. At one end of the spectrum in the United States are the status imposed regimes of community property and equitable distribution. At the other is a universe notionally regulated by contract. European civil law systems contemplate property ownership regimes which may dictate ownership both during the marriage and on its termination, or may even shift ownership from formal title during the marriage to contingent entitlement on its termination. Rosettenstein illuminates the choices available for modern divorce law through a detailed evaluation of the Roman law concept of *dos*, which was a bride's property contribution made pursuant to contract between the bride's *paterfamilias* (extended family) and the groom or his *paterfamilias*.

# PART I
# Fragile Nation States

# Chapter 1
# Relaxing Legal Norms to Restore Rights to Homes and Land in the Aftermath of War

Megan J. Ballard[1]

When sovereign states define property rights within their borders, they necessarily establish rules and procedures that claimants must follow to prove those rights. Such rules and procedures are often formal in nature. This chapter explores the extent to which post-conflict restitution of property might require a sovereign to relax formal legal norms related to proving property rights. Armed conflict causing widespread displacement often occurs where formal land registration systems, if they exist, are either incomplete or otherwise unreliable. Moreover, most people fleeing from violence do not take records with them to prove rights to the homes and land they abandon. This lack of property documentation can pose an obstacle to implementing legal remedies for the human rights violation of forced eviction once the conflict is resolved. To provide restitution or compensation to victims of forced eviction, the regime emerging after a conflict will likely need to allow flexibility in proving a person's pre-war property interests. Departing from traditional property norms might appear to impair the rule of law in a post-conflict society. To the contrary, this chapter suggests that relaxing the proof required to establish property rights actually enhances the rule of law in some contexts, when placed within the larger framework of transitional justice initiatives.

Part 1 of this chapter begins with a description of the global problem of displacement caused by armed conflict and the solution of voluntary return to a person's country or area of origin. This return solution, however, creates the problem of sustainability; displaced populations returned to their countries or communities need security, opportunities, services, and infrastructure in order to rebuild their lives. This sustainability problem gives rise to the partial solution of post-conflict property restitution. Part 2 of this chapter explores the legal framework supporting restitution of pre-war property rights. Post-conflict property restitution, however, generates problems of proof. When war destroys evidence, families forcibly displaced from their homes by armed conflict face

1 The author is grateful to Gonzaga University for a sabbatical award and a grant from the Gonzaga University Research Council, and to the J. William Fulbright Foreign Scholarship Board for a grant supporting some of the research in this chapter. Many thanks also to Professor Linda Rusch for her helpful comments on drafts, and to my research assistant, Michael Vander Giessen.

significant barriers in proving rights to the homes and land they abandoned. Part 3 explores these evidentiary problems and Part 4 considers how international mass claims programs have managed such obstacles. While the rules governing the administration of evidence in international mass claims programs attempt to address this problem by easing a victim's burden of proof, this approach may not be sufficient in a context void of documentary evidence. In Part 5, this chapter proposes the use of community-based evidence, that is, evidence gathered from a victim's former neighbors and community, to help fill the documentation gap. Reliance on community-based evidence to allocate property rights creates tension with established property rules, but is justified by the norms of transitional justice, as explained in Part 6 of this chapter.

Questions of sovereignty linger behind many aspects of post-conflict property restitution. International law instructs states to avoid forced evictions[2] and emerging international standards identify property restitution as the preferred remedy for unlawful forced evictions.[3] These doctrines may contribute to an "international property law" system under which international law affects the property rights of citizens of sovereign states.[4] The very idea of regulating conduct vis-à-vis property that occurs entirely within the boundaries of one nation can be viewed as inconsistent with sovereignty. Enforcement of these doctrines implicates sovereignty as well, whether within the context of a civil conflict that caused forced evictions or an international conflict with the same result. Indeed, the existence and enforcement of international legal standards has long raised fundamental questions of state sovereignty.[5] The narrower issue related to relaxing formal property norms to adequately remedy forced eviction overlaps with general international law and sovereignty concerns when a sovereign emerging after a war establishes a post-conflict property restitution program to comply with international legal principles.

---

2 U.N. Comm. on Econ., Soc. & Cultural Rts., General Comment No. 7: The Right to Adequate Housing: Forced Evictions ¶ 1, U.N. Doc. E/C.12/1997/4 (May 20, 1997). *See also* U.N. Comm'n on Hum. Rts., Forced Evictions, Res. 1993/77 (March 10, 1993) (affirming that "the practice of forced eviction constitutes a gross violation of human rights, in particular the right to adequate housing").

3 *See infra* Part 2.

4 John G. Sprankling, *The Emergence of International Property Law*, 90 N.C. L. Rev. 461, 468–70 (2012).

5 *E.g.*, *The Schooner Exch. v. McFaddon*, 11 U.S. (7 Cranch) 116, 116–17, 135–7 (1812); Jack Goldsmith & Daryl Levinson, *Law for States: International Law, Constitutional Law, Public Law*, 122 Harv. L. Rev. 1791, 1845–52 (2009); Helen Stacy, *Relational Sovereignty*, 55 Stan. L. Rev. 2029, 2030, 2043–4 (2003).

## Part 1. The Factual Context

By the end of 2012, the United Nations High Commissioner for Refugees (UNHCR) counted 45.2 million people forcibly displaced from their homes by conflict and persecution.[6] Over 7.6 million of these people were newly displaced during 2012.[7] Included in the total count are more than 15 million refugees[8] and 28.8 million internally displaced persons (IDPs), [9] many of whom have been uprooted by armed conflict.[10]

International law governing refugees and the protection of IDPs supports three "durable solutions" to displacement: voluntary return, resettlement to another place, and integration into a host community.[11] Of these solutions, the international community generally prefers return to a person's country or area of origin as the most sustainable option.[12]

---

6 U.N. High Comm'r for Refugees, *Global Trends 2012*, at 5 (2012) [hereinafter *UNHCR*].

7 *Id.* at 2

8 The United Nations Refugee Convention defines a refugee as any person who:

> owing to well-founded fear of being persecuted for reasons of race, religion, nationality, membership of a particular social group or political opinion, is outside the country of his nationality and is unable or, owing to such fear, is unwilling to avail himself of the protection of that country; or who, not having a nationality and being outside the country of his former habitual residence, is unable or, owing to such fear, is unwilling to return to it.

G.A. Res. 429(V) (Dec. 14, 1950);G.A. Res. 2198 (XXI) (Dec. 16, 1967).

9 *Id.* Internally displaced persons (IDPs) are:

> [P]ersons or groups of persons who have been forced or obliged to flee or to leave their homes or places of habitual residence, in particular as a result of, or in order to avoid the effects of armed conflict, situations of generalised violence, violations of human rights or natural or human-made disasters, and who have not crossed an internationally recognized State border.

U.N. Econ. & Soc. Council, Comm'n on Human Rights, *Guiding Principles on Internal Displacement,* Intro. ¶ 2, U.N. Doc. E/CN.4/1998/53/Add.2 (Feb. 11, 1998) [hereinafter *Internal Displacement Principles*].

10 *UNHCR, supra* note 6, at 5.

11 *Internal Displacement Principles, supra* note 9, Principle 28; U.N. High Comm'r for Refugees, *Framework for Durable Solutions for Refugees and Persons of Concern* 5–6 (2003). Historically, this right to return has not implied a right to return one's original home. Rhodri C. Williams, Int'l Ctr. for Transitional Justice, *The Contemporary Right to Property Restitution in the Context of Transitional Justice* 7 (2007) [hereinafter Williams, *Transitional Justice*].

12 Richard Black, *Return of Refugees: Retrospect and Prospect, in* Palestinian Refugee Repatriation: Global Perspectives 23, 28 (Michael Dumper ed., 2006) (noting that many refugees aspire to return); Giulia Paglione, *Individual Property Restitution: From Deng to Pinheiro – and the Challenges Ahead,* 20 Int'l J. Refugee L. 391, 403 (2008).

Communities and nations hosting displaced populations have only relatively recently emphasized return. After World War II, Western nations stressed integration into asylum communities or resettlement elsewhere, assuming that return was not feasible for refugees fleeing from communist regimes.[13] When the cold war began to thaw in the 1980s, United Nations (UN) agencies shifted strategy, maintaining that refugees from communist countries should return to promote post-conflict peace and development.[14] The momentum behind returning refugees to their countries of origin was fueled, in part, by a desire to counter an increase in migration from poor to rich nations.[15] In 2012, over 2 million displaced people were able to return to their countries or communities of origin.[16]

Despite its favored status, the solution of voluntary return is not in and of itself a complete solution to the problem of displacement. Populations returning to their countries or communities need shelter, jobs, education, and security, among other things.[17] Without minimal protections and resources, return may not be sustainable.[18] To these barriers associated with return, many in the international community find a partial solution in restoring property rights to a pre-war home. The idea is that displaced people will be more likely to return if they regain their former homes and land through a property restitution program.[19]

Restitution generally is a remedy intended to restore a person to his or her original position, prior to a loss or injury.[20] Restitution related to a loss of, or injury to, real property typically can involve monetary compensation, the return of real

13 Patricia Weiss Fagen, *UNHCR and Repatriation, in* Palestinian Refugee Repatriation: Global Perspectives 41, 43 (Michael Dumper ed., 2006).

14 *Id.* at 46.

15 Eric Rosand, *The Right to Return Under International Law Following Mass Dislocation: The Bosnia Precedent?,* 19 Mich. J. Int'l L. 1091, 1119–20 (1998).

16 *UNHCR, supra* note 6, at 6. There is no data on the number of returnees who were able to return to the specific home from which they had been displaced.

17 Rhodri C. Williams, *Post-Conflict Property Restitution and Refugee Return in Bosnia and Herzegovina: Implications for International Standard-setting and Practice,* 37 N.Y.U. J. Int'l L. & Pol. 441, 449 (2005) [hereinafter Williams, *Bosnia and Herzegovina*].

18 Williams, *Transitional Justice, supra* note 11, at 6.

19 The restoration of property rights does not guarantee that a displaced person will return to their home. Williams, *Bosnia and Herzegovina, supra* note 17, at 445 (noting that, while restitution was a "vital precondition for the actual return" of displaced people to Bosnia, many who regained their property rights chose not to return).

20 In the context of a violation of human rights or humanitarian law, restitution should restore the situation that existed prior to the violations. G.A. Res. 60/147, *Basic Principles and Guidelines on the Right to a Remedy and Reparation for Victims of Gross Violations of International Human Rights Law and Serious Violations of International Humanitarian Law* ¶ 19, U.N. Doc. A/RES/60/147 (Mar. 21, 2006) [hereinafter *Reparations Principles*]. *See also Tull v. United States*, 481 U.S. 412, 424 (1987) (defining restitution as a remedy designed to restore the status quo ante).

property wrongfully taken, or the provision of substantially equivalent property.[21] In a post-war context, however, restitution most often refers to the actual return of assets unlawfully seized.[22] The restitution of homes discussed in this chapter means the return of the very home from which a person was displaced.

## Part 2. Legal Framework of Restitution

There is no certain and general right to property restitution under international law for people displaced by conflict from their homes and land.[23] There is, however, an emerging—albeit disputed—entitlement to post-conflict property restitution.[24]

Many scholars and human rights practitioners identify the UN's *Principles on Housing and Property Restitution for Refugees and Displaced Persons* as a significant step towards solidifying a legal right to post-conflict property restitution.[25] In 2005, a sub-commission of the UN Commission on Human Rights

---

21 Restatement (Third) of Restitution and Unjust Enrichment § 1 cmts. a, e (2011).

22 Hans van Houtte, Bart Delmartino & Iasson Yi, *Post-War Restoration of Property Rights Under International Law* 250 (2008) (discussing restitution following an international conflict).

23 Megan J. Ballard, *Post-conflict Property Restitution: Flawed Legal and Theoretical Foundations*, 28 Berkeley J. Int'l L. 462, 479–80 (2010); Malcolm Langford & Khulekani Moyo, *Right, Remedy or Rhetoric? Land Restitution in International Law*, 28 Nordic J. of Hum. Rts. 143, 174 (2010); Paglione, *supra* note 12, at 393; Williams, *Transitional Justice*, *supra* note 11, at 8.

24 Susan Breau, *The International Law Rights to Home and Homeland, in* The Idea of Home in Law: Displacement and Dispossession 165, 194 (Lorna Fox O'Mahoney & James A. Sweeney, eds., 2011); Williams, *Transitional Justice*, *supra* note 11, at 8. Nonetheless, the Parliamentary Assembly of the Council of Europe suggested that member states take the Pinheiro Principles into account when resolving post-conflict property issues of refugees and IDPs. Eur. Parl. Ass. Res. 1708, ¶ 9 (Jan. 28, 2010), available at http://assembly.coe.int/main.asp?Link=/documents/adoptedtext/ta10/eres1708.htm. In addition, the Constitutional Court of Colombia has declared a binding right to property restitution, expressly adopting the UN Principles on Housing and Property Restitution for Refugees and Displaced Persons, among other soft law norms. Corte Constitucional, Oct. 5, 2007, *Rosmira Serrano Quintero v. Agencia Presidencial para la Acción Social y la Cooperación Internacional Acción Social*, [T-821/07 (Colom.), available at http://www.corteconstitucional.gov.co/relatoria/2007/T-821-07.htm.]

25 U.N. Econ. & Soc. Council, Sub-Comm'n on the Promotion & Prot. of Human Rts., Res. 2005/21, *Housing and Property Restitution for Refugees and Displaced Persons*, U.N. Doc. E/CN.4/Sub2/RES/2005/21 (Aug. 11, 2005) [hereinafter *Pinheiro Principles*]. *See, e.g.*, Anneke Smit, *The Property Rights of Refugees and Internally Displaced Persons: Beyond Restitution* 26 (2012) [hereinafter *Property Rights*]; Miriam J. Anderson, *The UN Principles on Housing and Property Restitution for Refugees and Displaced Persons (The Pinheiro Principles): Suggestions for Improved Applicability*, 24 J. Refugee Stud. 304, 304–305 (2011); Jose-Maria Arraiza & Massimo Moratti, *Getting the Property Questions Right:*

formally endorsed these Principles, commonly named the Pinheiro Principles after the UN Special Rapporteur on Housing and Property Restitution for Refugees and Internally Displaced Persons, Paulo Sérgio Pinheiro.[26] The Pinheiro Principles propose a legal framework, as well as administrative and enforcement options, for property restitution processes. One key recommendation is the restoration of housing, land, and property, or compensation if restitution is impossible, to people unlawfully deprived of their former property.[27]

Moreover, the Pinheiro Principles advise states to "prioritize restitution as the preferred remedy to displacement and as a key element of restorative justice," but they do not define "restitution."[28] An earlier report by Special Rapporteur Pinheiro, however, states that "restitution refers specifically to the return of arbitrarily or illegally confiscated housing or property to the original owner(s) or right holders."[29]

The resolution of the war in Bosnia-Herzegovina helped to shape the Pinheiro Principles.[30] In 1995, the Dayton Accords ending the hostilities established the

---

*Legal Policy Dilemmas in Post-Conflict Property Restitution in Kosovo*, (1999–2009), 21 Int'l J. of Refugee L. 421, 423 (2009); Breau, *supra* note 24, at 188; Paglione, *supra* note 12, at 391; Anneke Rachel Smit, *Housing and Property Restitution and IDP Return in Kosovo,* 44 Int'l Migration 63, 63 & 65 (2006); Dan E. Stigall, *Refugees and Legal Reform in Iraq: The Iraqi Civil Code, International Standards for Treatment of Displaced Persons, and the Art of Attainable Solutions*, 34 Rutgers L. Rec. 1, 3–4 (2009); Rhodri C. Williams, *Guiding Principle 29 and the Right to Restitution*, Forced Migration Rev., Dec. 2008, at 23, http://www.fmreview.org/FMRpdfs/GP10/GP10.pdf.

26 While the Pinheiro Principles specifically address displacement from "former homes, lands, properties or places of habitual residence," this chapter uses the term "property" to refer to the same. *Pinheiro Principles, supra* note 25, ¶ 1.1. The Preliminary Report to the Pinheiro Principles explains that the phrase "'housing and property' refers to housing and real property, including land." U.N. Econ. & Soc. Council, Sub-Comm'n on the Promotion & Prot. of Human Rts., *Preliminary Report of the Special Rapporteur, Paulo Sérgio Pinheiro, Submitted in Accordance with Sub-Commission Resolution 2002/7*, ¶ 4, U.N. Doc. E/CN.4/Sub.2/2003/11 (June 16, 2003) [hereinafter *Preliminary Report*]. It goes on to justify this definition on the basis that housing and real property restitution have received more attention from the international community than other types of property restitution because of the role of housing in securing the right to voluntary return of refugees and IDPs to their homes of origin. *Id.*

27 *Pinheiro Principles*, *supra* note 25, ¶¶ 1.2 and 2.1. Principle 21.1 allows compensation when a displaced person "knowingly and voluntarily" chooses compensation in lieu of restitution. *Id.* ¶ 21.1.

28 *Id.* ¶ 2.2.

29 *Preliminary Report*, *supra* note 26, ¶ 9.

30 Both the Working Paper and the Preliminary Report preceding the final Pinheiro Principles reflect the influence that the Bosnia experience had on crafting the Pinheiro Principles. The 2002 Working Paper, for example, includes a section on "Issues Requiring Further Study" expressly referencing problems encountered in Bosnia, such as the lack of independent local judicial systems. U.N. Econ. & Soc. Council, Sub-Comm'n on the

right of return for all refugees and displaced persons.[31] Moreover, the agreement set forth a specific right of restitution to pre-war property and established a quasi-international commission to facilitate the remedial program.[32] The institutions and procedures established to enforce these restitution rights represented the most comprehensive and systematized post-conflict restitution efforts ever implemented.[33]

In addition to the restitution experience in Bosnia, the Pinheiro Principles rest on at least four normative precursors: the right of refugees and IDPs to voluntarily return to their countries and areas of origin, the right to adequate housing, the duty of states to assist IDPs in recovering property abandoned because of displacement, and the right to a remedy for gross human rights violations. Various international treaties, declarations and other documents establish these first two norms—the rights to voluntary return and adequate housing.[34] These instruments, however,

---

Promotion & Prot. of Human Rts., *Working Paper of the Special Rapporteur, Paulo Sérgio Pinheiro, Submitted in Accordance with Sub-Commission Decision 2001/122,* ¶ 44, U.N. Doc. E/CN.4/Sub.2/2002/17 (June 12, 2002) [hereinafter *Working Paper*]; secondary occupation of abandoned housing, *Id.* ¶ 46; and abandonment laws implemented during the conflict that purported to terminate the property rights of persons who vacated their housing, *Id.* ¶ 49. The 2003 Preliminary Report includes a section reviewing property restitution in Bosnia to identify "best practices" and "common obstacles" in property restitution programs. *Preliminary Report*, *supra* note 26, ¶¶ 21–9. Notably, this review states that the Peace Accords ending the conflict in Bosnia "established principles which are of fundamental importance to this discussion." *Id.* ¶ 25.

31 General Framework Agreement on Peace in Bosnia-Herzegovina, Bosn.-Herz., Annex 7, art. 1, ¶ 1, 35 I.L.M. 75 (Dec. 14, 1995) [hereinafter Dayton Accords], *reprinted in* Housing, Land, and Property Restitution Rights of Refugees and Displaced Persons: Laws, Cases, and Materials 31 (Scott Leckie, ed., 2007) (stating in art. 1, ¶ 1 that "All refugees and displaced persons have the right freely to return to their homes of origin. They shall have the right to have restored to them property of which they were deprived in the course of hostilities since 1991 and to be compensated for any property that cannot be restored to them").

32 Dayton Accords, *supra* note 31.

33 Paglione, *supra* note 12, at 2 (asserting that the Dayton Accords, ending the hostilities in Bosnia, represented "the international community's first comprehensive attempt to enforce individual property restitution rights through the setting up of formal institutions and claims procedures"). While other states have established mechanisms for the return of property as part of negotiated peace agreements, no effort has been as far reaching and systematized as that in Bosnia and Herzegovina. Williams, *Bosnia and Herzegovina*, *supra* note 17, at 443.

34 Smit, *Property Rights*, *supra* note 25, at 9–33 (including a thorough review of the development of the right to return to a home of origin and to restitution of pre-conflict property).

fall short of identifying a right to return to a particular home.[35] Nonetheless, both influenced the Pinheiro Principles.[36]

The duty to protect property abandoned by IDPs is established in the UN Commission on Human Rights' 1998 *Guiding Principles on Internal Displacement* (Internal Displacement Principles).[37] The Pinheiro Principle's *travaux préparatoires* (preparatory works or drafting history) quote this document, highlighting the duty to assist IDPs who have returned, or those who have been resettled elsewhere, "to recover, to the extent possible, their property and possessions which they left behind or were dispossessed of upon their displacement."[38]

Finally, the UN General Assembly pronounced a right to a remedy for human rights violations in the 2005 Basic Principles and Guidelines on the Right to a Remedy and Reparation for Violations of International Human Rights and Humanitarian Law (Reparations Principles). These entitle victims of gross human rights violations, including victims of forced eviction, to a remedy.[39] Here again, the Pinheiro Principle's *travaux préparatoires* indicate reliance on the 2000 draft

---

35 Scott Leckie & Chris Huggins, *Conflict and Housing, Land, and Property Rights: A Handbook on Issues, Frameworks, and Solutions* 53 (2011); Breau, *supra* note 24, at 168.

36 *Preliminary Report*, *supra* note 26, ¶ 5 (discussing housing rights); *Pinheiro Principles*, *supra* note 25, ¶¶ 8 (right to housing) & 10 (right to return); *Working Paper*, *supra* note 30, at sections III and IV.

37 *Internal Displacement Principles*, *supra* note 9.

38 *Id.* ¶ 29.2; U.N. Econ. & Soc. Council, Sub-Comm'n on the Promotion & Prot. of Human Rts., *Progress Report of the Special Rapporteur, Paulo Sérgio Pinheiro, Addendum, Commentary on the Draft Principles on Housing and Property Restitution for Refugees and Displaced Persons*, ¶ 45, U.N. Doc. E/CN.4/Sub.2/2004/22/Add.1 (June 8, 2004) [hereinafter *Progress Report*] (noting in ¶ 1 that the Progress Report was intended to review the legal standards that supported the draft version of the Pinheiro Principles). Principle 29.2 of the Internal Displacement Principles states in full:

> Competent authorities have the duty and responsibility to assist returned and/or resettled internally displaced persons to recover, to the extent possible, their property and possessions which they left behind or were dispossessed of upon their displacement. When recovery of such property and possessions is not possible, competent authorities shall provide or assist these persons in obtaining appropriate compensation or another form of just reparation.

*Internal Displacement Principles*, *supra* note 9, at Principle 29.2.

39 *Reparations Principles*, *supra* note 20. Note that many authors refer to this report as the "Van Boven-Bassiouni Principles," but this chapter adopts a more descriptive reference. *See, e.g.*, *Transitional Justice and Displacement* (Roger Duthie, ed.) (2012). The Reparations Principles do not specifically mention remedying forced eviction, but the *Preliminary Report* to the Pinheiro Principles indicates that the Reparations Principles call for a remedy for victims of forced eviction. *Preliminary Report*, *supra* note 26, ¶ 7. The Progress Report defines "forced eviction" as "the permanent or temporary removal against their will of individuals, families and/or communities from the homes and/or land which they occupy, without the provision of, and access to, appropriate forms of legal or other protection." *Progress Report*, *supra* note 38, ¶ 10.

of these Reparations Principles.[40] The Reparations Principles discuss five forms of reparations, including restitution.[41] These principles state that restitution includes "the return to one's place of residence" and the restoration of property.[42]

Significantly, the Reparations Principles expressly adopt a "victim-oriented perspective" and advance a broad definition of reparations as a means to promote justice.[43] In doing so, the Reparations Principles advance the values and mechanisms of transitional justice.[44] This consideration of reparations, in general, and restitution, in particular, as contributing to transitional justice supports the argument set forth in Part 6 that a relaxation of evidentiary standards can advance the role of restitution in facilitating transitional justice.

Since the restitution experiment in Bosnia and the subsequent issuing of the Pinheiro Principles, the international community has increasingly emphasized post-conflict property restitution as part of a humanitarian and legal response to widespread displacement caused by armed conflict. Proponents suggest that restitution can enhance the rule of law in a post-conflict society, and link the remedy with promoting post-war peace and reconciliation as well as bolstering economic and social stability.[45]

Some academics and policymakers have criticized the international community's emphasis on post-conflict property restitution.[46] The gist of these concerns is that

---

40 *Progress Report*, *supra* note 38, ¶¶ 34 & 36.

41 In addition to restitution, the Reparations Principles include compensation, rehabilitation, satisfaction, and guarantees of non-repetition. *Reparations Principles*, *supra* note 20, ¶¶ 19–23. The Reparations Principles imply equivalency among these forms of reparations, rather than favoring restitution.

42 *Id.* ¶ 19.

43 *Id.* at Preamble & ¶ 15.

44 Jemima García-Godos, *Addressing Land Restitution In Transitional Justice*, 28 Nordic J. of Hum. Rts. L. 122, 131 (2010).

45 *See, e.g.*, Scott Leckie, *An Introduction to the Pinheiro Principles*, *in* Centre on Housing Rights & Evictions, The Pinheiro Principles 4 (2005) (stating that the international community recognizes "the direct links between housing, land and property restitution and peace, stability, reconciliation and economic development" and that this recognition "bolstered support for the human rights remedies offered to the displaced by restitution rights").

46 *See, e.g.*, Anderson, *supra* note 25, at 304 (pointing out six weaknesses of the Pinheiro Principles and suggesting amendments to address these flaws); Ballard, *supra* note 23, at 495 (cautioning that a focus on the technical features of restitution may undermine the sustainability of return and impair the legitimacy of a post-war state and the development of peace and stability); Langford & Moyo, *supra* note 23, at 151 (suggesting that restitution may favor formal property rights and disadvantage weaker rights); Paglione, *supra* note 12, at 403 (noting theoretical shortcomings of the Pinheiro Principles, primarily because the document does not address the meaning and substance of property restitution, and it ignores other types of redress aside from return); Sara Pantuliano & Samir Elhawary, *Humanitarian Policy Group Policy Brief 39 Unchartered Territory: Land, Conflict and Humanitarian Action* 3 (2009) (maintaining that restitution is only one of a number of

restitution should not be applied or prioritized in all conflict situations. Doing so may, for example, overshadow other solutions to displacement and allow states hosting refugee populations to avoid providing asylum.[47] In addition, restoring the status quo through restitution may not promote post-conflict peace and stability where land ownership is substantially unequal as it is in Colombia, for example.[48] Most families displaced by Colombia's decades-long violence farmed parcels with no security of tenure.[49] In that context, property redistribution, rather than restitution, may do more to advance peace and justice.

Post-conflict property restitution, despite the potential problems, may represent the best approach for remedying forced displacement in some societies recovering from war. Even when appropriate, however, there are a number of barriers associated with implementing the remedy. One of these barriers relates to the sufficiency of evidence available to establish a displaced person's right to a particular home and land.[50]

---

land-related issues that can arise in conflict settings and that "it is dangerous to limit engagement on land and property issues to the mechanical application of the Pinheiro Principles"); Daniel Fitzpatrick, Possession, Custom and Social Order, Property Rights in a Fragile State 29–30 (2011) (unpublished manuscript), *available at* http://works.bepress.com/context/daniel_fitzpatrick/article/1000/type/native/viewcontent (pointing to the difficulties of "implementing restitution in a historical context of colonization, invasion and complex population movement," such as East Timor); Rhodri C. Williams, *The Pinheiro Principles take a licking (and keep on ticking?)*, TerraNullius Weblog (Nov. 18, 2010), http://terra0nullius.wordpress.com/2010/11/18/the-pinheiro-principles-take-a-licking-and-keep-on-ticking (describing mounting criticism of the Pinheiro Principles).

47 Langford & Moyo, *supra* note 23, at 151; Paglione, *supra* note 12, at 408–409; Rhodri C. Williams, *Protection in the Past Tense: Restitution at the Juncture of Humanitarian Response to Displacement and Transitional Justice, in* Transitional Justice and Displacement 84, 94–6 (Roger Duthie ed., 2012) (summarizing critiques of post-conflict property restitution); Smit, *Property Rights*, *supra* note 25, at 3–5.

48 World Bank, *Colombia Land Policy in Transition* 9 (2004); Acción Social, *Project on Protection of Land and Patrimony of Internally Displaced Persons, Background Document for the "Workshop on the Protection of Land Rights and Patrimony of Internally Displaced Persons—Building on the Colombian Experience"* 9–11 (2010) (reporting that in 2001, 0.4 percent of landowners owned about 61.2 percent of total land in Colombia); David L. Attanasio & Nelson Camilo Sánchez, *Return Within the Bounds of the Pinheiro Principles: The Colombian Land Restitution Experience*, 11 Wash. U. Global Stud. L. Rev. 1, 15 (2012) (asserting that in 2004, 0.4 percent of landowners owned 62.3 percent of parcels larger than 500 hectares).

49 *Land and Violence in Colombia: This Land is Our Land, At Last the Government Tries to Reverse a Violent Agrarian "Counter-Reform,"* Economist (Sept. 16, 2010), available at http://www.economist.com/node/17043061.

50 The remainder of this chapter discusses homes and related land, specifically, rather than the broader category of property. Two reasons support this narrower discussion. First, the suggestion that property rights norms can be relaxed within a transitional justice initiative is based the international legal principle that forced eviction is a gross violation

## Part 3. Evidentiary Problems Associated with Restitution

People who have fled from their homes because of armed conflict often lack proof of any rights they may have to these homes. For example, about one-third of the restitution claimants in the aftermath of the war in Bosnia lacked proof of their pre-war property rights.[51] Similarly, over 60 percent of the Georgians who fled from secessionist violence in Abkhazia in the early 1990s report owning a home in Abkhazia but lack official documents to confirm ownership.[52] The problem of proof extends beyond formal ownership, as evidenced by the Pinheiro Principles' recommendation that restitution programs protect not just formal owners, but also the rights to housing of tenants and other non-owners.[53]

A variety of factors contribute to this proof problem. First, many areas embroiled in conflict lack formal land records. Recourse to official data to prove property rights then is not an option. In Colombia, for example, there is no cadastral information[54] for a significant portion of the country, including areas

---

of human rights. *See supra* note 39 and accompanying text. This principle is, in turn, based in large measure on a right to housing. *See supra* note 2. Second, the proposed community-based evidentiary solution requires a community of people occupying homes and land in proximity to one another.

51 Hans Das, *Restoring Property Rights in the Aftermath of War*, 53 Int'l & Comp. L. Q. 429, 438 (2004) [hereinafter *Restoring Property Rights*].

52 *Conciliation Resources, Displacement in Georgia: IDP Attitudes to Conflict, Return, and Justice* (2011) [hereinafter *Displacement Report*]. For information on the actual survey questions that were asked, *see* Conciliation Res. & Caucasus Research Res. Ctrs., *Survey: IDPs in Georgia – 2010* (2010), http://www.c-r.org/our-work/caucasus/documents/IDPs_2011/IDPs%20in%20Georgia%20Questionnaire%20ENG.pdf. For full results of the survey, *see* Conciliation Res. & Caucasus Research Res. Ctrs., IDPs in Georgia – June 2010 (June 30, 2010), http://www.c-r.org/our-work/caucasus/documents/IDPs_2011/IDPs%20in%20Georgia_Final.pdf.

53 *Pinheiro Principles*, *supra* note 25, ¶ 16. This proposal stems from the Principles' recognition that international law is more protective of housing rights than property ownership rights. *Working Paper*, *supra* note 30, ¶ 10; Leckie & Huggins, *supra* note 35, at 54–5 (explaining that "the right to adequate housing has been the most comprehensively legally clarified of all [housing, land, and property]-related rights," and citing to General Comments of the U.N. Committee on Economic, Social and Cultural Rights on the right to adequate housing). Restitution might provide an opportunity to formalize occupancy rights, but the premise of the remedy is to restore a person to the pre-conflict status quo. García-Godos, *supra note* 44, at 124 & 136.

54 A cadastre is a government land inventory, including the area, use, value, and ownership of each parcel, reflected on maps. Gerhard Larsson, *Land Registration and Cadastral Systems: Tools for Land Information and Management* 16 (1991). Unlike land title records held in U.S. county recording offices, cadastral records serve as a basis for land taxation and provide descriptions of parcel boundaries. *Id.* at 16–18.

from which people have been displaced by conflict.[55] Pinheiro acknowledged this problem in drafting his property restitution principles. A working paper leading up to the final version of the Pinheiro Principles recognizes that an absence of official property documentation will hinder the implementation of restitution programs and necessitate "formal investigation and verification procedures."[56] The Pinheiro Principles themselves suggest that "administrative and judicial authorities may independently establish the facts related to undocumented restitution claims" but propose no methods of doing so.[57]

Second, even in areas where a formal land registry exists, these records can be destroyed in a conflict (often intentionally); fraudulently altered; removed from the area; or simply be so poorly maintained that they provide no evidentiary value.[58] In Bosnia, for example, while some disagreement exists about the scope of archives destroyed, the war did result in damaged and altered property records.[59] One source claims that the war in Bosnia destroyed about a third of the books recording real property rights and tampering impaired other land records.[60] In Colombia, notary and land registry offices have been burnt down to destroy records.[61] Also in Colombia, the paper-based registration system for rural property was compromised by forced sales and fraudulent transfers after combatants seized territory.[62] Many of these transfers are cloaked in legality because of participation

55 Acción Social, *supra* note 48, at 1; Samir Elhawary, *Between War and Peace: Land and Humanitarian Action in Colombia* 6 HPG working paper (2007), *available at* http://www.odi.org.uk/resources/download/1912.pdf. *See also* William Neuman, *Displaced Residents Grapple with Hurdles of Going Home*, N.Y. Times, Dec. 3, 2012, at A6.

56 *Preliminary Report*, *supra* note 26, ¶ 51.

57 *Pinheiro Principles*, *supra* note 25, ¶ 15.7.

58 2 Hans Das & Hans van Houtte, *Post-War Restoration of Property Rights under International Law* 62 (2008). *See also* Maria Paula Saffon, *The Project of Land Restitution in Colombia: An Illustration of the Civilizing Force of Hypocrisy?*, Estud. Soci-Juríd. 109, 127 (2010) (calling Colombia's cadaster "extremely obsolete").

59 Hans van Houtte, *Mass Property Claim Resolution in a Post-War Society: The Commission for Real Property Claims in Bosnia and Herzegovina*, 48 Int'l & Comp. L. Q. 625, 636 (1999). Property records in Yugoslavia had been kept in two forms: land cadasters, containing information about the property; and property books, recording rights to real property, such as mortgages and other claims. *Id.* Many of the original property books were destroyed during World War II and never replaced. In addition, a number of property transactions were never recorded in the remaining property books. Das & van Houtte, *supra* note 58, at 62.

60 *Id.* Another source, however, indicates that the destruction of property records was "a relatively isolated phenomenon." Williams, *Bosnia and Herzegovina*, *supra* note 17, at 505.

61 Elhawary, *supra* note 55, at 6.

62 Interview with Clara María Sanín Posada, Superintendency of Notaries and Registries, in Bogotá, Colombia (May 4, 2011); Sebastián Albuja, *Internal Displacement Monitoring Centre, Building Momentum for Land Restoration: Towards Property Restitution for IDPs in Colombia* 8 (2010).

by notaries and property registrars.[63] In Kosovo, when the Serbians withdrew they took with them cadastral records, as well as other documents, to Serbian territory.[64]

Third, land records, even if they are maintained and survive a war intact and unaltered, may not reflect possessory rights of all people forcibly displaced from their homes. For example, many people displaced by war might have informally occupied land and not be included in official land records.[65]

Fourth, there may also be a dearth of documentation outside the land records that points to prior possession of a home. For example, many residents of rural areas or informal settlements may not be included in census data or may not officially receive electricity, gas, or water from a company with customer records. In fact, some victims of forced displacement have no formal identification, making it difficult even to prove that a claimant is who he or she purports to be.[66]

Fifth, even if a claimant once had a purchase contract or other document reflecting ownership or possession, there is a good chance that he or she will not have it when applying for a post-conflict property remedy. When people flee from their homes because of armed conflict, they rarely take with them documents that might prove a right to the property they are abandoning.[67] Documentary evidence that may have been left in an abandoned home can be lost when the home is destroyed, or ruined when someone else occupies the home in the victim's absence.

Finally, the passage of time separating forced displacement from a later restitution process can serve to compound evidentiary problems. Evidence that might have been available soon after displacement can be very difficult to gather

---

63 Interview with Clara María Sanín Posada, *supra* note 62; Comisión Nacional de Reparación y Reconciliación & Organización Internacional para las Migraciones, *Proyecto Piloto de Restitución de Bienes-Tierras y Retorno Integral a Mediano y Largo Plazo en el Corregimiento de Chengue, Municipio de Ovejas, Departamento de Sucre, Colombia* 9 (2011) (on file with author) [hereinafter *Pilot Project Chengue Report*].

64 Bjørn Vagle & Fernando de Medina-Rosales, *Norwegian Resource Bank for Democracy and Human Rights, An Evaluation of the Housing and Property Directorate in Kosovo* 35 (2006). While Serbian institutions initially refused to produce these documents, eventually Kosovo's Housing and Property Directorate (HPD) was able to secure access to them. *Id.* at 35. The Serbian Ministry of Justice and the HPD reached a formal agreement in December 2002 granting the HPD access to property records. Margaret Cordial & Knut Rosandhaug, *Post-Conflict Property Restitution: The Approach in Kosovo and Lessons Learned for Future International Practice* 65 (2009).

65 Colombia's cadaster does not include even formal tenancies. Saffon, *supra* note 58, at 127.

66 Internet (Skype) Interview with Peter Van der Auweraert, Head of Land, Property and Reparations Division, International Organization for Migration (Oct. 17, 2011) (discussing the lack of documentation among people displaced because of conflict in the Democratic Republic of Congo).

67 Das & van Houtte, *supra* note 58, at 60.

by the time a remedial process is established.[68] In addition, the original possessors displaced from their homes might die, leaving less informed heirs to submit a claim for restitution.[69]

## Part 4. Administration of Evidence in Mass Claims Tribunals

This problem of compiling proof to document losses caused by war is not new. Countries have paid war reparations to cover property damaged in international armed conflicts since the 1919 Treaty of Versailles.[70] A common effect of war is the deliberate or unintentional destruction of documents or items that could substantiate a claim for property loss or damage.[71] Accordingly, it is useful to consider past practices regarding questions of evidence.

States have relied on various settlement mechanisms to resolve post-war property claims, but international mass claims programs became a prominent means of resolving property issues beginning in the 1990s.[72] Examples include the international mass claims tribunals established to resolve claims for Swiss bank accounts dormant since World War II[73] and the commissions formed to govern property restitution claims after the wars in Bosnia and Herzegovina[74] and Kosovo.[75] All of these programs established following wars contend with limited evidence because of the destructive impact of conflict.[76] While not all post-conflict restitution programs have been or will be administered through an international mass claims process, considering how mass claims programs contend with evidentiary issues is instructive.

In administering the burden of proof, reparations commissions traditionally have held parties responsible for producing facts to prove their claims and contentions, regardless of the evidentiary problems that claimants might face due

---

68 Hans Das, *Claims for Looted Cultural Assets: Is There a Need for Specialized Rules of Evidence?* in Resolution of Cultural Property Disputes 193, 196 (Int'l Bureau of the Permanent Court of Arbitration, ed. 2003) [hereinafter *Looted Cultural Assets*].

69 *Id.* at 196–7.

70 van Houtte et al., *supra* note 22, at 14. Traditionally, states, not individuals, claimed losses. *Id.* at 17.

71 Das & van Houtte, *supra* note 58, at 60.

72 *Id.* at 1.

73 van Houtte et al., *supra* note 22, at 70–79 (discussing the two processes for dormant bank accounts and other claims).

74 *Id.* at 63–70 (addressing the Commission for Real Property Claims of Displaced Persons and Refugees).

75 *Id.* at 79–85 (describing Housing and Property Directorate and the Housing and Property Claims Commission).

76 Das & van Houtte, *supra* note 58, at 59 (noting that all but one international mass claims tribunals operated in the aftermath of armed conflict, a context that limits a claimant's ability to produce evidence).

to a war's destruction of records and the passage of time between the loss giving rise to the claim and the opportunity to assert the claim.[77] Historically, tribunals have made exceptions under the *probatio diabolica* (devil's proof) doctrine, which maintains that a party with the burden of proof cannot be required to discharge that burden if it is materially impossible to present the required proof.[78] Yet commissions have used this doctrine "sparingly and on a strictly ad hoc basis."[79]

More recently-created international mass claims commissions have creatively applied general burden of proof rules.[80] The Commission for Real Property Claims of Displaced Persons and Refugees (CRPC), established by the Dayton Peace Agreement for Bosnia and Herzegovina, required claimants to submit all evidence "available to them."[81] Similarly, the Kosovo process required claimants to produce all relevant documentation in a claimant's possession or reasonably available to a claimant.[82] These burdens are less onerous than the traditional requirement to prove the facts supporting a claim.[83]

Moreover, in both Bosnia and Kosovo, the adjudicating bodies themselves assumed an evidence-gathering and fact-finding role. In Bosnia, the CRPC collected pre-war cadastral and census data and sent CRPC staff to regional courts and cadastral offices to gather and verify additional information.[84] While many of the claims for restitution in Bosnia were determined through a domestic process, rather than through the CRPC's international claims resolution process, these domestic procedures also required local housing authorities to establish facts related to each claim.[85]

In Kosovo, the regulations governing the claims process similarly required the Housing and Property Directorate to collect evidence and verify documents submitted by a claimant.[86] Also, like the process in Bosnia, verification officers

77 Das, *Looted Cultural Assets*, *supra* note 68, at 202–205.

78 *Id.* at 205–206.

79 Das & van Houtte, *supra* note 58, at 86.

80 Das, *Looted Cultural Assets*, *supra* note 68, at 213.

81 *Id.* at 221 (quoting the Book of Regulations on the Conditions and Decision Making Procedure for Claims for Return of Real Property of Displaced Persons and Refugees).

82 Vagle & de Medina-Rosales, *supra* note 64, at 32. The rules governing the restitution process specifically stated that: "The claimant must submit with the Claim Form the originals or certified copies of any documents relevant to the claim which are in his/her possession, or which s/he can reasonably obtain from a public record." UNMIK Regulation No. 2000/60, *Residential Property Claims and The Rules of Procedure and Evidence of the Housing and Property Directorate and the Housing and Property Claims Commission* § 8.2 (Oct. 31, 2000), *available at* http://www.unmikonline.org/regulations/2000/reg60-00.htm.

83 Das, *Looted Cultural Assets*, *supra* note 68, at 221.

84 *Id.* at 222.

85 Williams, *Bosnia and Herzegovina*, *supra* note 17, at 504 & 507–508.

86 Cordial & Rosandhaug, *supra* note 64, at 76 (citing § 10.2 of UNMIK Regulation 2000/60).

went to courts, cadastral offices, and elsewhere to collect records and verify information.[87]

Not all post-conflict property restitution programs operate as international mass claims processes. For example, Iraq's Commission for the Resolution of Real Property Disputes, established to deal with property confiscation and destruction under Saddam Hussein's regime, is a purely domestic body and process.[88] Nonetheless, international organizations provided advice and guidance to Iraq in establishing this commission, as is typical of even purely domestic processes.[89] Iraq's quasi-judicial program still requires that the Commission review formal documentary evidence.[90]

Despite more recent leniency in applying burden of proof rules, international mass claims processes determining restitution claims still relied on documentary evidence, at least facially. Whether a property restitution program abides by rules governing international mass claims processes or not, some post-war claimants of property rights will likely find themselves in an impossible situation. Many survivors of war deserve some sort of remedy for the human rights violation of forced displacement, but some of these victims may not be able to produce evidence of prior property rights because the same conflict that resulted in the human rights violation also destroyed evidence of pre-war property entitlements. On the other hand, respondents and others deserve protection from fraudulent claims, and the process itself should be seen as legitimate and generate confidence in post-war governance.[91]

## Part 5. Alternative Solutions: Informal, Community-Based Evidence

One possible solution to this problem of a lack of reliable documentary evidence sufficient to match a claimant with his or her home is to gather evidence from people who formed the claimant's pre-displacement community. Community-based evidence can span an entire spectrum. On a very informal level, a person seeking verification of a victim's claim to a home can simply talk with former neighbors of the claimant to determine whether the person lived where he or she claimed to live. On the more formal end of the spectrum is social mapping, a process through which community members collectively map their territory (also

87 *Id.* at 66.

88 Peter Van der Auweraert, *Policy Challenges for Property Restitution in Transition—Iraq*, *in* Reparations for Victims of Genocide, War Crimes and Crimes against Humanity 459, 466 (Carla Ferstman et al., eds. 2009).

89 Van der Auweraert interview, *supra* note 66.

90 Van der Auweraert, *supra* note 88, at 477.

91 Das & van Houtte, *supra* note 58, at 60.

referred to as community mapping,[92] indigenous mapping,[93] cultural mapping,[94] counter-mapping,[95] or participatory mapping[96]).

Gathering and considering community-based evidence is not entirely new in programs attempting to catalogue or remedy forced displacement. Indeed, while not expressly authorized by governing procedures, even formal international claims commissions have relied on community-based evidence at times. This chapter proposes that the international actors involved in consulting with or establishing remedial programs expressly work to legitimate community-based evidence. By recognizing the important role of community-based evidence, the international community can highlight previous experiences and foster a transparent dialogue about various techniques and their related advantages and drawbacks.

On the informal end of the spectrum, verifying claims with neighbors seems to be fairly common, even if not expressly authorized by restitution program rules. While it might appear that this technique would be of minimal value in conflicts that pitted neighbors against neighbors, the experience in Bosnia instructs differently. In the Bosnian restitution process, local officials responsible for much of the restitution work often checked a person's claim against information provided informally by the claimant's pre-war neighbors who still resided near the victim's claimed home.[97] Given the nature of the ethnic cleansing that occurred during the war in Bosnia, the neighbors who later consulted with local officials on restitution claims may well have been a different ethnicity from those who fled. Yet these neighbors still provided evidence about claimants and their homes, perhaps out of recognition that restoring property rights does not necessarily equate with a victim's return to that home.

In the country of Georgia, the government undertook an effort to inventory homes abandoned because of conflict with two secessionist territories.[98] Government officials asked IDPs to complete an inventory questionnaire and to

---

92 Int'l Fund for Agricultural Development, *Participatory Mapping Guidelines* 6 (2009).

93 Margaret Wickens Pearce & Renee Pualani Louis, *Mapping Indigenous Depth of Place*, 32 Am. Indian Culture & Res. J. 107, 108 (2008).

94 Int'l Fund for Agricultural Development, *supra* note 92, at 8.

95 *Id.* at 10.

96 Pearce & Louis, *supra* note 93.

97 E-mails from Rhodri C. Williams, former Legal Advisor on property issues in the Human Rights Department of the Organization for Security & Cooperation in Europe Mission to Bosnia and Herzegovina (Oct. 2000 to May 2004) to Megan J. Ballard, Associate Professor of Law, Gonzaga University School of Law (Oct. 21, 2011, 1:17 a.m. PST & Oct. 23, 2011, 3:01 p.m. PST) (on file with author).

98 Decree of the President of Georgia No. 124, Concerning the Measures of Registration of the Rights on Immovable Property in the Autonomous Republic of Abkhazia and Tskhinvali Region (Feb. 14, 2006) (on file with author); Decree of the President of Georgia No. 255, Concerning the Rule of Preliminary Registration of the Immovable Property in the Autonomous Republic of Abkhazia and Tskhinvali Region (Apr. 8, 2006)

identify on satellite photos the homes from which they fled.[99] After one person identified a parcel on the photo, officials asked others filling out questionnaires at the same time if they knew who had resided in the home on that parcel.[100] Officials used information from former neighbors to corroborate or contradict a person's claim, particularly if an IDP lacked the required documentary evidence of pre-war property possession.[101]

Social mapping rests on the more formal end of the scale of community-based evidence, involving community participation in producing a map that reflects consensus on geographic features, names, boundaries, and other details.[102] The technique emerged in the 1970s within indigenous communities to document tribal sovereignty and protect tribal resources.[103] Social mapping applications have included collecting information on land use and occupancy; designing conservation plans; advancing conflict resolution over land and resources; and demarcating property claims.[104] Social mapping has only recently been used to help match property restitution claimants with the homes they were forced to abandon.[105]

Mirroring the broad array of terms used to describe social mapping are a wide range of processes. Often members of a community work with a technical expert facilitating the mapping exercise.[106] The process usually involves holding meetings with community members;[107] administering questionnaires about land

---

(on file with author). These two decrees called for the inventory and registration of IDP's land in Abkhazia and South Ossetia within the government's "My House" program.

99 Interview with Georgian government official familiar with the My House program (due to the sensitivity of this topic, the official asked to remain anonymous) in Tbilisi, Georgia (Oct. 21, 2010).

100 Interview with Georgian government official familiar with the My House program (due to the sensitivity of this topic, the official asked to remain anonymous), in Tbilisi, Georgia (Jan. 6, 2011).

101 *Id.*

102 Peter H. Herlihy & Gregory Knapp, *Maps of, by and for the Peoples of Latin America*, 62 Human Organization 303, 306 (2003).

103 Pearce & Louis, *supra* note 93, at 108.

104 Herlihy & Knapp, *supra* note 102, at 308.

105 Interview with Eduardo Medina, Property Restitution Manager, International Organization for Migration, in Bogotá, Colombia (May 4, 2011).

106 Herlihy & Knapp, *supra* note 102, at 307.

107 Francys Cárdenas, *¡Pedimos la Palabra! Propuesta Metodológica para la Exigibilidad del Derecho a la Tierra y al Territorio desde las Comunidades* 38–9 (2010); *Pilot Project Chengue Report*, *supra* note 63, at 36.

use and features;[108] having members of the community draw sketches of the land;[109] locating features and boundaries on scale maps or satellite or aerial photographs; and using a Global Positioning System (GPS) to demarcate boundaries.[110] Members of a community are sometimes trained to use GPS equipment, and measurements of boundaries can be done in the presence of neighbors and witnesses to ensure accuracy.[111] Such GPS measurements are practical only if community members can return, at least temporarily, to the affected land.[112] If feasible, information learned through social mapping processes can be integrated with a geographic information system, a computer-based system for storing and analyzing geographic information with related data.[113]

In Colombia between 1994 and 2000 social mapping demarcated collectively owned "indigenous reserves," and collectively owned Afro-Colombian territory.[114] The project, funded primarily through the World Bank, used social mapping to define collective boundaries and secure title to these territories.[115]

More recently, organizations have used social mapping to identify and title land in Colombia of rural communities forcibly displaced by the civil violence.[116] These organizations concluded three "Pilot Projects on Land Restitution" in 2010, with funding from the United States Agency for International Development (USAID). The projects used information learned from social mapping, cross referenced against governmental land records, to identify land use patterns and

108 Comisión Nacional de Reparación y Reconciliación & Organización Internacional para las Migraciones, *Proyecto Piloto de Restitución de Tierras Mampuján-Bolivar, Encuesta Circunstancias del Desplazamiento Forzado por la Violencia, Restitución de Bienes y Retorno*, undated survey instrument used in pilot restitution project for people displaced from the village of Mampuján (on file with author).

109 Int'l Fund for Agricultural Development, *supra* note 92, at 15 (involving community members drawing maps from memory).

110 John Corbett, et al., *Overview: Mapping for Change – the Emergence of a New Practice*, 54 Participatory Learning and Action 13, 14 (2006) (explaining that GPS can reliably identify locations using a "known coordinate system such as latitude and longitude").

111 Sylvanie Jardinet, *Capacity Development and PGIS for Land Demarcation: Innovations from Nicaragua*, 54 Participatory Learning and Action, *Mapping for Change: Practice, Technologies and Communication* 67, 69 (2006).

112 Cárdenas, *supra* note 107, at 38.

113 Int'l Fund for Agricultural Development, *supra* note 92, at 14.

114 Bettina Ng'weno, *On Titling Collective Property, Participation, and Natural Resource Management: Implementing Indigenous and Afro-Colombian Demands: A Review of Bank Experience in Colombia* 4–6, 36–7 (2000).

115 *Id.* at 7, 15–16 (reporting that a $39 million loan achieved titling of 4,100,271 hectares for 19,860 families, representing over 100,000 people, up to June 2000); Karl H. Offen, *The Territorial Turn: Making Black Territories in Pacific Colombia,* 2 J. of Latin Am. Geography 43, 60–61 (2003) (commenting on the role of social mapping in this project).

116 Interview with Sandra Pabón, Deputy Director, Demobilization and Reintegration, US Agency for International Development, in Bogotá, Colombia (Apr. 28, 2011); Interview with Eduardo Medina, *supra* note 105.

demarcate claims, as well as gather information on the circumstances surrounding displacement.[117] With information collected from social mapping, the pilot projects succeeded in working with government agencies to issue title to 202 properties.[118]

## Part 6. Limits to Community-Based Evidence and the Role of Transitional Justice

One of the primary concerns surrounding the use of community-based evidence is whether the information gathered is sufficiently reliable to grant a displaced person the legal right to an asserted prior home. The emphasis of international mass claims programs on documentary evidence seems to presume a substantial risk of fraud or error in a reparations process. Restitution experience, however, illustrates that fraud has not been a significant problem. Human rights workers and others involved in post-conflict property restitution or compensation processes estimate that about ten percent of claims are erroneous.[119] This estimate includes both claims that are fraudulent and those that are simply mistaken as to area, improvements, or other property details.[120]

On the formal end of the community-based evidence scale, experience has proven social mapping to be reliable. Both the World Bank and USAID have funded efforts to use the technique to identify the boundaries of parcels for which the Colombian government issued titles. Elsewhere in the world, international organizations and government agencies have used social mapping to determine land rights.[121] Social mapping specialists have endorsed it as "a remarkably successful methodology for producing accurate maps and descriptive data."[122] Under conditions that make social mapping feasible, this method might substitute for, or supplement, nonexistent or incomplete documentary evidence.

117 *Pilot Project Chengue Report*, *supra* note 63, at 16. The social mapping techniques included: workshops with each affected community; a day trip to the territory in question if the community had not already returned to the area; technical assistance from Colombian government's mapping agency (Instituto Geográfico Agustín Codazzi); and questionnaires for victims related to the land they were forced to abandon (land use, area, improvements, for example), abandoned personal property, and displacement circumstances (threats, violence in the area, forced sales, fraudulent transactions, for example). *Id.* at 16. Using social mapping to compile evidence of property rights for purposes of post-conflict property restitution or compensation can be accomplished through a day-trip to the affected land or, less reliably, with satellite or aerial photographs of the territory.

118 Interview with Medina, *supra* note 105.

119 Interview with Van der Auweraert, *supra* note 66. This estimate is a ball-park figure reflecting experiences where both a lesser and greater proportion of erroneous claims have been submitted.

120 *Id.*

121 Herlihy & Knapp, *supra* note 102, at 310.

122 *Id.* at 308.

On the informal end of the scale, authorities responsible for verifying pre-war housing rights have found reliable information gathered from discussions with neighbors of claimants.[123] In Bosnia, for example, local officials responsible for gathering evidence of pre-war housing rights relied on local knowledge of who had lived where and when to help substantiate undocumented property claims.[124]

The law in the United States governing the acquisition of property rights by prescription tacitly affirms the reliability of community-based evidence. Claimants often use evidence from neighbors to illustrate conspicuous occupancy, proving "open and notorious" possession.[125]

Even if community-based evidence is reliable in some contexts, this approach is not suitable for many post-conflict situations for a variety of reasons. First, social mapping works best with a cohesive community structure, requiring that members of a displaced community have fled to the same location.[126] Statements from neighbors, however, do not require social cohesion and have been found reliable even in the aftermath of conflicts that caused neighbors to turn against one another.[127] Nonetheless, evidence from neighbors also requires that they generally be together in one area. Moreover, at least with regard to social mapping, the process can be time and labor-intensive and can result in conflict within a community and among different communities with overlapping claims.[128]

Perhaps a more significant problem with relying on community-based evidence is tension with formal legal norms.[129] The state typically establishes property

---

123 E-mails from Williams, *supra* note 97.

124 *Id.*

125 *E.g.*, *Hill v. Carroll*, 730 S. 2d 230, 232 (Ala. Civ. App. 1998); *Nome 2000 v. Fagerstrom*, 799 P.2d 304, 308, 310 (Alaska 1990); *Alaska Nat'l Bank v. Linck*, 559 P.2d 1049, 1053 (Alaska 1977); *Morehead v. Parks*, 518 P.2d 544, 546, 548 (Kan. 1974); *Arnholt v. Carlisle*, No. 10CA91, 2011 WL 2436590, at *4 (Ohio Ct. App. June 6, 2011).

126 *See, e.g.*, Jardinet, *supra* note 111, at 72 (concluding that a well-organized community led to the success of a social mapping project in Nicaragua); Ng'weno, *supra* note 114, at 9 (noting that problems in the land titling process that used social mapping arose mainly in areas with weak community organization). Furthermore, in traditionally patriarchal societies, women's participation in social mapping may be constrained. *See, e.g.*, Lucy Hovil, *The Nexus between Displacement and Transitional Justice: A Gender-Justice Dimension in* Transitional Justice and Displacement 328, 348 (Roger Duthie, ed. 2012) (discussing problems displaced women have in proving property ownership for restitution purposes in patriarchal societies). Finally, community members must also be relatively safe in order to be concerned with social mapping.

127 *See supra* note 97 and accompanying text.

128 Int'l Fund for Agricultural Development, *supra* note 92, at 12.

129 Regardless of methods used to prove pre-displacement property rights, granting restitution itself may require relaxing domestic law related to, for example, statutes of limitation and continuous occupation requirements. Brookings-Bern Project on Internal Displacement, Protecting Internally Displaced Persons: A Manual for Law and Policymakers 177–8 (2008).

rights systems.[130] While positive law may not receive widespread legitimacy, or may compete with customary or religious law, a post-conflict regime might choose to uphold positive law for its stability and predictability, leaving changes in legal norms to the political process.[131] Reliance on even the more rigorous method of social mapping as a means of establishing rights over property likely deviates from the formal law of many jurisdictions. Moreover, on an international level, allowing community-based evidence would mean departing from the traditional mass claims programs approach to the administration of evidence. Such a divergence, however, could be justified under the *probatio diabolica* doctrine.[132]

The challenge that community-based evidence poses to positive legal norms can be overcome by considering this flexible approach as contributing to a transitional justice project. Social scientists and others considered transitional justice in the 1990s to involve legal responses during a period of political transformation from an authoritarian regime to a liberal democracy.[133] In this context, law was concerned with recognizing and guaranteeing fundamental rights denied during authoritarian rule.[134] More recently, however, transitional justice measures have been adopted after prolonged violence.[135] Here, the transition is away from violence and towards peace, during which time the goals of transitional justice are to promote the rule of law and strengthen the legitimacy of law and legal institutions.[136] This broader definition of transition, and the related goals of transitional justice, apply to the phase following many of the conflicts causing displacement and allow post-conflict restitution as an element of transitional justice programming.

Transitional justice in this context can encompass a range of processes and mechanisms related to a society's attempts to recognize past abuses, ensure accountability, serve justice, and achieve reconciliation.[137] Reparations, including restitution, are included among these transitional justice mechanisms and seek to recognize and address the harms suffered by victims of systematic human rights violations.

While victims of the human rights violation of forced eviction often prefer the remedy of restitution, transitional justice literature has only recently emphasized post-conflict property restitution as an explicit element of transitional justice

130 Leckie & Huggins, *supra* note 34, at 3.

131 *Id. See also* Ruti G. Teitel, *Transitional Justice* 12–13 (2000).

132 *See supra* note 78, and accompanying text.

133 Teitel, *supra* note 131, at 4–5; Rosario Figari Layús, *The Role of Transitional Justice in the Midst of Ongoing Armed Conflicts: The Case of Colombia* 12 (2010); Roger Duthie, *Incorporating Transitional Justice into the Response to Displacement in* Transitional Justice and Displacement 10, 12 (Roger Duthie, ed., 2012).

134 Layús, *supra* note 133, at 19.

135 *Id.* at 20.

136 *Id.* at 22.

137 Secretary-General, *Report of the Secretary-General, The Rule of Law and Transitional Justice in Conflict and Post-Conflict Societies* ¶ 8, U.N. Doc. S/2004/616 (Aug. 23, 2004).

efforts.[138] The Pinheiro Principles' focus on property restitution can be situated within a transitional justice framework. These Principles justify a right to restitution not only as an essential component of a refugee's right to return to his or her country of origin, but also as a remedy for illegal forced eviction.[139] Moreover, the foundation of the Pinheiro Principles includes the UN's Reparations Principles.[140] These Reparations Principles more explicitly contribute to a transitional justice project, inasmuch as they address a broader array of restorative mechanisms, including the right to justice and truth.[141] Consequently, a post-conflict property restitution program can support transitional justice goals.

Community-based evidence can be justified as a means to enable the remedy of restitution within a transitional justice process. In the case of social mapping, this technique is not only warranted by the norms of transitional justice, but can also enhance a transitional justice effort and help strengthen the rule of law. There are at least two ways in which social mapping to prove restitution claims can contribute to a broader transitional justice effort.

First, the method rests on victim participation. Indeed, victim participation in transitional justice reparations programs is crucial.[142] Giving victims a voice in identifying their rights can help lend legitimacy to a post-conflict legal system.

Second, a social mapping process that gathers information on the causes of displacement helps to enunciate the truth of the human rights violations behind forced displacement. Truth commissions serve an important role in addressing past human rights abuses as part of transitional justice initiatives.[143] In many conflicts, access to and control over land are both a root cause of civil strife and a strategy of waging war.[144] In communities with deep connections to the land, the human rights violation of forced displacement becomes more profound, pointing to a possibly greater need for truth seeking surrounding these abuses.[145]

---

138 García-Godos, *supra* note 44, at 124; Duthie, *supra* note 133, at 11.

139 Williams, *Transitional Justice*, *supra* note 11, at 8.

140 *See supra* note 40, and accompanying text.

141 *See supra* notes 43 & 44, and accompanying text.

142 Secretary-General, *Report of the Secretary-General, The Rule of Law and Transitional Justice in Conflict and Post-Conflict Societies* ¶ 26, U.N. Doc. S/2011/634 (Oct. 12, 2011) (asserting that "[r]eparations are arguably the most victim-centered justice mechanism available and the most significant means of making a difference in the lives of victims"). This report evaluates progress made since the Secretary-General's 2004 report on the rule of law and transitional justice, *supra* note 137.

143 Secretary-General, *supra* note 137, at ¶ 50 (defining truth commissions as "official, temporary, non-judicial fact-finding bodies that investigate a pattern of abuses of human rights or humanitarian law committed over a number of years").

144 Pantuliano & Elhawary, *supra* note 46, at 2.

145 *See, e.g.*, Comisión Nacional de Reparación y Reconciliación, *A Tierra en Disputa: Memorias de Despojo y Resistencia Campesina en la Costa Caribe* (1960–2010) (2010) (recounting forced displacement along the Caribbean coast of Colombia, as part of an independent historical memory project). *See also* Matilde González, *Local Histories:*

The social mapping used in the pilot restitution projects in Colombia did collect information from victims on the circumstances surrounding displacement, although titling property was the ultimate goal of those projects. At least one Colombian non-governmental organization also has undertaken social mapping of forcibly displaced communities in large measure to identify the political institutions that allowed the violations to occur and report the truth to society.[146] This project framed social mapping as part of the process of reclaiming truth and justice, as well as securing reparations.[147] The information gathered through social mapping can be especially useful for a later truth commission when some of the victims of displacement have died by the time a commission begins to operate.

The pilot restitution projects in Colombia that conducted social mapping provide an example, albeit a very unique one, of how state agencies relied on community-based evidence to allocate property rights despite inconsistent formal property norms. This example is unique because, while the conflict in Colombia remained unresolved during the administration of the pilot projects, Colombian legislation, presidential decrees, and Constitutional Court pronouncements had addressed reparations since 1997.[148] The pilot restitution projects were able to achieve recognition of the property rights of victims forcibly evicted from their property, in part because these projects emerged within the framework of the government's reparation and restitution policies.[149] Despite the fact that recognizing property rights, in some instances, went contrary to civil code provisions, the pilot projects maintained that doing so was justified in light of broad transitional justice policies already established in Colombia.[150]

It is unlikely that many post-conflict societies will have legislation, decrees, and judicial pronouncements establishing, even nominally, transitional justice

---

*A Methodology for Understanding Community Perspectives on Transitional Justice, in* Assessing the Impact of Transitional Justice: Challenges for Empirical Research (Hugo van der Merwe et al., eds., 2000) (emphasizing the importance of understanding how local communities experience conflict).

146 Cárdenas, *supra* note 107, at 10 (recounting the methodology that a victim's rights organization used in incorporating social mapping to help develop an "alternative cadaster" of displacement in Colombia).

147 *Id.*

148 Displacement Solutions, Comments on the Proposed Victims' Law and National Restitution Plan: Respecting and Protecting the Housing, Land and Property Restitution Rights of All Internally Displaced Persons in Colombia 5 (2008) (discussing attempts at formulating reparations plans since 1997).

149 *Pilot Project Chengue Report*, *supra* note 63, at 16. After completion of these pilot projects, Colombia adopted legislation in June 2011 establishing the outlines of a property restitution procedure. L. 1448, Junio 10, 2011, Diario Oficial [D.O.] 1, 3, 4 (Colom.) This law, referred to as the "Victims' and Land Restitution Law," shifts the burden of proof to the defendant or person opposing the restitution claim. *Id.* Art. 78. It remains to be seen how reversing the burden of proof will actually play out.

150 *Pilot Project Chengue Report*, *supra* note 63, at 20–21; 23.

policies by the time that a property restitution or compensation scheme is put in place. Institutions capable of establishing such policies are typically weakened by conflict.[151] Nonetheless, a remedial process for forced displacement can be more effective if it incorporates community-based evidence in the absence of conclusive documentary proof. The international community can encourage a post-war political order to authorize community-based evidence, when appropriate, as a provisional relaxation of established property norms within the framework of transitional justice initiatives.[152]

Justifying a departure from settled legal norms under the auspices of transitional justice will not be appropriate for every post-conflict context. For example, the Iraqi claims commission established to resolve property issues affirmatively decided to adopt a quasi-judicial commission, rather than an administrative process, and to rely on the Iraqi civil code.[153] The claims procedure is similar to that of an ordinary court, including a hearing, individual property valuations, and a right to appeal.[154] Iraqis chose this rigorous process, rather than a more flexible and speedy administrative process, in part, because the latter was too reminiscent of Saddam Hussein's methods.[155] For Iraqis, coming to terms with past abuses involved respecting the traditional role of the judiciary and relying on individual judicial determinations for allocating reparations.[156] In other words, relaxing property norms in some post-conflict contexts may not represent justice or lend legitimacy to law and legal institutions.

## Part 7. Conclusion

When a post-conflict restitution program is advisable, but documentation to match people with their homes is lacking, community-based evidence such as social mapping may ameliorate the problem. While doing so likely requires a departure from the property rules intended to foster predictability and stability, this kind of flexibility in a post-conflict society can be justified by, and contribute to transitional justice efforts.

Any post-conflict remedial process must be seen as legitimate by returnees, by those who may be occupying homes abandoned by force, and by the broader

151 Secretary-General, *supra* note 137, ¶ 27.

152 Such authorization may, in fact, be done as part of a larger package of temporary transitional measures to facilitate justice in a post-conflict setting. For example, a law requiring identification documents for education or health services may need to be suspended to facilitate access for returning IDPs and refugees who lack such documentation. Van der Auweraert interview, *supra* note 66.

153 Van der Auweraert, *supra* note 88, at 477.

154 *Id.*

155 *Id.*

156 Van der Auweraert interview, *supra* note 66.

society. If not, the transitional political order will be at risk and the system designed to remedy the human rights abuse of forced eviction may only engender a new set of grudges that will ignite later conflict.[157]

157 Van der Auweraert, *supra* note 88, at 469.

Chapter 2

# Property Endowments and Social Ordering: The Long Road to Land Law in East Timor

Daniel Fitzpatrick

An emerging body of literature considers the initial development of institutions and their path-dependent effects on economic growth.[1] Other literature analyses the origin of property institutions in small group settings.[2] Yet there is little on the initial development of property legislation, notwithstanding its path-dependent effects on economic development. While economic analysis asserts a baseline preference for simple legal rules of property, to reduce transaction costs for a broad audience,[3] there is little understanding of the variables affecting initial configurations of simplicity and complexity in the drafting of foundational property legislation. This chapter identifies incentives for social and political ordering, to avoid violent conflicts over scarce resources, as a key factor in the initial development of laws on land. In particular, the chapter describes incentives for initial property legislation, in systems emerging from violent conflict, to develop simple default rules of state title to land, and complex rules relating to private rights to land. The case study is the development of land law in East Timor, which provides an unusual opportunity to analyse new property rules in a new nation-state.

The analysis draws on recent work by North, Wallis, and Weingast on social ordering in circumstances of violence, particularly in terms of correlations between state stabilization and property rules that favor a political elite.[4] An elite coalition stabilizes the state, and solves the problem of violence, by co-

1 *See, e.g.*, Douglass C. North, *Institutions and Economic Growth: An Historical Introduction*, 17 World Dev. 1319–32 (1989); Daron Acemoglu et al., *Institutions as a Fundamental Cause of Long-Run Growth*, in 1A Handbook of Economic Growth 386–472 (Philippe Aghion & Stephen N. Durlauf eds, 2005).

2 *E.g.*, Robert C. Ellickson, *Property in Land*, 102 Yale L.J. 1315, 1333–4 (1993).

3 *See* Thomas W. Merrill & Henry E. Smith, *What Happened to Property in Law and Economics?*, 111 Yale L.J. 357, 359 (2001) ("property imposes an informational burden on large numbers of people .... As a consequence, property is required to come in standardized packages that the layperson can understand at low cost.").

4 Douglass North, Joseph Wallis & Barry Weingast, *Violence and the Rise of Open-Access Orders*, 20 Journal of Democracy 55, 59 (2009) [hereinafter North et al, *Open-Access Orders*]; Douglass North, Joseph Wallis & Barry Weingast, *Violence and Social Orders: A Conceptual Framework for Interpreting Recorded Human History* (2009) [hereinafter North et al, *Violence*].

opting "violence entrepreneurs" through inducements based on control over the mechanisms of the state, including the legal authority to grant privileged access to rights and resources. North, Wallis, and Weingast argue that flexible property rules may emerge in the aftermath of violent conflict as a tool to accommodate interest groups within a stabilizing elite, through readjustment of privileges in response to shifts in the balance of power.[5] A corollary—not explored by North, Wallis, and Weingast—is that members of the state-controlling elite have an incentive to adopt a bright-line default rule of state title to land, in order to extract rents from the grant of land concessions for economic development. The East Timor example supports the hypothesis of a relationship between state-stabilization and design choices in the initial development of land law. It also illustrates the pivotal role of a group outside the political elite—international legal advisers—which supported complexity/simplicity configurations in the new law not to obtain privileged access to rents, but as a result of cognitive preferences for imported legislative models, and professional incentives for legislative compromise.

No state can enforce property rights through coercion alone. All property systems require a foundation of social consensus because of the cooperation implicit in widespread respect for property entitlements.[6] A challenge for new post-conflict states or political orders is that rules emerging from elite-forming processes may not lend themselves to the development of a broad property consensus. The East Timor example illustrates the potential for chronic property uncertainty in post-conflict environments as legislative configurations of complexity and simplicity respond to a stabilizing elite and to imperatives to avoid state-destabilization, without reflecting or securing a foundation of social consensus. Merrill and Smith suggest that the social consensus required for a cooperative property system is more likely to coalesce around simple rules, such as deference to possession or respect for the first to possess.[7] The East Timor example illustrates the challenges of property rule simplicity in a post-conflict environment, as deference to possession creates conflict with prior possessors, and respect for prior possession requires costly investigations into title and forced evictions by a capable state. Even a simple default rule of state title to land will provoke resistance from long-term private users of land when there is a determination of state title, and local claims are overlooked in favor of investors receiving state leases or concessions.

---

5 North et al, *Violence*, *supra* note 4, at 77–8 ("Clear property rights make land more valuable, but they may also reduce the ability to use land as a tool to structure elite relationships in natural states. As a result, elites have conflicting interests in making land rights more secure. In fragile natural states, the flexible redistribution of land ownership and control can be used as a tool to balance interests within the coalition, especially as the balance of power shifts among prominent members.").

6 For a discussion *see* Thomas W. Merrill & Henry E. Smith, *The Morality of Property*, 48 Wm & Mary L. Rev. 1849, 1850–51 (2007) [hereinafter Merrill & Smith, *Morality of Property*].

7 *Id.* at 1851–2.

The chapter concludes that the political economy of rule formation may stabilize a post-conflict state but fail to create secure private property rights in land.

## Rule Formation and the Dynamics of State Stabilization

North, Wallis, and Weingast describe social order in terms of managing the "central problem of violence."[8] They distinguish between three basic types of social order: foraging order, limited access order, and open access order. Foraging order applies to small social groups characteristic of hunter-gathering societies. Once social organization moves beyond small groups the initial institutional response to violence is a limited access order, which forms through elite coalition with privileged access to rights and rents from resources. Limited access orders are fragile where realignments in power and access to means of violence affects the pay-offs of violence versus the benefits of membership of the elite.[9] While limited access orders are the "natural state" of institutional development, some societies have evolved into open access orders with equal access to privileges, resources and organizations, including the police and military, on the basis of minimal and impersonal criteria such as citizenship. Impersonal property exchange is a hallmark of open access orders.

Limited access orders respond to the threat of group violence by co-opting individuals and groups with access to means of violence. The imperative to stabilize the state leads to co-option of actors who could otherwise destabilize or de-legitimize the state.[10] The co-option process is facilitated by inducements based on privileged access to rents, which are benefits above ordinary returns from control of an asset.[11] As North, Wallis, and Weingast put it, privileged access to rents in a limited access order is not "simply a method of lining the pockets of the

8 North et al, *Open-Access Orders*, *supra* note 4, at 57–8.

9 *Id.* at 59–64.

10 North et al, *Open-Access Orders*, *supra* note 4, at 55, 59 ("Individuals and groups with access to violence form a dominant coalition, granting one another special privileges. These privileges—including limited access to organizations, valuable activities, and assets—create rents. By limiting access to these privileges, members of the dominant coalition create credible incentives to cooperate rather than fight among themselves."). The imperative to co-opt violence specialists applies to fragile states. *See* I. William Zartman, *Introduction: Posing the Problem of State Collapse*, *in* Collapsed States: the Disintegration and Restoration of Legitimate Authority 1, 5 (I. William Zartman ed., 1995) ("As the authoritative political institution, [the state] has lost its legitimacy, which is therefore up for grabs.").

11 North et al, *Open-Access Orders*, *supra* note 4, at 108 ("In a natural state, each non military elite either controls or enjoys privileged access to a vital function, such as religion, production, resources, trade, education, or the administration of justice. Because of their positions, privileges, and rents, the individual elites in the dominant coalition depend on the regime to keep entry limited.").

dominant coalition … [but] the essential means of controlling violence."[12] The elite formation process includes incentives to control the development and application of new laws on land. And the incentive to extract rents from minoritarian control of the state is heightened where members of the dominant elite have obligations to deliver state largesse to their sources of non-state authority, including the patron-client networks that provide them with the capacity to exercise or threaten group violence, and even more so where their position as privileged agents is precarious because of elite competition in an unstable socio-political environment.[13]

North, Wallis, and Weingast's typology of social ordering provides a framework for analyzing institutions that emerge in response to threats of group violence. In relation to property, they note the conflicting interests of a limited access elite: while secure rights makes resources more valuable for the elite, flexible property rights may serve to balance competing elite interests, particularly in the early phase of elite coalition-forming as the balance of power shifts among members of the elite.[14] The development of land law in England provides an example. After the Norman Conquest in 1066 there was a problem of social order where a distinct social group, the Normans, now controlled a new political entity, England.[15] The Normans avoided forced evictions by overlaying a feudal structure on the pre-existing system of landholdings. Landholders owed service, homage and fealty to new feudal landlords, who in turn owed service, homage and fealty to superior landlords or to the King himself. Initially the elite coalition of feudal landlords had a military purpose: to stabilize Norman control through obligations of military service to the King in exchange for the grant of land. The grant of land was personal as on death there was no inter-generational transfer and the land reverted to the control of the King. This flexible property arrangement facilitated royal control and capable military commanders. However, over time the lords demanded greater security of tenure through the right to devise land, first to a legal male heir, and later on trust or testamentary disposition to a choice of heirs.[16] Importantly, as the lords crystallized their property rights, the bulk of the population retained relatively insecure formal rights to land, at least until feudal tenants (in their various forms)

---

12 *Id.* at 59. *See also* Francis Fukuyama, *State-Building: Governance and World Order in the 21st Century* 6–7 (2004) (reversing Max Weber's definition of the state as the authority with the "legitimate use of force within a given territory" to highlight the lack of "enforcement" capacity as a central characteristic of state failure); Derick Brinkerhoff, *Rebuilding Governance in Failed States and Post-Conflict Societies: Core Concepts and Cross-Cutting Themes*, 25 Public Administration & Dev.1, 4 (2005) (State failure includes a "breakdown of law and order where state institutions lose their monopoly on the legitimate use of force and are unable to protect their citizens.").

13 North et al, *Violence*, *supra* note 4, at 42 ("Patron-client networks dominate the organizations within fragile natural states, and they are usually networks capable of using violence.").

14 *Id.* at 77–8.

15 *Id.* at 75.

16 *Id.* at 80–86.

obtained rights to prove their (better) title in the Royal Courts through the action of ejectment.[17]

The following case study of East Timor explores the relationship between state stabilization and property rules in a contemporary setting. It argues that, in a broad sense, the East Timorese analogue to flexible grants of feudal title is a default rule of state title to land, combined with complex rules of private property in land. The orthodox legal baseline of state (allodial) title to sovereign state territory suits elites seeking to extract rents from state control over resources. In particular, a rule that the state holds title to land without an owner places the burden of proving private title on private claimants, and creates opportunities for extraction of rents from the grants of rights to public land, including grants of licenses and concessions to commercial interests. Equally, while the proposed rules of private property in East Timor are not flexible—in the early feudal sense of *in personam* grants—they are complex because of the competing demands of groups with the capacity to destabilize the state, or disrupt the dominant coalition. The proposed private property rules reflect legislative compromises to accommodate competing interest groups, with access to means of violence, by establishing multiple pathways of argument, and leeways of adjudicatory choice, for respective sets of claim. The complex result, in a fragile state where determinations of contested title are likely to be slow, increases the likelihood that investment funds will flow through (rapid) personalized grant of state titles rather than impersonal exchange of (uncertain) private rights.

### *Rules of Possession and the Foundations of Property Cooperation*

Merrill and Smith argue that a property system is more likely to resolve the problem of social order through simple property principles because of the costs of communicating property information to a large audience.[18] Simple property rules facilitate the shared expectations of cooperation implicit in a property system. Merrill and Smith provide an example from the game-theoretic literature on rules of possession: those engaged in resource competition are more likely to reach a cooperative equilibrium where a simple rule of respect for possession supports expectations that those who have incurred costs to obtain possession will defend their possession more fiercely than those who simply wish to obtain possession.[19] The asymmetry of expectation leads to mutually reinforcing expectations of relative success, with possessors more likely to defend their claims with confidence and aggression, and other claimants more likely to forego their own claims in order to search for possessory claims elsewhere. Once both parties expect the other to

17 *Id.* at 84–5.

18 Merrill & Smith, *Morality of Property*, *supra* note 6.

19 *Id.* at 1858–59. *See also* Herbert Gintis, *The Evolution of Private Property*, 64 J. Econ. Behav. & Org. 1 (2007); Robert Sugden, *The Economics of Rights, Cooperation and Welfare* 70–71, 100–101 (1986).

follow the simple rule of respect for possession, there is a natural tendency towards cooperation as it is costly to break the cooperative pattern.[20]

Merrill and Smith nominate the first-in-time rule, which allocates entitlements to a first possessor, as a related example of a simple foundational rule of property.[21] A rule of first possession provides an easily understood response to the potential for violent resource competition. An example is the first car to enter a one-way bridge: it has the right of way as any other rule would be highly productive of social disorder.[22] Another example is the rule of first possession in the Californian gold mining districts. The rule granted rights to the first person to dig a hole and stake a claim.[23] McDowell, and Zerbe and Anderson, contend that the mining conditions of relative order were examples of Hayekian ordering in the absence of law.[24] Zerbe and Anderson characterize the first possession rule as a simple game-theoretic focal point that guided initial patterns of behavior and predictions of behavior, which then served to establish cooperative alternative to costly resource conflict.[25] McDowell also adopts game-theoretic analysis to suggest that the first possession rule created asymmetrical expectations of success in the event of competition, while providing new entrants with the option of obtaining new rights by digging a claim elsewhere.[26]

A simple rule that respects possession, or provides remedies for dispossession, facilitates shared expectations of cooperative behavior, which is essential for a property system to avoid high cost reliance on coercive enforcement. Merrill and Smith illustrate the requirement of cooperation in a large audience property system

20 *See* Richard A. Epstein, *A Taste for Privacy? Evolution and the Emergence of a Naturalistic Ethic*, 9 J. Legal Stud. 672–3 (1980) (discussing rule of deference to possession as an evolutionarily stable strategy); Sugden, *supra* note 19, at 52–4, 62, 70–71; Richard H. McAdams, *A Focal Point Theory of Expressive Law*, 86 Va. L. Rev.1649 (2000).

21 Merrill & Smith, *Morality of Property*, *supra* note 6, at 859.

22 *See* Andrea McDowell, *Real Property, Spontaneous Order, and Norms in the Gold Mines* 29 Law & Soc. Inquiry 771, 774 (2004); Robert Sugden, *Spontaneous Order*, 3 Journal of Economic Perspectives 85, 88–90 (1989).

23 Andrea McDowell, *From Commons to Claims: Property Rights in the California Gold Rush,* 14 Yale J.L. & Human.1, 27 (2002) ("The first arrivals ... had the first choice of claims, while the others were allowed to make their selections in the order of the date of their arrival.").

24 *See* McDowell, *supra* note 22, at 773 (The mining rules "were largely self-enforcing, as in Robert Sugden's game theory of 'spontaneous order'"); Richard O. Zerbe & C. Leigh Anderson, *Culture and Fairness in the Development of Institutions in the California Gold Fields,* 61 J. Economic Hist. 114, 115 (2001).

25 Zerbe & Anderson, *supra* note 24, at 115–16, 128. ("A focal point provides a coordination mechanism that, prior to the play of the game, has mutual significance to the players based on their common past experiences. These experiences, socially or culturally derived, help players to 'know' what to do, and to be able to predict what other players will do."). *See also* Sugden, *supra* note 19, at 70–1.

26 *See* McDowell, *supra* note 22, at 796.

through another automobile analogy.[27] In any given city, there are large numbers of cars with owners or drivers that are not known to other owners or drivers, or indeed to pedestrians or potential thieves. Self-help measures to protect car ownership, such as alarms or steering locks, do not establish a generally recognized duty not to interfere with another person's car. Equally, legal actions to enforce ownership—through prosecutions for theft or civil actions in trespass—may shape expectations but are relatively infrequent compared to the total number of cars. Neither law nor self-help can solve the problem of coordinated expectations of respect for property among a large group of unconnected people.[28] According to Merrill and Smith, a property system requires a robust moral consensus relating to property, which must be simple and easy-to-communicate because of the large and disconnected nature of the property audience. Simplicity is required because the collection of detailed information on rival claims in every particular situation would not facilitate the stability of expectations required for property cooperation. Moreover an interpretable standard—as opposed to a bright-line rule or principle—creates opportunities for multiple self-interested interpretations that also undermine the stable expectations required for cooperation.[29]

In the post-conflict circumstances of East Timor, as in other contemporary examples of armed conflicts, establishing the cooperative foundations of a property system is challenging as there is an implicit tension between rules favoring possession, and the provision of remedies for dispossession. Many of those in possession are secondary occupiers—people who occupied someone else's housing in circumstances of displacement. Conversely, those seeking restitution of possession include claimants that acquired title for value without notice of other claims, and claimants that acquired title through fraud or notice of previous acts of wrongful dispossession. In fact, due to the complex historical circumstances of East Timor, those seeking restitution of possession encompass different sets of claimant from different events of dispossession. These types of circumstances militate against a broad property consensus based either on a simple rule of possession, or a remedy for dispossession. A rule of possession that reflects expectations of aggressive defense by possessors denies the expectations of a dispossessed prior possessor. A remedy for dispossession—either of a first possessor or a successor to that title—requires enquiry into the acquisition of title and forced eviction of the current possessor. Hence, while the East Timorese state may stabilize around a dominant elite—enriching itself through control over the state land leasing and concessions process—the case study provides little foreseeable prospect of a private property system marked by broad cooperative respect for possession and impersonal exchanges of secure property rights.

---

27 Merrill & Smith, *Morality of Property*, *supra* note 6, at 1853–4.
28 *Id.* at 1854–5.
29 *Id.* at 1857.

## Moving Towards Law: The Development of Land Law in East Timor

Portugal held Timor as a colony from 1701 to 1974, interrupted by Japanese military occupation between 1942 and 1945. In 1975 the Indonesian military invaded East Timor, shortly after Portugal withdrew from all its colonies. From 1974 to 1999, at least 102,800 and as many as 183,000 East Timorese died from conflict-related causes. These deaths represented between 15 percent and 25 percent of East Timor's then population, a mortality rate equivalent to the killing fields of Cambodia.[30] Most deaths were due to the famine that resulted from forced relocations by the Indonesian military. Others resulted from targeted killings of East Timorese independence supporters by the Indonesian military and its proxies. In 1999 the Indonesian government agreed, over the objections of its military command, to hold a popular referendum on independence for East Timor. Almost 80 percent of East Timorese voted for independence, notwithstanding a campaign of intimidation planned by Indonesian military forces and executed by pro-Indonesian militia groups.

Following the vote, the Indonesian military and its militia proxies carried out a "scorched earth" campaign of property destruction and forced population displacement. Most land title offices and records were destroyed. More than half the housing stock was seriously damaged or destroyed. Over 400,000 people were internally displaced within East Timor itself, and a further 300,000 fled or were forcibly transported across the border to West Timor. This widespread displacement—more than 75 percent of the population—created a humanitarian crisis, while also reawakening cycles of land conflict as some took advantage of displacement or abandonment to repossess lands allegedly lost as a result of dispossession in either the Portuguese, Japanese and Indonesian periods of control of East Timor. Not surprisingly, in the capital city of Dili there was a rush to occupy habitable houses when displaced people returned to seek shelter. Much of the housing subject to ad hoc occupation had been held by Indonesian citizens, who fled once order was established by a UN-led military force (INTERFET).

As a result of the war-torn history of East Timor there are multiple bases for land claims, and a legacy of contestation over past events of possession and dispossession. The potential bases for private claims to land in contemporary East Timor include custom, possession, Portuguese title documents, Indonesian title documents, and eminent domain.[31] According to Indonesian government records, the colonial Portuguese Timor administration issued and registered

---

30 Commission for Reception, Truth and Reconciliation in East Timor (CAVR), *Chega! Report of the Commission for Reception, Truth and Reconciliation in Timor-Leste* 44 (2006).

31 *See* Daniel Fitzpatrick, *Land Claims in East Timor* 136 (2002). While on current statistics only around 8 percent of claimed land parcels are contested, these figures cover urban and peri-urban areas in districts targeted by a USAID-supported claims collection process. There has been no systematic claims collection in rural districts. Interview with

2,843 land titles between 1900 and 1974.[32] Between 1976 and 1996 the Indonesian administration issued and registered a total of 34,965 Indonesian property titles, covering approximately 10 percent of East Timor's total land mass. Most titles issued by the Portuguese and Indonesians took the form of limited term leases rather than indefinite ownership interests.[33] By 1998, according to de Sousa Xavier, the total number of Indonesian titles had increased to 44,091 titles.[34] In theory, these Indonesian titles included converted Portuguese titles pursuant to conversion regulations issued by the Indonesian government for East Timor. However the number of converted Portuguese titles was relatively small, as Indonesian government files record that only 142 out of a possible 1,503 in the capital city, Dili, were converted; and that, moreover, there was never any application for conversion by non-Indonesian citizens (i.e. East Timorese exiles in Portugal or Australia).[35]

On October 25, 1999 the United Nations Security Council passed Resolution No 1272, establishing the United Nations Transitional Authority in East Timor (UNTAET). Article 1 vested all legislative and executive authority with respect to East Timor, including the administration of justice, in the hands of UNTAET. After democratic elections East Timor attained independence in March 2002. The Fretilin party, which had been closely associated with the armed (Falantil) resistance to Indonesian occupation, formed the new government with a majority of ministers drawn from a group of Portuguese-speaking Timorese that had been exiles in Mozambique or Portugal during the Indonesian occupation. In 2006 political conflict between the Fretilin Prime Minister and the President, a former Falantil military leader, degenerated into circumstances of temporary state failure, as elements of the police and army engaged in armed combat, and latent tensions over post-1999 land occupations escalated into large-scale house burning and evictions in Dili.[36] In the lead up to the violent events of 2006, supporters of the Prime Minister and President had armed and funded competing private militia,

---

Nigel Thomson, Chef de Mission, USAID Strengthening Property Rights in Timor-Leste Project (Oct. 8, 2008).

32 Paulina da Cruz, *Studi Tentang Penguasaan dan Penggunaan Tanah Bekas Hak Portugis yang Ditunda Konversinya Dengan PP No. 34 Tahun 1992 di Kabupaten Dili Propinsi Timur-Timur* ("Study concerning the Control and Use of Former Portuguese Title Land that was Converted under Presidential Decision No. 34 of 1992 in the Dili Region of East Timor Province") 44 (n.d.1999) (unpublished thesis, Sekolah Tinggi Pertanahan Nasional Yogyakarta ("National Land College, Yogyakarta")) (on file with author).

33 *See* Fitzpatrick, *supra* note 31, at 88–9, 158–60.

34 Pedro de Sousa Xavier. *Aspek-Aspek Terbaru Pertanahan Timor Lorosae* ("Current Aspects concerning the land in Timor Lorosae") 2 (Mar. 1, 2000) (unpublished manuscript) (on file with author).

35 Da Cruz, *supra* note 32, at 11, 49.

36 For an overview that focuses on land and housing aspects of the crisis, *see* Andrew Harrington, *Ethnicity, Violence, & Land and Property Disputes in Timor-Leste,* 2007 East Timor L. J. 2.

which were associated with martial arts gangs and elements of the police and military. The conflict soon took on so-called "Easterner-Westerner" distinctions, which contributed to violent housing conflicts in Dili as "Westerners"—long-term residents of Dili—took advantage of widespread lawlessness to engage in tit-for-tat forced evictions of "Easterners," who had occupied houses largely owned by Indonesians before their departure in late 1999. The return of UN-led military and police forces led to restoration of order in 2007, the resignation of the Prime Minister, and the election of the President as Prime Minister under a coalition of parties known as the Association with a Parliamentary Majority (AMP). Fretilin is now the major opposition party.

The tragic events of 2006–2007 highlighted the fragility of the East Timorese state, and the relationship between state stability and post-displacement disputes over the possession of land and housing. The conflict over housing, in particular, increased appreciation among legal advisers and the political elite of the risks of disorder if the state attempted mass evictions as part of a program of restitution of pre-Independence titles to land. Until 2006, most international legal advisers advocated a simple rule of restitution of prior possession. Subsequently, a draft 2009 land law replaced restitution of titles with recognition of rights based on possession. East Timorese citizens could claim ownership on the basis of possession since December 31, 1998, even where there was a competing claim based on titles issued by the Portuguese or Indonesian administrations. The recognition of possession represented an acknowledgement of the likelihood of violent resistance to eviction by possessors, and the effects of further housing violence on state stability. However, the next year amendments to the draft re-introduced an element of restitution, as a result of recommendations by Portuguese legal advisers, while retaining a primary focus on recognition of possession.[37] Subsequent amendments also introduced concepts of community protection and community property, which were derived in part from Mozambican law. The following description of draft land laws for East Timor suggests that this layered complexity of private property rules is largely a product of concerns for state stability, including the need to accommodate possessory interests that may otherwise destabilize the state. It also reflects the complex political economy of legislative development in a fragile state, which requires compromizes among diverse interests—including international legal advisers—in order to increase the prospects for legislative approval.

### *The Draft UN Regulation of 2000: Restitution of Pre-Displacement Titles*

UNTAET Regulation No. 1 established a governing law for East Timor that maintained "the law as applied in East Timor prior to October 25, 1999," subject to certain international human rights standards.[38] This phrase was interpreted as a

37 Copies of the 2009 and 2010 draft regulations are on file with the author.

38 These standards included the Universal Declaration on Human Rights, the International Covenant on Civil and Political Rights, the International Covenant on

reference to Indonesian law, which had purported to adopt Portuguese law in East Timor after the Indonesian invasion in 1975.[39] The formulation of the governing law did not reflect international law arguments that Portugal, as the colonial power until 1974, retained sovereign authority over East Timor because Indonesia had a status as a belligerent occupier following its invasion in 1975.[40] UNTAET Regulation No. 1 applied Indonesian law—which had purported to apply and amend Portuguese law—as at October 25, 1999 rather than Portuguese law in East Timor as at April 1974.

In June 2000 the Land and Property Unit of UNTAET formulated a draft regulation to establish a land commission.[41] The regulation was prepared by lawyers from Australia and Canada, who at that time predominated in the Land and Property Unit. The regulation provided that applications for the registration of land rights, where there was no objection, were to be determined by reference to UNTAET Regulation No. 1, subject to obligations to reject an application where the right had not been acquired in good faith.[42] The reference to UNTAET Regulation No. 1 favored the restitution of Indonesian titles to land, with the qualification that land commission officers were to observe the international human rights standards set out in UNTAET Regulation No. 1. The result was a relatively bright-line approach based on restitution of titles to land in force as at October 25, 1999. Proponents of the draft regulation noted that—in formal terms—Indonesian law recognized and converted pre-1975 Portuguese titles in East Timor, which meant that restitution of Indonesian titles would not necessarily prejudice claims based on Portuguese titles.[43] However, as noted, very few Portuguese titles were converted to Indonesian titles after 1975.[44]

Restitution is a remedy for wrongful dispossession. On its face, it provides a simple response to the problem of population displacement. There is no great interpretive complexity to a rule providing that those who were displaced

---

Economic, Social and Cultural Rights, the Convention on Elimination of all Forms of Discrimination against Women, and the International Convention on the Rights of the Child (arts. 2, 3). UNTAET Regulation No. 1 is available at http://www.un.org/en/peacekeeping/missions/past/etimor/untaetR/etreg1.htm (last visited Dec, 27, 2012).

39 For a discussion, *see* Hansjörg Strohmeyer, *Collapse and Reconstruction of a Judicial System: The United Nations Missions in Kosovo and East Timor*, 95 Am. J. Int'l L. 46, 58–9 (2001).

40 *Id.* at 59. It seems clear that Indonesia had the status of a belligerent occupier, and sovereignty remained vested in the state of Portugal throughout the period of Indonesian occupation, Fitzpatrick, *supra* note 31, at 44–76.

41 A copy of this draft regulation is on file with the author.

42 UNTAET Draft Regulation § 12(d) (Nov. 24, 2000).

43 For a discussion of the conversion regulations, *see* Warren L. Wright, *A Note on Land Rights in East Timor*, 2004 East Timor available at: L. J. 1, http://www.eastimorlawjournal.org/ARTICLES/2004/land_rights_east_timor_conversion_indonesian_law_wright.html (last visited Dec. 27, 2012).

44 *See* Fitzpatrick, *supra* note 31, at 157–60

should go home. In international law, the 1998 UN Guiding Principles on Internal Displacement require competent authorities to protect property lost through displacement against illegal appropriation, occupation, or use,[45] and to establish the conditions and means to allow internally displaced persons to return voluntarily and safely to their homes, or else to resettle voluntarily in another part of the country.[46] In countries affected by ethnic cleansing or systematic racial discrimination—such as Bosnia-Herzegovina, Kosovo, and South Africa—there have been simple categories of displaced claimants with entitlements to restitution of property rights in land.[47] However, in East Timor there are multiple categories of potential claimants, including customary groups displaced by the Portuguese, Portuguese era title-holders dispossessed by the Indonesian administration, and Indonesian era title-holders displaced as a result of independence for East Timor.[48] While the law could focus on the most recent event of nation-wide displacement—in 1999 when the pro-Indonesian militia embarked on its campaign of violence—this would restore titles to Indonesian citizens and pro-Indonesian East Timorese, and thus restore a basic cause of conflict. In the event, these considerations led to rejection of the draft regulation by the UN Transitional Administrator in September 2001 (notwithstanding the obligations of the Guiding Principles on Internal Displacement).[49] Over time, as we shall see, they also led to consideration of a rule of adverse possession, as an alternative to restitution of pre-1999 titles to land.

45 U.N. Doc. E/CN.4/1998/53/Add.2, principle 21(3) (Feb. 11, 1998).

46 *Id.* principles 28, 29, 30. In 2005, the United Nations General Assembly "recognized" the Guiding Principles on Internal Displacement as "an important international framework." 2005 World Summit Outcome, G.A. Res. 60/1, ¶ 132, U.N. Doc. A/RES/60/1 (Oct. 24, 2005).

47 In relation to Bosnia-Herzegovina, *see* Rhodri C. Williams, *Post-Conflict Property Restitution and Refugee Return in Bosnia and Herzegovina: Implications for International Standard-Setting and Practice*, 37 N.Y.U. J. Int'l L. & Pol. 441, 448 (2005). In relation to Kosovo, *see* Alan Dodson & Veijo Heiskanen, *Housing and Property in Kosovo*, *in* Returning Home: Housing and Property Restitution Rights of Refugees and Displaced Persons 225, 233 (Scott Leckie ed., 2003). For a discussion of restitution in South Africa, *see* Bernadette Atuahene, *From Reparation to Restoration: Moving Beyond Restoring Property Rights to Restoring Political and Economic Visibility*, 60 SMU L. Rev. 1419 (2007); Bernadette Atuahene, *Property Rights & the Demands of Transformation*, 31 Mich. J. Int'l L. 765 (2010).

48 For a discussion and overview, *see* Fitzpatrick, *supra* note 31, at 1–21.

49 Warren L. Wright, *UNTAET Land Policy*, 2004 East Timor L. J. 2, available at: http://www.eastimorlawjournal.org/ARTICLES/2004/untaet_land_policy_east_timor_wright.html (last visited Dec. 27, 2012).

*Law Number 1 of 2003: The Bright-Line Rule of State Title to Land*

One year after independence, the National Parliament of East Timor approved Law No. 1 of 2003 on the regulation of state land and abandoned land.[50] This law is most significant for its definition of state land. The law defines land held under the "private domain" of the state to include unclaimed private land without an identifiable owner.[51] In civil law, the private domain of the state denotes land held by the state (and its agencies) under a private right of ownership. It contrasts with land in the "public domain" of the state, which includes public lands such as roads, waterways and foreshores. The inclusion of unowned land in the private domain of the state established a bright-line default: the burden of proving private title lies with the claimant. The bright-line default of state title to land reflected the incentives of key regulatory agents—political actors, government officials, and international legal advisers—to strengthen the state.[52]

Land laws that strengthen the state are consistent with aid donor objectives relating to international security and development.[53] Land law can be central to the territorialization of state power as it includes certain projections and assumptions of state sovereign authority.[54] In James Scott's well-known expression, government officials "see like a state" and interpret complex social relations with land through a legal lens of abstraction and objectification, as rights enforceable in autonomous terms, without the necessity of reference to cultural context or originating systems

50 Law 1/2003, Juridical Regime of Real Estate, Part I: Ownership over Real Estate [hereinafter Law 1/2003], http://www.mj.gov.tl/dntp/rel/DATA/UNMISET%20-%20Basic%20Land%20Law%2001%20-%202003/Law%202003-01%20-%20engl.pdf.

51 Law 1/2003 § 12(3). It also provides for temporary state administration of abandoned land, including the grant of leases to land defined as abandoned.

52 The definition of state land in East Timor provides a contrasting perspective to the literature on rent-seeking, which correlates fuzzy rules with enhanced opportunities to capture rents: *see* Carol M. Rose, *Crystals and Mud in Property Law*, 40 Stan. L. Rev. 577, 591 (1988) (citing J. Buchanan, *Rent Seeking and Profit Seeking,* in J. Buchanan, R. Tollison & G. Tullock, *Toward a Theory of the Rent Seeking Society* 3, 8–11 (1980)). In circumstances of minoritarian control of the state, a bright-line default rule of state ownership of land may enhance official rent-seeking opportunities by increasing the scope for determinations that land slated for leasing to investors is state rather than privately owned land.

53 *See* Patrick McAuslan, *Making law work: restructuring land relations in Africa,* 29 Development and Change 525, 525–7 (1998) (discussing the seminal importance of land reform to donors and from within recipient countries, wherein the reform of land law cohabitates seamlessly with "good governance").

54 Nancy Peluso, *Rubber Erasures, Rubber Producing Rights: Making Racialised Territories in West Kalimantan, Indonesia, in* The Politics of Possession: Property, Authority and Access to Natural Resources 46–78 (Thomas Sikor & Christian Lund eds, 2009).

of authority.[55] In similar vein, international legal advisers may also "look for a state" to facilitate strategies of exit and the achievement of program outputs.[56] The East Timor example suggests that the resulting focus on state-strengthening, including presumptive views of sovereign control over land, can interact with oligarchic processes of state formation to produce relatively well-defined forms of public property and more complex or interpretable rules of private property.[57]

Default presumptions of state ownership lie within orthodox common and civil law conceptual frameworks. Yet, in post-conflict circumstances of elite-formation, there are considerable incentives and opportunities for government officials to claim large areas as unowned land to facilitate rent extraction from the leasing of state land. Private claims are subject to widespread uncertainties because of population displacement, destruction of records, and undocumented forms of land holding. There may be investor interest in agribusiness developments. There will be economic pressures to generate employment and investment. In all these circumstances, a bright-line rule favoring state land may provide a low-cost interpretive pathway for government actors to obtain rents and grant land concessions to investors, who would otherwise face uncertain negotiations with purported groups of private landowners. Law No. 1 of 2003 allows this result as officials from the Land and Property Directorate may determine that an area of land lacks an identifiable owner and is therefore available for grant to an outside investor.[58]

### *The 2005 Draft Law on Private Land: Restitution and Recognition of Custom*

In September 2005 international legal consultants prepared a draft law on private land ownership, under the auspices of a US Agency for International Development

---

55 James Scott, *Seeing Like a State* (1998). *See, e.g.*, Debra McDougall, *The Unintended Consequences of Clarification: Development, Disputing, and the Dynamics of Community in Ranongga, Solomon Islands,* 52 Ethnohistory 81, 83 (2005) ("The legal articulation of property rights in the Solomons ... aims to transform complex, crosscutting, localized relationships into rights that are commensurable, predictable, and knowable to outsiders. It is an endeavor that has made little headway in the Solomons.").

56 *See, e.g.*, John Braithwaite et al., *Pillars and Shadows: Statebuilding as peacebuilding in Solomon Islands* 6 (2010) ("[The] focus has been on rebuilding the core pillars of the central state to the comparative neglect of the specific factors that fuelled conflict.").

57 This suggestion is put forward as a hypothesis that needs to be tested in other post-conflict contexts. At this stage the hypothesis is not a comprehensive theory of property rule formation in fragile state contexts as it does not include public choice considerations relating to the formation of coalitions to drive the property transition in question. Issues will include the development of coalitions, free riding and other questions of public choice in property transitions.

58 Such grants are subject to the risk of a private claim under yet-to-be legislated laws on private ownership.

(USAID) technical assistance program, and in consultation with the Ministry of Justice.[59] In general terms, the 2005 law continued the restitutionary approach of the UNTAET draft regulation. While the 2005 draft limited restitution to ownership titles issued under the Portuguese or Indonesian administrations, it provided for limited-term Portuguese or Indonesian titles to act as evidence for claims to "first adjudication" of ownership.[60]

Unlike the UNTAET draft regulation, the 2005 draft law allowed for first adjudication of ownership based on "possession and customary rights of ownership," provided there was no applicable Portuguese or Indonesian title claim.[61] This basis for claim did not establish a bright-line possessory rule, as it required proof of occupation for at least 20 years following "the practices of the community," and was subject to "no well-founded opposition from the community."[62] The draft also allowed communities to hold collective title to land and apply customary rules in administering their land, while respecting the principles of equality established in the law.[63] These provisions provided the first substantive legislative reference to possession, albeit in a customary context. They arose from increased awareness among international legal advisers of the social reality of customary landholdings in rural East Timor.[64] Outside urban areas most land is subject to customary forms of governance, with at least 26 distinct customary groups defined through language and ties of kinship.[65]

### *The Draft Law of 2006: Possessory Rights Outside a Customary Context*

East Timor's Minister of Justice rejected the 2005 draft law prepared under the USAID technical assistance program. It seems the qualified recognition of custom and communal titles to land inhibited the potential scope of state-owned land, and thus undercut the government's plans for agribusiness projects in rural districts.[66] The government commissioned a further draft in 2006, not long

---

59 Interview with Nigel Thomson, *supra* note 31.

60 Draft Land Law September 9 2005, art. 16. Eligible ownership titles must also have been the subject of registered claim by 10 March 2004, pursuant to Law No. 2003, and also have "evidence of legitimacy" (arts. 28, 43).

61 Draft Land Law Sept. 9, 2005, art. 29(3).

62 *Id.* art. 51(1). The draft law contemplated gradual extension of a government land administration system to all areas of East Timor. Until then, "communities" could continue to resort to customary rules provided they did not conflict with the Constitution and the law. *Id.* art. 3(5).

63 *Id.* art. 3.

64 Interview with Nigel Thomson, *supra* note 31.

65 Daniel Fitzpatrick & Susana Barnes, *The Relative Resilience of Property: First Possession and Order Without Law in East Timor*, 44 Law & Soc'y Rev. 205, 206 (2010) (summarizing ethnographic literature on origin groups in East Timor).

66 Interview with Ibere Lopez, Legal Adviser, USAID Strengthening Property Rights in Timor-Leste Project (Sept. 9, 2011).

before the outbreak of violent conflict in May 2006, which was prepared with the assistance of a lawyer from Brazil. The 2006 draft law provided much weaker recognition of customary relationships with land, as a result of explicit drafting instructions from the Prime Minister.[67] The draft law did not refer to custom but did recognize a "communal right of use." The draft did not define the incidents of a communal right of use. However, it stated that land subject to a communal right of use fell within the public domain of the state.[68] Moreover, "traditional institutions" had a right of participation—but by implication no right of veto—relating to natural resource exploitation.[69] It seems that the communal right of use was intended as an *in personam* interest, akin to a common law license. The flexibility reflected the government's desire for control over the allocation of rural land for investment projects.

As with the 2005 draft, the 2006 draft law provided for the restitution of ownership titles issued by the Portuguese or Indonesian administrations.[70] However, the law stated that restitution would not take place if there was a third party in possession of the claimed property, who had exercised peaceful possession for at least 10 years or peaceful and undisputed possession in good faith for at least 5 years.[71] For the first time, then, the 2006 draft law privileged some possessory claims over restitution of Portuguese or Indonesian ownership titles. This change in approach reflected the emerging belief of the lead Brazilian legal adviser, in particular, that restitution of Portuguese or Indonesian titles would result in large numbers of forced evictions and substantial risks of social conflict.[72] This belief proved somewhat prescient given the violent conflict over urban housing in 2006–2007 (see above).

### *The Draft Law of 2009–2010: Possessory Principles and State Stability*

The violence of 2006–2007 led to the fall of the Fretilin government and its replacement by a coalition government headed by Prime Minister Xanana Gusmao (the former President). The new government has significantly increased the grant of state land leases to investors notwithstanding the continuing absence of a legal framework to determine ownership of private land. For example, in January 2009, the Ministry of Agriculture purported to allocate over 100,000 hectares of rural land for bio-fuel developments under Memoranda of Understanding with foreign investors, even though the Minister of Justice has legal authority to grant

67 *Id.*

68 Draft Land Law n.d. 2006, art. 9(2).

69 *Id.* art. 9.

70 *Id.* art. 41. Those who acquired land from the holder of a Portuguese or Indonesian ownership title were also eligible for restitution, although this process was to "privilege" those who acquired in good faith. *Id.* art. 39.

71 *Id.* art. 47.

72 Interview with Ibere Lopez, *supra* note 66.

leases over state land not the Ministry of Agriculture.[73] There is also evidence of rent-seeking through the grant of state land leases. For example, the former Minister of Justice was accused of corruption in an official report by the Provedore (a corruption ombudsman) in 2010. Yet the Prime Minister did not suspend or dismiss the Minister until 2012. Moreover, the current head of the Land and Property Directorate, which makes initial determinations on the legal status of land (i.e. whether state or private), was the head of a leading martial arts gang implicated in the violence of 2006–2007; and yet he has been elevated to the status of Secretary of State for Land since the 2012 parliamentary elections.

The current coalition government rejected the draft 2006 land law prepared by the Fretilin government, and commissioned a further draft under the auspices of a second USAID technical assistance project, which again worked in conjunction with the Ministry of Justice. Ironically, the lead drafter was the Brazilian lawyer who had worked on the 2006 Fretilin draft.[74] The first version of the current draft law, issued in June 2009, did not allow for restitution of Portuguese or Indonesian titles at all, and provided for ownership based on long-term possession alone.[75] A claimant would receive an ownership right if she peacefully took possession of a vacant property before 26 April 2006, without the authority of the previous possessor; and maintained possession in good faith for at least 5 consecutive years. In this event, competing claimants holding Portuguese or Indonesian titles had a right to compensation only.

The privileging of possession over restitution in the draft 2009 law had an orthodox policy rationale: to reduce the costs of proving title. As in stable socio-political environments, the rule of adverse possession reduced the costs of proving rights in circumstances where other mechanisms of proof were lost or costly to establish.[76] Yet there were context-specific issues of social ordering affecting the design of the possessory rule, including a desire to minimize the likelihood of forced evictions, which would strain the enforcement capacity of a fragile and emergent state. Tom Merrill notes that this interest in preserving the peace, in circumstances where a possessor is more likely to resist re-occupation, has "distinct echoes of a frontier society."[77] In East Timor, the peace-preservation imperative also stems from the fragility of the state, where conflict over housing can intertwine with competitive racing for public authority among members of the political elite. Its effect on legal design involves a social ordering trade-off: the greater the risks of violent resistance to evictions, and the greater the fragility of

---

73 For a discussion, *see* Tim Anderson, *Privatising Land in Timor Leste*, Etan (Sept. 15, 2008), http://www.etan.org/et2008/9september/20/15land.htm.

74 The drafting process took place with the assistance of a working group that included Timorese lawyers and land experts.

75 Draft Land Law June 12, 2009.

76 *See* Thomas W. Merrill, *Property Rules, Liability Rules, and Adverse Possession*, 79 NW. U. L. Rev. 1122, 1122 (1984)

77 *Id.* at 1131.

the governing elite, the more likely a preference for rules favoring possession over remedies for prior dispossession.

In early 2010, the Minister of Justice commissioned Portuguese lawyers to review the 2009 draft law. The Portuguese legal advisers highlighted the importance of state fragility concerns, noting that the attribution of ownership to long-term possessors "avoids mass dispossessions (and therefore the social tensions that could arise)."[78] However, the advisers also noted the importance of meeting expectations of ownership, which suggested restitution of Portuguese or Indonesian-era ownership titles. They recommended restitution of pre-independence ownership titles while retaining ownership rights based on long-term possession. This result favors members of the Portuguese-speaking elite that had received ownership rather than limited term titles under the Portuguese administration.[79] The draft law as approved by the National Parliament of East Timor in February 2012 combines restitutionary and possessory principles.[80] Claims of ownership may be based on Portuguese or Indonesian ownership titles and, where there is no such title, on continuous, peaceful, and notorious possession that commenced on or before December 31, 1998.[81] On March 20, 2012 the President refused to assent to the law, and referred it back to Parliament with a list of proposed revisions. The Parliament did not have time to consider these revisions before parliamentary elections due in June 2012. As a result of the elections, the AMP coalition has formed government again, with a new President after Presidential elections in April 2012. On June 25, 2013, the Council of Ministers approved a draft law that has minor changes only to the draft approved by the National Parliament in February 2012. It is likely the draft law will be approved again by the Parliament and submitted for assent by the President in late 2013.

### *The Rule of Possession in Customary Districts*

Under the 2010 draft land law, "mere occupants" cannot acquire ownership rights to land by means of special adverse possession.[82] Mere occupants are defined to include people using land with no intention of acting as owners, people "who

78 Ana Belmarco & Joao Moucheira, *Work Mission in East Timor of the Technical Team from the Institute of Registers and of Notary of the Ministry of Justice of Portugal* (Dec. 2008) (on file with author).

79 Portuguese ownership titles were only granted to senior members of the indigenous colonial elite, including members of large landholding families that retain political influence in contemporary East Timor.

80 Draft Land Law Feb. 6, 2012.

81 *See id.* art. 22. It seems that the decision to push the commencement date of possession back to 31 December 1998 was motivated by a desire not to reward ad hoc occupiers of land after 1999, in part because of fears of renewed possessory conflicts in Dili. It may also be that the current coalition government was concerned not to recognize post-1999 claims to valuable coastal land by Fretilin-connected actors.

82 Draft Land Law n.d. 2010 art. 10(2).

took advantage of the tolerance of legitimate possessors," and representatives and agents of the legal possessor.[83] These categories establish distinctions between actual and legal possession that are common to civil and common law systems. They allow possessory doctrines to accommodate transactions such as bailment, leases and licenses. Unfortunately, and somewhat surprisingly, the draft 2010 law does not extend the distinction between mere occupants and legal possessors to customary districts. It defines possessors to include those who reside in, have erected buildings on, or have cultivated land claimed by another party based on the belief of ancestral customary domain, even when rent is being paid to that party.[84] This definition potentially allows persons that are not members of customary groups to claim alienable ownership of land within ancestral customary domains, even though they might otherwise fall within the definition of "mere occupant."

There are large numbers of relocated peoples living on land claimed by a customary group in East Timor. Many have occupied the land since before December 31, 1998, which entitles them to claim statutory ownership of land provided they have remained in possession. The application of a bright-line rule of possession to areas of customary domain will be highly contestable as a result of multiple events of population displacement in the history of East Timor. There are two broad categories of persons relocated to customary land during Portuguese or Indonesian times: those who have access to land pursuant to traditional agreement with the origin group; and those who occupied land during the war-torn years of the Indonesian occupation without contemporaneous agreement from origin house elders. While these categories are subject to a number of fine distinctions, and an evolving spectrum of relations between latecomers and first comer landholders, it is clear that entitlement to ownership on the basis of individual possession alone, with unrestricted powers to sell land to other Timorese citizens, will be inconsistent with localized understandings of relocatee rights and, in some cases, will lead to violent conflict should relocatees claim alienable rights of ownership.[85]

Reportedly, East Timor's Council of Ministers debated extension of a relatively bright-line rule of possession to customary districts at some length. The decision to apply the possessory rule, without reference to mere occupant distinctions, was made with one dissent—a Minister from the Socialist Party.[86] The Socialist Party is a member of the governing AMP coalition. In essence, the decision reflects a consensus among the political elite—including leaders of the opposition Fretilin Party—that the traditional authority of customary elders should not be recognized in the new institutional landscape of independent East Timor. There is longstanding elite antagonism to political acceptance of customary authority in rural areas in East Timor.[87] while members of the Council of Ministers are likely aware of the

83 *Id.* art. 10(1).
84 *Id.* art. 10(3).
85 *See* further Fitzpatrick & Barnes, *supra* note 65.
86 Interview with Ibere Lopez, *supra* note 66.
87 Fitzpatrick, *supra* note 31, at 24–42.

risks of conflict in rural districts, it seems that—unlike the case of urban housing conflicts—rural land conflict does not pose a sufficient threat to state stability to generate the development of complex or ambiguous law, including the retention of distinctions between mere occupancy and legal possession.

*Further Rule Complexity: Community Protection Zones and Community Property* The application of possessory principles to areas of ancestral customary domain takes place in conjunction with two new legal categories: community protection zones and community property. The notion of a community protection zone is borrowed from Mozambican law. Article 21 defines community protection zones as areas protected by the State for the purpose of safeguarding common interests of local communities.[88] In a community protection zone, the state has a number of protective obligations, including to ensure participatory and non-discriminatory customary practices, and to protect community ways of life.[89] Outside investment must also be preceded by community consultation.[90] These protective obligations apply irrespective of the nature of land ownership in a community protection zone.[91] In addition to individual rights based on possession or Portuguese or Indonesian statutory ownership, land in a community protection zone may be owned by the state or collectively by a community. Community-owned land is defined as land of common and shared use, organized in accordance with local practices and customs.[92] There is thus a complex, if not confusing, mosaic of legal landholdings in rural districts, which is overlaid by a wide-ranging set of protective obligations vested in the state.

At this stage, all domestic land actors in East Timor are unfamiliar with the notion of a "community protection zone." The notion of a community protection zone was taken from Mozambican law, primarily as a result of conversations among international legal advisers. There was a belief among international actors that key political and bureaucratic figures in East Timor would not support explicit recognition of customary structures, that a reference to Mozambique would provide legitimacy and a cognitive shortcut for East Timorese political figures who were exiles in Mozambique during the Indonesian occupation, and that the experience in Mozambique would provide a useful template for the implementation of Chapter V in East Timor.[93] The development of land law in Mozambique involved similar circumstances to East Timor of a former Portuguese colony emerging from

88 Protection areas have a broad potential reach as they include agricultural areas, either cultivated or fallow, forests, culturally relevant sites, pastures, water springs or areas with natural resources that are shared by the population and necessary for its subsistence. Draft Land Law Feb. 6, 2012, art. 21.

89 *Id.* art. 22.

90 *Id.* art. 25.

91 *Id.* art. 22.

92 *Id.* art. 25.

93 Interview with Ibere Lopez, *supra* note 66.

war, and a political elite antagonistic to recognition of customary authority. As is possible for community protection zones in East Timor, the state in Mozambique may grant state land leases to investors in rural areas subject to requirements of community consultation and partnership. The aim is not to grant bright-line collective rights of exclusion to customary landholders through recognition of customary rights to land, but to encourage "fuzzy" local processes of discussion and participation in development projects.

The importation of Mozambican legal concepts by foreign advisers had little to do with indigenous East Timorese processes of elite-formation. Community protection zones are not compatible with rent-seeking models of legislative development and their relationship with limited access orders. Their incorporation into the law reflects a conscious effort by foreign legal advisers to work within political constraints on recognizing customary rights to land, and elite desires for broad definitions of state land. However, their implementation will be influenced by the rent-seeking incentives of key actors in the state. In particular, at present there are no incentives for Land and Property Directorate officials to identify or demarcate community protection zones, in a timely or expansive manner, as that will trigger costly consultation and protection measures, and reduce the opportunity for rent-seeking gain from rapid grant of leases over state land.[94] A lower cost interpretive pathway will involve declaration by the Land and Property Directorate that an area sought by an investor is state land outside a community protection zone. This will allow the direct grant of rights to an investor, without incurring community protection zone obligations, including in particular the requirements of consultation prior to third-party economic activity. In fact, in a series of consultations with the author in 2011, senior officials at the Land and Property Directorate—who have tertiary qualifications in land administration from Indonesian institutions—repeatedly interpreted their scope by reference to Indonesian legal concepts that limit customary land to areas of actual residence and cultivation, with all other areas of untitled land categorized as state land. In Indonesia this interpretation has been the cause of chronic property rights uncertainty for rural communities, because it provides a basis for state claims to approximately 65 percent of the archipelago as state forest land, notwithstanding the presence of as many as 65 million occupants or habitual users of that land.[95]

94 The Land Law does not define the process of identifying community protection zones, or the line agency responsible for demarcating their boundaries. These lacunae will be filled by separate regulation or legislation. Based on conversations with a legal adviser in the Ministry of Justice, it is likely that the Land and Property Directorate will take responsibility for identifying and delineating community protection zones. This responsibility would be consistent with Land and Property Directorate authority over the demarcation of state land.

95 For a discussion, *see* Daniel Fitzpatrick, *Disputes and Pluralism in Modern Indonesian Land Law*, 22 Yale J. Int'l L. 171 (1997).

The first version of the 2010 draft law did not provide for customary ownership of land, whether individual or collective. After some debate, and criticism by a former UNTAET property lawyer, a second version included the possibility of collective ownership of land through incorporation as a cooperative. After further advice that customary groups were unlikely to form cooperatives, in circumstances of limited access to legal information, the draft law was amended to establish communities as juridical entities for the purposes of community property. A community may hold and register ownership of community property without the need for legal incorporation. Community property is defined as land acknowledged by the community as being of common and shared use, by a group of individuals or families, organized in accordance with local practices and customs.[96] As noted, a community may claim community property within a community protection zone.

Article 26 provides that the Land and Property Directorate shall assist each local community in the process of community property demarcation and consult with local and community authorities, as well as the elders residing locally, as sources of essential information. While community property may not be seized or alienated, a community may grant rights to community property, including leases to outside investors. Even more so than is the case with community protection zones, Land and Property Directorate staff have few incentives to identify and demarcate areas of community property in a timely or expansive manner. In conversations with the author, senior Land and Property Directorate officials also interpreted the notion of community property by reference to restrictive Indonesian conceptions of customary land (that is, limited to areas of actual residence and cultivation). There is little funding, capacity and political will to undertake any process for demarcating areas of community property. Wherever possible, the state is likely to grant rights directly to investors through claims of state land, or compulsory acquisition of private land, rather than facilitating agreements between a community and an outside investor. In these circumstances, the category of community property will likely not be a bright-line right of exclusion vested, in a customary community and enforced by agencies of the state, but a symbolic legal artefact—a product of compromises in the drafting of the law—that at best acts as an element in the localized negotiation of entitlements to customary land, and at worst contributes to widespread uncertainty and confusion surrounding the effects of private property rules in the draft law.

## Conclusion

This chapter suggests that the path-dependency of post-conflict property systems may be explained by tensions between elite processes of state stabilization, and the challenges of broad-based development of property legitimacy. The political economy of rule formulation in states emerging from violent conflict creates

96 Draft Land Law Feb. 6, 2012, art. 25.

incentives to develop simple default rules of state title to land, and complex rules relating to private rights to land. This configuration of property rules may manage the problem of group violence, but will do little to establish a system of secure private property rights. The analysis suggests that societies with histories of violent conflict may have legacy rules of private property complexity that developed in response to imperatives for state-stabilization. These legacy rules may be sub-optimal in the sense that they have higher information costs than a correspondingly simple rule. They may also prevent or inhibit the development of social consensus around simple private property principles. Yet complex rules of private property may be difficult to revise because they form part of the process of elite-formation that negated the threat of group violence in the first place. As a result, while there will be economic incentives to trend towards rule simplicity, there will also be contingent historical events that explain the divergent paths of different property systems.

## Acknowledgements

For insightful comments and conversations relating to earlier (and very different) drafts, I am grateful to Carol Rose, Bob Ellickson, Hanoch Dagan, Nestor Davidson, Frank Upham, Andrew McWilliam, Susana Barnes, Nigel Thompson, participants at the 2011 Association for Law, Property and Society Conference in Washington DC, participants at a Regulatory Institutions Network (RegNet) seminar in October 2010 (Australian National University), and members of the World Bank Justice for the Poor Program in East Timor and Solomon Islands. Research for this article was funded by a grant from the Australian Research Council (Discovery Project DP0556531—with Andrew McWilliam).

# Chapter 3
# Is there a Right to Territory in International Law?

Alexandra R. Harrington

Whether at the individual or national level, territory is and has been the key to legal identity throughout history. For example, at one point voting rights in the United States were tied to one's status as a property owner within one's community. Even now, in the domestic context, ownership of real property conveys a more vested interest in the community, since taxes that support everything from municipal works to schools are typically paid by those holding property within that community.

Internationally, property—this time in the form of territory that is acknowledged as belonging to a claiming entity rather than individually purchased or inherited land—is and has been essential for the assertion and recognition of statehood within the community of states. This territorial requirement has existed for centuries in one form or another, although it was given concrete and accepted form in the terms of the 1934 Montevideo Convention.[1]

Throughout history and until the present day, wars have been waged for territory, even for seemingly minute territorial gains. And, traditionally, title to territory has been transferred between conflicting states at the conclusion of hostilities, thereby ensuring that the territory and those who live in it were part of a valid state under international law.[2] During decolonization and then again after the fall of the Soviet Union, states withdrew their territorial claims over certain areas or simply dissolved, yet the international community was quick to ensure that the affected territories became part of a new, recognized political and governmental regime that was able to serve as a member of the international community.

These basic principles and practices of domestic and international law function on the premise that there is habitable, tangible land or territory that can be possessed and transferred according to the established laws and practices of the relevant putative state. And yet, the international community is facing a threat to these basic assumptions. Regardless of the reasons for it, it has been well established that global sea levels are rising[3] and that a series of territorial entities—particularly

---

1 Montevideo Convention on the Rights and Duties of States (1934).

2 James Crawford, *The Creation of States in International Law* 499–500 (2d ed. 2006).

3 *See* Intergovernmental Panel on Climate Change, *Climate Change 2007*: Synthesis Report 30–33 (2007).

small island developing states located in the Pacific and Caribbean Oceans—will either disappear or become uninhabitable as a result.[4] Indeed, the population of at least one island in Papua New Guinea has been forced to relocate to other domestic islands due to high sea levels.[5]

This chapter first discusses early concepts of territory and its link to sovereignty, as well as the evolution of these concepts, and then examines modern concepts of territory and sovereignty, with particular emphasis on the way in which this relationship has evolved from World War I onward. Next, it provides background on the known and anticipated effects of rising sea levels on states, especially vulnerable states, and efforts by some potentially affected states to purchase lands to which they intend to relocate their populations when necessary. It then focuses on the physical loss of territory due to environmental, rather than political, factors. This distinction is made because, throughout history, political changes to statehood[6] have been solved through negotiation and reallocation of territory; however, this is not possible when the change is environmental. This chapter posits that, in certain circumstances, validly existing states that are threatened with environmental territorial extinction should have a limited right to territory.

## Early Concepts of Territory and Sovereignty

Historically it has been possible for a group identity to exist without the explicit requirement of holding territory; however, in order to constitute any form of sovereign entity, the requirement of holding territory is and has been axiomatic.[7] This trend, and the growth of important concepts such as the permanency of sovereigns once established as part of the international community, are the subject of the following subsections. What is discernible throughout the evolution of legal thought regarding territory and sovereignty is the connection between the two entities and the necessity of territory to create sovereignty. At the same time, however, the focus on the difficulties attendant in defeating sovereignty at the international community level suggest that sovereignty, once established, was not meant to be easily done away with even when control over a designated territory was diminished or even lacking.

---

4 IRIN, *Papua New Guinea: The world's first climate change "refugees,"* http://irinnews.org/Report/78630/PAPUA-NEW-GUINEA-The-world-s-first-climate-change-refugees (last visited Mar. 12, 2012).

5 *Id.*

6 In this chapter, "political changes" to territory include transfers resulting from war, colonial and post-colonial territorial transfers, and transfers negotiated between states or the international community as a whole. Essentially, a political transfer is based on human action or activity.

7 *See* Ian Brownlie, *Principles of Public International Law* 70–71 (7th ed. 2008).

*Roman Law and Territory*

Many early aspects regarding the possession of territory and sovereignty over it originated under Roman law. One of the most important of these tenets was the method by which one could lay valid claim to territory. Originally, Roman law required that there be discovery of the territory and physical possession of the territory in order to assert a legally valid claim to it.[8] Later, however, this requirement was deemed to be overly onerous by the Emperor Justinian, who instead established that the intent to possess the entirety of an area was sufficient and that those claiming an area of territory were not required to physically take possession of the entire area if they had this intent.[9] Justinian also established the requirement that a claiming entity for a territory actively defend it in order to retain a valid claim to it, meaning that the claiming entity must manifest outward control over a claimed area of territory and defend it from invasion or attempted conquest by other states.[10] While this requirement does not specifically include the necessity of a military presence for valid claims to territory, it does assume that the claiming entity would defend the claimed territory from outside intervention through all necessary means, including military force.[11] As a corollary, under the laws crafted by Justinian, the failure to defend a territorial possession forfeits a claim over the territory in question.[12] In the context of war, the losing state may suffer a loss of title over some or all of its territory, depending upon the terms by which the war concludes.[13]

Thus, Roman law established the key concept that a claim over territory is not an absolute right and that such a claim could be lost through what amounted to abandonment—or at the very least negligence due to the failure of the state to adequately defend a claimed piece of territory—on the part of the claimant.[14] The good faith intent to take possession and, inferentially, to defend the territory at issue was, however, sufficient to preserve claims to and rights over territory.[15] Good faith was important here in that, if a state was aware that another state had already established a claim to the same piece of territory—for example through the erection of defensive buildings or the planting of a national flag—then the interest of the second-in-time state would not be valid.[16] What is particularly important for the purposes of this chapter is the importance of intent to claims

8 Ken MacMillan, *Sovereignty and Possession in the English New World: The Legal Foundations of Empire, 1576–1640*, at 61–2 (2006).

9 *Id.* at 111.

10 *Id.* at 111–12.

11 *See id.*

12 *Id.* at 122.

13 *See id.*

14 *See id.* at 111–12, 122.

15 *See id.*

16 *See id.*

to territory, particularly in instances where the claiming entity might not have physical possession of the entire territorial entity but did manifest the intent to assert possession.

Further, Roman law established the dichotomy between imperium and dominium, meaning the levels of control exerted over territory and its occupants by the state (represented by imperium) and exerted over territory by the state or other persons (represented by dominium).[17] Within this system, the entity exercising imperium over an area had supreme regulatory power over that area, although it could—and often would—delegate some power to lesser entities, such as administrative units, operating within that area.[18] Imperium and dominium reinforced each other, although the existence of dominium was guaranteed by and dependent upon the existence of imperium.[19]

### *Classical Legal Thought, Empire, and Territory*

The early tenets of Roman law vis-à-vis territory carried over to the political entities that followed its demise. When more organized forms of sovereignty and statehood emerged from the Middle Ages, more consolidated concepts of territory began to emerge as well. One concept that remained consistent, and indeed became more important during the advent of colonization, was that of imperium and dominium.[20] Indeed, imperium and dominium were essential aspects of the legal grounds for colonization in that the concept of imperium allowed the colonizing state to exercise complete control over all of its claimed territory—including newly conquered colonies—and the concept of dominium allowed administration by local entities without the need for copious state involvement.[21]

Some seventeenth- and eighteenth-century scholars, such as Grotius and Vattel, asserted that it was possible for a nation of people to exist under the sovereignty of another state without fully losing its identity.[22] In this situation, the nation would be located in a certain area but would either be subject to conquest by a larger entity or would become too small to sustain itself independently.[23] Grotius was adamant that sovereignty could not be extinguished easily or without deliberate agreement or other legal agreement.[24] Indeed, for Grotius, neither property nor sovereignty could easily be abandoned, although in situations where states joined

17 *Id.* at 6.

18 *Id.*

19 *Id.*

20 *Id.*

21 *Id.*

22 Hugo Grotius, *The Rights of War and Peace Including the Law of Nature and of Nations* 62, 71 (Cosmo Classics ed., 2007) (1625).

23 *Id.* at 117.

24 *Id.*

together to create a new entity or separated to form two new entities there would be a combination or separation, respectively, of sovereignty.[25]

Vattel, writing during the classical period for international law in the eighteenth century, asserted that a state retained its position in the international community even when it entered into an agreement for protection from another—presumably more powerful—state.[26] Vattel imputed a heavy burden on states to protect their populations and peoples, and gave those subject to state jurisdiction freedom of choice in that, were the state to split apart, these persons would not automatically be required to assume jurisdiction of the states where they found themselves located.[27] In this instance, subjects could assert nationality of either state that was formed as a result of the split.

During this period, Roman concepts of discovery and possession as necessary to support territorial claims were reinforced by a series of legal scholars who both reflected on the general state of law and sought to support the expansion of European states through colonization.[28] Eventually, this doctrine came to incorporate discovery and occupation, meaning that there was some manifest occupation that was able to be known by the outside world.[29] It was this emphasis on occupation and, from it, the requirement that a state be able to defend its territory, that many European states included military components and requirements in the charters establishing the exploration and trading companies that would, ultimately, give rise to colonization.[30]

Additionally, throughout this period, and indeed until the twentieth century, *terra nullius* was an accepted legal tenet. Under the doctrine of *terra nullius*, derived from Roman origins, land that was unclaimed—or unclaimed by civilized entities—was essentially free from any legal constraint and could thus be conquered upon discovery.[31] This doctrine was influential throughout the colonization process and was used by both the chartered exploration companies used by many European states to fund and undertake exploration and initial

25 *Id.* at 119–20.

26 Emer de Vattel, *The Law of Nations* 85 (Bela Kapossy et al., 2008) (1758). In this way, Vattel qualified the Roman concept that territorial rights could only be maintained through defense by the claiming entity. The state entering into a protection agreement presumably did so willingly and as a means of protecting its territorial interests, which were typically not merged into those of the more powerful state. *Id.*

27 *Id.*

28 *See id.* at 213.

29 *Id.* Occupation required a manifested claim to the territory under color of right by the claiming state, such as by erecting a state flag or creating defensive positions within the area. *See* Brownlie, *supra* note 7 at 133–5. The idea of occupation was to signal to the rest of the world community that the area was already occupied by another state, and thus not *terra nullius* open for occupation. *Id.*

30 *See generally* H.V. Bowen, *The Business of Empire: The East India Company and Imperial Britain, 1756–1833* (2006).

31 MacMillan, *supra* note 8, ch. 3; Crawford, *supra* note 2, at 258.

colonial exploits and by the European states which gradually stepped in to take control from these companies and assert direct jurisdiction over colonies around the world.[32] Under the doctrine of *terra nullius* that was established during this time, the presence of indigenous communities on a piece of territory was not sufficient to bar the classification of that territory as *terra nullius* because the indigenous communities were typically not thought of as "civilized" state actors capable of holding or asserting territorial rights.[33]

The period of colonization and empire stressed the acquisition of territory and did not contemplate the loss of territory unless it was at the hands of a competing colonizing state. Even then, the impact was rarely felt in a direct manner, except where the territorial loss was accompanied by the loss of life. Thus, international law at this time stressed doctrines of discovery and occupation for the acquisition of land and required the persistent presence of the colonizing state or its agents in order to maintain control over territory. In the event that control over territory shifted, this was a political shift in that it shifted between states and did not simply disappear.

## Territory in Modern International Law

### *World War I*

By the end of World War I, the international community began its slow dismantling of colonialism, with the exception of the Italian colonial efforts that occurred during the interwar period. One of the key instruments of this dismantling effort was the Treaty of Versailles ("the Treaty").[34]

The Treaty had the immediate effect of creating the League of Nations which, while ultimately regarded as a failure on many levels, was designated as an international organization which would oversee territorial disputes between states.[35] The terms of the Treaty evidence an understanding of territorial loss which was purely political—through conquest by another state—and sought to prevent this form of territorial loss through mediation mechanisms.[36] Additionally, should territorial loss be regarded as the result of warfare between or impacting a member state of the League of Nations, the Treaty required that economic and/or military actions be taken by the entirety of the League members.[37]

The end of World War I saw colonies of the defeated states stripped from their original colonizers and placed under the jurisdiction of a designated mandatory

32 Malcolm N. Shaw, *International Law* 502–8 (6th ed. 2008).
33 MacMillan, *supra* note 8, at 8–10.
34 *See* Treaty of Versailles (1919).
35 *See id.* arts. 1–30.
36 *Id.* art. 10.
37 *Id.* art. 16.

state.[38] The mandatory state was a victorious state that was charged with overseeing the territory and peoples in assigned colonial areas with the goal of ultimately preparing these states for self-governance.[39] Thus, territorial loss was political in this instance and these territories were immediately placed under the jurisdiction of another state rather than interminably lost.[40] The mandate system established by the Treaty created three forms of mandates—classes A-C—which were assigned according to their presumed ability to work toward self-government, and largely split control of these areas between the British and French governments.[41] Despite this grant of control, the mandatory states were required to report to a specialized organ of the League regarding their work within the mandates on a yearly basis.[42] Further, the intent of the mandate system was not to effect the permanent transfer of these territories to the mandatory state, but rather to assign the mandate states to the mandatory states in the form of a temporary protectorate.[43] However, the goals of the Treaty were not quickly realized, and the majority of mandate areas were still under the control of their assigned mandatory state at the commencement of World War II.[44]

The terms of the Treaty directly imposed political territorial loss, as portions of territory that were held or acquired by the defeated states during the war were reassigned to other states. In some instances, areas such as the Free City of Danzig (Gdansk) and the Saar Basin, were placed under international administration for a set number of years.[45] The international administration system for these areas emphasized the political existence of these areas—and the territory on which they were located—and affirmed the classical law concept that a member of the international community could continue to exist even when there was a change to sovereign control.

Additionally, the Treaty and others treaties associated with the end of World War I[46] "freed" a good deal of territory, in that they legally reestablished and recognized states that had existed but were under the control of prior defeated states.[47] Similarly, the Treaties of Sevres and Lausanne, addressing the surrender of the Ottoman Empire, contained elements of political losses and involved the

38 *Id.* art. 22.

39 *Id.*

40 *Id.*

41 Crawford, *supra* note 2, at 568–74.

42 Treaty of Versailles art. 22 (1919).

43 *Id.*

44 Crawford, *supra* note 2, ch. 13.

45 Treaty of Versailles art. 50 annex ch. II; art. 100 (1919).

46 Although the end of World War I is viewed as synonymous with the Treaty of Versailles, the Treaty of Versailles was a peace treaty among only some of the states involved in the conflict. Other treaties also played a key role in the cessation of hostilities, including the Treaty of Lausanne and the Treaty of Sevres, which primarily addressed the cessation of hostilities with the Ottoman Empire.

47 *See generally* Treaty of Versailles (1919).

transfer of title over territory to other states or the appropriate mandatory regime rather than the physical loss of territory due to environmental factors.[48]

With the end of colonization and the beginning of decolonization, the doctrine of *terra nullius* was nullified as an actively accepted doctrine for asserting title over territory. In essence, the nullification of *terra nullius* meant that, globally, all territory was deemed to belong to someone,[49] and that thus there was an existing entity which could claim rights to it, thereby doing away with a key justification that had been used during the colonial period.

### *The Montevideo Factors*

In 1934, the Montevideo Convention on the Rights and Duties of States, which contained what are commonly referred to as the Montevideo factors of statehood, was enacted by the International Conference of the American States.[50] Under the terms of the Montevideo Convention there are four essential factors for state validity under modern international law: a permanent population, a defined territory, an effective government, and capacity to enter into international relations.[51]

The permanent population requirement is fluid in that there is no requisite size for the claimed population to qualify as a state.[52] There is, however, some limitation in that these populations cannot be transient, such as nomadic populations, and instead must be permanently located within the territory of the claiming state.[53] The territorial requirement again is not subject to any particular size restrictions and, further, it has been established that the borders of a claimed state can still be in flux at the time that statehood is recognized, provided that there is a demonstrated area over which the claiming entity can assert territorial control.[54] Effective government is again a rather fluid concept in that the claiming state must be able to demonstrate that it can govern the population effectively; however, this does not mean that the claiming state must demonstrate a fully functioning government or a government of a particular ideology, such as democracy.[55] As long as a loose governmental apparatus can be demonstrated, the effective government requirement is typically met.[56] Finally, it should be noted that the international capacity requirement is by far the most political, in

48 *See* Treaty of Sevres (1920); Treaty of Lausanne (1923).

49 With the exception of the things such as the high seas and Antarctica, which were deemed to be *res communis*, and thus incapable of ownership by a particular state; rather they are owned by the entire world community. *See* Brownlie, *supra* note 7, at 105, 169.

50 *See* Montevideo Convention, *supra* note 1.

51 *Id.*

52 Shaw, *supra* note 32, at 199.

53 *See id.*; Brownlie, *supra* note 7, at 70–71.

54 Shaw, *supra* note 32, at 199.

55 *Id.*; Brownlie, *supra* note 7, at 71.

56 *Id.*

that entities which have otherwise fulfilled the requisite elements for statehood have still been denied statehood recognition by the international community due to their lack of favorability with the international community overall.[57] This was perhaps best illustrated by the failed bid of Rhodesia to become a state in the 1960s.[58] Although Rhodesia technically fulfilled the territorial, population, and governmental elements of statehood, it was still denied official recognition as a state on the grounds of international capacity because the government of Rhodesia was organized on a system that embraced and implemented apartheid as the official policy of the claimed state, which the international community would not endorse or recognize.[59]

Despite its age and limited signatories,[60] the Montevideo Convention has supplied the enduring statehood test used by international law.[61] In the years since the elucidation of the Montevideo factors, scholars have suggested many other potential considerations for statehood evaluation,[62] yet none have been as indelible. Scholars have offered many opinions as to the weighting and interdependence of these factors,[63] although none of these opinions has been subsequently adopted to clarify the questions raised in this chapter regarding the existence of a right to territory for already established states. Once a state has been found to exist as a matter of international law as a result of the international community's acquiescence under the capacity prong of the Montevideo factors, the question of its territory becomes indelibly entwined with its sovereignty. Domestically, the state is regarded as the legitimate actor within its territory due to its sovereignty, and international law and actors will not interfere in this sovereignty unless a dire circumstance occurs.[64] Internationally, the recognition of state sovereignty through territory makes a state a legitimate member of the international community and gives it a voice within that community.[65] As such, international law uses territory as a factor to determine statehood and then uses statehood to recognize and legitimatize territory and its control.

It should be noted that international law and the international community has recognized anomalies in the application of the Montevideo factors once a

57 Shaw, *supra* note 32, at 200–204.

58 *Id.* at 469–70.

59 *Id.*

60 The signatories to the Montevideo Convention were: Argentina, Bolivia, Brazil, Chile, Colombia, Cuba, the Dominican Republic, Ecuador, El Salvador, Guatemala, Haiti, Honduras, Mexico, Nicaragua, Panama, Paraguay, Peru, United States, Uruguay, and Venezuela. *See* Convention on Rights and Duties of States, http://avalon.law.yale.edu/20th_century/intam03.asp (last visited July 21, 2012).

61 *See* Crawford, *supra* note 2, at 45–6.

62 *See id.* at 62–95; Restatement (Third) of Foreign Relations Law of the United States § 202 (1987).

63 *See, e.g.*, Crawford, *supra* note 2 at 45–62

64 *See id.* at 17–19.

65 *See id.*

state is established. Over time, it has become a well-established principle that the non-recognition of a state's government by other states (for example where a government comes to power through a coup) does not result in the non-recognition or negation of the state itself although this non-recognition directly relates to a state's capacity.[66] The same is true where a government in exile is regarded as the legitimate government of the state as a matter of law.[67] Further, Somalia has provided an important lesson. For several years, multiple entities have claimed to be the legitimate governing bodies of Somalia, resulting in a situation where no one is the effective governing body.[68] However, the international community maintains that, as a matter of international law, the state of Somalia still exists although its territory is controlled by various factions.[69]

### *World War II and Decolonization*

The Treaty of Versailles, and particularly the League of Nations that it created, was intended to prevent a repeat of the worldwide conflict that had ravaged Europe in particular as a result of World War I. However, for many reasons, the League of Nations was unable to live up to the charge it was given and it was only a matter of decades before another, more global, war broke out. This war would forever change the face of international law and would highlight the importance of the international community working together to combat human rights violations and the overall concept of the use of force in all but the direst situations.

At the end of World War II, the majority of mandate territories established by the Treaty of Versailles and the League of Nations were still under the control of their mandatory states.[70] When the League of Nations was replaced by the United Nations as the world's preeminent international organization in 1945, the mandatory system was replaced with the trusteeship system.[71] This system had a more cognizable goal of decolonizing existing mandate territories, as well as existing colonies that were vested in the victorious European states, in a timely fashion.[72] The new trusteeship system was not without controversy, and indeed there were several cases brought before the International Court of Justice in which states challenged the ability of the League of Nations mandate system to be unilaterally transformed into a portion of the United Nations' functions and

---

66 *See id.* at 34.

67 *See id.* For example, after the democratically elected government of Haiti under Jean Bertrand Aristide was deposed in 2004, the majority of the international community still regarded it as the official government.

68 *See id.* at 91–2.

69 *See id.*

70 *Id.* at 586–601.

71 *Id.* at 565–95.

72 *Id.*

jurisdiction.[73] The International Court of Justice was consistent in its holdings that allowed for transference of jurisdiction from the League of Nations to the United Nations.[74]

From its inception until the 1990s, the United Nations Trusteeship Council oversaw the gradual decolonization of all areas held in trust.[75] The underlying principle of the Trusteeship Council and decolonization generally was the principle of self-determination of peoples.[76] This principle did not necessarily involve the creation of new states for peoples who wished to and were able to exert their own identity and self-determination within the larger framework of an existing entity, although for the former mandate territories which then became trust territories there was a preference for statehood and self-determination as a territorial and political combination.[77] Indeed, this preference was manifest in the accepted legal tenet that the strength of statehood claims asserted by a trust territory could generally be weaker than another claimed entity and still be accepted by the international community.[78]

Thus, from the end of World War II to the 1990s, when Palau became the last trust territory to attain independent statehood status, international law promised former mandate and trust territories that they would be and were entitled to independence and self-government.[79] In this sense, the focus of statehood was on population and political will, as there was already some form of established territorial area over which these entities could assert rights, even if the exact contours of this territorial area were unsettled at the time of independence and recognition of statehood, for example in the creation of the state of Israel.[80] The grant of independence and the ability of peoples to assert their own identities and

---

73 South West Africa Cases, Second Phase, Judgment, 1966 I.C.J. 6; Legal Consequences for States of the Continued Presence of South Africa in Namibia (South West Africa) notwithstanding Security Council Res. 276 (1970), Advisory Opinion, 1971 I.C.J. 16.

74 *See id.*

75 Crawford, *supra* note 2, at 565–95.

76 *Id.*

77 *Id.* at 107–31.

78 *Id.*

79 *See* United Nations, *Trusteeship Council*: http://www.un.org/en/mainbodies/trusteeship/ (last visited Mar. 12, 2012).

80 *See* Crawford, *supra* note 2, at 48–9. Israel is perhaps the ultimate example of this principle because of the continuously disputed contours of its territory and borders. The creation of the State of Israel is a very clear example of political use of territory, since, while many of the arguments for the creation of a Jewish homeland centered on historical persecution and the need to escape it, there was no assertion that the Jews as a population would be without a place to live in the event that Israel was not created. Further, the potential future creation of a Palestinian state would be political in nature because it would result from political negotiations between the Palestinian and Israeli governing apparatuses, informed by the will of their respective constituencies rather than by the exigencies of

place within the international community was thus given primacy to any potential territorial questions, provided that these questions did not involve the entirety of the claimed state.

*Post-Cold War and Territory*

The unification of East and West Germany and the fall of the Soviet Union resulted in a drastic reshaping of the international community. The unification of Germany in many ways could be argued to serve as the union of two anomalous territorial entities, as the partition of Germany following World War II was the result of political factors and imposed agreements that, unlike mandates and trusteeships, did not have an intended terminal point. This partition was also anomalous in that it was regarded as a temporary solution and morphed into a decades-long coexistence—with periods of flared tensions—that resulted in what was essentially a stalemate until there was a significant will to reunify.[81] It should be noted that, in this context, the two German states came together under the rubric of the Federal Republic of Germany (known more commonly as West Germany), and that the German Democratic Republic (known more commonly as East Germany) brought with it territory as well as a significant debt load. In this sense, there was a territorial loss, in that the territory comprising the German Democratic Republic was lost, although it was absorbed into the Federal Republic of Germany rather than being lost as a matter of law and fact.

The fall of the Soviet Union, following fast on the heels of German reunification, threatened modern concepts of statehood and raised the question of whether a validly recognized state in the international community could disappear.[82] This question was reiterated with the Balkan wars of the 1990s and the disintegration of Yugoslavia.[83] These situations resulted in the fundamental international law tenet that states will not, as a matter of law, be considered extinct or fully disintegrated entities in terms of their rights and obligations and, as a result, a successor state must be designated.[84] A designated successor entity of the dissolved state is deemed to exist and it is this state that has the ability to claim the rights and responsibilities of the dissolved former state, even where the dissolved former state has been broken into new several state entities.[85] Thus, for example, the Russian Federation became the successor entity of the Union of Soviet Socialist Republics although several other states emerged from the dissolution of the Soviet Union.[86]

---

environmentally caused territorial loss and attempts by some potentially impacted states to find an alternative home.

81 Shaw, *supra* note 32, at 228.

82 *See* Crawford, *supra* note 2, at 705–14.

83 *See id.*

84 *See id.*

85 *See Id.*

86 *See id.* at 705.

These new principles of international law are important to the discussion of whether a right to territory exists because they demonstrate that, once created and recognized, international law does not allow for the disappearance of states as political or legal entities.[87] To date, the situations in which such disappearances threatened to occur were essentially political. Even though the USSR ceased to exist, the territory upon which that state was based continued to exist, albeit under a different name and political system, thus the continuation of the state's rights and obligations under a different name was not difficult to fathom from the perspective of law or reality.

However logical these new principles of international law and statecraft might be, they have not been tested in a situation where the state's territory literally disappears from the habitable world. Yet, many of the same concerns regarding the rights and obligations incurred by and owed by and to the state would be the same. There would also be new questions of the continuance of a state's rights over the submerged territory on which it used to reside, its retained interests in the sea beds and nautical boundaries which it could formerly claim, and the rights to natural resources located in the submerged land. Some legal scholars have argued that the loss of a state's physical territory would signify the end of the state per se as a matter of international law.[88] However, it is the author's view that this assessment is at best a deceptively easy way to view a nuanced and multi-faceted problem and at worst a recipe for legal disaster for states, their citizens, and the international community generally. In a legal system which shuns statelessness and the extinction of states, to say that the disappearance of a state's territory extinguishes the state is contradictory and does not take into account the full extent of the issues faced.

The fall of the Soviet Union in some ways was unremarkable from the strict public international law standpoint as it followed the accepted requirements for state dissolution, complete with the designation of a recognized successor state.[89] In many other ways, however, the fall of the Soviet Union was quite remarkable from the territorial perspective in that it gave life to myriad states that had been suppressed as part of the Soviet Union.[90] This meant that territorial claims and interests emerged, or, perhaps more appropriately, re-emerged, and, alongside them, there emerged claims to self-determination and general territorial independence as a matter of right for minority and other groups. In some instances

---

87 *See id.* at ch. 17.

88 *See, e.g.*, Rosemary Rayfuse, *International Law and Disappearing States: Utilising Maritime Entitlements to Overcome the Statehood Dilemma*, Univ. New South Wales Faculty of Law Res. Series (2010), http://law.bepress.com/unswwps-flrps10/art52/ (last visited July 21, 2012); Ben Saul & Jane Adams, *An Insecure Climate for Human Security? Climate-Induced Displacement and International Law*, Univ. Sydney Law School, Legal Studies Res. Paper 08/131, http://ssrn.com/abstract=1292605 (last visited Mar. 12, 2012).

89 Brownlie, *supra* note 7, at 649–70.

90 Shaw, *supra* note 32, at 240–41.

these claims have gone unaddressed, while in others they have resulted in the creation of areas with increased autonomy within existing states.[91] Further, old Soviet outposts, such as the port city of Kaliningrad, still exist and sovereignty over them has devolved to the Russian Federation although they exist completely within the territory of another state.[92] Territorial disintegration and questions of statehood and sovereignty have continued to be of paramount importance since the fall of the Soviet Union, as evidenced by the violent breakup of Yugoslavia.[93]

## The Disappearing State

Regardless of one's views as to its cause, it is very difficult to deny the existence of climate change, particularly in terms of the steadily rising sea levels across the world.[94] This chapter does not seek to assert a particular cause for rising sea levels, as to do so would arguably detract from the central point of the arguments asserted, which address the existence of a right to territory for already existing states in the international system when the loss of territory that they are faced with is the result of environmental factors rather than political factors. Instead, this chapter accepts scientific findings that sea levels are rising across the globe and that, unabated, this trend has and will steadily become problematic in terms of territorial use and habitability in the future.

Several examples highlight the impact of rising sea levels on issues of territory and habitability. As mentioned previously, at least one island in the 151 island chain[95] which comprises the Pacific state of Papua New Guinea has become uninhabitable due to higher sea levels.[96] This resulted in the relocation of the inhabitants of the island to other parts of Papua New Guinea.[97]

Beyond this, there are several more concrete international law examples of the territorial issues associated with the potential disappearance of states due to climate change. In 2008, the then-president of the Maldives, Mohamed Nasheed, made global headlines when he announced plans to examine the possibility of buying land in Australia, India or Sri Lanka to which he planned to relocate the population of the Maldives when the island nation became uninhabitable due to rising sea

91 A prime example of this is the status of Abkhazia within the Republic of Georgia.

92 *See Regions and territories: Kaliningrad*, http://news.bbc.co.uk/2/hi/europe/country_profiles/6177003.stm (last visited Mar. 12, 2012); *see also* European Union External Action Service, *Kaliningrad*, http://www.eeas.europa.eu/russia/kaliningrad_en.htm (last visited Mar. 12, 2012).

93 *See* Noel Malcolm, *Bosnia: A Short History* (1996).

94 *See* Intergovernmental Panel on Climate Change, *supra* note 3, at 30–33.

95 Papua New Guinea, *UN System-wide Earthwatch Island Directory*, http://islands.unep.ch/CHD.htm (last visited July 21, 2012).

96 IRIN, *supra* note 4.

97 *Id.*

levels.[98] Although to date this goal has remained unrealized, it nevertheless demonstrates the reality of the issue as well as the myriad legal issues associated with it—for example, what the status of the purchased territory would be, whether the Maldives would be able to reconstitute itself as a state within the confines of the purchased territory, what the legal rights of those already living in the areas contemplated for purchase would be, and what the immigration and citizen rights would be for the citizens of the Maldives who relocated to the purchased territory. Similarly, the Kiribati—another small island state that is projected to be uninhabitable due to sea level changes within several decades—has recently announced that it is considering attempting to purchase land in Fiji for the purpose of relocating its population.[99] Again, the same legal issues are implicated without any particular form of domestic or international guidance.

Further, in all these examples there is a vacuum in which international law would need to operate. This vacuum involves the standing of the relocating state/entity as a matter of law, since there would be no guarantee that the international community would continue to recognize the valid statehood of a state that left the territory over which it had exercised sovereignty at the time of its statehood grant [100] in favor of territory located in another recognized state. This issue would become particularly troublesome in the event that the target state (such as Australia or Fiji) refused to grant title to the territory outright and instead insisted on a long-term lease of the territory, similar to the types of leases used for foreign military bases. Thus, there would be a significant question as to whether the disappearing state would lose its statehood due to the loss of its territory where this territorial loss is environmental rather than political, and where the lost territory would not be recovered and claimed by another political entity, as has been the norm throughout political and legal history.

In this context, it is necessary to examine whether there is an inherent right to territory for recognized states in the international system where the loss of their territory is the result of non-political factors beyond their control and the territory would not be reconstituted as part of another state. In other words, does the grant of statehood after a showing that a state fulfills the Montevideo factors create a right to continuation through territorial relocation when all other elements of the factors remain the same? Or is the physically disappearing state doomed to disappear as a matter of law as well?

---

98 *See Plan for new Maldives homeland* (Nov. 10, 2008), http://news.bbc.co.uk/2/hi/south_asia/7719501.stm (last visited Mar. 12, 2012).

99 *See* Nick Perry, *Entire Pacific nation could one day move to Fiji,* Yahoo! News (Mar. 9, 2012), http://news.yahoo.com/entire-pacific-nation-could-one-day-move-fiji-044612426.html (last visited Mar. 12, 2012).

100 Although there is no official statehood granting entity, the primary organization that is responsible for ensuring the place of an identified state in the world community is the United Nations during the process of deciding whether to admit the claiming state to the United Nations. Brownlie, *supra* note 7, at 94.

## The Right to Territory

When examining laws regarding territory it is imperative to look to Roman law, as it is the font of much current law and understanding of territorial standing. Roman law established that it was possible to validly lose territory, and required discovery and occupation in order for a valid claim to territory to exist. At the same time, Roman law under and after Justinian took a more pragmatic understanding of the need to occupy claimed territory by doing away with the requirement for physical occupation of the entirety of claimed territory.

Further, Roman law established the concept of imperium and dominium which would continue to form the foundation of international law through the colonial period and, it can be argued, still informs modern international law. As a matter of law, the combination of imperium and dominium means that the state will exercise imperium over the entirety of an area while at the same time allowing internal entities to exercise control over part of its territory at the domestic level through dominium. However, without territory over which to exert control both forms of control are rendered moot.

Throughout the works of classical legal writers there are several consistent threads regarding territory. Classical writers continued to endorse the need for discovery, possession and occupation in order to claim continuous title territory. These writers also recognized that nations and peoples could continue to exist within the larger apparatus of another state,[101] although they would necessarily lose a certain amount of standing and sovereignty as a result of being co-opted into the larger state. Additionally, there was an understanding that, in the event of a new alliance between a state or nation and another state, it would still be able to exert a place within the international community unless there was an express statement to the contrary.[102] In other words, there was a presumption that, once a recognized part of the international community, this status was very difficult to extinguish.

The eventual shunning of *terra nullius* as a valid doctrine in international law meant that all land must belong to a state. At the same time, beginning with the mandate system and decolonization, the idea of self-determination arguably included the inherent assumption that there was a territory for all validly recognized people. Together, these doctrines have worked well in terms of establishing statehood for areas which had been the subject of colonial control and which sought to become independent states. Although the doctrine of self-determination has recently come under criticism in recent examples of national minorities and others seeking to further breakdown other states and being denied

101 For example, Grotius highlights the entities which existed as part of the Roman Empire. *See* Grotius, *supra* note 22, at 64–5.

102 *See* Samuel Pufendorf, *Two Books of the Elements of Universal Jurisprudence* book I definition II (Liberty Fund ed., 2009) (1660).

statehood despite making self-determination-based claims,[103] it was validly used to establish many states in the current international system including those small island developing states that are most at risk because of rising sea levels associated with climate change.[104]

Additionally, history has shown that the loss of territory and/or statehood is typically a political loss in that the territory at issue has not physically disappeared but rather is incorporated into the territory of another state. The issue of states physically disappearing due to environmental loss is thus a break with traditionally understood and imposed concepts of territorial loss as a matter of law.

Taken together, the past and the present in international law and the practices of the international community suggest that there is indeed a place for the recognition of a limited right to territory for states that are facing the loss of their territory as a result of environmental factors. The contours of the right as proposed are quite nuanced: the territory lost would have to be sufficient to render the majority of the state uninhabitable[105]; the right would not mean that the international community as a whole would be required to pay for territory to which the state would relocate[106]—rather, the recognition of the right comes with the concomitant duty of the international community not to withdraw recognition of statehood[107] for the state which must relocate and to provide such assistance as is practical; the right would not mean that the state losing territory could name any particular area to which it wished to relocate and automatically receive that area[108]—rather, the state would need to seek territory that is similar to its current territory and which the state that currently holds sovereignty over the territory is willing to give up; and the right would only apply where all other factors of statehood are still fulfilled by the territorially threatened state.

In essence, the right is meant to encompass existing and historically validated tenets of international law. It does so by acknowledging the place of possession

---

103 Crawford, *supra* note 2, at 107–31.

104 *Id.*

105 Thus, in the situation of Papua New Guinea, the right to territory would not be implicated because the majority of the state territory would still be habitable. The choice of a majority of the territory being uninhabitable rather than the entirety of the territory being uninhabitable is made in realization of the fact that there would be a significant issue of population control—or lack thereof—where the majority of the state's territory becomes uninhabitable. Thus, rather than waiting for the entirety of the state's territory to become uninhabitable, it is asserted that the majority should suffice to trigger the right to territory proposed by this chapter.

106 This would negate the possibility of using the right to territory as a means for redistribution of property or wealth.

107 It should be noted that there is a question of how the international community would actually withdraw recognition without a successor state to designate, as there is no formal tribunal which would render this decision.

108 For example, the government of the Maldives could not assert a right to take part of the island of Manhattan for the purposes of relocation.

and occupation as grounds for valid claims to territory and also acknowledging that the mere inability to exert control over territory due to factors beyond the state's control should not invalidate the ability of the state to exist as a legitimate state in the international community. Further, the right allows for the continuation of imperium and dominium in their modern forms, as without territory the state under present law could not be a valid entity under international law and thus could not exert control over or protect citizens at the internal level. The right also incorporates the statements of classical legal writers regarding the difficulty of extinguishing the place of a state within the international community and the ability of a state or nation to exist even within the confines of a larger state.

The proposed right to territory is necessarily limited and is designed to ensure that there is continuity of statehood and stability within the international system. Its goal is to preserve the statehood of otherwise valid states that are threatened by environmental disappearance and to protect the international system from disruption when these states become uninhabitable. The purpose of the right is to establish that these states have the right to reestablish themselves as existing states on an alternate piece of territory without facing questions of their status within international law and without the need to petition for statehood anew based on their new territory and location.

## Conclusion

The unfortunate reality of rising sea levels—whatever their cause—is that many states, particularly small island developing states that have only recently entered the international community as independent states, are facing the possibility that their territories will be uninhabitable in the not too distant future.

Although such a situation would have been unimaginable to the crafters of Roman law or classical law scholars, all of these schools provide insights into and justifications for territory that gives support for the idea of a limited right to territory as a matter of international law. Further, the process of decolonization and implementing the principle of self-determination should be viewed as reasons to provide support for and to states which are threatened by a loss of territory through no fault of their own where this loss is environmental rather than political. As explained throughout the chapter, the former is a loss which cannot be controlled and which involves the permanent loss of territory, while the latter is a form of territorial loss for one state while another state gains the territory—for example through the shifting of a border following conflict. Political losses of territory will seldom threaten the territorial existence of a state but the same cannot be said of environmental losses.

The right to territory advocated in this chapter is necessarily limited and intended for use only in the direst of situations. It is not meant as the precursor to a larger redistributive right, nor is it meant as a coercive right in terms of requiring the international community to give or fund the purchase of territory. Instead, the right is intended to ensure that an otherwise valid state in the international community is not invalidated or required to seek statehood again when it finds that it must physically relocate to another territory or face uninhabitability. Thus, the right to territory advocated in this chapter requires the international community to uphold its agreement in terms of recognition and the lack of a defined area of territory needed for control in instances where a state is seeking to continue on as a state within the international community.

# PART II
# New Worlds

# Chapter 4
# Outer Space and the Non-Appropriation Principle

Steven Freeland

## Introduction: The Legal Context of Outer Space

On October 4, 1957, the Soviets launched a space object, Sputnik I, which orbited the Earth over 1,400 times during the following three months. Thus began humankind's adventures in outer space. This milestone heralded the dawn of the space age, over the ensuing decades giving rise to the development of fundamental principles that would underpin the legal regulation of the exploration and use of outer space.

The Sputnik journey highlighted almost immediately some difficult and controversial legal questions, involving previously undetermined concepts. Some earlier scholarship considered the nature and scope of laws that might apply to the exploration and use of outer space, but only at a hypothetical level.[1] However, history changed forever on that day in 1957. Suddenly, the reality of humankind's aspirations and capabilities with respect to outer space became apparent. The world had to react, quickly, to an unprecedented event in an unregulated legal environment, particularly because it was clear that this was just the dawn of a quest to undertake a wide range of space activities. First and foremost, Sputnik necessitated a clarification as to the legal categorization of outer space for the purposes of international law.

As a preliminary matter, to categorize outer space one would naturally expect to require a legal definition of what constitutes outer space; that is, where does outer space begin? Indeed, this was the first issue that the United Nations put to the newly established United Nations Committee on the Peaceful Uses of Outer Space (UNCOPUOS), the principal multilateral body involved in the development of international space law.[2] Whilst many theories have been proposed since then, quite remarkably (at least for those not involved in the diplomatic discussions), the

1 For a summary of the main academic theories relating to space law in the period prior to the launch of Sputnik I, *see* Francis Lyall & Paul B. Larsen, *Space Law: A Treatise* 3–9 (2009).

2 UNCOPUOS, established by the General Assembly in 1959, currently has 70 Members, which makes it "one of the largest Committees in the United Nations," http://www.unoosa.org/oosa/en /COPUOS/members.html (accessed 11 Aug., 2011).

question of where air space "ends" and outer space "begins" has thus far remained unanswered from an international legal viewpoint.

At other levels tentative answers are emerging. National laws have specified a "demarcation" in national law,[3] followed more recently and significantly by some emerging international practice.[4] If such state practice is eventually extensively adopted and followed elsewhere, ultimately, we will have evidence tending towards the creation of a new customary international rule, but at present the issue still remains uncertain.

However, notwithstanding the lack of a clear definition of outer space, a number of fundamental legal principles relating to the exploration and use of outer space emerged quickly, although the negotiations directed towards expressing these into a conventional form took more time. This was due to a number of causes, including the unique environment with which it would have to deal, the very significant political and strategic factors at play, and the rapid growth of space-related technology that followed almost immediately from the Sputnik success.

In general terms, the fundamental international legal principles that regulate the exploration and use of outer space have served to allow for a significantly improved standard of living for humanity through the use of space technology. For example, important scientific questions concerning environmental protection and the effects of climate change on the Earth are addressed by fleets of Earth-observation satellites, and the use of satellite data is vital to facilitate relief efforts in regions that suffer natural or technological disaster. The prospects for the future use and exploration of outer space offer both tremendous opportunities and challenges for humankind. Law at the international level, and increasingly at the national level, will continue to be at the forefront in this regard.

The law of outer space has developed as a discrete body of law within general public international law. Since the launch of Sputnik 1, this process of evolution has been largely driven by the need to agree on rules to regulate activities in this new "frontier." A substantial body of international and domestic law principles

3 For example, the Australian Space Activities Act 1998 (Cth) § 8 incorporates into the definitions of a "launch", a "launch vehicle," a "return" and a "space object," a reference to "the distance of 100 [kilometres] above mean sea level. " For a detailed analysis of the Australian legislation, *see* Steven Freeland, *Difficulties of Implementing National Space Legislation Exemplified by the Australian Approach*, in "Project 2001 Plus" - Global and European Challenges for Air and Space Law at the Edge of the 21st Century 65 (Stephan Hobe et al. eds, 2006).

4 In 2008, Russia and China, with the support of a significant group of other states, submitted a draft Treaty on the Prevention of the Placement of Weapons in Outer Space, the Threat or Use of Force Against Outer Space Objects (PPWT) to a meeting of the United Nations Conference on Disarmament in Geneva. Article I (a) of the PPWT defines outer space as the "space beyond the elevation of approximately 100 km above ocean level of the Earth. " For more details on the PPWT, *see* Steven Freeland, *The 2008 Russia / China Proposal for a Treaty to Ban Weapons in Space: A Missed Opportunity or an Opening Gambit?*, 51 Proceedings of the Colloquium on the Law of Outer Space 261 (2008).

dealing with many aspects of the use and exploration of outer space have evolved. These principles are primarily found in a number of United Nations sponsored multilateral treaties, United Nations General Assembly Resolutions, an expanding range of national legislation, decisions by national courts, bilateral arrangements, and determinations by intergovernmental organizations. There are also a number of foundational principles that reflect customary international law.

Through the auspices of the UNCOPUOS, states have concluded five main multilateral treaties. These are:

i. 1967 Treaty on Principles Governing the Activities of States in the Exploration and Use of Outer Space, including the Moon and other Celestial Bodies;[5]
ii. 1968 Agreement on the Rescue of Astronauts, the Return of Astronauts and the Return of Objects Launched into Outer Space;[6]
iii. 1972 Convention on International Liability for Damage Caused by Space Objects;[7]
iv. 1975 Convention on Registration of Objects Launched into Outer Space;[8] and
v. 1979 Agreement Governing the Activities of States on the Moon and other Celestial Bodies.[9]

These five treaties deal with various important issues relating to outer space. When assessing them, it is important to bear in mind that they were formulated in the Cold War era, when only a relatively small number of countries had space faring capability, a situation that has changed over time. In general terms, the international legal principles they contain provide for the non-appropriation of outer space by any one state, the freedom of the use and exploration of outer space, a liability regime applicable in the case of damage caused by space objects, the return of space objects and the safety and rescue of astronauts, the notification to and registration of space activities with the United Nations, the scientific investigation and exploitation of the natural resources of outer space, and the settlement of disputes arising from outer space activities.

Although the drafters of the treaties contemplated that non-governmental entities might also undertake space activities, the responsibility for such activities was imposed, from an international law perspective, on states. Article VI of the Outer Space Treaty imposes "international responsibility" on states for "national activities in outer space," undertaken either by "governmental agencies or by non-governmental entities."

5 610 U.N.T.S. 205 [hereinafter Outer Space Treaty].
6 672 U.N.T.S. 119.
7 961 U.N.T.S. 187 [hereinafter Liability Convention].
8 1023 U.N.T.S. 15.
9 1363 U.N.T.S 3 [hereinafter Moon Agreement].

The provision then specifies that the "activities of non-governmental entities in outer space" require "authorization and continuing supervision by the appropriate State Party," but does not specify the mechanism for such authorization and supervision, simply imposing the obligation on states.

In addition, the United Nations General Assembly has adopted five main sets of principles, each of which relates to specific aspects of the use of outer space. These are:

i. 1963 Declaration of Legal Principles Governing the Activities of States in the Exploration and Use of Outer Space;[10]
ii. 1982 Principles Governing the Use by States of Artificial Earth Satellites for International Direct Television Broadcasting;[11]
iii. 1986 Principles Relating to Remote Sensing of the Earth from Outer Space;[12]
iv. 1992 Principles Relevant to the Use of Nuclear Power Sources in Outer Space;[13]
v. 1996 Declaration on International Cooperation in the Exploration and Use of Outer Space for the Benefit and in the Interest of All States, Taking into Particular Account the Needs of Developing Countries.[14]

These sets of principles provide for the application of international law and promotion of international cooperation and understanding in space activities, the dissemination and exchange of information through transnational direct television broadcasting via satellites and remote satellite observations of Earth, and general standards regulating the safe use of nuclear power sources necessary for the exploration and use of outer space.

The five main sets of principles have largely been considered as constituting "soft law,"[15] although a number of specific provisions may now also represent customary international law.[16] In addition, a number of more recent soft law

10 G.A. Res. 1962 (XVIII), U.N. Doc. A/RES/1962 (Dec. 13, 1963).

11 G.A. Res.37/92, U.N. Doc. A/RES/37/92 (Dec. 10, 1982).

12 G.A. Res.41/65, U.N. Doc. A/RES/41/65 (Dec. 3, 1986).

13 G.A. Res. 47/68, U.N. Doc. A/RES/47/68 (Dec. 14, 1992).

14 G.A. Res.51/122, U.N. Doc. A/RES/51/122 (Dec. 13, 1996).

15 *See* Steven Freeland, *For better or for worse? The use of "soft law" within the international legal regulation of outer space*, 36 Annals of Air and Space Law 409 (2011).

16 *See* Ricky J. Lee & Steven Freeland, *The Crystallisation of General Assembly Space Declarations into Customary International Law*, 46 Proceedings of the Colloquium on the Law of Outer Space 122 (2004).

instruments set out further guidelines for the use of nuclear power sources in outer space[17] and space debris.[18]

## State Acceptance of the Non-Appropriation Principle

Although the Soviet Union did not seek the permission of any other state to undertake the Sputnik mission, there were no significant international protests asserting that this artificial satellite had infringed any country's sovereignty as it circled the earth. The almost total international inaction that stemmed from the Sputnik mission confirmed that this new frontier for human activity—outer space—did not possess the traditional elements of sovereignty that had already been well established under the binding international law principles that regulated land, sea and air space on Earth. Instead, states apparently assumed that outer space was to be regarded as an area beyond territorial sovereignty.

Describing the early emergence of this customary international principle, Judge Manfred Lachs of the International Court of Justice observed in 1969, shortly after adoption of the first United Nations Space Law Treaty, that:[19]

> The first instruments that men sent into outer space traversed the air space of States and circled above them in outer space, yet the launching States sought no permission, nor did the other States protest. This is how the freedom of movement into outer space, and in it, came to be established and recognised as law within a remarkably short period of time.

Almost immediately after humankind began its quest to explore and use outer space, a number of foundational principles of the international law of outer space were born—in particular the so-called "common interest," "freedom," and "non-appropriation" principles. These principles were later incorporated into the terms of the United Nations Space Law Treaties,[20] with the result that they also constitute binding conventional rules, codifying what had already amounted to principles of customary international law. In essence, the community of states, including both of the major space-faring states of the time, had accepted that outer space was to be regarded as being similar to a *res communis omnium*.[21]

---

17 *See* UNCOPUOS Scientific & Technical Subcomm. & Int'l Atomic Energy Agency, *Safety Framework for Nuclear Power Source Applications in Outer Space* (2009), http://www.fas.org/nuke/space/iaea-space.pdf (last visited Dec. 28, 2012).

18 *See, e.g.*, G.A. Res. 62/217, U.N. Doc. A/RES/62/217 (Dec. 22, 2007); G.A. Res. 65/97, U.N. Doc. A/RES/65/97 (Dec. 10, 2010).

19 *North Sea Continental Shelf Cases* (*Ger. v. Den. & Ger. v. Neth.*), 1969 I.C.J. 3, 230 (dissenting opinion of Judge Lachs).

20 *See, e.g.*, Outer Space Treaty, *supra* note 5, arts. I, II.

21 Antonio Cassese. *International Law* 95 (2d ed, 2005).

These three fundamental rules underpinning the international law of outer space represent a significant departure from the legal rules relating to air space, which is categorized as constituting part of the "territory" of the underlying state. The territorial nature of air space is reflected in the principal air law treaties. For example, reaffirming the principle already acknowledged as early as in 1919,[22] the 1944 Convention on International Civil Aviation[23] provides that "every state has complete and exclusive sovereignty over the air space above its territory."[24]

The International Court of Justice has concluded that this characteristic of air space also represents customary international law.[25] As a consequence, civil and commercial aircraft have only certain limited rights to enter the air space of another state,[26] in contrast to the freedom principle relating to outer space.[27] As noted above, the fact that a demarcation between air space and outer space has not yet definitively emerged—at least thus far—has not in practice led to any significant confusion as to "which law" might apply in particular circumstances.[28]

The degree to which international law governs outer space is not entirely clear. The Outer Space Treaty affirms that activities in space are to be carried on "in accordance with international law,"[29] but the fact that most existing international law at the time developed for "terrestrial" purposes meant that it was not readily or directly applicable in every respect to this new paradigm of human endeavour. Moreover, the non-sovereignty aspect of outer space meant that any then existent national law (which, in any event, did not at that time specifically address

---

22 *See* Convention on the Regulation of Aerial Navigation, Oct. 13, 1919, 11 L.N.T.S. 173.

23 15 U.N.T.S. 295 [hereinafter Chicago Convention].

24 *Id.* art 1. For the purposes of the Chicago Convention, the territory of a state is regarded as "the land areas and territorial waters adjacent thereto under the sovereignty, suzerainty, protection or mandate of such State." *Id.*, art 2.

25 In Case Concerning Military and Paramilitary Activities in and against Nicaragua (Nicar. v. U.S.),Judgment, 1986 I.C.J. 14,128, the court noted that "[t]he principle of respect for territorial sovereignty is also directly infringed by the unauthorized overflight of a State's territory by aircraft belonging to or under the control of the government of another State."

26 *See* Chicago Convention, *supra* note 23, arts. 5, 6.

27 Of course, any space activities requiring a launch from Earth or a return to Earth involve a "use" of air space. In this respect, the law of air space becomes relevant if the space object of one state travels through the air space of another state. *See also* Liability Convention, *supra* note 7, art. II (convention applies *inter alia* to "aircraft in flight,", i.e, in air space).

28 However, as the range of activities in outer space becomes ever broader, the issue will become more important in relation not only to the broad principles of international space law, but also on a practical level—for example, to the regulation of commercial sub-orbital space tourism activities, which, at least under current technological constraints, involve paying passengers being taken to an altitude slightly in excess of 100 kilometres above the earth.*See* Steven Freeland, *Fly Me to the Moon: How Will International Law Cope with Commercial Space Tourism?*, 11 Melb. J. Int'l L. 90 (2010).

29 Outer Space Treaty, *supra* note 5, art. III.

space-related issues) would not *prima facie* apply to this frontier, and would not be the appropriate legal basis upon which to establish the initial framework for regulating the conduct of humankind's activities in outer space. It was clear, therefore, that, at the dawn of the development of "space law," specific international binding rules would be required to address the particular characteristics and legal categorization of outer space.

## Codification of the Non-Appropriation Principle: Article II of the Outer Space Treaty

Article II of the Outer Space Treaty encompasses the so-called "non-appropriation" principle, which is regarded as one of the most fundamental rules regulating the exploration and use of outer space. The provision reads:

> Outer space, including the moon and other celestial bodies, is not subject to national appropriation by claim of sovereignty, by means of use or occupation, or by any other means.[30]

In general terms, Article II confirms that outer space (which includes the Moon and other celestial bodies) is not subject to ownership rights and prohibits *inter alia* any sovereign or territorial claims to outer space. Outer space therefore is not to be regarded as "territorial," a principle that, by the time the treaty was concluded in 1967, was already well accepted in practice.

Indeed, by the time that the Outer Space Treaty was finalized, both major space superpowers of the time, the United States and the Soviet Union, had already been engaged in an extensive range of space activities; yet neither had made a claim to sovereignty over any part of outer space, including celestial bodies, notwithstanding the planting by the Apollo 11 astronauts of an American flag on the surface of the moon.[31] As a result, although it was of great importance to formalize this principle of non-appropriation of outer space, the drafting process leading to the finalization of Article II of the Outer Space Treaty was relatively

---

30 *Id.* art. II. For a detailed analysis of *Article II, see* Steven Freeland & Ram Jakhu, Article II, in 1 Cologne Commentary on Space Law 44 (Stephan Hobe et al. eds, 2009). Much of the following discussion in this chapter also appears in that analysis.

31 This is to be compared with the situation in Antarctica, which had seen a series of sovereign claims by several states in the period leading up to the finalization in 1959 of the Antarctic Treaty, 402 U.N.T.S. 71. Article IV of the Antarctic Treaty has the effect of suspending all claims to territorial sovereignty in Antarctica for the duration of that instrument, as well as prohibiting any "new claim, or enlargement of an existing claim. " The Protocol on Environmental Protection to the Antarctic Treaty, 30 I.L.M. 1455, which came into force in 1998, augments the Antarctic Treaty by protecting Antarctica from commercial mining for a period of 50 years.

uncontroversial, particularly given its early acceptance as a fundamental concept by these two space faring states.

It is no coincidence that the non-appropriation principle is set out immediately following Article I of the Outer Space Treaty, which elaborates on the "common interest" and "freedom" principles and confirms that the exploration and use of outer space is to be undertaken "for the benefit and in the interests of all countries" and freely "by all states without discrimination of any kind, on a basis of equality and in accordance with international law." In general terms, the primary intent of Article II was to reinforce these important concepts by confirming that principles of territorial sovereignty do not apply to outer space. Not only does this reflect the practice of states from virtually the beginning of the space age,[32] but it also helps to protect outer space from the possibility of conflict driven by territorial or colonizing ambitions.

In this regard, the United States delegate to UNCOPUOS, Mr. Herbert Reis, reiterated the specific object and purpose of Article II on 31 July 1969, just a matter of days after the Apollo 11 astronauts had landed on the Moon, as follows:

> The negotiating history of the Treaty shows that the purpose of this provision (i.e. Article II) was to prohibit a repetition of the race for the acquisition of national sovereignty over overseas territories that developed in the sixteenth, seventeenth, eighteenth and nineteenth centuries. The Treaty makes clear that no user of space may lay claim to, or seek to establish, national sovereignty over outer space.[33]

In this regard, the sentiments reflected in Article II of the Outer Space Treaty are fundamental to the regulation of outer space and its exploration and use for peaceful purposes. It is for these reasons that a binding principle of non-appropriation is an essential element of international space law, to be preserved and followed in the conduct of all activities in outer space.

Unlike the corresponding provision in United Nations Convention on the Law of the Sea (UNCLOS) dealing with the high seas, Article II does not expressly limit itself to the purported actions of states;[34] rather, the provision is drafted in

---

32 One notable exception is the Bogota Declaration, issued in 1976 by a number of equatorial states, including Brazil, Colombia, the Congo, Ecuador, Indonesia, Kenya, Uganda, and Zaire. The countries claimed sovereign rights over segments of the geostationary synchronous orbits above their respective territories. They asserted their claims principally because of the lack of an accepted delimitation between airspace and outer space. Such assertions were strenuously opposed by other states and have not been successful.

33 Cited from Erik N. Valters, *Perspectives in the Emerging Law of Satellite Communications*, 5 Stan. J. Int'l Studies 53, 66–7 (1970)

34 But note UNCLOS, art. 137(1), Dec. 10, 1982, 1833 U.N.T.S. 397, provides:

> No State shall claim or exercise sovereignty or sovereign rights over any part of the Area or its resources, nor shall any State or *natural or juridical person*

more general terms, in that it seeks to prohibit specific actions that constitute a "national appropriation."[35] With the obvious exception of the reference to "by claim of sovereignty," there is no express limitation in Article II *only* to the actions of states. This has, over the years, given rise to frequent debate among commentators as to the precise scope of the prohibition and, more particularly, the extent (if at all) to which "private property rights"[36] may exist in outer space, notwithstanding (or perhaps as a result of) the terms of Article II. These questions call for an examination of the precise terms of the provision.

*"National Appropriation"*

This term represents a combination of public law ("national") and private law ("appropriation") concepts. The expression "national appropriation" was first used in 1961 by the United Nations General Assembly,[37] and served to complement the other fundamental concept of the freedom of exploration and use of outer space. The negotiating history of the Outer Space Treaty clearly shows that most of the delegates participating in those discussions were of the opinion that Article II prohibited both public and private appropriation. They made clear statements welcoming the fact that there was broad agreement that neither state sovereignty, nor private proprietary claims, apply to outer space. In this regard, of particular importance is the position of the United States Government which, from the beginning of the space age, has maintained the view that outer space must remain free from exclusive property or private rights.

President Lyndon B. Johnson, in his 1967 Letter of Transmittal to the United States Senate for its consent to the ratification of the Outer Space Treaty, recalled:

> In November 1958, President Dwight D. Eisenhower asked me to appear before the United Nations to present the U.S. resolution [on outer space] ... On that occasion, speaking for the United States, I said: "Today, outer space is free.

---

appropriate any part thereof. No such claim or exercise of sovereignty or sovereign rights nor such appropriation shall be recognized (emphasis added).

35 The Chinese version of the Outer Space Treaty, however, differs in this respect from all other versions, in that it prohibits appropriation "through the state by asserting sovereignty, use, occupation or any other means." In accordance with Article XVII of the Outer Space Treaty, the Chinese version is "equally authentic" with all other versions. But the fact that the other four versions (English, Russian, French and Spanish) all concur on the text of the provision is significant, "the more so if they include the languages which were mostly used in negotiations of the [Outer Space Treaty]." Vladimir Kopal, *Comments on the issue of "Adequacy of the Current Legal and Regulatory Framework Relating to the Extraction and Appropriation of Natural Resources of the Moon," in* Proceedings of the Policy and Law Relating to Outer Space Resources: Examples of the Moon, Mars, and Other Celestial Bodies Workshop 227, 230 (McGill Univ. Inst. of Air & Space Law 2006).

36 David J. Harris, *Cases and Materials on International Law* 252 (6th ed. 2004).

37 G.A. Res.1721 (XVI), ¶ 1(b), U.N. Doc. A/RES/1721(XVI)A (Dec. 20, 1961).

> It is unscarred by conflict. No nation holds a concession there. It must remain this way. We of the United States do not acknowledge that there are landlords of outer space who can presume to bargain with the nations of the Earth on the price of access to this domain … " I believe those words remain valid today.[38]

Under the provisions of the Outer Space Treaty, all space activities are to be classified only either as "national" (whether carried out by governmental or by non-governmental entities) or "international" (carried out by international or inter-governmental organizations). During the discussions on the treaty, the United States was of the view that, in addition to states, private companies must be allowed to undertake the exploration and use of outer space. On the other hand, the Soviet Union adamantly opposed any such involvement by private entities. Eventually, however, it accepted such a role by the private sector, after being assured that the non-governmental entities would participate only when they were authorized by appropriate states, which would also continuously supervise their activities. Without such an assurance, an agreement on this issue would have not been possible.

In this regard, it is generally agreed that private entities and individuals are also covered by the prohibitions contained in Article II of the Outer Space Treaty. This interpretation draws support from the words "or by any other means" at the end of the provision. This "catch-all" phrase has the effect of preventing a state from using other types of entities to carry out a relevant act of appropriation in its stead.[39] Thus, private claims to "own" the Moon or other celestial bodies, and subsequent attempts to "sell" parts of those to other persons, are without legal foundation.[40]

It is to be noted that Article II provides that outer space "is not subject to" such national appropriation. In other words, no action, either by a state or a private entity or natural person—be it a claim of sovereignty, a use or occupation, or "any other means"—will ever sustain a claim that it gives rise to a right of ownership over any part of outer space.

---

38 Treaty on Outer Space: Hearings before the S. Comm. on Foreign Relations, 90th Cong. 105–106 (1967).

39 There is not, however, unanimity on this point; for a contrary view, written before the finalization of the Moon Agreement, *see, for example,* Stephen Gorove, *Interpreting Article II of the Outer Space Treaty*, 37 Fordham L. Rev. 349, 351 (1969): "the [Outer Space Treaty] in its present form appears to contain no prohibition regarding individual appropriation or acquisition by a private association or an international organization … [in relation to] any part of outer space, including the Moon and other celestial bodies."

40 For more detail, *see* Freeland & Jakhu, *supra* note 30, at 55–8.

### *"Claim of Sovereignty"*

As noted above, there is no particular controversy in relation to prohibiting an appropriation by a state's claim of sovereignty. It has been the established practice of the major space faring states that, *contra* traditional notions of territory on Earth, no state could subject any part of outer space, including the Moon and other celestial bodies, to its sovereign control or regard it as part of its territory. This prohibition has served to protect outer space from colonization by states, which itself represents an important element in the peaceful exploration and use of outer space.

### *"Use or Occupation"*

The *use* or *occupation* of outer space in this context thus relates back to the general prohibition of "national appropriation." The concept of "use" in Article II must be considered in light of the terms of Article I of the Outer Space Treaty, which applies the freedom principle to the use of outer space, and further provides that it "shall be the province of all mankind." In other words, the use of outer space is open to all states, and their non-governmental entities and natural persons, in relation to whose activities in outer space the states remain internationally responsible by virtue of Article VI of the Outer Space Treaty. Those activities are subject to any specific restrictions or prohibitions that may be provided for, either within the space treaties themselves, or under customary international law.

However, since Article II provides that outer space "is not subject to" appropriation by way of use, it follows that no amount of the use of outer space will ever suffice to justify, from a legal viewpoint, a claim of ownership rights over the whole, or over any part of outer space, including the Moon and other celestial bodies. Thus, for example, the exploitation of the natural resources of the Moon and other celestial bodies constitutes a "use" of outer space that is contemplated by the freedom principle specified in the Outer Space Treaty, subject to any other qualifications set out in the space treaties. However, for the purposes of Article II of the Outer Space Treaty, this use does not and can never be such as to constitute a "national appropriation" giving rise to ownership rights.

On the other hand, this is not to say that all uses of outer space are without limitation. For example, the placing in orbit around the Earth of an object carrying nuclear weapons or a weapon of mass destruction may constitute a "use" of outer space; yet it is clear that such actions are expressly prohibited by virtue of the terms of Article IV of the Outer Space Treaty.

Of more relevance is a situation where the exploitation of the natural resources of a celestial body—say, a small asteroid—is of such a scale that, in effect, the celestial body is exploited "out of existence." This use of outer space, whilst not constituting an appropriation within the scope of Article II, would still be unlawful, because it would, in all likelihood, violate other principles of international space law, such as the requirement that it be "for the benefit and in the interests" of all states and that due regard is to be paid to the corresponding interests of all other states.[41]

In similar vein, it also follows that no amount of "occupation" of any part of outer space can constitute an appropriation. The term "occupation" includes one of the traditional international law modes by which states can acquire terrestrial territory, where a state may seek to claim a legitimate legal interest in territory originally of a *terra nullius* nature, if it can show that it had subsequently exercised sufficient "continuous and peaceful effective control" over that territory.[42] Similarly, a display of continuous and peaceful effective control may lead a state to claim territory that was initially part of the sovereignty of another state, under the international law principle of "prescription."[43] However, these modes of acquisition, as well as the concept of "continuous and peaceful effective control" giving rise to ownership rights, are not applicable to, or compatible with the *res communis* nature of outer space.

Moreover, Article II of the Outer Space Treaty equally applies to any other form of occupation. There are, for example, no "squatters rights" associated with remaining in a particular part of outer space for any period of time.[44]

### *"Any Other Means"*

The expression "any other means" represents a "catch all" phrase designed to ensure that there are no other methods distinct from sovereign claims, uses, and occupations that sanction national appropriation in the sense it is used in Article II. This expression, carefully and intentionally asserted at the end of Article II, leaves no room for any form or shape of appropriation of outer space by whatsoever means.

---

41 *See* Outer Space Treaty, *supra* note 5, arts. I, IX. In addition, due "regard shall be paid to the interests of present and future generations" as required under the Moon Agreement, *supra* note 9, art. 4.

42 *See, e.g., Clipperton Island Case* (*Fr. v. Mex.*), 2 R.I.A.A. 1105 (Perm. Ct. Arb. 1931).

43 *See, e.g., Island of Palmas Case* (*Neth. v. U.S.*), 2 R.I.A.A. 829 (Perm. Ct. Arb. 1928).

44 During the negotiation of the Outer Space Treaty, the delegate from France, Mr. Deleau, sought clarification of the scope of the term "use" as included in the treaty; that is. did this '"term imply use for exploration purposes, such as the launching of satellites, or did it mean use in the sense of exploitation, which would involve far more complex issues?": UNCOPUOS, Legal Subcomm., Fifth Sess., July 20, 1966, at 8, U.N. Doc. A/AC.105/C.2/SR.63 (Oct. 20, 1966). In response to this question, the delegate from the Soviet Union, Mr. Morozov, explained that "no human activity on the moon or any other celestial body could be taken as justification for national appropriation."*Id.* at 10.

This does not, however, prevent the states parties to the Moon Agreement and their authorized private entities from removing and using the natural resources and other substances of the Moon and celestial bodies, but only for "scientific investigations" and in "quantities appropriate for the support of their missions."[45] It should also be noted that Article II does not exclude the possibility that other forms of rights and interests, such as intellectual property rights, may also exist in relation to activities in outer space.

## Implications of Article II

It is imperative that all states respect the broad meaning and scope of non-appropriation of outer space, including the Moon and other celestial bodies. Any substantive deviation from this principle would have grave implications for the international regulatory regime of outer space. Any act of appropriation, be it by way of actions by states, private entities, or natural persons, would have the effect of excluding others from enjoying free access to outer space as guaranteed by the freedom principle.[46] In addition, if some states were to appropriate outer space or a part if it, it would be inconsistent with the common interest principle, according to which outer space must be explored and used for the benefit and in the interests of all countries.

Moreover, allowing private entities to appropriate outer space, or a part of it, would defeat the very purpose of Article II, which contains comprehensive provisions prohibiting appropriation.

Above all, Article II along with the provisions of Articles I(1) and (2) of the Outer Space Treaty, has created a "balance of interests" of space powers and non-space powers.[47] Any attempt to appropriate outer space would upset that balance and could thus threaten the rule of law established for the governance of outer space. Therefore, the Outer Space Treaty in general and Article II in particular,

45 Moon Agreement, *supra* note 9, art. 6(2).

46 Outer Space Treaty, *supra* note 5, art. I(2).

47 After the completion of the draft Outer Space Treaty in UNCOPUOS, the U.S. delegate, Mr. Goldberg, underlined that the "spirit of compromise shown by the space Powers and the other Powers had produced a treaty which established a *fair balance* between the interests and obligations of all concerned, including the countries which had as yet undertaken no space activities." Official Records of the General Assembly, Twenty-First Session, First Committee, Summary Records of Meetings, Meeting 1492, at 427 (Dec. 17, 1966) (emphasis added). Similarly, the delegate of Brazil, Mr. de Carvalho Silvos, stressed "the necessity of maintaining a proper balance between the rights and obligations of the space Powers and those of non- space Powers. " *Id.* at 432. The Soviet delegate, Mr. Morozov, responded by emphasising the "principle of equality between space and non-space Powers, to which the Brazilian representative just referred." UNCOPUOS, Legal Subcomm., Fifth Sess., July 21, 1966, at 9, U.N. Doc A/AC.105/C.2/SR. 64 (Oct. 24, 1966).

should—subject to the well-established rules of interpretation of a treaty[48]—be interpreted, applied and respected to maintain that balance.

However, it must be noted that the Outer Space Treaty prohibits (via Article II) "appropriation by use," but not the "use" of outer space, which is guaranteed. Thus in practice, it may be more complex and difficult to draw a line between "use" and "appropriation by use," although such complexity must not nullify the legal principle of non-appropriation. Some more recent "uses" of outer space that are pertinent to these considerations are briefly referred to below:

### *Possible "Exploitation" of Lunar Resources*

Recently, there has emerged a renewed global interest in the exploration and eventual exploitation of the natural resources of the Moon and other celestial bodies. Several states have started launching or are actively planning the launch of their missions to the Moon and Mars. A question arises as to whether Article II of the Outer Space Treaty would inhibit such exploration and exploitation. In other words, how should Article II be applied, interpreted or changed for, or within the context of, an appropriate legal regime that would be conducive to the exploration and exploitation of the natural resources of the Moon and other celestial bodies, particularly by private enterprises?

In addition to the Outer Space Treaty, the exploration and exploitation rights in natural resources of the Moon and other celestial bodies are currently governed by the provisions of the Moon Agreement, which is designed to initiate the discussions on, and elaborate the details of an international regime, once the exploitation of the natural resources of the Moon is imminent.

As discussed above, the meaning, nature and scope of the principle of non-appropriation in Article II is very broad and to a large extent inflexible. On the other hand, the terms of the Moon Agreement suggest that the exploitation of the natural resources of the Moon (and other celestial bodies within the solar system) does *not* constitute a means of appropriation. Article 11(2) of the Moon Agreement replicates the prohibitions contained in Article II of the Outer Space Treaty. Yet one of the principal objects and purposes of the Moon Agreement is to promote the "exploitation" of the natural resources of the Moon through the establishment of an international regime.[49]

It is clear, therefore, that the prohibition of national appropriation in Article 11(2) of the Moon Agreement does not in and of itself restrict the exploitation of natural resources, which will also involve removal of such resources from their

48 The Vienna Convention on the Law of Treaties (VCLT), 1155 U.N.T.S. 331, sets out clear principles for the interpretation of a treaty. Its general rule of interpretation, which also represents customary international law, provides *inter alia* that a "treaty shall be interpreted in good faith in accordance with the ordinary meaning to be given to the terms of the treaty in their context and in the light of its object and purpose." *Id.* art 31(1).

49 Moon Agreement, *supra* note 9, preamble, arts. 11(5), 11(7).

"place" on the Moon.[50] Having said this, the conduct of such exploitation will always remain subject to the general principles of international space law and is to be carried out in a manner compatible with the purposes of the yet-to-be-established international regime, which are set out in Article 11(7) of the Moon Agreement,[51] as well as with the right to collect and remove "samples," as is provided for by Article 6(2) of the same instrument.[52]

### *Regulation of the Geostationary Orbit*

The allocation of exploitation rights in the geostationary orbit[53] is governed under an international allotment regime created through the International Telecommunication Union (ITU), the oldest specialized agency of the United Nations.[54] Beside radio frequencies, orbital "slots" in the geostationary orbit are indispensable for space systems to work. This orbit, an integral part of outer space, is an international natural resource to be shared by all states on an equitable basis.[55]

---

50 Natural resources "in place, shall [not] become property of any State." Moon Agreement, *supra* note 9, art. 11(3).

51 Article 11(7) of the Moon Agreement provides:

The main purposes of the international regime to be established shall include:

> (a) The orderly and safe development of the natural resources of the moon;
> (b) The rational management of those resources;
> (c) The expansion of opportunities in the use of those resources;
> (d) An equitable sharing by all States Parties in the benefits derived from those resources, whereby the interests and needs of the developing countries, as well as the efforts of those countries which have contributed either directly or indirectly to the exploration of the moon, shall be given special consideration.

52 For more detail, *see* Freeland & Jakhu, *supra* note 30; Stephan Hobe, Ram Jakhu & Steven Freeland, *The Appropriateness of the Moon Agreement for Lunar Exploration and Use*, Proceedings of the International Institute of Space Law 562 (2010).

53 The geostationary orbit is an equatorial orbit approximately 36,000 kilometres above the surface of the Earth, whose orbit follows the Earth's rotation at the same speed and direction as that of the Earth. As a result, a satellite in the geostationary orbit appears motionless in the sky, thus making it the most appropriate orbit for many communications and television satellites, towards which a (large) number of satellite dishes and/or ground stations are pointed.

54 There are currently 193 Member States and 742 Sector (mainly non-state) Members and Associates of the ITU.

55 Article 44 (2) of the Constitution of International Telecommunication Union specifies *inter alia* that:

> [i]n using frequency bands for radio services, Member States shall bear in mind that radio frequencies and any associated orbits, including the geostationary-satellite orbit, are limited natural resources and that they must be used rationally, efficiently and economically, in conformity with the provisions of the Radio Regulations, so that countries or groups of countries may have equitable access

The international community, through the ITU, has devised an extensive and complex regulatory regime that ensures equitable allocation of the orbital positions to all satellite operators through their respective states. As the demand for the geostationary orbital usage increases, the ITU actively updates this regime through regularly scheduled intergovernmental conferences in which the private sector has increasingly participated, leading to revisions of its Radio Regulations. states have almost universally adhered to the international treaties. Detailed rules included in the Radio Regulations allow all states equitably to use, but not appropriate, this international resource.[56]

Recent attempts to "hoard" geostationary slots through registration with the ITU of so-called "paper satellites,"[57] which might be considered a form of appropriation, is now being controlled by extensive and rigid regulations. The ITU regime has adopted new rules incorporating concepts like "use it or lose it" for access to the orbit and "user must pay" for the advantages to which it gives rise. In addition, the state that desires interference-free access to a particular orbital position must convincingly show its intention to use the desired position and must actually use it within a predetermined, fixed period of time.

## Concluding Comments

From the first moment of humankind's steps into outer space, it became important to determine the plethora of legal issues relevant to the ongoing use and exploration of this new frontier. A primary concept that emerged in the early days of space law was the consensus among states that outer space was different than traditional 'territory'. The well-accepted 'modes' that dictate how states might claim to have 'acquired' territory in specific circumstances under the general principles of public international law that had evolved well before the launch of Sputnik 1, were developed to apply to terrestrial acquisition and were inappropriate for the regulation of outer space. In this regard, the legal characterization of outer space follows that of the high seas; for both the law regards as invalid any claim of sovereignty.[58]

---

to those orbits and frequencies, taking into account the special needs of the developing countries and the geographical situation of particular countries.

56 For a discussion of the ITU regime, *see* Ram Jakhu, *Safeguarding the Concept of Public Service and the Global Public Interest in Telecommunications*, 5 Singapore J. Int' & Comp. L. 71 (2001).

57 "Paper-satellites" are those systems that are registered with the ITU for the purpose of acquiring or holding on to the registered radio frequencies and associated geostationary orbital positions, but which, in all likelihood, will not be utilized, at least in the way initially envisaged by the ITU at the time that it allocated the particular orbital position. *See, e.g.*, Don Riddick, *Why does Tonga own Outer Space?*, 19 Air & Space L. 15 (1994).

58 Article 89 of UNCLOS provides:" No state may validly purport to subject any part of the high seas to its sovereignty."

This gave rise to the principle of non-appropriation of outer space, including the Moon and other celestial bodies, as subsequently incorporated in Article II of the Outer Space Treaty, which is one of the most fundamental tenets of international space law. It is also a rule of customary international law and is thus applicable to all states, whether or not they are parties to the Outer Space Treaty. All states are therefore under an obligation not only to comply themselves with the principles set out in Article II, but also to ensure that their respective non-governmental entities do not in any manner or form act contrary to this important legal norm.

Undoubtedly, the letter and spirit of the non-appropriation principle has proven to be, and remains, an indispensable provision necessary to achieve and maintain a proper legal order and conflict-free use of outer space for the benefit and in the interests of all countries. Our use of outer space should reflect underlying notions of cooperation and shared benefit, which must remain as the cornerstones in this next phase of human achievement.

## Chapter 5

# Property and Sovereignty in Virtual Worlds

Wian Erlank

The term "virtual world" carries many different meanings, but perhaps the easiest one to understand is "an alternative non-physical world, in contrast to the real, physical world we live in".[1] Most often a virtual world refers to an online environment that simulates the real world to some degree in a digitally represented format. Examples of such virtual worlds include *Second Life*, which is a socially oriented world, and *World of Warcraft* (*WoW*), which is an entertainment oriented virtual world. Whereas a very abstract virtual world may be represented only as a text-based interface, the modern tendency is for a virtual world to be a three dimensional and highly visually detailed representation of a digital environment.[2]

The developer of a virtual world has dual roles, serving first as initial creator and then as governor of the virtual world. All virtual worlds have inhabitants. They are the players who purchase the right to enter the world created by the developer, thus subjecting themselves to the developer's governance. This results in relationships between the inhabitants (players) of virtual worlds and their sovereigns (developers) that are often uneasy. Although the parties share mutual interests in the success and continuation of the virtual world enterprise, they have differing perspectives. Players generally desire stability. Their expectations, which can be described as claims to property, relate to stability both in the virtual world environment and in their acquisitions within that world. The developer, in contrast, primarily wants to achieve and maintain sovereign control. Both parties have valid concerns regarding their perceived interests, which both seek to protect via some mechanism. The protective mechanism inevitably is a legal system. Since virtual worlds mimic the real world in terms of social interaction and are ultimately populated by avatars controlled by humans, it is logical that the need for control of and in a virtual world, ultimately results in the implementation of some form of legal system. Because developers are responsible for the development of the in-game legal system, they have the opportunity to shape the legal relations to their advantage. As designers, they plan, create, and implement the legal system of their virtual world in order to regulate the (physical) virtual environment, enhance

1 Wian Erlank, *Lecture: Introduction to Virtual Property* 3 (Oct. 19, 2009), http://ssrn.com/abstract=1491118.

2 For an in-depth discussion of the history and development of virtual worlds, *see* Wian Erlank, *Virtual Property* ch. 2 (2012) (unpublished LLD dissertation, University of Stellenbosch).

the game-play experience, and control the in-world legal system and social interactions inside it.

In the real world, the sources of law derive from a collection of (depending on the specific legal system and country) common law, legislation, judge-made law, civil codes, constitutions, customary law, and case law.[3] Compared to the large number of possible legal sources in the real world, the sources of virtual-world laws are more restricted. Like the real world, virtual worlds are also subject to a combination of rules, regulations and legal norms, which provide the foundation for the virtual world's legal system. These rules, regulations, and legal norms constitute "virtual law."[4] The term "virtual law" is sometimes defined narrowly as laws that only exist inside the virtual environment,[5] but this chapter uses the term more broadly to include two additional components: laws that pertain to the virtual environment but also apply outside of the virtual environment, and real world regulation of virtual worlds.[6] With this in mind, the sources of virtual law are derived from computer program code, contracts, customary or user created law, as well as some real world regulation.

The developer achieves sovereign control of its virtual world by manipulating the sources of virtual world law. The first source is the program code, which forms the very basis of the virtual world.[7] Binary computer code (ones and zeros) produces rules that specify the virtual world environment. Through the program

---

3 This chapter discusses only western democratic legal systems. For an account of how eastern legal systems deal with the issues, *see* Ung-gi Yoon, *Real Money Trading in MMORPG Items from a Legal and Policy Perspective,* 1 J. Korean Judicature 418 (2008), *available at* http://ssrn.com/ abstract=1113327.

4 For a general discussion of the field of virtual law *see* Benjamin Tyson Duranske, *Virtual Law: Navigating the Legal Landscape of Virtual Worlds* 14 (2008); Lawrence Lessig, *Code: And other Laws of Cyberspace* 6 (1999) [hereinafter Code]; Bobby Glushko, *Tales of the (Virtual) City: Governing Property Disputes in Virtual Worlds,* 22 Berkeley Tech. L.J. 501, 509–17 (2007); James Grimmelmann, *Virtual Worlds as Comparative Law*, 49 N.Y.L. Sch. L. Rev. 147, 147–84 (2004); F. Gregory Lastowka & Dan Hunter, *The Laws of the Virtual Worlds*, 92 Calif. L. Rev. 1, 1–74 (2004); Peter Edelmann, *Framing Virtual Law* (2005), http://www.digra.org:8080/Plone/dl/db/06278.45351.pdf; Jennifer L. Mnookin, *Virtual(ly) Law: The Emergence of Law in LambdaMOO*, 2 J. Computer-Mediated Comm. (Special Issue) P1 (1996), http://jcmc.indiana.edu/vol2/issue1/lambda.html; Daniel Terdiman, *Laying Down the Virtual Law,* Wired (Nov. 13, 2003), http://www.wired.com/gaming/gamingreviews/news/2003/11/61188.

5 In this case, virtual law is used in the narrow sense as referring to laws that relate to "internal governance structures … that appear in some virtual worlds." *See* Duranske, *supra* note 4.

6 Virtual law can also be used in the wider sense as referring to "internet law" or all law that broadly applies to virtual worlds. *See id.* This wider approach will include both the second and third types mentioned above.

7 For an illuminating discussion on computer code and its effects on the laws of virtual worlds *see* Code, *supra* note 4 as well as its sequel, Lawrence Lessig, *Code: And Other Laws of Cyberspace, Version 2.0* (2006) [hereinafter Code: Version 2.0]. *See also*

code as law, the developer achieves full and absolute control over virtual world relationships.[8] The developer has the power to change the code at any stage without any input or opposition by the players. The players are mostly powerless to oppose such action.[9] The second source of virtual law consists of the contracts that developers force players to enter into before they may participate in a virtual world. These contracts are usually manifested in so-called "End User License Agreements" (EULAs) and "Terms of Service" (TOSs).[10] Developers use both foundational contracts to create rights and obligations concerning the virtual world, shaping the legal relations to their advantage. Most real world legal relationships that have anything to do with interaction with a virtual world are governed solely by contract.[11] This chapter analyzes parts of the foundational contracts of *World of Warcraft (WoW)* and *Second Life* to illustrate how a virtual world operates on a contracts-based rights system.

Using the two vehicles of the EULA and TOS in tandem, the developer limits and in most cases prevents the creation and vesting of property rights in the players. Through program code and the two foundational contracts, developers act as sovereigns, particularly by limiting players' acquisition of property rights. In most virtual worlds, the developers of the world assume sovereign, god-like powers to regulate the world and to exclude players from acquiring property rights or interests inside the virtual worlds.

A third source of virtual law deserves brief mention. Players create customary law amongst themselves outside of the developer's influence. This could also be referred to as common law, but common in the communal sense, and not in the real world common-law sense. Although of lesser importance than program code and

---

Ben Pollitzer, *Serious Business: When Virtual Items Gain Real World Value* 20–22 (Dec. 1, 2007), http://ssrn.com/abstract=1090048 (succinctly describing how code works).

8 *See generally* Code: Version 2.0, *supra* note 7; Code, *supra* note 4; Andrew E. Jankowich, *Property and Democracy in Virtual Worlds*, 11 B.U.J. Sci. & Tech. L. 173 (2005); Pollitzer, *supra* note 7.

9 While players are mostly powerless, some remedies are available. For example, a player may choose to withdraw from the virtual world. However, this is not a very effective remedy, unless it is coordinated as a mass-exodus that results in the eventual financial failure of the virtual world.

10 Jankowich, *supra* note 8, at 177. *See also* Glushko, *supra* note 4, at 514; Jason T. Kunze, *Regulating Virtual Worlds Optimally: The Model End User License Agreement,* 7 Nw. J. Tech. & Intell. Prop. 102, 103 (2008); Pollitzer, *supra* note 7, at 22; Kristina Denapolis, *Real Concerns in Virtual Property* 10 (July 1, 2005), http://ssrn.com/ abstract=1154234.

11 Jankowich extensively discusses the governance issues of virtual worlds, mentioning the problems that developers face when confronted with conflicts between themselves and players. He questions Lessig's assumption that all legal relations in a virtual world are primarily governed by the computer code as law and, if that fails, is governed by the "catch-all restrictions of the end user license agreement ("EULA") or terms of service ("TOS") that participants agree to when joining the virtual world." Jankowich, *supra* note 8, at 177. *See also* Code, *supra* note 4.

the EULA and TOS contracts, customary law serves as a realm where the players may achieve a limited amount of autonomy and may on occasion protect property-like expectations.

## Computer Code as Law

The rules created by program code contribute to the body of virtual world law.[12] The virtual world is built upon the fundamental building blocks of computer code. This code is at its essence just a list of instructions and rules that form a coherent structure when implemented in its final form. The most basic forms of computer programming are construed around commands such as IF, AND, THEN, DO, BUT, and OR. For example, code for a game might provide: "IF a player picks up a sword AND the sword is cursed THEN the player dies BUT IF the player is wearing a protective charm THEN he only loses 10 health points." This method of programming leaves no room for interpretation. The rules of the virtual world are clear and they are embedded into the program code. In this sense the code laws are similar to the laws of nature because they are unchangeable (by the avatar), inevitable (for the avatar), and also not open for negotiation or interpretation. In other words, the laws do not need to be enforced by external influence of the developer. The results are inevitable and, unlike in the real world, there is no room for maneuver when a player interacts with the program code.[13]

In a virtual world there is no meaningful distinction between software and law. What the software does not allow is impossible. This leads to an area of law in virtual worlds where "there is no room for mediation because any 'legal' mediation embodied in the software immediately becomes part of the 'natural' world."[14] This means that a player's property rights are guaranteed by the programming. As the "owner" of a virtual sword, an avatar has guaranteed protection and enforcement of her rights in the sword against all other players by means of the game-code.[15] While the player "owns" the sword, no other player can interfere with her right, or even make use of it. This is generally true, but as in real life, property rights

12 *See* Code: Version 2.0, *supra* note 7, at 5; Code, *supra* note 4, at 6; Jankowich, *supra* note 8, at 177; Pollitzer, *supra* note 7, at 20.

13 The crux of the matter is that due to the unique nature of coded law, any rule that the developer wishes to implement into the game-design will be uncircumventable. This would mean that the implementation of code-based laws will always be similar to the laws of nature in the real world. In other words, in a virtual world code rules that resemble real world legal rules (like ownership) can also function like natural laws. For example, game code can make theft impossible in a virtual world, while this is not feasible in the real world. This issue is discussed in more detail below.

14 Grimmelmann, *supra* note 4, at 150. *See generally* Lawrence Lessig, *The Law of the Horse: What Cyberlaw Might Teach*, 113 Harv L. Rev. 501, 522, 531; Code, *supra* note 4.

15 Grimmelmann, *supra* note 4, at 150.

are not totally absolute or exclusive in a virtual world. A player's property rights will be guaranteed only to the extent that the software does so.[16] For example, the game design and software for the virtual world of *Ultima Online* enables players to steal from one another.[17]

Planning the virtual world legal system begins before any program code is actually typed. The game designers create rules as they plan the basic functions and operation of the virtual world. For example, a designer must decide what happens when a player picks up an item.[18] The designer might conceive of two options: the item becomes part of the things that the avatar carries around on a permanent basis (that is, the avatar has permanent possession of the item, which cannot be relinquished), or the avatar has control over the item only as long as he carries it around. This duality of choice is then coded into the game and leaves the player with no other options besides the two that this designer envisioned.

A more complex example of the creation of such a property rule arises if the designers consider allowing players to store items that they have gathered.[19] The designer could decide to allow a player to have a house where he could store items that he bought or acquired in the game. To make the storage function of the house work, practical decisions must be made. Will an item that is put down by the player inside the house stay inside the house (that is, have permanence)[20] or will it disappear? Who will be allowed inside the house? Will only the player be allowed to access the inside of the house, which in effect will safeguard his belongings, or will other people have access to the house? If so, what happens when someone else comes into the house? Can the player who uses the house for storage keep other people out? Can he prevent people who do in fact come in from taking items that he has put down in the house? What happens if a visitor drops one of his items in

---

16 This is if the virtual law is derived from the computer code. It is also possible that players create legal norms between themselves that are not designed or enforced by the code-based legal norms. This aspect is addressed in more detail below at Contracts: EULAs and TOSs.

17 Grimmelmann, *supra* note 4, at 150 n. 11; F. Gregory Lastowka & Dan Hunter, *Virtual Crimes,* 49 N.Y.L. Sch. L. Rev. 293, 309 (2004). Certain virtual worlds even include the class of "thief" as one of the types of avatar that a player can choose to create. For an in-depth discussion of the "thief" class and attributes relating to thievery in some other classes like "rogues", "swashbucklers" and "assassins", *see* Forum Contributors, *Thief-classes in MMOs,* The Pub at MMORPG.COM (Mar. 15, 2008), http://www.mmorpg.com/discussion2.cfm/thread/170724/Thiefclasses-in-MMOs.html.

18 See the discussion on the acquisition of virtual property in Wian Erlank, *Acquisition of Ownership inside Virtual Worlds,* De Jure (forthcoming 2013) (manuscript at 11–20), http://papers.ssrn.com/sol3/papers.cfm?abstract_id=2019110.

19 Grimmelmann, *supra* note 4, at 150–54.

20 For more information about requirements or *essentialia* of virtual worlds in general and the requirement of persistence or permanence in particular *see* Lastowka & Hunter, *supra* note 4, at 1, 5–6; Erlank, *supra* note 1, at 3.

another player's house? Does it become the property of the house-owner, or does it stay the property of the original player?

To address these practical issues, the designer makes policy decisions about how the game will handle the problem. As soon as the policies are implemented in the game by programming into the code, virtual law is created.[21] Because the policies are within the game code, usually a player cannot circumvent them. If the code determines that one can only enter one's own house in the game, there is absolutely no way of entering the house of another person and, by inference, it is impossible to steal items in another person's house. Unfortunately, even in the virtual world there are always exceptions. One of these exceptions is that someone might illegally modify the code to get access to something that was not intended by the programmers.[22] In essence, the only way to break the laws that are coded into the game is to "hack" the system.[23] This distinguishes these laws from the laws of nature, which can never be altered, and thus renders them closer to laws in the real world, which can be broken.[24]

---

21 Edelmann, *supra* note 4, at 5.

22 An example of this could be something as innocuous as changing a part of the game's URL (website address) and thereby being able to buy virtual real estate for a cheaper price. For an example of this *see* Gigs Taggart, *ANALYSIS: Bragg v. Linden et al - A virtual property dispute*, The Seventh Sun (June 2007), http://theseventhsun.com/0607_braggAnalysis2.htm.

23 For more information about the different hacking methods *see* Lastowka & Hunter, *supra* note 17, at 298, 313; Chun Feng, *Playing with Shadows – Exposing the Black Market for Online Game Password Theft*, 207, 209 (Oct. 2008), http://download.microsoft.com/download/4/b/8/4b83fed7-ad1e-4d1f-abfe-bf9c121397b5/Feng-VB2008.pdf. This is such an important issue that developers tend to address it in the EULA. For example, *WoW*'s EULA states that one is not allowed to "…use cheats, automation software (bots), hacks, mods or any other unauthorized third-party software designed to modify the World of Warcraft experience…" Blizzard Entertainment, World of Warcraft End User License Agreement, Additional License Limitations, B. (Aug. 22 2012), http://www.worldofwarcraft.com/legal/eula.html [hereinafter Blizzard EULA]. This clause is important for the everyday governing purposes of the virtual world. Players who make use of hacks, cheats or other methods to circumvent the normal code-based rules are able to gain an unfair advantage over other players in the game. By making use of these methods, players could bypass the intended gameplay and programmed virtual laws of the game. Because of this problem, it is specifically prohibited in the EULA. Such players could also disturb the enjoyment of gameplay for the other players. If this is allowed to continue without abatement, it could cause the collapse of a whole virtual world if the general player population decides to move to a competing virtual world.

24 Although this is an example of where code as law is similar to real world law, the analogy is not totally accurate. When a player "hacks" the code-level law to change one of the unchangeable laws of the game, it is closer to performing real magic in the real world than to just breaking the law. An example is the act of levitation in the real world. The law of gravity determines that a person cannot levitate on earth, but if a magician were to break this unbreakable rule of nature and uses magic to levitate himself, he would not merely be

The beauty of code as rules is that, even though these design issues and questions tend to lead to ever-increasing complexity, they do not suffer from the cognitive problems associated with the enforcement of such a complex rule-set in the real-life environment. In the real world, an increasingly complex set of rules creates the risk of great discretion in enforcement;[25] in the virtual code-based world it stays simple. No matter how complex the rule-set becomes, the outcome is not open to discretion and will always be decided according to a binary and objective test by the computer. Software does not have the discretion of a judge. Therefore every software decision embedded in code is pre-determined.[26]

## Contracts: EULAs and TOSs

Most developers make use of a combination of EULAs and TOS agreements to create the contractual relationship between themselves and the virtual world participants or players.[27] The EULA is designed to regulate the player-developer relationship in the real world. It sets forth the player's real-world rights and obligations. The TOS on the other hand is normally used to regulate player behavior inside the virtual world, announcing norms that all gamers must follow in their actions taken inside the virtual world.

Although the two contractual mechanisms have different functions, they are usually closely related. Developers often state that the EULA includes the TOS by reference and *vice versa*. The two legal documents tend to mirror each other to a large degree, with only some paragraphs left out in the one, or included in the other. These instruments are sometimes referred to as click-wrap agreements[28] because they force a player to accept the whole content of the contract by clicking on a button that normally says "I agree."[29] The player is left with only two choices when confronted by the EULA or TOS: she clicks on the "I agree" button and

---

making a choice to break a law, but in fact doing the impossible. The same can be said for a player who changes the code based rules by hacking the system. See generally Lastowka & Hunter, *supra* note 17; Ung-gi Yoon, *South Korea and indirect reliance on IP Law: real money trading in MMORPG items*, 3 J. Intell. Prop. L. & Prac. 174 (2008).

25 Grimmelmann, *supra* note 4, at 153; Edelmann, *supra* note 4, at 5. *See generally* Code, *supra* note 4.

26 Grimmelmann, *supra* note 4, at 150–54; Edelmann, *supra* note 4, at 5–6.

27 *See* Edelmann, *supra* note 4, at 4; Denapolis, *supra* note 10, at 10. *See generally* Daniel C. Miller, *Determining Ownership in Virtual Worlds: Copyright and License Agreements*, 22 Rev. Litig. 435 (2003).

28 These agreements are similar to shrink-wrap agreements. Both click-wrap and shrink-wrap agreements are examples of contracts of adhesion. *See generally* Tana Pistorius, *Click-Wrap and Web-Wrap Agreements*,16 SAMLJ 568 (2004).

29 See, for example, the concluding statement to *WoW*'s EULA, which states that "I hereby acknowledge that I have read and understand the foregoing License Agreement and agree that by clicking 'Accept' or installing the Game Client I am acknowledging my

accepts all the terms of the contract, or she cannot progress with the installation of the client software, nor access the game. The "wrap" part refers to packaging if the player purchases goods (usually software contained on a CD or DVD) rather than downloading information. The player must break some form of seal or wrapping to access the contents, thereby expressing her intention to enter into the contract.[30]

With a EULA or TOS, the developer retains the right to modify unilaterally the terms of the contracts. If a player does not like this, the only available remedy is to stop participating in the game. Even though this might sound like an unfair practice and possibly immoral and illegal, a considerable number of courts have held that such unilateral modification clauses are legal and enforceable.[31]

The EULA is arguably the most important source of virtual law that exists at the moment.[32] It fulfills a dual function. In the virtual world it is a primary source of law that regulates and legislates player behavior and that creates the legal relationships between players and developer. It also regulates the legal relationship between the player and developer in the real world.[33] Contrary to the non-circumventable laws derived from the program code, many rules contained in the EULA are not enforceable in the game by the code. This is due to the nature of the rules that tend to deal more with cross-world relationships between player and developer than in-game code-based laws. For example, if the EULA prohibits the sale of virtual property in the real world, and a player disregards this and still buys virtual property in the real world, rather than earning it or buying it in the game, the game code cannot know or do anything about such extrinsic transactions.[34]

---

agreement to be bound by the terms and conditions of this License Agreement." Blizzard EULA, *supra* note 23.

30 This seems to be an accepted method of expressing intent to enter into a contract under South African Law. The Electronic Communications and Transactions Act 25 of 2002 § 24(2) (S. Afr.) [hereinafter ECT Act] is construed by Pistorius as being "designed to include statutory recognition of the click-wrap and web-wrap mechanisms for expressing intent, but it is nevertheless open-ended and neutral." Tana Pistorius, *Monitoring, Interception and Big Boss in the Workplace: Is the Devil in the Details?,* 12(1) Potchefstroom Elec. L.J. 1, 18 (2009).

31 This was decided in the United States in cases like *ProCD, Inc. v. Zeidenberg*, 86 F.3d 1447 (7th Cir. 1996) and *Groff v. America Online, Inc.*, No. PC 97-0331, 1998 WL 307001 (R.I. Super. Ct. May 27,1998), amongst others. For more information about this topic, case discussions, and some good background discussions *see* Berkman Center for Internet & Society, *E-Commerce: An Introduction, Transactions,* http://cyber.law.harvard.edu/olds/ecommerce/transactions.html

32 Jankowich, *supra* note 8, at 177. *See also* Glushko, *supra* note 4, at 252; Pollitzer, *supra* note 7, at 19, 22; Kunze, *supra* note 10, at 103; Denapolis, *supra* note 10, at 10.

33 *See generally*, Joshua A.T. Fairfield, *Anti-social Contracts: The Contractual Governance of Virtual Worlds,* 53 McGill L.J. 427 (2008).

34 This is typically called real money trade (RMT). See the discussion below about forcing players to make use of the in-game trading mechanisms, as well as Yoon, *supra* note 3.

### *EULA of WoW*[35] *and TOS of Second Life*

In order to fully understand the effect that a EULA/TOS combination has as a source of virtual law, I will look at the EULA/TOS combination of the two largest and most important virtual worlds used in this research. These virtual worlds are Blizzard's *World of Warcraft* (*WoW*) and Linden Lab's *Second Life*. It is illuminating to analyze certain clauses of the EULA and TOS to see how these instruments try to anticipate and deal with both real world and virtual world problems. As mentioned above, the TOS[36] mostly regulates the in-game relationship between the player and developer, as well as the relationships between players inside the virtual world. However, generally speaking the TOS often tends to overlap with the EULA and may contain a large collection of regulatory material addressing ownership of in-game virtual items, control and ownership rights in the account as well as a comprehensive code of conduct to which the player is bound. In this regard, the EULA and TOS fulfill the same function and the relationship between the developer and player is regulated in the same manner as in the EULA.

In *Second Life*, the TOS fulfills much of the same functions as the EULA together with the TOS in *WoW*. The biggest difference between the two is that in *WoW*, Blizzard tries to remove all possible rights that a player might have regarding in-world virtual property, as well as almost all the obligations that Blizzard might possibly have towards the player. In contrast, Linden Lab has chosen to explicitly give players the illusion[37] of having certain property rights to the virtual world property in *Second Life*. However, even though this is the principle behind most of *Second Life*, Linden Lab tries to restrict the effect of acceptance of these virtual property rights to the virtual world.

*World of Warcraft* is a leveling game[38] in which the focus is on the playing of the actual game (the gameplay). In this virtual world, the developer of *WoW* (Blizzard), created the virtual world solely for entertainment purposes. Even

35 I have decided to use the *WoW* EULA that was in operation at the time when I started with the writing of this chapter. It is not important for the academic discussions of these EULAs that the most recent version should be included, since the changes are usually very superficial and the discussions about the clauses are of a general nature.

36 In *WoW* the TOS is referred to as the Terms of Use Agreement (TOU).

37 Since I have started writing this chapter, the position taken by *Second Life* has changed quite a bit. This is reflected in the different versions of the TOS which Linden Lab has implemented during the past three years. With each new version of the TOS the concept of having property rights in *Second Life* has been watered down and the amount of legalese and sub-clauses has grown. In the final version of 2010 (to which I will be referring in the following section) Linden Lab has continued to dilute the concept of virtual property by just leaving a player with the illusion that he or she has any property rights in the virtual world.

38 "Leveling" usually entails that a player starts out in the game at level one. Once he or she "levels", his or her power increases and the game continues. Once the player has accumulated enough experience he or she will level up to the second level, etc. This strategy forms the basis of most of the entertainment orientated virtual worlds.

though players may view it as "just a game,"[39] Blizzard views it purely as a commercial enterprise. It is clear from the EULA that the developer's first and foremost purpose with the EULA is to protect its own (financial) interests.[40]

In order to get this protection, the developers cast the contract into the form of a license agreement. When the player buys the game from a store or online vendor, she gets (according to the developer) a licensed right to play the game and to make use of the developer's intellectual property for that purpose. If she agrees to and adheres to a certain number of pre-set conditions, she is allowed to play the game. Usually one condition is that the player must pay a monthly access fee to gain entry into the virtual world. If the player does not pay this fee, she is left with a very expensive set of CDs or DVDs, with little[41] economic value.

Another very important reason why developers want to retain as much control as possible over their players is that they initially[42] envisaged that revenue generated from monthly access fees and some in-game sales of virtual property items would account for their profits. However, the effect of the internal economy (of a virtual world) on the external economic market has been quite substantial and most of these external market transactions are bypassing the revenue streams of the developers due to unauthorized trade outside of the virtual worlds. As a consequence, the developers try to enforce policies enabling them to profit from these transactions.[43] For example, by creating in-game trading mechanisms and platforms, the developer is able to tax every transaction that takes place.

Linden Lab created *Second Life* to provide a venue for socialization and social networking. Although a player can use *Second Life* for entertainment purposes, there is a lot more happening in the virtual world than "just playing a game."[44] Players often take *Second Life* quite seriously, pursuing diverse purposes such as research, simulations,[45] and even helping with the treatment of medical conditions.[46] Another serious part of the *Second Life* experience is commerce. For this reason Linden Lab tries to control the in-world economic effects of the commercial transactions among players.

---

39 Erez Reuveni, *On Virtual Worlds: Copyright and Contract Law at the Dawn of the Virtual Age*, 82 Ind. L.J. 261, 308 (2007).

40 Which is an obvious goal and justification for a company that is commercially driven and accountable to its shareholders.

41 The player can theoretically resell the installation disks to another player and as such can recoup the cost of the physical media.

42 This would have been when the commercial possibilities of virtual worlds were only being discovered.

43 See the more comprehensive discussion below at Power, control, and lawmaking.

44 Reuveni, *supra* note 39.

45 Simulations often focus on military or scientific training scenarios.

46 As an example, one of the private islands in *Second Life* is called "Brigadoon." This is a safe, virtual environment where people with Asperger's syndrome and their caregivers can interact. *See* Jonathan Silverstein, *A World Where Anything Is Possible*, ABC News (Aug. 9, 2005), http://abcnews.go.com/Technology/FutureTech/story?id=1019818.

*License and Copyright Terms of WoW and Second Life*

The opening paragraph of the *WoW* EULA[47] makes it clear that a player only gets a license to use the software, with no ownership rights. If the player does not accept the terms of the EULA within 30 days after purchase, he may request a full refund of the purchase price. There is no mention of the consequences of a player deciding not to accept a subsequent developer change to the EULA.

The copyright section states that the developer (Blizzard) retains all copyright in the game in all its related forms.[48] Blizzard even states that it retains copyright in any files or software that it gives to the players to enable them (the players) to modify the game. The intent is not to allow a player to assert copyright in her own creative efforts to change the game, for example by creating a unique avatar.

The developer enforces its right to the sole provision and management of the game[49] by prohibiting players from making use of the *WoW* software to run on servers that are not managed by the developer. A "catch-all" clause prohibits any player actions except those explicitly allowed by the EULA.

The *Second Life* contracts largely mirror the ones of *WoW* with respect to the player's license and the developer's retention of copyright,[50] but unlike *WoW* the

---

47 "Important! Please read carefully. This software is licensed, not sold. By installing, copying or otherwise using the game (defined below), you agree to be bound by the terms of this agreement. If you do not agree to the terms of this agreement, you are not permitted to install, copy or use the game. If you reject the terms of this agreement within thirty (30) days after your purchase, you may call (800)757-7707 to request a full refund of the purchase price." Blizzard EULA, *supra* note 23.

48 "This software program, and any files that are delivered to you by Blizzard Entertainment, Inc. (via on-line transmission or otherwise) to 'patch,' update, or otherwise modify the software program, as well as any printed materials and any on-line or electronic documentation (the 'Manual'), and any and all copies and derivative works of such software program and Manual (collectively, with the 'Game Client' defined below, the 'Game') is the copyrighted work of Blizzard Entertainment, Inc. or its licensors (collectively referred to herein as 'Blizzard'). Any and all uses of the Game are governed by the terms of this End User License Agreement (the 'License Agreement' or 'Agreement')." Blizzard EULA, *supra* note 23.

49 "The Game may only be played by obtaining from Blizzard access to the World of Warcraft massively multi-player on-line role-playing game service (the 'Service'), which is subject to a separate Terms of Use agreement (the 'Terms of Use') incorporated into this Agreement by this reference. The Game is distributed solely for use by authorized end users according to the terms of this License Agreement. Any use, reproduction, modification or distribution of the Game not expressly authorized by the terms of the License Agreement is expressly prohibited." Blizzard EULA, *supra* note 23.

50 "Welcome to Second Life! This agreement (this 'Agreement' or the 'Terms of Service') describes the terms on which Linden Research, Inc. and Linden Research United Kingdom, Ltd. (collectively 'Linden Lab') offer you access to Second Life. 'Second Life' or the 'Service' means the multi-user online service offered by Linden Lab, including its Websites, Servers, Linden Software, Linden In-World Content, and User Content (as those

*Second Life* documentation does not refer to a refund for a player who decides not to accept the agreement. Here is a prime example of the developer's intention to create only a contractual relationship between itself and the player.[51] The developer defines the right of the player to use the game-client as a "limited, non-exclusive license."[52] The developer limits the possible property rights of the player by explicitly prohibiting the use of the virtual property contained in the game for any security purposes or any transfer of the game property to any third parties.[53]

### *Ownership and Transfer Issues*[54] *of WoW and Second Life*

A large section of the EULA deals with issues of ownership.[55] This includes the different iterations of things in which the developer is holding intellectual

---

terms are defined in this Agreement). This offer is conditioned on your agreement to all of the terms and conditions contained in the Terms of Service, including the policies and terms linked to or otherwise referenced in this Agreement. By using Second Life, you agree to and accept these Terms of Service. If you do not so agree, you should decline this Agreement, in which case you are prohibited from accessing or using Second Life." Linden Lab, Terms of Service (Dec. 15, 2010), http://secondlife.com/corporate/tos.php [hereinafter Linden Lab TOS].

51 "If you agree to this License Agreement, you may install the computer software (hereafter referred to as the 'Game Client') onto your computer for purposes of playing the Game by registering for and accessing an account with the Service (the 'Account'). Subject to your agreement to and continuing compliance with this License Agreement, Blizzard hereby grants, and you hereby accept, a limited, non-exclusive license to (a) install the Game Client on one or more computers owned by you or under your legitimate control, and (b) use the Game Client in conjunction with the Service for your non-commercial entertainment purposes only. All use of the Game Client is subject to this License Agreement and to the Terms of Use agreement, both of which you must accept before you can use your Account to play the Game." Blizzard EULA, *supra* note 23.

52 *Second Life* takes this one step further and states that "Linden Lab hereby grants you a non-exclusive, non-transferable, non-sublicenseable, limited, revocable license to access and use the Service as set forth in these Terms of Service and expressly conditioned upon you and each of your Accounts remaining active, in good standing, and in full compliance with these Terms of Service." Linden Lab TOS, *supra* note 50, at 7.7.

53 "[You may not] sell, grant a security interest in or transfer reproductions of the Game to other parties in any way not expressly authorized herein, or rent, lease or license the Game to others." Blizzard EULA, *supra* note 23.

54 For some practical examples as a discussion of transfer of ownership in virtual worlds, *see* Erlank, *supra* note 18.

55 "A. All title, ownership rights and intellectual property rights in and to the Game and all copies thereof (including without limitation any titles, computer code, themes, objects, characters, character names, stories, dialog, catch phrases, locations, concepts, artwork, character inventories, structural or landscape designs, animations, sounds, musical compositions and recordings, audio-visual effects, storylines, character likenesses, methods of operation, moral rights, and any related documentation) are owned or licensed by

property rights, which is of specific relevance to the legal system and governance of a virtual world.[56] A section of the *WoW* EULA deals with the transfer of rights and obligations under the license agreement. Even though a player might view her software purchase as only incidental to playing the game, the developer approaches this issue differently. The EULA section gives the player an explicit right to transfer all of her rights and obligations under the license agreement to another person, in contrast to the strict control that the developer exerts over its intellectual property. In effect, the developer acknowledges that a player owns a property interest in the game, which the player may use for economic benefit. Even though the EULA elsewhere prohibits the practice of selling anything derived from the game for a commercial purpose, here the developer explicitly permits a player to transfer her in-game interests. Even though a player has played the game with the intention of deriving commercial benefit from the eventual selling of the game, the EULA allows the sale of in-game interests if the buyer receives both the physical game media and the account. It should be noted that the requirement that the player must transfer the physical media might create some complications in the real world. Often a player does not possess any physical media because she downloaded the game-client directly from the internet and never made a physical copy. The right-to-transfer provision requires that the transferring player delete all copies and installations of the game in her possession or control. This only applies to the game-client and does not affect the player's virtual patrimony or account. The only embargo that the developers are placing on the transfer is a virtual-world

---

Blizzard. The Game is protected by the copyright laws of the United States, international treaties and conventions, and other laws. The Game may contain materials licensed by third parties, and the licensors of those materials may enforce their rights in the event of any violation of this License Agreement. B. You may permanently transfer all of your rights and obligations under the License Agreement to another only by physically transferring the original media (for example, the CD-ROM or DVD you purchased), all original packaging, and all Manuals or other documentation distributed with the Game; provided, however, that you permanently delete all copies and installations of the Game in your possession or control, and that the recipient agrees to the terms of this License Agreement. The transferor (i.e., you), and not Blizzard, agrees to be solely responsible for any taxes, fees, charges, duties, withholdings, assessments, and the like, together with any interest, penalties, and additions imposed in connection with such transfer." Blizzard EULA, *supra* note 23, at Ownership. *Second Life* follows a similar formula and regulates the transfer of an account as follows: "13.2 You may not assign your Account; we may assign this Agreement. You may not assign this Agreement or your Account without the prior written consent of Linden Lab. You may not transfer or sublicense any licenses granted by Linden Lab in this Agreement without the prior written consent of Linden Lab, except solely to the extent this Agreement permits transfer of the Linden Dollar Licenses and Virtual Land Licenses. Linden Lab may assign this Agreement, in whole or in part, and all related rights, licenses, benefits and obligations, without restriction, including the right to sublicense any rights and licenses under this Agreement." Linden Lab TOS, *supra* note 50, at 13.

56 Blizzard EULA, *supra* note 23, at Ownership.

*nemo plus iuris* rule,[57] which forces the new player receiving the transferred rights also to accept the obligations connected to it.[58]

Even though the *WoW* right-to-transfer paragraph seems to cover all the bases for developer regulation of transfers of virtual world patrimony, there is one problem area that lies beyond the developer's control. The developer cannot force non-contracting third parties to abide by the rules contained in the EULA and TOS. This is an uncontroversial situation in normal contractual relations. As a general rule, a contract creates obligations between the contracting parties, which do not affect third parties.[59] Third persons who are strangers to the EULA and TOS are not subject to the contract terms, but they might be liable if they are infringing on the developer's virtual property rights, whose parameters are defined at least in part by the EULA and TOS. This distinction is illustrated by the South Korean case of *Webzen v. ItemBay*,[60] in which a developer tried to force a company that catered to the real-world sale and exchange of virtual items to stop providing the services. The court held that the company was not bound by the developer's EULA because it was not a party to that contract and only provided services outside the virtual world. In essence, the developer was asking the court for property-like protection of its virtual interests and therefore for the contract to have third-party effect. The outcome in *Webzen*, however, demonstrates that even though developers often see their powers as absolute, they are sometimes stumped by the realities of the real world.

One of the most prominent features in *Second Life* is the possibility of acquiring, selling, renting, improving, and developing virtual land. *Second Life*'s TOS describes virtual land with attributes that mirror real-world land in both form and function, but then relabels it as something else in order to prevent legal consequences and liabilities.[61] First, the TOS explicitly endows virtual land with characteristics that mirror real-world land: players have the rights to acquire, use, and transfer the asset.[62] But the player who acquires "Virtual Land" obtains only

57 The *nemo plus iuris* rule refers to the principle that a person cannot transfer more rights to another person than he or she as transferor already has.

58 In other words, the person acquiring the rights is also bound by the contractual obligations into which the initial contractant entered into with the developer.

59 Also commonly referred to as privity of contract.

60 Western Seoul District Court [Dist. Ct.], Dec. 26, 2002 (S. Kor.).It is discussed by Yoon, but the discussion contains no more specific reference to a case name or reporter than what has been provided here. *See* Yoon, *supra* note 3, at manuscript 22–3.

61 "Virtual Land is the graphical representation of three-dimensional virtual world space. When you acquire Virtual Land, you obtain a limited license to access and use certain features of the Service associated with Virtual Land stored on our Servers. Virtual Land is available for Purchase or distribution at Linden Lab's discretion, and is not redeemable for monetary value from Linden Lab." Linden Lab TOS, *supra* note 50, at 6.

62 "The Service includes a component of In-World virtual space that is stored on our Servers and made available in the form of virtual units ('Virtual Land'). This 'Virtual Land' constitutes a limited license to access and use certain features of our Service as set

"a limited license to access and use certain features of the Service associated with Virtual Land stored on our Servers." The restriction to a "limited license" is then reinforced by the developer's statement that players do not get "a real property right or actual real estate" in *Second Life*.[63] Even though the form and function of virtual land in *Second Life* follows that of real-world property, the developer explicitly denies and prevents the vesting of such rights in the players.[64]

### *EULAs and TOSs in Other Virtual Worlds*

The contract terms imposed upon players in *WoW* and *Second Life* are not unique. Similar terms appear in EULAs and TOSs that govern other virtual worlds. Developers use both contracts to prevent the recognition of virtual property rights of players. From the discussion above it has also become clear that an

---

forth below. Linden Lab may or may not charge fees for the right to acquire, transfer or access Virtual Land, and these fees may change at any time. When you acquire Virtual Land, Linden Lab hereby grants you a limited license ('Virtual Land License') to access and use features of the Service associated with the virtual unit(s) of space corresponding to the identifiers of the Virtual Land within the Service as designated by Linden Lab… The Virtual Land License is transferable by the holder to any other user provided that both users and the proposed transfer comply with these Terms of Service, maintain their accounts in good standing, and are not delinquent on any Account payment requirements. Except as expressly permitted by this Agreement, this Virtual Land License may not otherwise be encumbered, conveyed or made subject to any right of survivorship or other disposition and any attempted disposition in violation of these Terms of Service is null and void. Linden Lab may revoke the Virtual Land License at any time without notice, refund or compensation in the event that: (i) Linden Lab determines that fraud, illegal conduct or any other violations of these Terms of Service or other Second Life policies is associated with the holder's Account or Virtual Land; or (ii) the holder becomes delinquent on any of that user's Account's payment requirements, ceases to maintain an active Account or terminates this Agreement. …" Linden Lab TOS, *supra* note 50, at 6.

63 "You acknowledge that Virtual Land is a limited license right and is not a real property right or actual real estate, and it is not redeemable for any sum of money from Linden Lab. You acknowledge that the use of the words 'Buy,' 'Sell' and similar terms carry the same meaning of referring to the transfer of the Virtual Land License as they do with respect to the Linden Dollar License. You agree that Linden Lab has the right to manage, regulate, control, modify and/or eliminate such Virtual Land as it sees fit and that Linden Lab shall have no liability to you based on its exercise of such right." Linden Lab TOS, *supra* note 50, at 5–6.

64 It is interesting to note how developers are becoming more and more aggressive in their efforts to deny the existence of such rights and the increasingly complicated legal steps that they take to prevent this. This leads to one of the important questions as to the justifications for the acceptance of virtual property and the associated rights. The question could be asked whether, even though the EULA and TOS contractually denied the creation, existence and vesting of property rights, normative justifications should not override the contractual terms and give real world recognition to such rights.

important aspect to keep in mind when thinking about virtual worlds and the legal repercussions of the phenomena, is that virtual worlds that are run as a commercial enterprise are just that—commercial enterprises. Because of this, the relationship between player and developer is regulated by contract and one needs to view the rights and relationships between the various parties and participants in the virtual worlds in the same frame of mind.[65]

## Customary Law[66]

In a virtual world unexpected things can happen. An example is the emergence of a third source of virtual-world law in the form of customary rules developed by the players themselves.[67] A group of players may combine and agree amongst themselves to act according to a set of unwritten rules, or sometimes they spontaneously start to do things in a certain manner. Any new player who subsequently enters the virtual world and spends some time getting to know the ropes will invariably pay close attention to the way in which other players are doing things. In this manner, in-game customary law arises. These unwritten rules and customs are external to the governing function of the developer and no reference to these rules will be found in the EULA or TOS. The developers are not directly involved in the settlement of any disputes originating between players regarding these rules. Players normally find methods of settling these differences in their own way.[68]

The determining factor of the effectiveness of a virtual-world customary law rule is whether it can be enforced.[69] A rule incapable of being enforced might just as well not exist. In the virtual world, the enforcement mechanisms are often not only quite amusing, but also effective.[70] One example of effective enforcement is

65 *See* Jack M. Balkin, *Virtual Liberty: Freedom to Design and Freedom to Play in Virtual Worlds*, 90 Va. L. Rev. 2043, 2047 (2004) (arguing developers should be subjected to consumer protection laws due to commoditization of the virtual world).

66 In a virtual world, customary law refers to law created by the users of a virtual world (through custom) as opposed to the coded law created by the developer.

67 Edelmann, *supra* note 4, at 7–9.

68 James Grimmelmann, *Virtual World Feudalism*, 118 Yale L.J. Pocket Part 126, 128 (2009), http://yalelawjournal.org/images/pdfs/740.pdf; David R. Johnson & David Post, *Law and Borders - The Rise of Law in Cyberspace*, 48 Stan. L. Rev. 1367, 1389–90. *See also* Edelmann, *supra* note 4, at 7–9.

69 Tamir Maltz, *Customary Law & Power in Internet Communities*, 2 J. Computer-Med. Comm. (Special Issue) P1 (1996), http://jcmc.indiana.edu/vol2/issue1/custom.html.

70 For example, players often resort to self-help if they are unable to get help from the developers. They do this to discipline other players who do not technically transgress the games' rules, but do transgress the unwritten common law of the players. *See* Mikael Jakobsson & T. L. Taylor, *The Sopranos Meets Everquest: Social Networking in Massively*

when players shun another player who does not follow the customs of the game.[71] This might not sound like an effective mechanism, but if a player's success in a game is linked to her ability to find and participate as a member of a social group, shunning a player will have a devastating effect on that player's progress in the game.[72] Harassment[73] as an alternative form of policing is also quite popular. In a game with a time-based element, a group of players may direct their avatars to surround an errant player's avatar, causing a total loss of virtual assets for that player.[74] In some real-world contexts, self-help is frowned upon, but if the action of self-help inside the virtual world has no influence in the real world, then it should not be viewed with the same trepidation as in the real world. The fact of the matter is that it is commonly done by groups of players inside the virtual world, and the practice is deemed to be exceptionally effective.[75]

---

*Multiplayer Online Games*, 17 FineArt Forum, Aug. 2003, http://tltaylor.com/wp-content/uploads/2009/07/JT-SopranosMeetsEQ.pdf. *See also* Maltz, *supra* note 69.

71 As in the real world, social pressure as an enforcement mechanism is used to regulate player behavior. For a real world example of how neighbors often resolve disputes amongst themselves by relying on informal and decentralized forms of control (making use of the example of cattle trespass and how this is resolved informally and often with self-help), *see* Robert Ellickson, *Order Without Law: How Neighbors Settle Disputes* 40–64 (1994).

72 Susan P. Crawford, *Who's in Charge of Who I Am?: Identity and Law Online*, 49 N.Y.L. Sch. L. Rev. 211, 228 (2004); Raphael Koster, *The Man Behind the Curtain*, Raph Koster's Website (May 11, 1998), http://www.raphkoster.com/gaming/essay5.shtml.

73 However, one should take note of the very real possibility that self-help in the form of social pressure as an enforcement mechanism can quickly become problematic, especially when it forms the basis for anti-social behavior that spills over into the real world. Examples of such anti-social behavior include the online assault and harassment of minorities, women, people of color, and any other vulnerable individual. Because of the safety of anonymity that the internet can provide, anonymous online groups are free to terrorize victims by publishing lies, doctored photographs, sensitive personal information, and even threats of physical or sexual violence against a person. *See* Danielle Keats Citron, *Cyber Civil Rights*, 89 B.U. L. Rev. 61, 63–81 (2009).

74 In the now-extinct virtual world of *The Sims Online*, there was a virtual mafia. The mafia was available for hire to make a player an offer he could not refuse. If he did refuse to cooperate, the members of the mafia would surround the player and effectively bar the player from earning virtual money or attending to the maintenance needs of his or her virtual property. This could result in a huge financial loss for the player if his assets deteriorated beyond repair, and sometimes the player would lose his or her virtual work. *See* Dawn C. Chmielewski, *Mobs move into 'Sims Online' power vacuum*, SiliconValley.com (June 5, 2003), http://msl1.mit.edu/furdlog/docs/2003-06-05_sivalley_sims. *See also* Urizenus Sklar, Interview with SSG's SnowWhite, Alphaville Herald (Nov. 26, 2003) http://alphavilleherald.com/2003/11/interview_with__1-10.html; Edelmann, *supra* note 4, at 8.

75 For an in-depth discussion on how these self-help mechanisms function and the uniquely effective and acceptable use thereof (in cyberspace) *see* Maltz, *supra* note 69,

Another form of user-created law is the formation of guilds in most of the virtual worlds. The guilds draw up their own codes of conduct and enforce them without the help of the developer.[76] In other instances, players form a virtual posse of vigilantes that hunt down wrongdoers and subject them to the same harm that they have inflicted on others.[77] As illustrated by these examples, players by themselves create and enforce a lively and innovative informal legal system.

## Power, Control, and Lawmaking[78]

The developer of a virtual world usually performs the functions of governance, not only out of necessity, but also out of commercial interest.[79] The ability to perform these functions normally derives from the contractual terms in the EULA and TOS. The players and participants in virtual worlds often view the developer's reliance on contractual terms as problematic because they lack bargaining position and input in the creation of the contract. However, the use of contract by a developer to regulate its world is not necessarily problematic, but negative effects flow from the way in which developers implement their contracts.[80] The biggest of these problems seems to be that developers forget that they are not gods or sovereigns. Even though they have virtual sovereignty inside the boundaries of their own creations, they are still themselves subject to the control, regulation, and laws of their respective real world governments.[81]

---

discussing the history, effectiveness, methods, and the fact that these forms of self-help are generally based on the consensus of the virtual community at large.

76 *See* Johnson & Post, *supra* note 68, at 1389–90, comparing this development to that of the *Lex Mercatoria* or Law Merchant in the Middle Ages. They argue that virtual worlds face a similar problem to the occurrence of jurisdictional confusion in the Middle Ages, where merchants were unable to take their disputes to the local noble. Since the local noble was unable to understand the complex subject matter at hand (that was executed beyond his control), the merchants eventually developed a new legal system amongst themselves. The idea behind the *Lex Mercatoria* was that "people who cared most about and best understood their new creation formed and championed this new law, which did not destroy or replace existing law … " They argue that this same phenomenon is developing in Cyberspace (virtual worlds) at the moment.

77 Lastowka & Hunter, *supra* note 4, at 70.

78 Only the issues applicable to a virtual world created and maintained as a revenue-generating venture by the developers are dealt with in this discussion. For a more detailed discussion of the differentiation that has to be made between revenue-generating and non-revenue generating virtual worlds and in particular the differing rights that should be recognized in each, *see* W Erlank, *Virtual Property – Protection and Remedies* 9–19 2012 *in* Property Law Perspectives (Bram Akkermans & Eveline Ramaekers eds)

79 Jankowich, *supra* note 8, at 179.

80 *Id.* at 178.

81 *Id.* at 179; Balkin, *supra* note 65, at 2046.

A different approach to this problem of unequal contracting positions posits that developers see themselves not as virtual governments, but as customer-service providers.[82] Castronova[83] and Jankowich[84] argue that the problem stems from the nature of the developer's creations. Developers need players to populate the virtual worlds they have created, because a virtual world without players is useless when the developer has the commercial objective of making money. Because players necessarily take active roles in the continuous development and running of the virtual world, they are left with a high level of self-perception.[85] This self-perception is markedly lower in console-type[86] games that do not provide for much player-autonomy and usually do not comprise a virtual world in the strict sense.[87] On the other hand, in the virtual world this self-perception stems from the vast self-determination capacity that a virtual world player receives. Indeed, the developer usually actively markets this autonomy as an attractive benefit and selling feature of its virtual world.[88] While the developer tries to regulate its relationship with the players by labeling its contribution in the virtual world as the provision of services, the player perceives the developer's role as one of providing a governing function.[89] Therefore, "in their minds, the players are not customers,

82 Jankowich, *supra* note 8, at 178; Edward Castronova, *On Virtual Economies*, 3 Int'l J. Computer Gaming Res., (Dec. 2003), http://www.gamestudies.org/0302/castronova/.

83 Castronova, *supra* note 82.

84 Jankowich, *supra* note 8, at 178.

85 In other words, players perceive themselves to be permanent active participants in the virtual world and not merely temporary visitors. Jancovich describes this in terms of increased player autonomy. *See id.*

86 Typical game consoles include the Xbox 360 from Microsoft, the Playstation 3 by Sony and the Wii by Nintendo. These console gaming systems usually provide for single player gaming and sometimes for multiplayer gaming (that does not connect to virtual environments which has all the features of a virtual world). Usually the requirement of permanence is absent from these games. To date, these gaming consoles have not seriously been used to participate in virtual world gaming.

87 In other words, the console-game usually would not have all the *indicia* of a virtual world. For a discussion of the *indicia* or *essentialia* of virtual worlds, *see* generally Erlank, *supra* note 2; Charles Blazer, *The Five Indicia of Virtual Property*, 5 Pierce L. Rev. 137 (2006); Joshua A. T. Fairfield, *Virtual Property,* 85 B.U. L. Rev. 1047 (2005).

88 For example, the game *Asheron's Call* contains the following description of what awaits the prospective player: "Welcome to the online role-playing game Asheron's Call, where thousands of players inhabit a beautiful 3D fantasy world to make friends and seek out perilous adventure. Customize your alter ego with a unique appearance and balance of heroic skills, then enter a magical frontier of terrible monsters, breathtaking vistas, and fast alliances. With over 500 square miles that offer ever more wonders to explore, Asheron's Call gives you a world of unparalleled scope and freedom, the richest setting yet for creating your personal saga or joining your friends in an epic campaign." *See About Asheron's Call: Features*, Asheron's Call, (2009), http://ac.turbine.com/index.php?option=com_content&view=category&layout=blog&id=34& Itemid=64&NavItemid=56.

89 Castronova, *supra* note 82.

but citizens with corresponding rights."[90] In effect, the big question is one about rights. How do the parties perceive their rights and obligations, and what is the actual situation? Jankowich argues that the EULAs and TOSs are insufficient for regulating the long-term relationships between developers and players.[91] These agreements fail to provide for all the needs of the participants, and any ad hoc rulemaking that developers use to address issues not covered in the EULA or TOS will most likely result in unsatisfactory and arbitrary solutions.[92]

Although I agree in principle with the position taken by Castronova and Jankowich that developers view themselves as customer service providers, I think that the problem lies more in the way that developers see players not only as the recipients of services but as their subjects, which they can both govern and control from their omnipotent position. In the real world the gamer would be seen as a consumer who in certain instances is protected by real-world law to help equalize the skewed relationship between consumer and developer.[93] However, in the virtual world the developer becomes the enterprise, government, and god.[94] In effect the developer inherently acquires the role of judge, jury, and executioner of the gamer. This feeling of powerlessness has led some players to seek help outside of the governance structure of the virtual world when they believe that their in-game rights are too limited.[95] Jankowich explains that the "absence of a robust legal system in a complex environment like a virtual world inhabited by people with very limited rights will lead those people to search for environments where they have greater power."[96]

The disparity in power and control between the developer and its players has temporal dimensions. There are five stages at which the developer might have differing levels of influence and governing control. The first stage is the creation of the virtual world. The second is the testing stage. The third is the stage that occurs during the normal running of the virtual world. The fourth stage is the maintenance stage. Finally, there could be a stage in which the virtual world is destroyed.

The developer needs to have creative control to create the world.[97] While the virtual world is being created this is only of interest to the developer and does not

---

90 *Id.* This idea was already present in the early days of the development of virtual worlds. *See* Raphael Koster, *Declaring the Rights of Players*, Raph Koster's Website (Aug. 27, 2000), http://www.raphkoster.com/gaming/playerrights.shtml; Koster, *supra* note 72.

91 Jankowich, *supra* note 8, at 178.

92 *Id.* at 179.

93 *See* Balkin, *supra* note 65, at 2048–50.

94 Kunze, *supra* note 11, at 107; Jankowich, *supra* note 8, at 185; Kevin Deenihan, Leave Those Orcs Alone: Property Rights in Virtual Worlds 5 (Mar. 26, 2008), http://ssrn.com/abstract=1113402. For a more comprehensive discussion of what Grimmelmann refers to as "The God Problem", *see* Grimmelmann, *supra* note 4, at 174.

95 Jankowich, *supra* note 8, at 179.

96 *Id.*

97 Richard A. Bartle, *Pitfalls of Virtual Property,* The Themis Group, 9–13 (2004), http://www.themis-group.com/uploads/Pitfalls%20of%20Virtual%20Property.pdf.

affect anyone else. If the developer is held back in any way during this creative phase, the virtual world would ultimately not come into existence and the legal question would remain moot. Even though the potential players do not really have an interest in the game at this stage, the state and community in the real world where the developer is located might have a legitimate interest in the development of the virtual world.[98] If the topic, idea, theme, or implementation of the virtual world is *contra bonos mores*, or even criminal, the state and society will have the power to censure and possibly stop the further development of the virtual world.[99]

During the testing phase of the virtual world, the developer constantly makes changes to and fine-tunes the program code. Some unexpected error might occur, causing unintended consequences in the virtual world. At this stage the developer approaches either the general public or a select group of gamers to test the game in its *beta* state.[100] The developer always makes it clear that the virtual world is a work in progress, and players should expect interruptions in their gameplay experience. The virtual world can be reset or reverted to the initial stages at any time. At this stage the enterprise does not qualify as a virtual world because it is non-permanent.[101] The gamers who take part in this testing stage do so voluntarily and usually do not pay for the privilege of being the first people to experience the new virtual world. The developers make it quite clear that the gameplay might change drastically at any stage, and that the leveling of avatars during the testing phase could at any time revert to the initial stages.[102] Developers also explicitly state that the items acquired by players during the testing stages will not be transferred to

---

98 Balkin, *supra* note 65, at 2048–50, 2053.

99 Although this might sound like a highly theoretical issue, there are a number of games that were developed and marketed with themes that are so abhorrent that even in a liberal society, they are viewed as not only extremely distasteful, but possibly criminal in some states. Examples that spring to mind are the games where the game's sole purpose is to rape women. Another game puts the player in the shoes of a terrorist who has the liberty of killing many innocent civilians at an airport. For more detail about these and other games *see* Nic Simmonds, *5 Most Offensive Games Ever* My Gaming (Nov. 20, 2009), http://mygaming.co.za/news/news/4868-5-most-offensive-games-ever.html Another area where the state might want to interfere at this stage is where the state decides that the general idea or effect of the game would be against state policy. For example, China is hindering the launch of the new *WOW* expansion because certain elements of the game, such as skeleton characters, were seen as unacceptable for the government. *See* AFP, *China Tightens Supervision of Online Games*, Google News (Nov. 19, 2009), http://www.google.com/hostednews/afp/article/ALeqM5gZyJ5KJqIzPv4X-BUXuyae8nsaMQ.

100 *See, e.g.*, Star Wars: The Old Republic Game, Launch FAQ, http://www.swtor.com/info/faq/game#top.

101 For more details about the characteristic of permanence see the discussion about the characteristics of a virtual world in Lastowka & Hunter, *supra* note 4. *See also* Erlank, *supra* note 2.

102 An explicit notice to this effect is normally incorporated into the trial version's EULA.

the world when it launches for the broad public.[103] During the testing stages, these items might at any time disappear from the avatar's collected possessions.

In the third stage, when the virtual world is functioning properly and the general public has started participating, the developer still needs to manage the general administrative tasks required by a virtual world. Disputes between gamers need to be arbitrated when they have concerns about issues affecting the virtual world or the interests of the developers. The developer must be able to take action against players whose actions create problems for other players, have detrimental effects for the virtual world, or create problems regarding real world state regulation.[104] The developer must manage any problems that crop up on a daily basis due to the expansion of the virtual world or the unforeseen development of in-game.[105]

---

103 For example, the Game Testing Terms and Conditions for *Star Wars: The Old Republic* state that "(L) You acknowledge and agree that BWA reserves the right to change/add/remove items collected or updated, modify or remove any items in the Game at any time and without warning." Bioware "Game Testing Terms and Conditions for Star Wars: The Old Republic:" 2011 *Star Wars: The Old Republic* at https://account.swtor.com/user/register/ (last visited July 5, 2011).

104 *WoW*'s EULA states that one is not allowed to "…use cheats, automation software (bots), hacks, mods or any other unauthorized third-party software designed to modify the World of Warcraft experience…" Blizzard EULA, *supra* note 23, at Additional License Limitations, B. Another reason why a developer would want to include a clause to this effect would be to comply with the laws of the state where the server is hosted. For example, see the disclaimer by Second Life about it being a U.S. based service: "13.1 Second Life is a United States-based service. Linden Lab makes no representation that any aspect of the Service is appropriate or available for use outside of the United States. Those who access the Service from other locations are responsible for compliance with applicable local laws. The Linden Software is subject to applicable export laws and restrictions." Linden Lab TOS, *supra* note 50. Some of the modifications (mods) or hacks are often used to render the avatars nude or to enable the avatars to engage in sexual practices. *See generally* Nelson Williams, *World of Warcraft Nude Mods and Clothing Patches*, Vox ex Machina (Nov. 28, 2008), http://www.voxexmachina.com/mods/world-of-warcraft-nude-mods-and-clothing-patches/; Mike Jackson, *WoW Police Hunting down Sexual Role-Play*, CVG (Aug. 5, 2010), http://www.computerandvideogames.com/article.php?id=258879. Also compare with *supra* note 99.

105 An example of this would be where some type of error or omission in the programming is (legally) exploited by a number of players. If it is creating problems for the virtual world it would need to be rectified. An example is the case of *Bragg v. Linden Research, Inc.*, 487 F. Supp. 2d 593 (E.D.Pa. 2007), where the plaintiff *Second Life* player found a way to bypass the normal virtual real estate auctioning system and exploited this to his benefit by buying virtual land at rock-bottom prices. When the developers discovered this exploit, they closed the loophole and froze all of his assets in the game. *See also* Kunze, *supra* note 11, at 102. This could be especially troubling where there are minors who also participate in the virtual world. Developers therefore use this clause to enforce compliance with their rules and censor or prohibit certain behavior.

The fourth stage, maintenance, refers to substantial work or modification taken by the developer to stabilize or transform the virtual world. In the highly competitive market of Massively Multiplayer Online Role Playing Games (MMORPGs) a developer must periodically upgrade a virtual world to keep the players resident there. One of the ways to achieve this is by implementing a "patch"[106] to the client-side program that runs on the player's computer. Sometimes this takes the form of an automatic update from the developer's servers when the player logs onto the game. It could also take the form of either an optional or mandatory piece of software that players have to download from the server and install by themselves. Sometimes the patch is sufficient to address maintenance problems without affecting the general game experience for the player. Sometimes, however, the developer uses a patch to force players to accept changes that they ordinarily would have rejected. In many instances such a patch includes an updated version of the EULA or TOS. Many patches are mandatory in the sense that players must accept and install them in order to continue participating in the game. Although this is not usually problematic, it can lead to abuse.

The final stage is the end of the world. Sometimes a virtual world faces a digital Armageddon and shuts down forever. This has happened in a few instances, the shutdown of *The Sims Online*[107] being a prominent example. Even though this is a highly undesirable situation for the players, a developer wants the power to shut down the game if necessary. For some developers this is sufficiently important that they include a specific clause in the EULA reserving the right to discontinue the virtual world at their discretion.[108] Purely financial reasons sometimes motivate

106 A patch in this sense refers to an additional piece of software that is released after the initial launch of the main program. This patch is then used to fix any problems that have manifested in the meantime. It could also be used to improve or change certain minor elements of the program.

107 The Sims Online (TSO) was a popular and well populated virtual world that was discontinued by the developer without much warning and against strong opposition from the players. For a detailed discussion about this event and the backlash by players *see* Daniel Terdiman, *'EA Land' Closing just Weeks after Debut*, CNET (Apr. 29, 2008), http://news.cnet.com/8301-13772_3-9931757-52.html; Erlank, *supra* note 3. *See also The Sims Online,* Virtual World Review, http://www.virtualworldsreview.com/thesimsonline/

108 For example, *WoW*'s EULA states that "(t)his License Agreement is effective until terminated. You may terminate the License Agreement at any time by (i) permanently destroying all copies of the Game in your possession or control; (ii) removing the Game Client from your hard drive; and (iii) notifying Blizzard of your intention to terminate this License Agreement. Blizzard may terminate this Agreement at any time for any reason or no reason. Upon termination for any reason, all licenses granted herein shall immediately terminate and you must immediately and permanently destroy all copies of the Game in your possession and control and remove the Game Client from your hard drive." Blizzard EULA, *supra* note 23, at Termination. The termination clause fulfills an essential function in the governing of a virtual world. It gives certainty to the developer about the point at which the contractual relationship between it and the player has come to an end. However, this

developers to shut down a virtual world.[109] For example, the costs of operating a virtual world that is underperforming as a financial investment could be better spent on another project or virtual world. Such a decision to reinvest funds might stem from pressure from shareholders in the developer, even if the developer's managers might otherwise continue the game. Although the shut-down decision may make financial and logical sense from the developer's perspective, due to the nature of the virtual world as a vehicle for social interaction and considering that it is often designed to be addictive, a developer arguably should have a social responsibility to continue supplying players with access to the virtual world that they have come to rely on.[110]

---

specific termination clause does not provide any certainty to the contract. The requirement that is expected from the player to publicize termination of the agreement is problematic. It is unclear whether any single action specified above, that is, destruction, removal, or notification is the essential element to publicize this fact. Due to the unclear semantics, it could be construed that any of these actions could constitute such publication. If all three requirements are met, it creates a massive onus on the player. The transfer clause discussed above did not require that the developer be notified of the transfer. It now seems strange that the termination would require such explicit notification. Even more problematic for the player is the fact that the developer gives itself not only the right to terminate the agreement at any time, but also to do so for "any reason or no reason." Such clauses that clearly put the player at a disadvantage could be construed to be *mala fide* and *contra bonos mores*. While a person may shrug such imperious tactics off when it only applies to issues inside a virtual world, this clause also has a cross-border element. The contract affects the player-developer relationship in the real world and not only in the virtual world. If one were to accept the value of virtual property interests and vested economic, social, and sentimental value that a player has in a virtual world, such actions by developers could lead to gross misuse. Problems like "expropriation" of virtual property interests would appear and the affected player(s) would need to be able to find redress somewhere. Nothing in the clause includes references to a form of compensation or other remedy that a player can rely upon if the developer chooses to end the agreement. At the very least one should expect that a player whose license has been unfairly or otherwise terminated by a unilateral action from the developer should at least be able to get compensation for the physical game media that he or she could lose.

109 See the discussion about the implications of these actions when viewed from a normative perspective as a consideration for the justification of allocating property rights in virtual resources (or not) in Lastowka & Hunter, *supra* note 4, at 43–50. *See also* Erlank, *supra* note 3, at ch. 4; Erlank, *supra* note 78.

110 See the discussion about the social elements and effects of virtual worlds in Fairfield, *supra* note 87, at 1059–60; Lastowka & Hunter, *supra* note 4, at 27; Erlank, *supra* note 3, at ch. 4. Many of these virtual worlds and games are intentionally designed to be addictive and therefore developers should be held accountable for the wellbeing of the players if and when they decide to end a virtual world. *See* Nick Yee, *The Virtual Skinner Box*, Nick Yee's HomePage, http://www.nickyee.com/eqt/skinner.html, as well as Nick Yee, *The Norrathian Scrolls: A Study of EverQuest*, Nick Yee's HomePage, http://www.nickyee.com/eqt/home.html, for Yee's analysis of both quantitative and qualitative statistical data from *Everquest* where he also includes interviews with players regarding their levels of

Players of course prefer not to witness the sudden destruction of their virtual world; they would like to participate in the decision-making process before this happens. Sometimes they might be willing to help rescue a virtual world that faces financial problems, or they might be willing to take over the running of the game themselves and allow the developer to exit.[111] This last alternative usually requires the developer's consent because the EULA prohibits players from using the source-code of the virtual world for non-licensed purposes. But developers are faced with a distinct challenge, since players often get their hands on the code, which they sometimes run on their own unlicensed servers. Even though these unlicensed servers do not have any interaction with the properly licensed version of the virtual world, many players are content to make use of them.[112] The existence of unlicensed servers represents more of a problem for virtual worlds that cater for *ad hoc* multiplayer games than for those that are socially orientated.

## Conclusion

The sources of virtual law form the basis for the governance of virtual worlds. The laws created by the first source of virtual law, the computer code, do not need to be enforced, since the enforcement is automatically done by the game itself. There is no room for circumventing the rules as the outcome of any given set of rules and actions is always pre-determined by the code. This creates certainty in the legal system of the game. The second source is in-game customary law developed by the players themselves outside of the developer's influence. The creation process of such law is sometimes spontaneous, but at other times carefully planned. Customary law is also policed and enforced by the players themselves, without the intervention or help of the developers. Such enforcement is surprisingly effective and innovative, although occasionally problems of self-help and vigilantism arise. Another important source of virtual law is contractual terms contained in EULAs and TOSs. In the EULA the developer creates and controls rights and obligations concerning the virtual world. As the most important source of virtual property, the EULA gives rise to (and is subject to) real world law and is the point of reference for discussing the legal relationship between player and developer.

---

addiction to the virtual world. *See also* Reuveni, *supra* note 39, at 303 (asserting virtual worlds are more than just entertainment).

111 Bartle, *supra* note 97, at 12–13. When the virtual world of *Earth and Beyond* shut down, the players attempted to buy the hardware and software from the developer to ensure the continuation of the world. However, the developer could not be convinced to sell.

112 This would only be a satisfactory solution if players decide to join such an unlicensed server without any benefit from their previous playing experience on the proper virtual world server. They would have to recreate their avatars from scratch, level up from the start and also have to start accumulating all their virtual property from the beginning.

The sources of virtual law provide the foundation, both legal and technological, for the governance and management of virtual worlds. The application of these sources of law, in both the real and virtual worlds, undergoes constant change and refinement. An in-game legal system, which is essential to the running of any virtual world, affects both developers and players with regard to power, control, and executive lawmaking. One of the most contentious legal issues between players and developers of a virtual world stems directly from the developer's reliance on the sources of virtual law to prohibit the vesting of property rights in players. The current application and enforcement of EULAs results in unfair bargaining positions between players and developers. However, with some modification of the problematic aspects of the EULAs—which take into account the concerns and needs of the players, especially regarding the recognition of property rights—the current system of virtual law will continue to provide an effective means of virtual world governance.

# PART III
# The Arts

# Chapter 6
# Property and Sovereignty in HBO's *Deadwood*[1]

Michael B. Kent, Jr. and Lance McMillian

"Property and sovereignty, as every student knows, belong to entirely different branches of the law."[2] So wrote legal philosopher Morris Cohen in 1928. Of course, Cohen's purpose in making this statement was largely so that he could refute it. As he made clear in the same work, property and sovereignty in reality are intertwined: "[W]e must not overlook the actual fact that dominion over things is also *imperium* over fellow human beings."[3]

The interconnection between property and sovereignty was on full display in the critically acclaimed television series *Deadwood*, which ran on HBO from 2004 to 2006. The series portrayed the fictional saga of what is now Deadwood, South Dakota,[4] from its inception as a lawless mining camp to its evolution as a *bona fide* town complete with budding government and social institutions. As series creator David Milch has explained, the show is about "the development of law and order, or, specifically, how does order develop without law."[5] Because the community of Deadwood is founded on the gold that rests in the nearby hills, the assignment and protection of gold claims serve as the central focus in the evolution from anarchy to established legal order. Thus, the show has a lot to say about property's relationship to human society generally and its relationship to the concept of sovereignty in particular.

---

1 This book chapter is a modified version of our article, *The World of* Deadwood*: Property Rights and the Search for Human Identity*, 20 S. Cal. Interdisciplinary L. J. 489 (2011).

2 Morris R. Cohen, *Property and Sovereignty*, 13 Cornell L. Q. 8, 8 (1928).

3 *Id.* at 13 (emphasis in original).

4 *Deadwood* actually is a mix of the factual and the fictional. Deadwood is a real place that originated with the discovery of gold in the Black Hills. Many of the show's characters—Al Swearengen, Seth Bullock, Wild Bill Hickok, and George Hearst—are historical figures, while others (Alma Garrett, most prominently) are not. The show itself makes only a slight pretense to historical accuracy. Rather, *Deadwood* is a vehicle for its creator, David Milch, to tell his stories.

5 Allen Barra, *The Man Who Made* Deadwood: http://www.americanheritage.com/content/man-who-made-%C2%91deadwood%C2%92 (last visited Dec. 19, 2012).

In its most common application, the term "sovereignty" refers to political rule exercised through some governmental agency.[6] In a broader sense, however, "sovereignty" refers simply to power and control, both over things and over other human beings.[7] Indeed, Cohen himself described property in terms of a "sovereign power compelling service and obedience,"[8] suggesting that control over things also bestows certain power in relation to people. *Deadwood* shows how property relates to sovereignty in both senses of the latter term. As an initial matter, *Deadwood* invokes ancient debates over who has the power to create and define property in the first instance. Second, the series demonstrates the important role that property plays in establishing political sovereignty, as well as in the relationship between government and its citizens. Finally, *Deadwood* reveals how property creates a sphere of personal sovereignty in its owners.

Stories are powerful teaching tools because they marry information and context.[9] Moreover, by supplying a picture of law in action, film and television marshal the power of the visual to make law more real, less abstract. By seeing how the application of law affects characters we know and care about, we become more attuned to the potential effects of legal decisions in the real world. By reflecting on the story of *Deadwood*, the relationship between property and sovereignty is reinforced in new and interesting ways.

## Labor, Possession, and the Power to Create Property

What is property, and who has the power to create and define it? These questions occupy a prominent place in the story of *Deadwood*, and therefore, serve as obvious starting points for discussing *Deadwood*'s portrayal of the relationship between property and sovereignty. At issue is the age-old controversy about whether property is a natural right that focuses on an individual's relationship to things or, alternatively, whether it is a creature of positive law that focuses primarily on relationships between individuals. The early episodes of the series reflect a decidedly naturalist view.

The narrative of *Deadwood* begins in 1876. Bare wilderness only a short time before the viewer joins the story, the camp of Deadwood has just arisen from

6 *See, e.g.*, Random House Webster's *Unabridged Dictionary* 1826 (2d ed. 1999) (defining "sovereignty" as "supreme and independent power or authority in government as possessed or claimed by a state or community").

7 *See* Cohen, *supra* note 2, at 12–13 (discussing sovereignty in terms of power).

8 *Id.* at 12.

9 *See* Chip Heath & Dan Heath, *Made To Stick: Why Some Ideas Survive and Others Die* 204–37 (2008) (describing the role of stories in the spread of new ideas); *see also* Lance McMillian, The Death of Law: A Cinematic Vision, 32 U. Ark. L. Rock L. Rev. 1, 11 (2009) (explaining why the "broad reach of popular culture inevitably shapes popular opinions about the law").

the mud. Its existence is geographical fortuity. Deadwood sits in close proximity to the Black Hills, where gold has been discovered. This gold draws a ragtag group of miners, pioneers, and entrepreneurs who come to the camp to fulfill two interrelated purposes—to strike it rich and to live autonomously, free from the rules that govern more civilized places.

Both of these aims are made possible, to varying degrees, by the unique political circumstances in which the camp initially finds itself. Having formed organically on land that legally belongs to the Sioux,[10] the camp remains outside the jurisdiction of any recognized US government. It has no mayor, no council, no sheriff, nor any other trappings of an organized state. It is free, unincorporated, unencumbered, and unassociated. It exists, in other words, in something of a state of nature.

Despite this lack of formal government or legal institutions, the camp serves the purposes of its residents. In law's absence, custom and community norms control, and a functioning market quickly develops. Autonomy appears to be working, and the people of Deadwood seem pleased with the emerging course of dealing. A system of property develops, under which there is a shared recognition of claims to the gold and the surrounding land on which the camp is situated.

An exchange early in the first season of the series between camp founder Al Swearengen and newcomer Seth Bullock is revealing. Swearengen is the owner of the Gem Saloon and the unofficial leader of the camp. Bullock, a former marshal in the Montana territory, has recently arrived in Deadwood where he and his partner have plans to open a hardware store catering to the miners. The aspiring entrepreneurs quickly identify the perfect plot of land for their new endeavor, which is owned by Swearengen. Negotiations follow, but abruptly end when Swearengen becomes distrustful of Bullock's long-term intentions.[11] Negotiations later resume, and a deal is finally struck after Swearengen becomes convinced that Bullock will not threaten the former's interests. What does the convincing, in large part, is Bullock's agreement not to form any business venture with a competing saloon in the camp, not to use the plot for activities that would compete with Swearengen's business, and to give Swearengen the first right to repurchase the plot should it ever come up for sale.[12] This brief discussion explicitly raises basic property questions of rights of first refusal, covenants not to compete, and servitudes. But how are these agreements enforced? And why is the plot under consideration Swearengen's to sell in the first instance? Deeds do not exist. Transactions are secured by handshakes. When expectations go asunder, there are

10 The Fort Laramie Treaty of 1868 set apart what is now the entire State of South Dakota, along with portions of several other states, "for the absolute and undisturbed use and occupation" of the Sioux. Treaty with The Sioux, Apr. 29, 1868, U.S.-Sioux, 15 Stat. 635, art. 2; *see United States v. Sioux Nation of Indians*, 448 U.S. 371, 374 (1980) (discussing Fort Laramie Treaty).

11 *Deadwood: Deep Water* (HBO television broadcast Mar. 28, 2004).

12 *Deadwood: Reconnoitering the Rim* (HBO television broadcast Apr. 4, 2004).

no courts to which to appeal. What power has created these property rights, and what power will enforce them?

Here we see, however imperfectly, a naturalist theory of property at work. Under this theory, the authority to create and define property does not come from any official law or political regime but rather exists naturally, apart from any legal conventions. This view of property enjoys a long pedigree in Western thinking, but perhaps the most famous explanation of it, at least in the American context,[13] was developed by English philosopher John Locke.

Locke posited that property was a God-given right that existed in the state of nature apart from and antecedent to the formation of political society.[14] Although this divine grant initially gave the fruits of the earth to humanity in common, the natural order also included a means by which persons might appropriate these common benefits for their own individual good.[15] For Locke, this power to acquire property rested in each person's own labor.[16] Locke suggested that "every man has a *property* in his own *person*," which "nobody has any right to but himself" and which includes "[t]he labor of his body, and the works of his hands."[17] Thus, by laboring, an individual extends the scope of his property beyond himself to reach the objects of his labor, removing them from the commons and rendering them

---

13 Many scholars have noted that Locke's conception of property enjoyed wide influence in the formative years of American law and politics. *See, e.g.*, Laura S. Underkuffler, *On Property: An Essay*, 100 Yale L. J. 127, 138 (1990) ("Locke's views exerted a powerful influence on the American Founders and on the early years of American jurisprudence."). Examples of this influence can be seen in the writings of James Madison, *see* James Madison, *Property* (1792), *reprinted in* 1 The Founders' Constitution 598 (Philip B. Kurland & Ralph Lerner eds, 1987), and Justice Paterson's 1795 opinion in *Vanhorne's Lessee v. Dorrance*, 2 U.S. (2 Dall.) 304, 310 (C.C.D. Pa. 1795) (linking property acquisition to "labour and industry" and stating that "preservation of property ... is a primary object of the social compact"). More recent examples of Lockean influence can be found in *Ruckelshaus v. Monsanto Co.*, 467 U.S. 986, 1003 (1984) (citing Locke's theory in discussing property rights in trade secrets), and *Washlefske v. Winston*, 234 F.3d 179, 184 & n.2 (4th Cir. 2000) (citing Locke's theory for proposition that "private citizens ordinarily have a constitutionally protected property interest in the wages earned from their labor under employment contracts").

14 John Locke, *Second Treatise of Government* § 4, at 8 (C.B. Macpherson ed., Hackett Publishing Co. 1980) (1690); *id.* § 26, at 18–19.

15 *Id.* § 26, at 18–19.

16 *Id.* § 27, at 19.

17 *Id.*

his own.[18] In Locke's own words, "As much land as a man tills, plants, improves, cultivates, and can use the product of, so much is his property."[19]

Thus, the sovereign power to create property is vested in the value-adding labor of each individual person.[20] The reason that an individual who cultivates a field is said to own that field, for example, is because it is her value-adding activity that accounts for the real worth of the field, which would be worthless apart from the things it could produce.[21] The use of the field to create valuable commodities sets that field apart as valuable itself, and this value-adding use justifies the acquisition of the field by the user. To protect that acquisition, other rights must also be implied—for example, the right to transfer both the field and the things it produces, as well as the right to keep others from interfering with the value-adding means of production.[22] Taken together, these rights form the heart of the idea of property "as a unified whole of rights concentrated in the thing owned."[23] And this group of rights, initially created by the power of an individual's labor, can be viewed as giving the user the additional power of possession—defined as dominion and control—over the thing itself.[24]

---

18 *Id.* Locke included a caveat, however, that labor created property "at least where there is enough, and as good, left in common to others." *Id.* Many scholars have noted that this caveat, called the "Lockean proviso," emphasizes the relationship between the labor-based view of property and equal opportunity for all laborers. *See, e.g.*, Joseph William Singer, *Original Acquisition of Property: From Conquest & Possession to Democracy & Equal Opportunity*, 86 Ind. L. J. 763, 765 (2011). Moreover, the idea that all laborers must have equal opportunity to acquire property raises the question of whether Locke's theory is more appropriate for explaining property rights in resources taken from land (such as crops) rather than in the land itself. *Cf.* Bret Boyce, *Property as a Natural Right and as a Conventional Right in Constitutional Law*, 29 Loy. L.A. Int'l & Comp. L. Rev. 201, 224 (2007). As noted in the next sentence, however, Locke applied the labor theory to land and not just to the things that land might produce.

19 *Id.* § 32, at 21.

20 *See* Anupam Chander, *The New, New Property*, 81 Tex. L. Rev. 715, 741–3 (2003) (linking Lockean concept of labor with value-adding activity); Adam Mossoff, *Locke's Labor Lost*, 9 U. Chi. L. Sch. Roundtable 155, 159–63 (2002) (explaining Locke's theory in terms of "value-creating activity").

21 Mossoff, *supra* note 20, at 161.

22 *See* Adam Mossoff, *What Is Property? Putting the Pieces Back Together*, 45 Ariz. L. Rev. 371, 402–403 (2003) ("The substantive role of acquisition, use and disposal derive from the fact that property is a consequent of the actions necessary to maintain life and liberty. The formal role of exclusion derives from the fact that property cannot do what it is supposed to do—maintain one's life and liberty—if the owner cannot prevent other people in society from appropriating the property.")

23 Eric Claeys, *Takings and Private Property on the Rehnquist Court*, 99 Nw. U. L. Rev. 187, 193 (2004).

24 *See Blacks' Law Dictionary* 1201 (8th ed. 2004) (defining "possession" in terms of dominion and control).

The initial settlers in Deadwood seem to fall squarely within this natural law tradition. In the early days of the camp, gold claims are established by a simple precept: you work it, you own it.[25] There is no law, and there is no government, but there is property, created by the sweat equity of those who got there "first." The idea that property originates from labor, not law, obviously reflects a Lockean perspective, one that Swearengen makes explicit early in the show's first season. Noting the increasing presence of newcomers to the camp, Swearengen complains: "Where were they when Dan and me were chopping trees in this gulch? Hands all blistered. Bucktooth ... beavers rolling around in the creek. Slappin' their tails in the water like we was hired entertainment."[26] For Swearengen, the authority that created the property being sought out by these later interlopers was the same value-adding labor of those who created the camp in the first instance.

A similar spirit of freedom, self-reliance, and self-interest animates a conversation between Swearengen and a gold prospector named Ellsworth in one of the very first scenes in the series. During their exchange, Ellsworth declares his independence: "I stand before you today beholden to no human ... , and workin' a payin' ... gold claim. Not the U.S. government sayin' I'm trespassin', or the savage... red man himself, or any of these ... passin' themselves off as prospectors had better try to stop me."[27] Ellsworth's labor creates an expectation in his mind that the land upon which he works belongs to him alone—not the Sioux (the legal possessors of the land), the federal government, or other prospectors in the area. Significantly, Ellsworth's claim is not simply to the gold he brings out of the ground; rather, in Lockean fashion, that claim extends to the ground itself, over which Ellsworth asserts the dominion and control associated with integrated possessory rights. His labor gives him property in the gold already mined, any gold that may be mined in the future, and the ground in which that gold is located.[28] This mindset of acquisition and possession through personal conquest provides

---

25 As illustrated below in our example of Ellsworth, we (and the characters in *Deadwood*) use the term "gold claims" to refer not only to gold already removed from the earth, but also to the continued right to exploit the vein from which that gold originated, as well as to ownership of the land in which the vein is located.

26 *Deadwood; Reconnoitering the Rim*, *supra* note 12.

27 *Deadwood: Deadwood* (HBO television broadcast Mar. 2, 2004).

28 Federal law in place when the story of *Deadwood* takes place presents both similarities to and distinctions from the expectations of the story's characters. The basic system governing mining operations was established by the General Mining Law of 1872, which is still in effect. *See* Act of May 10, 1872, ch. 152, 17 Stat. 91 (codified as amended at 30 U.S.C. §§ 22–30, 33–5, 37, 39–43, and 47). According to a leading treatise, "[t]he fundamental basis" of this system is "the right of self-initiation," granting legal protections to those claimants that located and pursued valuable minerals. 1 American Law of Mining § 30.01 (2d ed. 2010). Thus, like the Lockean views of *Deadwood*'s founders, the system seemed to reward labor, an unsurprising result for a system that itself was premised on the local customs of miners. *See id.* Unlike the expectations in *Deadwood*, however, the General Mining Law primarily gave the claimant property rights in the minerals themselves and not

a living example of Locke's state of nature in action. Property rights come from labor, not law, and therefore create a sovereignty that exists apart from law or political institutions.

## Positivism, Exclusion, and the State's Power to Redefine Property

Nonetheless, another view of property and the authority on which it depends is at work in *Deadwood.* If the early settlers reflect, however imperfectly, a Lockean attitude toward the creation of property, then later arrivals to the camp reflect the alternative view that property is defined by the political power of the state. In context, this makes perfect sense. The idea of Deadwood—a world based on the power of labor rather than law—works best when meaningful economic opportunity is available to all.[29] When this condition exists, self-interest produces a rough conformity that benefits the camp's pioneers. But what happens when the saturation point is reached and there are no more plots to buy or gold claims to develop through one's labor? Many arrive too late to enjoy the spoils of the initial financial windfall. The interest of this later group is not to safeguard the fruits of its (or anyone else's) labor, but rather to appropriate and utilize, for good or ill, the wealth of those who came before. To satisfy this goal, the authority to define property must rest somewhere other than with each individual possessor.

The idea that property is an institution created by positive law primarily to regulate social relations between individuals also has a long history in Western thought, and is perhaps the dominant view among modern American scholars. Reflecting a broadly-held understanding among legal scholars, for example, Charles Reich offered the following description: "Property is not a natural right but a deliberate construction by society. If such an institution did not exist, it would be necessary to create it, in order to have the kind of society we wish."[30]

Perhaps the most accessible example of this positivist notion lies in the "bundle" metaphor so widely used in current discussions about property.[31] Made popular by the legal realists of the early twentieth century,[32] this metaphor holds that property is not fundamentally about one's rights in or to a thing. Rather,

---

the land in which they were contained. Acquiring fee simple title to the land required a further step—obtaining a patent from the federal government. *See id.*

29 Here again, we see Locke's theory in action, specifically the "Lockean proviso" connecting labor with equal opportunity. *See supra* note 18.

30 Charles A. Reich, *The New Property*, 73 Yale L. J. 733, 771–2 (1964).

31 *See* Thomas W. Merrill & Henry E. Smith, *The Morality of Property*, 48 Wm. & Mary L. Rev. 1849, 1870 (2007) (indicating that modern legal thought takes "as self-evident [the proposition] that property is a bundle of rights, the content of which is whatever lawmakers decide it should be").

32 *See* Thomas W. Merrill & Henry E. Smith, *What Happened to Property in Law and Economics?*, 111 Yale L. J. 357, 365 (2001) (stating that bundle metaphor "became popular among the legal realists of the 1920s and 1930s"); Adam Mossoff, *The Use and Abuse*

property is an amalgam of various rights and duties that ultimately serve to define and regulate one's relationships with other people, with any particular thing being only of secondary importance.[33] According to this metaphor, property is dependent on the social context in which it occurs and the legal rules that define that context, which can be changed as circumstances require. For this reason, the configuration of the bundle that forms property in any given instance is subject to wide variation. "[P]roperty," as noted by one scholar, "is simply the label for whatever 'bundle of sticks' the individual has been granted" by the legal system,[34] and the particular sticks included in the bundle are contingent on the given milieu in which they operate. In short, it is the political sovereignty of the state that creates property, and that sovereignty can reshape property as it deems best to meet changing circumstances.

Once property is defined in this manner, however, certain theoretical problems necessarily arise. If property is merely any set of entitlements bestowed by the state, then the question becomes whether "property" has any real meaning at all.[35] To overcome this dilemma, the legal realists and their successors had to link the bundle theory to some core principle that, more or less, would normally be expected to exist in the relationships they categorized as property.[36] The principle that best serves that function is the right to exclude others, which has become the chief component of property in modern American thinking.[37]

---

*of IP at the Birth of the Administrative State*, 157 U. Pa. L. Rev. 2001, 2008–13 (2009) (discussing connections between legal realists and positivist bundle theory).

33 *See* Bruce Ackerman, *Private Property and the Constitution* 27 (1977) ("[P]roperty is not a thing, but a set of legal relations between persons governing the use of things."); Felix S. Cohen, *Dialogue on Private Property*, 9 Rutgers L. Rev. 357, 363 (1954) ("Property ... is basically a set of relations among men, which may or may not involve external physical objects."); Wesley Newcomb Hohfeld, *Fundamental Legal Conceptions as Applied in Judicial Reasoning*, 26 Yale L. J. 710, 743 (1917) ("[T]he supposed single right *in rem* correlating with 'a duty' on 'all' persons really involves as many separate and distinct 'right—duty' relations as there are persons subject to a duty"); Merrill & Smith, *supra* note 32, at 357–8 (identifying as "conventional wisdom" the notion that "[p]roperty is a composite of legal relations that holds between persons and only secondarily or incidentally involves a 'thing.'").

34 Edward L. Rubin, *Due Process and the Administrative State*, 72 Cal. L. Rev. 1044, 1086 (1984).

35 *See* Thomas C. Grey, *The Disintegration of Property*, in Nomos XXII: Property 69, 81 (J. Roland Pennock & John W. Chapman eds, 1980) (indicating that "ultimate consequence" of this type thinking is "that property ceases to be an important category in legal and political theory").

36 *See* Cohen, *supra* note 33, at 378 (discussing need to "get rid of the confusion of nominalism").

37 *See, e.g.*, *Kaiser Aetna v. United States*, 444 U.S. 164, 176 (1979) (describing right to exclude as "one of the most essential sticks in the bundle of rights commonly characterized as property"); Thomas W. Merrill, *Property and the Right to Exclude*, 77 Neb. L. Rev. 730, 730 (1998) (calling right to exclude "the *sine qua non*" of property).

This is not to say that the right to exclude is entirely a product of positivist notions, or that it holds no importance to the naturalist concept of property. Indeed, under a Lockean approach, the right to exclude others is vital to the idea of property because the rights of a laborer to acquire and use that property are of little moment if he cannot prevent others from doing the same.[38] Nevertheless, while important to the naturalist view, exclusion plays a somewhat secondary or derivative function, with acquisition, use, and disposal constituting "the more fundamental rights."[39]

In the positivist conception, however, at least as it has developed in American thinking about property, exclusion assumes a more central place. If property is defined as a set of state-sanctioned relationships between persons, then it seems logical that the right to exclude would receive primary attention. As Adam Mossoff has explained, "[t]he social-relations view of the concept of property thus leads to identify the right to exclude as the essential element or 'stick' of property because this is the only formal element of this concept that reflects its social function."[40] Exclusion touches the relational aspect of property to a greater degree than any of the other principles usually mentioned as composing the bundle. Moreover, this right to exclude others, created and enforced by the state, provides a certain value to the relationship described as property that does not exist where the exclusion right is absent.[41] In short, the right to exclude others is deemed essential because, by and large, it is this state-sanctioned exclusion that distinguishes a relationship as property in the first instance. For the modern positivist, where the law gives no such right or where there is no social context in which to implement it, property does not exist. Thus, while the bundle can be configured and reconfigured by the lawmaker to deal with the exigencies of any particular set of circumstances, at

---

It should be noted that Professor Merrill is neither a legal realist nor a proponent of the bundle metaphor, and he argues for the predominance of exclusion on other grounds. *See id.* at 734–54.

38 *Cf.* Mossoff, *supra* note 22, at 402–3 (discussing "formal role of exclusion" as connected to "substantive role of acquisition, use and disposal").

39 *Id.* at 390; *see also* Alfred C. Yen, *Restoring the Natural Law: Copyright as Labor and Possession*, 51 Ohio St. L. J. 517, 523–4 (1990) (indicating that "the English natural law of property developed [from] the Roman doctrines of possession and the moral philosophy of Locke," such that labor was transformed into property "only if the fruits of that labor were considered capable of permanent possession").

40 Mossoff, *supra* note 22, at 396.

41 *See, e.g.*, *Hybritech, Inc. v. Abbott Labs.*, 849 F.2d 1446, 1456 (Fed. Cir. 1988) (stating that "the principal value of a patent is its statutory right to exclude"); *United States v. Williams*, 15 C.M.R. 241, 245 (C.M.A. 1954) ("[T]he right to exclude others from the use of property of any sort, real or personal, may well be deemed the chief ingredient of its value.").

the end of the day, the bundle normally needs at least some exclusion right to qualify as property.[42]

In *Deadwood*, this positivist view of property is embodied most directly in the form of two latecomers who arrive in the camp early in the show's second season—Hugo Jarry and Francis Wolcott. Jarry is an official with the Dakota territorial government who uses his position to cast doubt as to whether the government will honor existing gold claims should Deadwood be annexed into the territory. Jarry accomplishes this aim in a public notice that both suggests that the existing claims will be presumed legitimate, while simultaneously stating that this "presumption shall be subject to qualification" by undisclosed "mitigating facts."[43] The two statements stand in marked tension with one another. In effect, Jarry is telling the people of Deadwood, "Your title is safe until the politicians decide otherwise."

The locals understand this message and do not take kindly to it. A mob forms, attacks Jarry, and appears ready to kill him until Bullock intervenes to restore order. Jarry quickly leaves town, but the disquiet he unleashed remains in his wake. Naturally, the greater the doubt concerning the legal standing of the existing gold claims, the less value these claims have on the open market. This economic reality plays right into the hands of Francis Wolcott, the right hand man of gold tycoon George Hearst.

The mere mention of Hearst's name inspires fear and reverence in those that hear it. The owner of Deadwood's primary hotel, E. B. Farnum, tries to scam Wolcott but withers when he learns that Wolcott is in Hearst's employ. To make up for the aborted fraud, Farnum agrees to do Wolcott's bidding and spread rumors among the people of Deadwood calling into question "the validity of the present titles to the claims."[44] This misdirection, combined with Jarry's official pronouncement, causes a panic among those holding gold claims, which is Wolcott's intended result. Using Hearst's money, Wolcott capitalizes on this development and purchases most of the existing gold claims at discount prices. Hearst's mining operations begin almost immediately.

In many ways, Jarry and Wolcott can be viewed as representing a more positivist outlook than is revealed by Deadwood's leaders. Where Al Swearengen looks back to days when the first few settlers fashioned the camp out of the surrounding wilderness, Jarry and Wolcott see the camp's future as a part of the Dakota Territory and the United States, with all of the social implications that such a relationship entails. Both men, of course, are corrupt exploiters of the first order,

---

42 Of course, the right to exclude is not absolute either. *See, e.g.*, *Pruneyard Shopping Ctr. v. Robins*, 447 U.S. 74, 82–4 (1980) (rejecting argument that constitutional property rights were infringed even while acknowledging that state "literally" had taken right to exclude); *State v. Shack*, 277 A.2d 369, 372 (N.J. 1971) (holding that right to exclude is limited under certain circumstances).

43 *Deadwood: Complications* (Formerly "*Difficulties*") (HBO broadcast Apr. 3, 2005).

44 *Deadwood: New Money* (HBO broadcast Mar. 20, 2005).

and it is clear that getting the camp's gold into their hands (or the hands of those whose bidding they do) is of primary importance. But this shouldn't completely overshadow the larger reality. Once legitimated, Deadwood will serve several important functions, from a strategic military outpost to a burgeoning center of "civilization" in the heart of Indian country. And the gold, too, will serve important functions, bolstering the financial stability and influence of the territory, serving as a catalyst for investment and economic activity, and providing the means by which the camp might indeed be transformed into a town. What difference does it make, these characters might ask, if a few pockets happen to get lined in the process? For them, the gold in Deadwood ultimately means progress. Thus, with the prospect of law still in nascent form, the gold to which the camp owes its existence is evolving, below the surface, from a thing acquired and possessed via the hard work of autonomous individuals to a complex engine of social change and transformation.

For this transformation to take place, however, the property rights in the gold cannot remain stagnant. For Jarry and Wolcott to achieve their ends, the gold claims must be redefined, or at least be susceptible to redefinition, to accommodate the new order. Consider again the public notice posted by Jarry. Although it seems to acknowledge Deadwood's preexisting property regime, the notice simultaneously suggests that any rights acquired under that regime will be subject to alteration by the territorial government. Property, in Jarry's view, is not some indissoluble right of the natural order. Rather, echoing a positivist viewpoint, Jarry's notice implies that property is a construction of the law that is designed to meet specific societal contexts. As those contexts change, so too does property. Property is, in other words, a bundle of legal rights, and the existence and definition of that bundle depend on how the law is structured and restructured over time. In this view, as the unruly mining camp of Deadwood transforms into a civilized member of the Dakota Territory, it is only to be expected that the rights and relationships that make up the bundle will undergo some transformation as well. The independent residents of Deadwood naturally chafe at this idea, and their discomfort is only made worse by the maneuverings of Jarry and Wolcott, who use the law not only to regulate the prior relationships but to turn them completely on their heads. Panic and instability follow.[45]

---

45 One intended lesson of this story arc is to highlight the disjunction between law and order. In Season One, order exists in Deadwood without the presence of law. In Season Two, the fear of law creates disorder and confusion. Milch explains:

> A misapprehension that can distort one's understanding of Deadwood—and the world in which we live today—arises from the way that law and order are commonly conjoined. The phrase 'law and order' can easily create the impression that these two very different social phenomena arise from the common human impulse, or that they are somehow one and the same. Law and order are not the same. It is common for us to try to retroactively apply the sanction of law to the

Importantly, however, Jarry and Wolcott do not overtly steal the claims. They do not engage in acts of trespass, nor do they ride in with armed gunmen. Even in the context of their exploitative activities, these men attempt to attain their goals through recognizable channels. The gold claims they are after ultimately are purchased, not taken. Thus, unlike many of the legal realists for whom property was an empty concept, Jarry and Wolcott tacitly acknowledge that property has *some* meaning. It is malleable, to be sure, and can be changed by the state as the state deems best, but it means *something*. The actions of these men suggest that, while many of the expectations of the camp's early residents will be up for grabs once law officially arrives in Deadwood, the ability of the claimants to exclude others will largely remain intact.

This concern for exclusion seems to underlie not only the strategy to purchase the claims (rather than simply squat on them), but to do so as quickly as possible. Inasmuch as the right to exclude essentially characterizes property from a social-relations point of view, to deny such a right would be to admit that the gold claims were not property. And that admission would mean that the claims were valueless, both to the initial settlers and to anyone who came after. At the same time, it is concern over this same right to exclude that pushes Jarry and Wolcott to act quickly, procuring the claims before annexation occurs and formal mechanisms for enforcement exist. Thus, Jarry and Wolcott appear to reflect the modern perspective about property—it is a set of social relationships between persons, chiefly defined by and given legal effect through the ability of some of those persons to exclude others from engaging in certain conduct or behavior. So long as these exclusion rights exist, the relationship qualifies as property, regardless of how else it might change. And at the end of the day, the relationship derives its value not primarily from any individual's labor or possession, but from the sovereign authority of the state itself.

## Property, Sovereignty, and the Social Compact

So far, we have seen two different, yet intimately related, stories unfold in *Deadwood*. First, there is the internal narrative, which focuses on the ideas of power and property within the early life of the camp itself. Second, there is the external narrative, which focuses on outsiders and their quite different understandings of

---

> things we do to maintain order. Our desire for order comes first, and law comes afterward.

David Milch, *Deadwood: Stories of the Black Hills* 121 (2006). The people of Deadwood seek the protection of law to protect the old order they established in law's vacuum, that is, the Lockean transformation from the state of nature to the social compact. Jarry, on the other hand, sees law as a positivist tool to create a new order based on new understandings. In both cases, the end is the creation of a recognizable order. Law is merely the means of accomplishing this objective.

these same concepts. It is obvious that these two stories are on a collision course with each other. The discovery of the gold has not only motivated the early settlers, it also has prompted the federal government to begin negotiating a new treaty with the Sioux that will officially cede the land to the United States. The prospect of cession, in turn, has watered the mouths not only of other settlers and prospectors, but also of the powers that be in the nearby Dakota Territory. Talk of annexation into Dakota is prevalent, and as demonstrated above, territorial officials like Jarry seem ambivalent toward the property claims of Deadwood's current residents. Even in the lawless wilderness, Deadwood is never truly alone.

In the face of these realities, the question for the camp's early settlers becomes how they can preserve the property and power that has already been created. Having developed their property through a Lockean labor theory, Deadwood's residents respond to the new threats by again acting in Lockean fashion—they decide to form a civil government of their own.

Locke's theory conjectured that all persons initially lived in a state of nature apart from any organized political society.[46] In this state of nature, each person enjoyed the freedom to decide for himself how to arrange his own affairs, including the use and disposition of his person and possessions.[47] So long as individuals remained in the state of nature, however, this freedom lacked stability because every individual enjoyed exactly the same freedom. None had authority to settle disputes or regulate conduct for the mutual benefit of all.[48] For this reason, the rights enjoyed in the state of nature were always in danger, being "constantly exposed to the invasion of others."[49] To obtain greater security for these rights, people united together "for the mutual *preservation* of their lives, liberties and estates," which Locke called "by the general name, *property*."[50] Thus, for Locke, the primary purpose for which individuals create and submit to formal government "*is the preservation of their property*."[51]

This theory aptly describes the course of the early camp fathers. Existing in something of a state of nature, these pioneers initially enjoy a sense of power and freedom not existing in more civilized communities. But that context quickly becomes exposed by outside forces that do not clearly recognize the preexisting arrangements. Thus, the camp finds itself in a situation where its property and power are threatened by the very autonomy and lack of government that served as a draw to most of its early settlers.

---

46 Locke, *supra* note 14, § 4, at 8.

47 *Id.*

48 *Id.*; *see also id.* § 123, at 66 (positing that, "in the state of nature," every person's rights are "constantly exposed to the invasion of others" such that "the enjoyment of the property he has in this state is very unsafe, very unsecure").

49 *Id.* § 123, at 66.

50 *Id.*

51 *Id.* § 124, at 66.

To protect against that threat, Swearengen initiates a meeting of the camp's leaders. Reflecting the autonomous nature of the camp, there is considerable confusion as to who should attend. This matter is settled by a basic rule in keeping with the camp's individualistic mindset: basically, show up and you're in. At the meeting, Swearengen explains the situation. The camp needs an "informal municipal organization" complete with "titles and departments" to help ward off the possibility that the territorial officials will appoint a government of "their cousins to rob and steal from us." [52] The hope is that having its own government in place will assist the camp in reaching a favorable peace with the outsiders that threaten harm. Although the residents lack a true desire for real government, they reluctantly acquiesce to a modicum of government for the purpose of protecting what they already have (chiefly, their property and the power it bestows). Reflecting on the prospect of government and civilization coming to Deadwood, Bullock comments, "I'd settle for property rights," suggesting that the primary reason to have the former is to ensure protection of the latter.[53] In short, the men give up some of their sovereignty in order to protect the remainder of it.

## Property and Personal Power

That property itself, however created or defined, bestows sovereignty to its owner is a point that *Deadwood* vividly portrays. And to the extent that sovereignty means power, in the world of *Deadwood*, no one has more sovereignty than George Hearst.

Hearst arrives in the camp at the end of the show's second season and quickly becomes the dominant member of the community. Unlike many people, however, Hearst does not seek power for its own sake. Rather, for Hearst, power is just a means to his singular end of obtaining more gold, or as he calls it, "the color." This relentless pursuit is not merely—or even primarily—economic. Because of his prowess at discovering gold, Hearst earned the nickname "boy-the-earth-talks-to" from the Indians.[54] There is an almost religious relationship between the earth and Hearst that represents the driving force of Hearst's life. Everything is about the color; nothing else matters.

And that includes other people. Hearst is utterly ruthless with those who stand between him and his passion. A shocking scene between Hearst and Swearengen occurs early in the third season of the series. Hearst wants the one gold claim in town that has thus far eluded him—that belonging to the young and attractive widow, Alma Garrett, who inherited the claim from her husband in the early, labor-oriented days of the camp. Hearst enlists Swearengen's help to obtain the claim with these menacing words: "I'll not name how you would benefit from the action

52 *Deadwood: No Other Sons or Daughters* (HBO broadcast May 16, 2004).
53 *Deadwood: Here Was a Man* (HBO broadcast Apr. 11, 2004).
54 *Deadwood: Boy-the-Earth-Talks-To* (HBO broadcast May 22, 2005).

I wish you to take, saying only instead that it's my will. To which I will have you bend."[55] When the defiant Swearengen resists, Hearst cuts one of his fingers off. The normally larger-than-life Swearengen, the camp's founder and leader, temporarily becomes a humbled and insecure mess in the aftermath.

Hearst embarks on a campaign to obtain the Garrett claim by asserting psychological dominance over the entire camp. To do this, Hearst primarily employs a strategy of terror. First, he orders the murder of a miner named Pasco who sought to unionize Hearst's workers. Next, he arranges for the body of the dead man to be left in the middle of Deadwood's main street with a knife in his chest.[56] The obvious message: "I can do whatever I want to do, and you cannot stop me." Bullock, now sheriff, is enraged at Hearst's brazenness. When Bullock confronts Hearst, the latter tells Bullock to go "fuck [himself]" and talks of killing him. Bullock then arrests Hearst for threatening a peace officer and fittingly places him in a cell that shares Pasco's corpse. The community reaction to the arrest is telling of the power that Hearst holds. Instead of celebrating Bullock's willingness to stand up to the town bully, the fear is that Bullock's rashness may spur Hearst to destroy Deadwood. Hearst's mission to instill fear in the populace has succeeded.

The camp's leaders come together to consider a response to Hearst's actions. Is violence the answer? Not yet. As an alternative, the passive-aggressive course of action is chosen. A.W. Merrick, owner and operator of the Deadwood newspaper, publishes a letter from Bullock to Pasco's mother informing her of her son's murder. Because everyone knows that Hearst is behind the killing, the purpose behind printing the letter is to place a bright spotlight on the human costs of Hearst's barbarism. This message of condemnation is not lost on Hearst. He responds by hiring twenty-five Pinkerton agents to serve as his muscle in town. If the murder of Pasco was a play to establish psychological dominance over Deadwood, the Pinkerton gambit represents an effort to assert physical dominance, as well. Almost immediately, one of the Pinkerton agents pistol whips Merrick and trashes the newspaper offices in retaliation for publishing the Bullock letter.

Additionally, Hearst uses his power to influence the coming elections that the territorial government has promised Deadwood's residents. Hearst tells the territorial official Jarry, "Elections cannot inconvenience me. They ratify my will or I neuter them."[57] In the case of Deadwood, the election serves to ratify Hearst's will. At his bidding, hundreds of US soldiers are purposely stationed near Deadwood in the weeks prior to the election so as to become eligible to vote. Working through the corrupt Jarry, Hearst instructs the soldiers how to vote, thereby dictating the electoral outcome.

Hearst's central concern, however, remains obtaining the Garrett gold claim. Knowing Hearst's intent, a naïve Alma first attempts to reach out to Hearst by

55 *Deadwood: I Am Not the Fine Man You Take Me For* (HBO broadcast June 18, 2006).

56 *Deadwood: A Two-Headed Beast* (HBO broadcast July 9, 2006).

57 *Deadwood: A Constant Throb* (HBO broadcast Aug. 13, 2006).

proposing a business partnership between the two of them. The mere idea offends Hearst greatly, and he almost rapes Alma in response. Growing more cognizant of the type of man Hearst is, Alma nevertheless digs in her heels and refuses to sell, which only ratchets up the tension even more. One day, as Alma walks to the bank that she founded with her gold money, gun shots are fired at her. Swearengen protects her, then encourages her to complete her walk in a defiant stand to the Hearst forces.[58] More Pinkertons arrive in the camp, one of whom murders the gold prospector Ellsworth, who is now Alma's second husband. Alma has no choice but to sell, which she does with a gun at the back of her head.

What allows Hearst to behave in such a manner? Simply put, it is the property he owns and the power that such property provides. As the earlier parts of this chapter demonstrate, there is much truth in Charles Reich's statement that "property guards the troubled boundary between individual man and the state."[59] Equally true, regardless of whether one views property in positivist or naturalist terms, is that property often tends to the troubled boundary between an individual and his neighbors. The ability of an individual to control valuable or value-producing objects necessarily speaks to the power that individual has vis-à-vis others.

Looking first at its relationship to external power, Anglo-American thought has long associated property with the ability to withstand outside coercion. In his *Commentaries on the Laws of England*, for example, William Blackstone described property in terms that made its connection to personal freedom obvious. Property consisted of "the free use, enjoyment, and disposal of all [an individual's] acquisitions, without any control or diminution, save only by the laws of the land." [60] Thus, property bestows on its owner a unique sphere of sovereignty that allows him a certain amount of liberty. To quote Reich again:

> Property draws a circle around the activities of each private individual or organization. Within that circle, the owner has a greater degree of freedom than without. Outside, he must justify or explain his actions, and show his authority. Within, he is the master, and the state must explain and justify any interference ... .

Thus, property performs the function of maintaining independence, dignity and pluralism in society by creating zones within which the majority has to yield to the owner.[61]

Importantly, the circle drawn by property not only protects the owner from governmental intrusion, but also allows him to enlist the government in helping ward off intrusions by other private actors.[62] Where the owner can be sure that

58 *Id.*

59 Reich, *supra* note 30, at 733.

60 1 William Blackstone, *Commentaries on the Laws of England*, *138.

61 Reich, *supra* note 30, at 771.

62 R. Wilson Freyermuth et al., *Property and Lawyering* 5 (2d ed. 2006).

this sphere of sovereignty will be recognized and enforced, property fosters self-sufficiency, predictability, and order by "afford[ing] day-to-day protection in the ordinary affairs of life."[63]

In addition to protecting against external power, however, property also enables the individual to exert power himself. By creating this sphere of sovereignty, property vests the owner with authority to decide whether, how, and when to utilize and exploit the thing that is owned.[64] To return to the words of Morris Cohen: "If then somebody else wants to use the food, the house, the land, or the plow which the law calls mine, he has to get my consent. To the extent that these things are necessary to the life of my neighbor, the law thus confers on me a power, limited but real, to make him do what I want."[65] The exercise of this power can have profound effects on the rights of others. Property includes, to varying degrees, the ability to influence resource allocation, economic production, the actions of other persons, and the mechanisms of governance. Abuse of this ability can easily lead to a myopic view that ignores, or in some cases exploits, the rights and interests of other persons or groups. Large aggregations of property can make this abuse easier to undertake and more intense in its effects.[66] Property, then, might be viewed as a double-edged sword, providing the means with which to resist power and, at the same time, the means of exerting it.

This dual nature of property is apparent in the foregoing narrative about George Hearst. It is Hearst's ownership of other gold claims located elsewhere that gives him the political sway he enjoys over Jarry and Dakota's other territorial leaders, who not only post the notice that destabilizes the claims in Deadwood, but who also help rig the promised elections according to Hearst's designs.[67] It is his newfound ownership of the gold in Deadwood itself that supplies the audacity for Hearst's actions once present in the camp, allowing him to interfere with the freedom of the press, murder and maim those who stand in his way, pressure the previously untouchable Swearengen, and attempt to terrorize Alma Garrett. Hearst is a personification of what can happen when property, and the sovereignty and influence that it helps create, are abused. Moreover, the vastness of Hearst's property only creates a larger sphere of sovereignty and influence that makes his efforts to manipulate and ignore the rights of other people easier to accomplish. This truth is recognized by Bullock's deputy sheriff, who angrily labels Hearst's

63 Reich, *supra* note 30, at 771.

64 *See* Michael B. Kent, Jr., *Pavesich, Property and Privacy: The Common Origins of Property Rights and Privacy Rights in Georgia*, 2 John Marshall L. J. 1, 21 (2009) (describing property rights in terms of these attributes).

65 Cohen, *supra* note 2, at 12.

66 *Cf.* Walter Hamilton, *Property—According to Locke*, 41 Yale L. J. 864, 877–8 (1932) (discussing property in context of industrialization).

67 The bastardized version of the Golden Rule has figurative and literal meaning here: "He who has the gold makes the rules." *See e.g.*, Stacy D. Phillips, *Divorce: It's All About Control—How To Win The Emotional, Psychological and Legal Wars* 20 (2005).

agent Wolcott, "Mr. Amalgamation and Capital."[68] In Hearst, the worst potential of property as a tool for tyranny is on full display.

But the sphere of sovereignty created by property has a positive aspect, as well, which *Deadwood* also reveals. The power provided by property can be used as a positive force for freedom. As noted earlier, until the very end of the series, one claim remains outside the grasp of Hearst's control—that of Alma Garrett—and it is this claim that ultimately provides whatever liberty the town continues to enjoy. As the only landowner in Deadwood whose holdings can in any way compete with Hearst's, Garrett's claim acts as a counterbalance to the Hearst machine and begins to exemplify the town's deeply held desire for independence. Her gold claim provides Garrett with a sphere of sovereignty that, if not exactly comparable to Hearst's, nonetheless prevents him from exercising complete control. Garrett's claim represents the freedom that property provides, a freedom from undue interference resulting from a circle of power that allows people to go about their ordinary lives, even in the face of oppression.[69] Here, we see property as a source of liberty. Even as Hearst uses his property to threaten and coerce, Garrett's property serves as the town's protection against those threats. Garrett's gold claim, a vestige of the labor-based view of the town's pioneers, acts as the community's last, best hope for independence. And as the town coalesces around the strength and freedom her claim provides, the identities of the town's residents (and the town itself) are changing.

## Property, Sovereignty, and Identity

The dual nature of property also suggests that it speaks, in some manner, to its owner's persona, character, and identity. Inasmuch as property bestows power on its owner, whether that power is defensive or offensive in nature, it relates to who he is as a person. So, too, does the manner in which he chooses to exercise that power, or whether he even exercises it at all. These ideas lead to a final topic raised by *Deadwood*—the relationship between property, sovereignty, and personal and community identity.

Modern discussions of this subject conventionally begin with German philosopher G.W.F. Hegel. Hegel's thought describes "a person" as "a consciously

---

68 *Deadwood: Amalgamation and Capital* (HBO broadcast May 1, 2005). Interestingly, Wolcott responds with a series of questions that suggest his own recognition that property can be viewed in both positive and negative terms: "Mr. Utter, are you a student of Hume? Smith? A disciple of Karl Marx?" *Id.* These questions also suggest that there may be more similarity between Hearst and the early residents of Deadwood than the deputy cares to admit; that is, both the pioneers and Hearst were drawn to Deadwood by the hope of utilizing property, and the sovereignty it produces, for their own individual purposes.

69 *See* Reich, *supra* note 30, at 771.

free will ... consist[ing] in a formal, simple and pure reference to itself as a separate and independent unit."[70] A chief problem for the person, however, concerns how this will is manifested. Because the individual lives in a world of physical objects external to his will, he needs some objective means of expressing that will. Otherwise, he is at risk of being only "something subjective," which ultimately "contradicts and destroys" his nature.[71] To achieve full realization, the person must express his will in some material way through these external objects,[72] and the mechanism by which that expression occurs is property.[73] By exerting power over the external object, the person gains possession of it, and this possession results in "a tangible existence" by which the abstract will becomes "an actual will."[74] For Hegel, this self-actualization is a necessary first step in becoming a fully developed individual, which starts in a person's relation to external things and progresses to higher relations with other persons—specifically in the group context of family and state.[75] For Hegel, then, property is an essential expression of personhood and individuality that leads to higher and better expressions of groups and communities.

In American thinking about property, Hegel's theory has found its most prominent voice in Margaret Jane Radin's *Property and Personhood*.[76] Radin argued that Hegel's system offered three primary insights relating to property regimes. First, Hegel's view of self-actualization by exerting power over the material world underscored not only "the ongoing relationships" between persons and their physical environments, but also "that these relationships can be very close to a person's center and sanity."[77] Second, Hegel's concept of this self-actualization as leading to fuller relationships with other persons implied that "certain groups are likely to be constitutive of their members in the sense that the members find self-determination only within the groups."[78] Finally, Hegel's theory supported the intuitive notion "that certain kinds of property relationships can be presumed to bear close bonds to personhood."[79] For Radin, these insights suggested that property, in certain contexts, can be more than just an object or a

70 G.W.F. Hegel, *Philosophy of Right* ¶ 35, at 2 (S.W. Dyde, trans., Cosimo Classics 2008) (1821).

71 *Id.* ¶ 39, at 3.

72 *Id.* ¶ 41, at 4.

73 *Id.* ¶¶ 44–5, at 6–7.

74 *Id.* ¶ 45, at 7.

75 *See* Margaret Jane Radin, *Property and Personhood*, 34 Stan. L. Rev. 957, 972–7 (1982) (discussing Hegel's theory); Peter G. Stillman, *Hegel's Analysis of Property in the* Philosophy of Right, 10 Cardozo L. Rev. 1031, 1035–41 (1989) (same).

76 Radin, *supra* note 75.

77 *Id.* at 977.

78 *Id.* at 978.

79 *Id.*

set of rights. It also can be something that is "almost part of [oneself],"[80] which is inextricably wrapped up in "human flourishing."[81]

From this idea that certain types of property can help define individual identity, it is but a small leap to consider how property might also shape the identity of an entire community. Indeed, Radin allowed for this when she mentioned that property claims by "a minority group or some group outside the American mainstream" might be stronger because the claimed property rights would be "more clearly necessary to their being able to constitute themselves as a group and hence as persons within that group."[82] Other scholars have extended this idea to argue for a "peoplehood" view that protects property based on the degree to which it serves to identify a particular group, such as Native Americans.[83] Property plays a vital role in identifying not only the individual self but also the community in which that individual participates because the two, ultimately, are inseparable.[84]

The relationship between property, power, and community identity also finds support in early American political philosophy. Republicanism, a philosophical tradition prevalent during America's formative years, promoted the idea that government should advance the best interests of the entire political community. Doing so, of course, occasionally necessitated the subordination of individual interests to the needs of the commonwealth.[85] This tradition depended on the concept of public virtue, the ability of every citizen to give "himself totally to the good of the public as a whole."[86] Virtue, in turn, required that no citizen should be dependent upon another, lest he be corrupted by that dependency and act in the interests of those to which he was beholden, rather than in the common interest.[87]

For republicans, a significant mechanism for fostering this type of virtue was private property, in large part because of the power and individual sovereignty that it bestows.[88] Property ownership advanced virtue by instilling values important to the preservation of autonomous and responsible citizens: "an attachment to

80 *Id.* at 959.

81 *See* Margaret Jane Radin, *Market Inalienability*, 100 Harv. L. Rev. 1849, 1904 (1987) (linking "personhood" to "concept of human flourishing").

82 Radin, *supra*, note 75, at 1013.

83 *See, e.g.*, Kristen A. Carpenter, *Real Property and Peoplehood*, 27 Stan. Envtl. L.J. 313, 344–64 (2008).

84 *See* Gregory S. Alexander & Eduardo M. Peñalver, *Properties of Community*, 10 Theoretical Inq. L. 127, 139 (2009) ("Each of our identities is inextricably connected in some sense with others with whom we are bound as members of one or typically more communities.").

85 *See, e.g.*, Forrest McDonald, *Novus Ordo Seclorum*, 70–71 (1985); *see also* 1 Alfred H. Kelly et al., *The American Constitution* 67 (7th ed. 1991).

86 McDonald, *supra* note 85, at 71.

87 *See id.* at 70–71.

88 *See id.* at 74–5.

community, self-sufficiency, stability, and wisdom."[89] As one commentator has explained: "Only a person who was independent in this sense, who could transcend selfish considerations and resist manipulation by men ambitious for power, was truly free politically to act for the good of the commonwealth."[90] Thus, we see that, philosophically at least, property, power, and the identities of both individuals and communities are intertwined.

These philosophical notions are displayed practically in *Deadwood*, where the gold seems to be the driving agent behind almost all of the characters' activities. In Hegelian fashion, the residents of Deadwood seem to find initial actualization by relating to and exerting power over their physical environments. The surrounding gold deposits act as the catalyst that both draws them to the camp and determines their actions once there. The gold becomes a part of who they are as persons. But in their individualistic quests for the gold, something else happens—a community begins to emerge. Their separate relationships with the gold—an external commodity—begin to bind them together in deep and powerful ways. The gold not only becomes a part of each individual's own personal story, it also entwines those stories with the stories of others, forming a common narrative in the process. In *Deadwood*, we see the personhood theory of property in action—the residents' individual relationships to property become bound up with the individuals themselves, and those individuals eventually become bound up with each other, forming a larger collective also linked to (and by) property. New identities begin to take shape.

Thus, in *Deadwood*, property and the power it provides simultaneously serve as means for promoting both individual freedom and community welfare. The prospect for wealth and autonomy draws people to Deadwood, and as these people are increasingly connected through their shared pursuits, social relationships become richer. The wilderness is transformed into a camp, which itself is transformed into a town. The promise of personal prosperity and power enables a more communitarian outlook.[91] Bullock, who comes to the camp as an individualistic entrepreneur, ends up as the town's pillar of stability and justice. Calamity Jane, a dysfunctional drunk who arrives in camp seemingly to escape conventional society, becomes the camp's Florence Nightingale during a smallpox epidemic. Alma Garrett, who at one point complains that "my life is living me, and

---

89 Daniel A. Farber & Suzanna Sherry, *A History of the American Constitution* 13 (2d. 2005).

90 1 Kelly et al., *supra* note 85, at 37.

91 As explained by one commentator: "In Deadwood, when people get together, social life becomes rationalized along economic lines, people seek ways in which to specialize their service, and the social life of the camp moves, sometimes in fits and starts, toward peace." Jordan J. Ballor, *A Law Beyond Law: Life Together in* Deadwood, Religion & Liberty, Summer 2007, at 4, 5. The examples of Seth Bullock, Calamity Jane, and Alma Garrett discussed in this paragraph are all raised in Ballor's article.

soon will be over, and not a moment of it will have been my own,"[92] nonetheless remains in Deadwood and uses her position to form a bank "for the good of the camp."[93] Her second husband, Ellsworth, puts a finer point on this, noting to Alma's adopted daughter that her mother is a "service to the camp, turning her mine into houses and the like getting built, businesses begun. Some for people that'll never know her name."[94] And when Hearst threatens Garrett's claim, the rest of the town rallies to her rescue, including some of her former enemies who had designs on her claim themselves.[95]

We see in these examples a budding virtue of the type promoted by the civic republicans; that is, the ability of individual persons to give of themselves for the greater good. Just as republican thinking viewed property as essential to the fostering of such virtue, so in *Deadwood* do we find property at the center of the camp's virtuous transformation.

## Conclusion

Unique in popular culture, *Deadwood* tells the story of how property rights are birthed, maintained through the uncertain years of adolescence, and ultimately legally recognized in adulthood through the rise of the state. In many ways, this story is the story of America. David Milch, the visionary behind *Deadwood*, explains this connection:

> Deadwood, like other gold rush towns, was a kind of reenactment of the founding of our country. When gold was discovered, there was a rush into a new territory, followed by a collective regression from society—thus, the Wild West. And later, there was a regeneration of society seemingly *de novo*, from new. That happens in the hopes that the contradictions of the old social order will finally be resolved. But once the news comes of a strike, settlement patterns immediately change. Waves of prospectors and parasites, merchants, fortune hunters, displaced persons, and government bureaucrats rush in to this new space, bringing with them all the old forms of civilization from which the first wave of adventurers had fled.[96]

Property creates law because property cannot long survive without law. The state of nature matures into the social compact, where law—not labor—defines the contours of property rights. This tradeoff, the reason that the residents of Deadwood relinquish their autonomy, is the securing of what each citizen already

92 *Deadwood: Boy-the-Earth-Talks-To* (HBO broadcast May 22, 2005).
93 *Deadwood: Something Very Expensive* (HBO broadcast Apr. 10, 2005).
94 *Deadwood: Full Faith and Credit* (HBO broadcast July 2, 2006).
95 *Deadwood: A Constant Throb* (HBO broadcast Aug. 13, 2006).
96 Milch, *supra* note 45, at 41, 43.

believes to be his. The purposes for which government is created thus act as a limit on the state's ability to reshape those interests. Law's power, in turn, derives from the sovereignty of those institutions that sustain order in law's name. Property and sovereignty, therefore, depend upon one another. Government exists because property exists first; property exists because government exists to recognize and protect it.

# Chapter 7

# *American Scenery* and American Sovereignty: A Quantitative Analysis of Landscape and Property before the Civil War

Anna Elizabeth Lineberger and Alfred L. Brophy

## Introduction: Property Rights and Stages of Civilization

In his 1850 address to the South Carolina Institute at its annual fair, Georgia Supreme Court Justice Joseph Henry Lumpkin spoke of the wonders of the progress of the mid-nineteenth century. "[T]he success of Daguerre in producing in a moment, by the light of heaven, the most exquisite likenesses—the annihilations of time and space by the steam car and the electronic telegraph, are now considered ordinary events."[1] Lumpkin spoke for his age in his celebration of technological progress and in his astonishment at the speed of change and what might yet be accomplished. The printing press and the availability of inexpensive paper were "republicanizing knowledge," so that "within the life of the present generation, science and the arts will accomplish wonders of which it hath not entered into the heart of man to conceive."[2] The change was coming rapidly; "[c]enturies have become years — years minutes."[3]

In particular, the change allowed humans to subdue the earth and thus fulfill a divine mission. Subduing nature was a positive image for Lumpkin. As he told the South Carolina Institute audience:

> To *subdue*, then, is not to destroy and devastate this beautiful and magnificent habitation of our race; but to clear the forests—drain the swamps—remove the stones and convert them into fences, walls and fixtures—set the orchards—open the rivers—tunnel the mountains—fill up the vallies—make the crooked places straight, the rough places smooth, and web the land with highways for travel and transportation—erect school houses, churches, private residences and

1 Joseph H. Lumpkin, *An Address Delivered Before the South-Carolina Institute at Its Second Annual Fair* 6–7 (1851). The Institute was a society formed to promote arts, mechanics, and industry.

2 *Id.* at 7.

3 *Id.* at 6.

> public edifices—and thus cultivate, improve and adorn the earth, the place of our abode, to the highest attainable perfection.[4]

Many European Americans of the pre-Civil War era spoke of subduing nature and of humans' dominion over the earth. In an address to the Whig and Cliosophic Literary Societies at Princeton in 1850, North Carolina Congressman Abraham Venable pointed to the "wonderful results of mechanical labor" to demonstrate that "with reason, God gave to man dominion over the creatures ... ."[5] Venable found in the technological development of the era confirmation of the virtues of subduing nature:

> Agricultural industry, walking side by side in all its progress, receiving improved implements, and labor-saving expedients, has caused the earth to smile in plenty, and the heart of man to rejoice in abundance. In this peaceful march, streams have gushed out in the desert, and the solitary place has been glad for them. The world's fair now in progress is no collection of military heroes, enthroned on pyramids of human skulls, assembled to recount scenes of butchery and bloodshed; no congress of political economists and statesmen to ascertain how much may yet be wrung by taxes from a burdened and down-trodden people, or what is the point of oppression which may be approached without incurring the hazard of rebellious uprising … . It is the spontaneous acknowledgement of the civilized world, that all avocations are indeed secondary to those two great and leading ones, which employ mechanical and agricultural labor.[6]

The language of subduing, of gaining by labor and the wresting of profits, was part of a civilizing mission that Americans spoke about in the years leading into the Civil War. They celebrated how far modern society had advanced from the wild and unimproved nature. They drew comparison of modern society, with fields, fences, and grand structures, to the wild and unimproved nature that Native Americans inhabited.

Such distinctions were important in justifying European-American ownership of land. In 1832 when the Alabama Supreme Court decided a case that limited the property rights of natives, it contrasted the improvements of modern Alabama with the terrain when it was inhabited only by Natives:

---

4 *Id.* at 9–10.

5 Abraham W. Venable, *Address Delivered Before the American Whig and Cliosophic Societies of the College of New Jersey* 28 (1851).

6 *Id.* at 28–9. Earlier in the address Venable spoke about the respect owed to ancestors who, "by a successful conflict with the savage, the forest and the elements, subdued a wilderness, and gave it to us for a home." *Id.* at 14. And he also spoke about the reverence of monuments of the past. *Id.* at 18.

> [W]hen we contemplate the change which has been wrought in this once savage wilderness, by the arts, the industry, and the superior knowledge of the new population; when we visit our thronged cities, smiling fields, and happy habitations; when we contemplate our numerous bays and harbors, once the resort only of the wild fowl and the inhabitants of the deep; now studded with ships and vessels of all sizes and nations, pouring upon these lands the rich and extensive commerce of a whole world; when, instead of a roving tribe of hunters, we behold a powerful nation of agriculturists, as free in every desirable liberty, as their savage predecessors; when our happy political institutions and the religion of the Bible, have displaced their barbarous laws, and wretched superstitions; can we wish these effects of civilization, religion, and the arts, to disappear, and the dark forests and roaming Indian again to possess the land?[7]

That brought together in one place the images of cities, fields, ships, commerce, and Christianity in contrast with the "dark forests" before white people arrived. Such imagery was part of the intellectual support for colonization. Similarly, the Alabama Supreme Court had a very distinct image of how society progressed, from the wild nature of the "dark forests and roaming Indian" to the cultivated fields of the European-American settlers. Only nine years before in 1823, Chief Justice Marshall had invoked similar imagery to explain the ways that settlers justified taking away land from Native Americans in the case *Johnson v. McIntosh.*[8]

Tennessee Supreme Court Justice John Catron, who later served on the United States Supreme Court, wrote in similar terms in *State v. Foreman*[9] about the difference between white civilization and Native savagery. He concluded that part of the process of civilizing was putting Native Americans and enslaved African Americans under the control of white people:

> Thus surrounded by savages destroying each other, for mere pastime, with the fierceness of wild beasts, a colony was attempted in their midst on the coast of Carolina, and, after a struggle of about three-fourths of a century, was fairly crowned with success. This great effort to build up a civilized community was accomplished partly by compacts with the Indians, partly by laws passed for their government, but mainly by the sword. The tribes found inland have passed under the dominion, and melted away under the influence and superior powers, mental and moral, of the white man, as did the savages of Europe, Asia, and Africa pass under the dominion of the Romans, and as will him of Australasia, Africa, and the Rocky Mountains be compelled to submit to the stroke of fate sooner or later—to accept a master or perish. It is the destiny of man. Ignorance and division cannot stand before science and combination, nor can the civilized community exist by the side of a savage foe. And foes to each other, and foes

7 *Caldwell v. State*, 1 Stew. & P. 327, 445 (Ala. 1832).
8 21 U.S. (8 Wheat.) 543 (1823).
9 16 Tenn. (8 Yer.) 256 (1835).

> to all men, our ancestors found the North American savages, the main business of their lives being war, and that a war of extermination (the foe taking no prisoners, save for the exercise of a refined cruelty—to burn him at the stake); a people that had no government, and with whom the right of the strongest alone was respected.[10]

Catron then explained the control that European settlers exercised "by the law and the sword" and concluded that those rights of dominion had passed down to Catron's generation and to the Tennessee government:

> The philosopher and jurist of the quiet city may easily prove that such a people had undoubted rights of soil and of sovereignty, and sympathy and eloquence may, as in the Cherokee case, powerfully urge their adoption on the courts of justice—forgetting that it was impossible for our ancestors to recognize the rights claimed; that they had actually, by law and the sword, established what their charters granted—dominion over all abiding within their limits--and this upon a principle admitting of no countervailing right, that of self-preservation. They were obliged to conquer and to govern, or to perish. Such rights as they acquired were transmitted to us, unless they have been impaired by the American Revolution, or the institutions, laws, and treaties consequent upon the Revolution. If so, to the destruction of sovereignty it can be safely affirmed, the people of North Carolina and Tennessee have been overreached by indirect provisions in the federal Constitution, treaties, and acts of Congress of which they were unaware for nearly fifty years after we declared ourselves independent of Great Britain.[11]

Catron depicted the world as binary, as shifting from Native savagery to European and later white American civilization. However, in the nineteenth century, Americans more frequently spoke of stages of civilization. In fact, "progress of civilization" was a phrase in wide circulation in pre-Civil War America. It constituted part of the popular idea that societies travelled through stages of civilization, that western European countries had reached the highest state of civilization, and that they were destined to scale even greater heights. This was part of the romantic era's understanding of stages of historical development and its calibration of rights to the particular status of civilization.[12] For in surveying the record of human history, Europeans and Americans of the first half of the nineteenth century hoped to unlock the methods of human progress.[13] Leading

10 *Id.* at 270–71.

11 *Id.* at 271.

12 *See, e.g.*, *The Progress of Civilization*, 11 Yale Literary Magazine 172–6 (1846); John C. Lord, *Lectures on the Progress of Civilization and Government* (1851).

13 *See, e.g.*, W. Cooke Taylor, *The Natural History of Society in the Barbarous and Civilized State* (1840); *Essays on the Progress of Nations, in Civilization, Productive*

historians of the era, like François Guizot, framed the evolution of society in terms of stages, ascribing the passage to higher stages to a series of events, including the security of property rights, the education of the people, and the presence of political liberties.[14]

American historians, building on European historians, told similar stories. E.L. Magoon's 1854 book, *Westward Empire: or, The Great Drama of Human Progress*, [15] focused on the ways that European-American society had improved as it went westward. This picture was heavily influenced by Protestant thought, but it was also a story of the conquering of property and the sweeping away of Native people in the process. Other works by leading pre-Civil War historians, like William and Mary Professor Thomas R. Dew's *The Laws, Customs, Institutions, and Manners of Ancient and Modern Nations*, [16] also depicted stages of progress in civilization. Dew's narrative was one where property rights, including property rights in other human beings, and commerce were central to the growth of civilization and freedom, at least for white people.

Amory Dwight Mayo explained this in New York in 1858 by comparing the Hudson River Valley at the time European settlers arrived with its current state of cultivation. He did this in an unusual setting—in an address at the dedication of Green Hill Cemetery in Amsterdam, northwest of Albany in the Hudson River Valley. At the cemetery, it was easy to recall how much New York had progressed in the generations since the beginning of the eighteenth century. The land was no longer inhabited by Native Americans, who were buried with their faces "turned towards the east, as in prophetic foresight of the coming civilization … .."[17] Through "patient fortitude" the Hudson River Valley's settlers had "subdued the wilderness" and with "patriotic devotion saved" the valley "for the heritage of freemen."[18] Mayo then looked to the future to "behold in vision the scene that shall gladden the eyes of your descendants a century and a half from today."[19] He predicted those far-off generations would find "[a] garden valley more enchanting that any Eden of the past, peopled by a race that in power and opportunity shall surpass our largest prophecy."[20] The cemetery was the best act citizens of the town had ever undertaken, which promised to grow in beauty over the generations and

---

*Industry, Wealth and Population* (1852); Neil Arnott, *A Survey of Human Progress: From the Savage State to the Highest Civilization Yet Attained* (1861).

14 François Guizot, *The History of Civilization: From the Fall of the Roman Empire to the French Revolution* (1846).

15 E.L. Magoon, *Westward Empire: or, The Great Drama of Human Progress* (1854).

16 Thomas R. Dew, *The Laws, Customs, Institutions, and Manners of Ancient and Modern Nations* (1852).

17 A.D. Mayo, *The American Cemetery: An Address Delivered at the Dedication of Green Hill Cemetery* 4 (1858).

18 *Id.* at 4.

19 *Id.* at 4–5.

20 *Id.* at 5.

appeal "to the holiest and calmest sentiments of our being, through the spectacle of enchanting natural scenery, and the associations of the beloved on earth … .."[21]

Mayo explained that the cemetery was part of establishing the principles of democracy and republicanism because it brought people together in death. The cemetery was a symbol of republicanism and a creator of it:

> All things are tending, at least in the more advanced portions of our country, to a broad and pure republicanism, founded on the christian law of love; and what emblem can be more significant of this happy tendency than the American Cemetery, constructed by the money, taste and sentiment of the whole people; containing the dust of the earliest generations removed thither with pious care; receiving the body of every citizen when his earthly work is done, and he steps down from his little eminence of worldly distinction, to mingle with the great democracy of death.[22]

Mayo's praise for the cemetery was extreme. The cemetery represented the progress of American society in general, serving as "a powerful aid in teaching the people the christian view of life and death; as a perpetual preacher on the relations of those who live in this world, and in the world of souls."[23] Cemeteries offered the opportunity for creating beauty and order, which represented a high point in American thought about civilization. Cemeteries became places of cultivated gardens and beauty. In fact, antebellum Americans often celebrated the ways that they had improved upon nature—and in particular how beauty itself was uplifting.[24]

One sign of the progression of society from ancient times to the present was the use of human energy to beautify nature and to convert nature to serve human purposes. In comparing the past with the present, for instance, President George Junkin of Washington College in Lexington, Virginia, remarked that "intelligence and physical prowess which then spent its force in desolating the earth and subduing nations for tyrants, is now expended in beautifying the earth and conquering nature for man."[25] Junkin, thus, linked subduing nature and beauty.

Antebellum Americans believed that property rights and commerce were at the center of the progress. For instance, Virginia Senator Robert M.T. Hunter remarked at the Virginia Military Institute's graduation in 1857 "that the educated, intelligent Anglo-Saxon merchant, whether of the senior or the junior branches of

21 *Id.* at 5.

22 *Id.* at 8.

23 *Id.*

24 Eugenius Nisbet, *Thoughts on the Beautiful: An Address Delivered at the Commencement of the Griffin Synodical Female College* (1857).

25 George Junkin, *An Apology for Collegiate Education Being the Baccalaureate Address Delivered on Commencement Day of Washington College* 19 (1851).

the family, is a prime agent in the work of human civilization … ."[26] Many others celebrated the role that the market played in bringing civilization, though they also sometimes recognized that it brought problems as well. Ralph Waldo Emerson's address on the "Young American" celebrated the power of trade to bring about reform, like the end of feudalism, and he looked forward to the day when it would tear down slavery as well: [27]

> The philosopher and lover of man have much harm to say of trade; but the historian will see that trade was the principle of Liberty; that trade planted America and destroyed Feudalism; that it makes peace and keeps peace, and it will abolish slavery. We complain of its oppression of the poor, and of its building up a new aristocracy on the ruins of the aristocracy it destroyed. But the aristocracy of trade has no permanence, is not entailed, was the result of toil and talent, the result of merit of some kind, and is continually falling, like the waves of the sea, before new claims of the same sort.[28]

## Progress and Fine Art

The catalytic role of property and commerce in the development of civilization, evidenced in the writings of jurists and political theorists, appeared in the fine art of the era. In this volume on property and sovereignty, we want to suggest that the landscape art of the pre-Civil War era reflected the dominant ethos that property should be developed and that development led to progress. For instance, landscape artist Thomas Cole's series of five paintings, *The Course of Empire,* first displayed in 1836, depicted the cycle that many believed that a civilization passed through—from the savage state, to the pastoral, to consummation, decline, and, ultimately, desolation.[29] That was a cyclical image, of growth and then decline. Many Whig thinkers were, in fact, concerned that the United States might decline, largely through an excess of democracy. President Henry Ruffner of Washington College in Lexington, Virginia, spoke about the threats to the United States in

---

26 Robert M. T. Hunter, *Address Delivered Before the Two Literary Societies of the Virginia Military Institute* 31 (1857). *See also* Alfred L. Brophy, *Considering William and Mary's History with Slavery: The Case of Thomas Roderick Dew*, 16 Wm. & Mary Bill Rts. J. 1091, 1119–20 (2008) (discussing attitudes towards property in antebellum era political thought).

27 Ralph Waldo Emerson, *Essays and Lectures* 213 (Joel Porte ed., 1983).

28 *Id.* at 221.

29 Cole's series of *Course of Empire* is *reprinted in* Angela Miller, *The Empire of the Eye: Landscape Representation and American Cultural Politics, 1825–1875,* at 27–32 (1993). *See also* Albert Boime, *The Magisterial Gaze: Manifest Destiny and American Landscape Painting* (1991).

his inaugural address in 1837. He invoked the specter of retrenchment from civilization if education was neglected:

> [E]very thing connected with civilization would retrace its steps; the awful gloom of the dark ages would again settle over the face of society; & mankind would again sink down into the barbarism from which they had emerged. ... [G]overnment would be converted into lawless violence; insecurity of rights would destroy industry; agriculture, manufactures and commerce, would no longer support a numerous & thriving population; misery in all the shapes of famine, robbery and war, would desolate the earth, and reduce the fair realms of civilization to a wilderness of scattered barbarians.[30]

Yet, Cole's depiction of decline was at odds with the beliefs of many Americans. When Justice Levi Woodbury of the United States Supreme Court spoke about "progress" at Dartmouth in 1844 he told the students that Cole's final landscape was wrong. There would not be decline in the United States, but continued progress.[31] This was in some ways related to the Whig concern over democracy, which saw threats to American society from the loosening of traditional hierarchy; whereas Democrats like Woodbury were thinking optatively that progress would go on forever. The image of progress (and sometimes decline), then, appeared in landscape art. In fact, the art of the pre-Civil War era reflected Americans' political theory, such as the ways that societies progressed through religion, trade, and economic progress. And in the case of Cole, that there might be decline through an excess of democracy or a lack of virtue.[32]

The image of progress often included subduing the earth, wresting bounties from it, and improving upon nature. In this mission, all manner of technologies were important, from the steam engine to the printing press, to the intellectual technology of law.[33] In particular, property law facilitated commerce and investment. The claims were grand: progress through property and technology was remaking the world. Washington College President George Junkin's address at Rutgers linked the United States with Providence and found that technology was making it possible to subdue the world and spread the cause of liberty:

---

30 Henry Ruffner, *Inaugural Address* 21 (1837).

31 *See* Levi Woodbury, *On Progress: An Oration Before the Phi Beta Kappa Society of Dartmouth College* (1844), *reprinted in* 3 Writings of Levi Woodbury 75, 77 (1852).

32 *See* Alfred L. Brophy, *Property and Progress: Antebellum Landscape Art and Property Law*, 40 McGeorge L. Rev. 603, 641–6 (2009) (discussing Course of Empire).

33 Stephen D. Davis & Alfred L. Brophy, *"The Most Solemn Act of My Life": Family, Property, Will, and Trust in the Antebellum South*, 62 Ala. L. Rev. 757, 789–91 (2011) (viewing wills and trusts as part of the technology used to generate economic development in antebellum era).

> The Sublime Porte long since doffed his turban to the American ship-wright. The Czar of all the Russias sits *tete-a-tete* with an American Engineer. His Imperial Majesty of the Brazils buys American engineering talent at royal prices. Scientific France pays her most profound obeisance, as the American iron horse gulps up the waters of the Seine, and thunders along in the suburbs of the civilized world. Even proud old mother England seems ashamed of her own very natural jealousy upon sight of her oldest daughter passing her in the race of improvement, and winning the applause of the nations; and shows no fidgety nervousness at the thundering roar of American cars on English rails, or American lightning snapping into her ears intelligence from Paris or Vienna, Sevastopol or St. Petersburg. Why should the old lady be any longer jealous? Is not she like her daughter an iron nation? Is not the Anglo-Saxon race an *iron race*? Is it not by working as an artificer in this peculiarly Anglo-Saxon product, it has placed itself upon its lofty iron throne, as protector of humanity — as Guardian of the Liberties of the world?[34]

Images of landscape served grand purposes. They showed the progress of civilization, they inspired patriotic sentiments, and they linked America's mission with Providence. George Junkin invoked romantic imagery of the American landscape to link nature with human development, which in turn linked to God and freedom:

> One hundred millions of freemen, spread over a mighty continent, with a commercial and martial marine whose eagle wings darken all the billows of all the seas; with an agriculture and a mechanism firm as the pillars of our everlasting hills; with a militia, the true *gens-d'arme* of freedom—over ten millions: with seven thousand miles of coast facing all the oceans, indented all along with harbors and bristling with batteries, and breasts ready to man them; and with a Washington—if, indeed, among a hundred millions we can find him—at the head of a government, the most energetic, though not the quickest conceivable. From such a body politic, with gigantic skeleton of huge granite mountains, with veins and arteries of vast rivers and railroads, and all under the control of electric nerves, terminating in the central deposit of life, what may not the world expect? What ought to be her doings in the eyes of humanity? What does God, who placed us in this position, expect of us?[35]

Similarly, Henry Ruffner, Junkin's predecessor as president of Washington College, delivered an address a few days after Junkin's, on July 4, 1856, in western Virginia. Ruffner's address appealed to Union for economic as well as sentimental reasons. He described the image of a grand republic decades hence—seventy

---

34 George Junkin, *An Address Delivered Before the Literary Societies of Rutgers College* 16 (1856).

35 *Id.* at 29–30.

years forward, just as his audience was then seventy years past the signing of the Declaration of Independence.[36] Art—whether oratory or visual—was part of a constitutional vision that sought to harness positive attitudes towards Union. Artwork, thus, served as a piece of the constitutional culture.[37]

## *American Scenery* and the Signs of Progress

We have two goals as we continue to explore Lumpkin's and Venable's insight that the American settlers were subduing the earth. First, we trace out in some detail how landscape art of the pre-Civil War era depicted humans subduing and putting their stamp on the land. For instance, the art of the era often portrayed the technologies Americans used, such as railroads, steam boats, and bridges, and the various stages Americans passed through in the process of subduing nature, from the rude state of nature to the well-ordered cities with respectable homes and manicured gardens.

To do this, we turn to two books of landscape art of the pre-Civil War period, bearing the same title, which were published fourteen years apart. The first is Nathaniel Parker Willis' 1840 *American Scenery*.[38] The second is Thomas Addison Richards' 1854 *American Scenery*.[39] We examine the 118 landscape prints in Willis and the 32 in Richards to provide a systematic assessment of the ways that landscape artists depicted how Americans had subdued nature and improved upon it, to use a term common at the time. This illustrates the centrality of landscape art to the United States' nationalizing mission, as numerous works of art history have recognized.[40]

Our second goal is to link that landscape art to property law. We view the landscape art as the dependent variable of culture, which also found expression in property law. The landscape art serves as a gauge of the issues of importance for American property law. We can learn something more about how property law assisted development by "reading" it in conjunction with other evidence of the culture, such as landscape art. Thus, our foray into quantitative art history may assist our understanding of legal history, particularly the preference of judges for economic development and for robust constitutional protection of private property.

---

36 Henry Ruffner, *Union Speech; Delivered at Kanawha Sabines, Va.* 7 (1856).

37 *See generally* Jason Mazzone, *The Creation of a Constitutional Culture*, 40 Tulsa L. Rev. 671 (2004).

38 N.P. Willis, *American Scenery: Or, Land, Lake, and River—Illustrations of Transatlantic Nature* (2 vols) [hereinafter Willis].

39 T. Addison Richards, *American Scenery: Illustrated* (1854) [hereinafter Richards]..

40 Examples are Neil Harris, *The Artist in American Society: The Formative Years, 1790–1860* (1966) and Angela Miller, *supra* note 29.

### Nathaniel Parker Willis' 1840 *American Scenery* and Thomas Addison Richards' 1854 *American Scenery*

Nathaniel Parker Willis published *American Scenery: Or, Land, Lake and River Illustrations of Transatlantic Nature* in 1840, when he was thirty-four years old. Born in 1806 in Maine, Willis grew up in Boston, and then was educated at Yale.[41] He had a long-standing interest in scenery and its relation to American history. In 1828 he edited two volumes of historical sketches.[42] The two volumes of *American Scenery*, prepared while Willis traveled the United States in the late 1830s, present essays and poetry on the places he visited, along with prints prepared by William R. Bartlett.[43]

Despite the subtitle, which focuses on nature, Willis acknowledges that in the United States, landscape images more often are about the future than the past. In Europe, landscape often depicted ruins of ancient buildings, along with nature. But in the United States, the images were rarely of the past; instead, the landscape artist sees "a valley laden down like a harvest waggon with a virgin vegetation, untrodden and luxuriant; and his first thought is of the villages that will soon sparkle on the hill-sides, the axes that will ring from the woodlands, and the mills, bridges, canals, and railroads, that will span and border the stream that now runs through sedge and wild-flowers."[44] Willis summed this up: In the United States the artist "looks upon all external objects as exponents of the future. In Europe they are only exponents of the past."[45] *American Scenery's* 118 landscape prints, then, range from scenes of wild and uninhabited nature through modern civilization.

Our second object of study is T. Addison Richards' 1854 book, also titled *American Scenery*. Richards, born in London in 1820, moved with his family to the United States in 1831. After first living in New York, the family moved to South Carolina, and later in 1837 to Georgia where his father served as a Baptist minister. In 1841 Addison and his brother William published *Georgia Scenery*, a book containing many scenes of wild and uninhabited nature in Georgia.[46] Shortly afterward, Addison moved north to New York City, where his career as a landscape

---

41 Thomas N. Baker, *Sentiment and Celebrity: Nathaniel Parker Willis and the Trials of Literary Fame* (1999).

42 *The Legendary: Consisting of Original Pieces, Principally Illustrative of American History, Scenery, and Manners* (N.P. Willis ed., 1828).

43 As is true for the artwork, the majority of the passages center upon the disorder of nature, the lifestyle of the "ordered" human as separate from the land, and the adoration of human improvements upon the land. Along the same lines, the definition of nature derived from these passages also assumes human structures are a part of the "natural scenery."

44 1 Willis, *supra* note 38 at 2.

45 *Id.*

46 In *American Scenery*, Richards incorporated some of engravings he had used in *Georgia Scenery*, including "The Falls of Tallulah" and the "Medical College of Georgia." *See also* Richards' *The Night Funeral of a Slave*, *in* Educational Repository and Family Monthly 720 (1860).

artist blossomed. The prints in the Richards volume, like those in Willis, were prepared by William Bartlett. Thus, while the authors of the text are different, the images that we discuss here were created by the same person; in fact several the prints in Richards had appeared first in Willis.[47]

*Categorizing American Scenery*

In order to get a systemic understanding of Willis' and later Richards' American landscape scenes, we examined the 118 prints in Willis' *American Scenery* and the 32 prints in Richards' *American Scenery*. For each scene, we first recorded whether the scene contained nature, humans, structures, or a combination of these three elements. Overall, each category was represented fairly evenly throughout each of the scenes from the collection. Out of 150 total prints, 142 included nature, 132 included people, and 116 included structures. Only eight prints included no scenes of nature. Those prints showed a giant hotel in Saratoga Springs, the Medical College of Georgia, and streets and buildings in Boston, Massachusetts, Ballston Springs, Virginia, Philadelphia, Pennsylvania, and Washington, DC.[48]

Next we refined our categories further to describe the predominant characteristics of each print by using two additional variables. First, we assessed the amount of the print dedicated to nature, humans, and structures. Here we gauged the relative significance of the three elements assessed in the analysis. Structures were a significant portion of 88 prints. People appeared in significant

47 The repeats are "Narrows, From Staten Island," Richards, *supra* note 39 at 31, 1 Willis, *supra* note 38 at 34; "New York, From Weehawken," Richards, *supra* note 39 at 53, 2 Willis, *supra* note 38 at 30; "Columbia Bridge," Richards, *supra* note 39 at 127, 1 Willis, *supra* note 38 at 87; "Niagara Falls," Richards, *supra* note 39 at 211, 1 Willis, *supra* note 38 at 45; "Susquehanna," Richards,, *supra* 39, at 257, as known as "View of Northumberland," 2 Willis, *supra* note 38, at 63and "The Connecticut River," Richards, *supra* note 39 at 295, 1 Willis, *supra* note 38 at 10. After *American Scenery*, Addison Richards published a smaller version known as *The Romance of American Landscape* in 1854, and then a less expensive travel guide, *Appletons' Illustrated Hand-book of American Travel*, in 1857.

It is helpful to read Addison's work in conjunction with his brother, William C. Richards, who also wrote frequently about the progress of American society. In fact, William Richards delivered a revealing literary address at South Carolina's Erskine College in 1853, which focused on the multiple ways that technology improved the lives and morals of Americans. That same year William also published *A Day in the New York Crystal Palace, and How to Make the Most of It* (1853).

48 The images were "The Colonnade of Congress Hall (Saratoga Springs)," 1 Willis, *supra* note 38 at 20; "Medical College, Georgia," Richards, *supra* note 39 at 71; "View of State Street, Boston," 1 Willis, *supra* note 38 at 42; "View of Faneuiel Hall," *id.* at 57; "Ballston Springs," *id.* at 128; "View of the United States Bank," 2 Willis, *supra* note 38 at 73; "The Exchange, and Girard's Bank, Philadelphia," Richards, *supra* note 39 at 53; "Principal Front of the Capitol, Washington," *id.* at 55.

ways in 48 prints. Only seven prints featured all three.[49] Such prints included the "Palisades on the Hudson River," which included numerous steamboats and other vessels, the river and the cliffs of the Palisades, and the crew and passengers on the ships. Another print, "Tomb of Kosciusko," presents patrons of a local park picnicking on a hillside overlooking a mountain lake with sailboats, near a monument to Thad Kosciusko, a Revolutionary war hero. Another print featuring all three elements, the "Columbia Bridge on the Susquehanna," (Figure 7.1) depicts travelers overlooking the river and admiring the bridge.[50]

**Figure 7.1 "Columbia Bridge on the Susquehanna"**

Finally we considered the stages of development. We divided the prints into five stages of development that roughly paralleled how pre-Civil War Americans wrote about the stages of civilization. Our categories were: the savage state or state of nature; humans in nature; human structures in nature; civilization; and finally

49 "The Palisades - Hudson River," 1 Willis, *supra* note 38 at 14; "Tomb of Kosciusko," *id.* at 30; "Columbia Bridge, over the Susquehanna," *id.* at 87; "Washington's House, Mount Vernon," Richards, *supra* note 39 at 38; "View of Baltimore," *id.* at 51; "Brock's Monument, from the American Side," *id.* at 75; "The Park Fountain, New York," *id.* at 21.

50 The print appeared in 1 Willis, *supra* note 38 at 87 and in Richards, *supra* note 39 at 127. This illustration is available at http://blurblawg.typepad.com/.a/6a00e54f871a9c88330162fe0d0fdd970d-popup

consummation, shown by vistas of civilization. Savage state or state of nature included wild and uninhabited nature, such as plants, animals, rivers, trees, clouds, or Native Americans by themselves. Humans in nature emphasizes human activity in a scene, such as people sailing or farming. The next stage, human structures, focused on objects such as steamboats, bridges, and buildings in an otherwise "wild" environment. The fourth stage, "civilization," included nature improved by humans, such as scenes of parks and city blocks. A vista of civilization, what we identify as the consummation, was a rendering of a city sprawling over the landscape.[51]

For this analysis, we coded the dominant stage of civilization, even though some prints had several stages of civilization. Although nature appeared in many of the prints, it was only the focus of 27 scenes—less than 20 percent of the set. Humans and their activities overwhelmingly represented the focus of the sample set. Of the 150 total scenes, humans or their structures in nature are the focus of 69 scenes, almost half. An emphasis on civilization, including a vista of civilization, was represented by 54 scenes, just over one third. Table 7.1 presents the breakdown of the Willis and Richards landscapes according to the stages of civilization.

**Table 7.1 Stages of civilization in American scenery landscapes**

| | Savage State or Nature | European-Americans in Nature | Human Structures in Nature | Civilization | Vista of Civilization | Total Prints |
|---|---|---|---|---|---|---|
| Richards | 10 (31.2%) | 7 (21.9%) | 6 (18.8%) | 5 (15.6%) | 4 (12.5%) | **32** |
| Willis (v1) | 15 (22.7%) | 16 (24.2%) | 15 (22.7%) | 12 (18.2%) | 8 (12.1%) | **66** |
| Willis (v2) | 2 (3.8%) | 11 (21.2%) | 14 (26.9%) | 12 (23.1%) | 13 (25%) | **52** |
| **Total:** | **27** | **34** | **35** | **29** | **25** | **150** |

## *Stages of Civilization in Willis'* American Scenery

Willis' landscapes spanned the spectrum of stages of civilization. We have ordered our discussion along the lines of stages of development, beginning with wild and untamed nature. Seventeen of Willis' prints fall into that category. Niagara Falls

51 Another vantage on this appears in N. P. Willis, *Letters from Under a Bridge, And Poems* (1840). In addition to a portrait of Willis and a frontispiece of his homestead, there were nine illustrations—three of gardens or parks; four scenes of the Susquehanna River, which showed various stages of industrial development, one of the Schuykill Water Works, and one of the Valley of Wyoming. All revealed substantial development and improvement upon nature. Again, the prints were prepared by William Bartlett.

was a repeat favorite for Willis; it accounted for fourteen scenes in the two volumes. The first scene in the entire collection, "Niagara Falls, from the Ferry," reveals Willis' awe over the magnitude and power of the Falls. "The tremendous power of the Fall," Willis wrote, "as well as the height, realizes [man's] utmost expectations." The ferry "toss[ed] like an egg-shell on the heaving and convulsed water" and the crew of "athletic men" worked even to "keep the boat up against [the tide] with difficulty."[52]

The second appearance of Niagara, "The Rapids Above the Falls of Niagara," highlights the wild nature and immense power of the water.[53] Although the accompanying narrative begins by describing a battle, it quickly turns to its primary purpose: illustrating human folly by telling of the impact of the rapids on a boat, the boat's cargo, and a sole surviving goose. Willis concludes with a description of the rapids:

> The torture of the Rapids, the clinging curves with which they embrace the small rocky islands that live amid the surge, the sudden calmness at the brow of the cataract, and the infernal writhe and whiteness with which they reappear, powerless from the depths of the abyss, all seem, to the excited imagination of the gazer, like the natural effects of impending ruin, desperate resolution, and fearful agony, on the minds and frames of mortals.[54]

Boats in peril are a staple of Willis' repertoire, featured in these two examples and in many other scenes. The final boat adventure in the collection, however, displays a more confident person in his vessel amongst a similarly raging nature. "Lighthouse Near Caldwell's Landing"[55] depicts stormy waters and deck hands in the foreground and waves bombarding the low-lying docks of the New York harbor. The focus, however, is on a large sailboat in the center, its sails highlighted with a radiant glow. The sailboat piloted by its captain glides effortlessly through the choppy waters, destined to finish their course despite the storm. Strangely, the narrative Willis wrote to accompany this scene is more akin to "if lighthouses could talk;" it retells a tragic and dramatic story of a military leader's wife whose vanity all but ruined her soldier-husband's hard-fought reputation. The only relationship the story has to the lighthouse is simply the fact of its non-momentous passing on the couple's way up the river to West Point. Nevertheless, the scene speaks for itself by displaying the rage of a storm, its impact upon the natural landscape of the New York harbor, juxtaposed by humans boldly and fearlessly brooking no interference with their journey.

Other scenes emphasize human improvement upon nature. For instance, a serene and picturesque mountain lake in "Caldwell, Lake George" shows that

---

52 1 Willis, *supra* note 38 at 4.

53 *Id.* at 16.

54 *Id.*at 17.

55 *Id.*at 64.

humans were interrupting the beauty and tranquility of the lake's waters. "Before it became a part of the fashionable tour, this lake was a solitude, appropriated more particularly by the deer and the eagle. Both have nearly disappeared."[56] The "peppering of fancy sportsmen" and "echo of the steam-boat … ha[ve] now taken the place of the noiseless canoe."[57] After this compliment to the transformation of nature, Willis describes the human-made "adornments" that are still missing from the landscape:

> To complete the scenery of this lake, the efforts of cultivation are obviously wanting. The hand of the husbandman has already begun to clear these grounds; and will, at no great distance of time, adorn them with all the smiling scenes of agriculture. It does not demand the gift of prophecy to foresee, that the villas of opulence and refinement will, within half a century, add here all the elegances of art to the beauty and majesty of nature.[58]

Humans may and should improve nature, the primary theme of "Caldwell, Lake George," but the scene also presents a different, more radical vision. Rather than emphasize the compatibility of nature and humans, Willis envisages humans often living separately from nature. From the opposite end of the spectrum, he indirectly contrasts the wildness of nature by his characterization of human designs. In "View of State Street, Boston," Willis described "modern" improvements to human designs: "Alterations and additions have of late years greatly improved the appearance of Boston. The streets … wide and commodious; the old wooden structures … replaced by handsome buildings of stone or brick. In the western part, particularly, there is much neatness and elegance."[59] By contrast, nowhere does he describe nature as "elegant," "handsome" or "neat."

Willis presented images of wild nature and ordered human culture beside each other. The description of the Massachusetts scene from "The View from Mount Holyoke" demonstrates that often there can be order mixed with disorder:

> The view immediately below presents a singular phase of the scenery of the river, which seems here to possess a soul for beauty, and loiters, enamored and unwilling to flow on, in the bosom of a meadow which has no parallel in New England for loveliness and fertility … . The meadow is almost entirely unfenced … forming a foreground to one of the most sunny and cheerful villages in Massachusetts.[60]

56 *Id.* at 70.
57 *Id.* at 70.
58 *Id.* at 71.
59 *Id.* at 42.
60 *Id.* at 10.

Thus, despite the pleasantries of the river meandering through the field alluded to by the passage, the contrast with the structured society reflected by the village and cleared meadow is quite at odds with the naturalistic theme. Willis describes the landscape's history:

> The town was surrounded with palisadoes (i.e. the town was fortified) … [S] everal forts were built within the town. Still their dwellings were often burnt, their women and children carried into captivity, and their time was divided between war and agriculture.[61]

Meanwhile, the river meanders through a field. Often the prints contain elements of both the theme that nature is wild and the theme that humans can improve upon it, too. "The Narrows at Staten Island," New York, had progressed beyond their disarrayed beginnings:

> At this day there stands a villa on every picturesque point; a thriving town lies on the left shore; [with] hospitals and private sanitary establishments…[L] ittle fleets of merchantmen … fly rapidly and skilfully [along with] a constant succession of steam-boats, gaily painted and beautifully modeled … [O]nly two hundred years ago [this place] 'was wild and rough; a thick forest covered the parts where anything would grow; its beach was broken and sandy, and full of inlets; its interior presented hills of stony and sandy alluvion, masses of rock, ponds, swamps, and marshes.'[62]

Another New York scene, the "Village of Sing Sing," shows a similar combination of the two themes of wild nature and the ways that humans improve upon it. Willis describes the land as "quite desolate" and the people distrusting, not kind, and overall unhappy. It "is a rough country in natural surface, but since the [1780's] … its vicinity to New York, and the ready market for produce, have changed its character to a thriving agricultural district."[63] Another print, "Descent into the Valley of Wyoming" (Figure 7.2, overleaf) shows the stages of civilization. In the foreground is a simple rude road leading down into the civilized and distant valley; the town of Wilkes Barre appears in the distance.[64]

Willis' descriptions similarly praise humans for enhancing nature. This is distinguished from the earlier theme of humans improving upon nature in the sense that the works of nature and humans are not at odds; rather humans and their structures adorn the landscape, as if they were there from the beginning.

---

61 *Id.* at 12.

62 *Id.* at 35.

63 *Id.* at 50.

64 Descent into the Valley of Wyoming, *Id.* at 53. The illustration is available at http://blurblawg.typepad.com/.a/6a00e54f871a9c88330162fce75a4b970d-popup

For example, in the passage from "Boston, From Dorchester Heights," Willis describes the commanding view:

> The bay, with its fortified islands … beautiful from its shape and from the brightness of its water; the city, clustering upon its heights, rises in graceful lines to the pinnacled State House; and the country to the left is all that is lovely in cultivation, sprinkled here and there with gay and thrifty-looking villages … [T]he suburbs of Boston will soon sparkle with villas on every hill side within the horizon.[65]

**Figure 7.2 "Descent into the Valley of Wyoming"**

Just like sunlight on the water of the surrounding bay, the villas enhance the hillside. This scene focuses on human structures with nature providing only the backdrop. Another scene, "Peekskill Landing," depicts a landing on the Hudson, which was the way that travelers could go off into the world. In the foreground is a rude dirt road; off in the distance are sailboats and the rest of the world. Willis viewed Peekskill Landing like an "outstretched hand from the interior of the country."[66] With an emphasis on the coming and going of travelers, this scene focuses on the life of people.

In *American Scenery* Willis showed many landscapes as scary and in need of development and portrayed others as high points of modern civilization. The

65 1 Willis, *supra* note 38 at 57.
66 *Id.* at 61.

landscape pictures conveyed how Americans had triumphed over nature in the eras of agricultural and urban expansion and the development of markets. Landscape art, then, illustrated the values of development of land and the course that Americans were pursuing of building a commercial republic of well-ordered fields and cities. Although *American Scenery* does not directly speak to the roles played by the sovereign in fashioning property laws that facilitated the transformation of the American natural landscape, the volumes implicitly celebrate the means used to achieve the end.

## Thomas Addison Richards' 1854 *American Scenery*

Just as with Willis' 1840 *American Scenery*, Richards' volume 14 years later reveals a hierarchy of development of land. It begins with images of wild and essentially uninhabited nature, such as the "Falls of Towalaga" in Georgia, "Bison and Elk, River Scene in the South-West," and the "Lake in the Adirondacks, New York".[67] Nearly a third of the prints in Richards were about wild nature or the savage state, which is substantially more than those in Willis' earlier volume. Given the relatively small number of prints, it is perhaps unwise to draw too many comparisons between the volumes, but one might consider several hypotheses here. First, the earlier and larger volume may have needed to focus more on the ways that Americans had improved the land; and then, fourteen years later, the next volume could focus more on nostalgic scenes. Perhaps that hypothesis relies upon too much change in attitudes in a short compass; another hypothesis is that Richards, who started life in the south, had more of an interest in the southern and rural scenes than did Willis.

Whatever the origin of the differences in proportions, Richards also has images of increasing progress. He has images of the savage state (such as the "Falls of Tallulah," where a Native American hunts with a bow and arrow).[68] The next stage of development is shown with European Americans crossing nature, such as "Washington crossing the Allegheny on a log raft, scene in the backwoods." Others show European Americans interacting with natives, such as "St. Regis Indian Village."[69] The next stage seems to be European Americans visiting nature, such as the print of "Niagara Falls."[70] Even higher stages of development appeared when technology conquered nature, such as the "Columbia Bridge over Susquehanna," (Illustration 1) which repeated a print that appeared in Willis.[71] There are also

67 Richards, *supra* note 39 at 9, 181, 235,

68 *Id.* at 81. One might also think of the "Elk Horn Pyramid" here, a pyramid of Elk horns constructed by Native Americans. *Id.* at 13.

69 *Id.* at 65, 165.

70 *Id.* at 211.

71 *Id.* at 127; 1 Willis, *supra* note 38 at 87.

images of Americans visiting improved places, like the "Park Fountain," in New York and the "Medical College of Georgia." [72]

Sometimes a single print shows several the stages of progress. The "Susquehanna," also known as "View of Northumberland (on the Susquehanna)" (Figure 7.3) appeared in both Willis and Richards. It shows the stages of civilization, from a peddler walking about the canal, to the canal boats, to the thriving city in the background.[73]

**Figure 7.3 "View of Northumberland (on the Susquehanna)"**

The highest stage of civilization appeared in landscapes of cities that had improvement as far as the eye could see, such as "Narrows from Staten Island, New York from Weehawken."[74]

The results of the commercial republic appear in Richards' landscapes of cities. Houses, merchant buildings, churches, government buildings, ships, and well-dressed humans meld together. Richards also depicts scenes of well-ordered nature, such as the ox-bow in the "Connecticut River," with fields, orchards, and

72 Richards, *supra* note 39 at 21, 71.

73 *Id.* at 257; 2 Willis, *supra* note 38 at 63 . The illustration is available at http://blurblawg.typepad.com/.a/6a00e54f871a9c883301675f015472970b-popup

74 Richards, *supra* note 39 at 31; 1 Willis, *supra* note 38 at 34.

fences.[75] And "Rock Mountain," shows rows of planted trees on the left, drifting off to as yet unimproved nature on the right.[76]

The landscapes in Richards reveal a similar span of stages of civilization as Willis' images. Only one third of the scenes (10 of 32) emphasize nature. Over two-thirds (23/32 or 71.9 percent) of the scenes include some significant elements of nature. Almost half focus on people.

Both the order and focus of the narratives in *American Scenery* demonstrate a noteworthy shift in Richards' perceptions of nature. At the onset, Richards informs the reader of his knowledge, "a brief, but he hopes an intelligent, glimpse at the varying characteristics of the beautiful natural scenery of our country."[77] He then describes his intentions for the book: to share "a more genial topic—the Romance and Reality of American Landscape—its physique and morale, its historic tradition, its poetic legend, its incident, adventure, and suggestion."[78] Here Richards exposes his view of the supreme status of humans: "Since the halcyon days when Adam and Eve rejoiced with exceeding joy beneath the glorious skies of Paradise, Nature has ever shared bountifully in the love and adoration of man. This feeling is an instinct, no less than a refinement, in our souls."[79]

A frequent, underlying assumption is that humans and nature are compatible and intertwined, yet they are also distinct from each other. The beginning of Chapter 3, titled "The Romance of American Landscape," provides an example. The chapter begins with Richards' praise of Virginia's shores, but quickly turns to the shores' historical interactions with people and events:

> 'Old Virginia's shore' ... a noble theme, regarded in any and every light; whether we consider the adventurous incidents of her early history, the bravery and gallantry of her people, and their signal services to our country in every phase and period of its life; or whether we explore its rich and varied stores of natural beauties and wonders.[80]

After expounding upon the natural features of the Virginia landscape before him, Richards then observes how frequently humans focus on themselves. He ponders, "Is it not strange that while Virginia is no less singularly interesting in her physical than in her moral aspect, she has won so little of the attention of our landscapists?"[81] He follows by recounting the options before him, and the neglect of painters to seize the opportunities:

75 Richards, *supra* note 39 at 295.
76 *Id.* at 245.
77 *Id.* at 7.
78 *Id.* at 16.
79 *Id.* at 19.
80 *Id.* at 41–2.
81 *Id.* at 48.

> [F]rom the alluvial plains of the eastern division, through the picturesque hills and dales of the middle region, onward to the noble summits of the Blue Ridge, with their intervening valleys and mountain streams and waterfalls, the white-cotton umbrella of the artist has scarcely ever been seen to temper its sunshine, except in a few instances of particularly notable interest—as the Natural Bridge, and the grand views near Harper's Ferry. The landscape of Virginia is everywhere suggestive; and, even in the least varied regions, continually rises to the beauty of a fine picture… Verily, we painters have too much neglected our duties and privileges in this case.[82]

Richards then offers a reason behind such apathy. Artists find travel to the northern American landscapes easier due to the predominant starting point of New York City.

The title of Chapter 3, "The Romance of American Landscape," at first appears to be a misnomer given the contents of the chapter. Based on the title of the book, *American Scenery*, one would expect descriptive narratives of the landscapes in America, the alluring aspects of nature's beauty, its colors and topography, and her siren song to humans. In fact, the reference to "romance" has nothing to do with the American landscape apart from the individuals who inhabit it. The chapter is replete with love stories and a brave young maiden named "Little Emma." The chapter might have been more appropriately titled "The Romance *in* American Landscape."

As Richards continues his journey, he experiences diversity in the people, the cultures, and the landscapes. His newly expanded horizons result in his equally expanded perceptions as his travels continue. Richards first describes the story of a young woman named Gabrielle St. Pierre, who left French society with her father for the western forest of America. Richards seems to be genuinely intrigued by the rebellious attitude of Gabrielle towards society, and despite calling her a "wild daughter, rugged in nature," his opinion is broadened by the lessons Gabrielle has learned from living in both worlds:

> Here, in the solemn ministrations of God's first temples—the grand primeval forests—and amidst the dangers and privations with which she had to contend, she grew up a thoughtful and truthful spirit, with earnest and daring purpose; while a longer breathing of the poisoned and demoralizing atmosphere of the court of Louis, might have degraded her into a reckless and unscrupulous woman of fashion and intrigue.[83]

Gabrielle likewise describes the broadening of her perception based upon her life experiences. Not missing the city life in Paris, she speaks of the hills and valleys which:

82 *Id.* at 49.
83 *Id.* at 77.

> repay [her] wit with much more instructive and agreeable talk than the silly tattle of the drawing-room. The song of the birds is pleasanter to me than the false flatteries of heartless admirers, and the fragrance of the pure mountain air more grateful than the perform of lovers' sighs.[84]

For a book and era that praises humans, particularly their fashioning of an ordered society, it is no surprise Richards was intrigued by such a counter-cultural young woman as Gabrielle.

The further south Richards travels, the more nature becomes a focus of both his scenes and his narratives. This is also true of Willis, for which human scenes from the south focused on nature. The fifth chapter of Richards, set in the south, praises the beauty of nature without human improvements. Particularly speaking of the low country, Richards describes his experience with this unique landscape and the "dreary humour of the sleeping lowlands."[85] He is enchanted by this landscape:

> [N]ot so much for the contrast it offers to the general character of our scenery, as for its own intrinsic charms. There is to me a marvelous attraction in the beauty of the broad savannas, seemingly interminable in the hazy atmosphere which wraps them in such peaceful and poetic repose; and which, with the luxuriant vegetation and the wealth of forest flowers, soothe the feeling and fancy, but yet keep them delightfully wakeful and active.[86]

Referring to the South, Richards also applauds the "material wealth" that contributes to the economy. In the story of Georgia's Nacoochee Valley, Richards describes the landscape as "useful as well as ornamental; its soil yielding to the tiller rich returns, not only of luscious grains and fruits, but of pure gold."[87] Richards also finds a void of social refinement and education. He wrote of his expectation that soon there would be development of education and society:

> [T]he influx of new and broader ideas, carried thither by the increasing current of travel, and by enlarged industry and ambition, will soon lift the people above the gross ignorance in which they at present so contentedly rest. In no part of our Union is the mental condition of the peasantry so low as among the inhabitants of the Southern mountain lands …[88]

However, Richards' prejudices were checked by speaking with a local woodsman who wisely informed him that civilization had stretched to Georgia's woods:

---

84 *Id.* at 81.
85 *Id.* at 102–3.
86 *Id.* at 102.
87 *Id.* at 113.
88 *Id.* at 113.

> It is not alone … in your great cities that the romance of thought and action is to be found. Even in these thinly peopled woods, the observant eye may read life's histories, its smiles and tears, in the perpetual rehearsal of all the acts and scenes in both the comedy and tragedy of life.[89]

## Linking Landscape Art to Property Law

The prints in the volumes of *American Scenery* authored by Willis and Richards tell us much about American attitudes towards the development of property. But how are they related to law? The landscape artists themselves were often explicit about the ways that civilization connected to the subduing of nature. South Carolina artist Charles Fraser's 1828 address at the College of Charleston explained the roles that education, government, and technology played in wringing a multitude of bounties from nature:

> The freedom of the government disposes and enables its citizens to improve these advantages to their greatest extent. Our Atlantic cities display the happiest combinations of wealth and refinement. Agriculture spreads its many coloured mantle over our fields. The forests of the West vanish before the arm of enterprize—and civilization is subduing the savage wanderers of the wilderness. Canals and roads, like arteries, are rapidly circulating the vital aliment of commercial health and vigour, and connecting the remotest districts of the interior with the great emporiums of trade.[90]

Art supported constitutional thought at a high level of generality. It linked patriotic sentiments to romantic imagery of the United States.

We want to link the images to the general pro-development, pro-market law of the era. That is, we view the images as another set of data points to illuminate how the ideology of the Whig political party promoted the development of property and of law. This was a story of harnessing technology like steam and the technology of law to promote development. All worked together to form a robust pro-market culture. There were many—sometimes Whigs, often Democrats—who were ambivalent about the development of the era, including some landscape artists. However, the central tendency of the era was in favor of development.

In other instances, the objects of art are directly linked to property law because they are the subject of lawsuits. For instance, there was frequent litigation over the appropriate measure of damages for land taken through eminent domain for

89 *Id.* at 124.

90 Charles Fraser, *An Address … At the Laying of the Corner Stone of a New College Edifice … 12th January, 1828*, 7 (1828). *See also* E.L. Magoon, *Scenery and Mind*, *in* The Home Book of the Picturesque: or American Scenery, Art, and Literature 1 (1852).

the construction of roads, canals, and railroads.[91] The economic importance of transportation often exerted pressure to limit the damages for eminent domain.[92] Judges similarly limited the liability of railroads for disturbances to their neighbors. For instance, the Kentucky Supreme Court denied a request for an injunction against a railroad that was causing a significant disturbance of its neighbors. Instead, the neighbors were left with a claim only for money damages.[93]

Some sense of how American judges thought about civilization appears in an obscure 1860 New York insurance case, *Casler v. Connecticut Mutual Life Insurance*.[94] The insured died on a trail to California in 1850 and the insurance company objected to paying on the policy, which covered people only if they perished within the "settled limits of the United States." The question then became, whether "settled limits" implied only geographic boundaries—as in the established geographic boundary of the country—or whether that meant, as the insurance company argued, within the limits of settlement in the United States (or what one dissenting jurist referred to as "civilization"). By the time the case was decided in 1860, a majority of the judges on the panel took a broad interpretation and concluded that the insured died within the settled geographic boundaries of the country. Civilization was spreading and it was irrelevant whether the insured died in a place with many or with few people, so long as he died within the geographic boundaries of the United States. The result in *Casler* suggests that civilization had a broad meaning and that the United States was thought of as settled, even in places where nature still presented many dangers.

As the process of physical settlement went along, legislatures and courts were also modifying rules related to property to facilitate civilization. For instance, the Illinois Supreme Court concluded that an Illinois statute that required railroads to fence their tracks to keep out cattle was both constitutional (that is, not an impairment of the railroads' contract rights under their charters) and part of the regularization of rules of corporations and of civilization.[95] Similarly, a New York court found that the married women's property acts, which gave women autonomy over their separate property had emerged "as civilization and refinement advanced, and the true position of woman as a member of society came to be better understood and acknowledged … "[96] The result was a rule that the "husband has

91 *See, e.g., Mifflin v. Railroad Co.*, 16 Pa. 182 (1851) (interpreting damages for land taken under charter that provided for eminent domain in construction of road in light of a new charter that provided for converting the road into a railroad); *Case of Philadelphia & Trenton R.R.*, 6 Whart. 25 (Pa. 1840) (interpreting damages for land taken for railroad).

92 *Jerome v. Ross*, 7 Johns. Ch. 315, 341–2, 345 (N.Y. Ch. 1823) (emphasizing public interest in the construction of a canal). *See also* Leah M. Green, *The Erie Canal and the American Imagination: The Erie Canal's Effects on American Legal Development, 1817–1869*, 56 Ala. L. Rev. 1167 (2005).

93 *Lexington & Ohio R.R. v. Applegate*, 38 Ky. (8 Dana) 289 (1839).

94 *Casler v. Connecticut Mut. Life Ins. Co.*, 22 N.Y. 427 (1860).

95 *Ohio & Mississippi R.R. v. McClelland*, 25 Ill. 140 (1860).

96 *Winans v. Peebles*, 31 Barb. 371, 376–7 (N.Y. Gen. Term 1860).

been deprived of all right to the property of his wife, and all dominion over it, except by her free or voluntary consent or grant."[97] Similarly, Justice Joseph Henry Lumpkin of Georgia turned to the centrality of commerce and its role in civilization in admitting a merchant's book accounts as evidence. "The credit system of the world, upon which the rapidly developing commerce and civilization of the world, so materially depends, I say this as contradistinguished from the cash system, rests mainly upon the foundation to which I have just referred."[98] In many cases in the years before the Civil War, jurists invoked the word "civilization" in praising recent law reform.

As Americans celebrated the roles of technology from the axe to steam in subduing nature, we also drew upon the technology of law to help with that process. The effect of civilization and law appeared in the order brought to the landscapes, from fences to buildings and other human structures on the land.

As with other landscapes of the era, like William Sonntag's now missing series *The Progress of Civilization*,[99] the landscapes in *American Scenery* are optimistic. They present pictures of continual upward progress; this is also the picture that judges and lawyers presented. The artwork presents a vision and at the center of that vision is a nation ordered through law. Central to that vision were stable property rights and gradually evolving property rules that promoted commerce. In contrast to the eighteenth century writers who spoke of humans as thriving in a state of nature, Chancellor James Kent's *Commentaries* explained that property and civilization were related. "Man was fitted and intended by the author of his being for society and for the acquisition and enjoyment of property."[100]

> The sense of property is graciously bestowed on mankind, for the purpose of rousing them from sloth, and stimulating them to action; and so long as the right of acquisition is exercised in conformity to the social relations, and the moral obligations which spring from them, it ought to be sacredly protected. The natural and active sense of property pervades the foundations of social improvement. It leads to the cultivation of the earth, the institution of government, the establishment of justice, the acquisition of the comforts of life, the growth of the useful arts, the spirit of commerce, the productions of taste, the erections of charity, and the display of the benevolent affections.[101]

As Kent explained to generations of American lawyers through his *Commentaries on American Law*, the evolution of property rights occurred alongside the evolution of society, from the "savage state" to "polished nations."[102]

---

97 *Id.* at 377.
98 *Ganahl v. Shore*, 24 Ga. 17, 25 (1858).
99 Miller, *supra* note 29, at 138–42.
100 2 James Kent, *Commentaries on American Law* 318 (5th ed. 1844).
101 *Id.* at 319.
102 *Id.* at 318.

The artwork of *American Scenery* illustrates that evolution from wild nature to refined cities in mid-nineteenth century America. As landscape art depicted the dominion that Americans exercised over the land, it helped confirm the cultural support for that dominion. It served as a graphic measure of how Americans thought about their relationship to property and to nature, as well as the centrality of law in facilitating sovereignty over land and people.

**Acknowledgements**

The authors would like to thank Jim Smith for his help on issues big and small and his characteristically insightful edits and good humor.

# PART IV
# Regulatory Property

Chapter 8

# The Rise and Fall of the "Underclass": Ideology and Governmental Exclusion of the Poor through Zoning

David Ray Papke

During the final quarter of the twentieth century a striking number of journalists, sociologists, and politicians came to conceptualize the 10–12 percent of the American population living in impoverished center-cities as an "underclass." The conceptualization and the concomitant label carried with it a pronounced sympathy for the underclass and its plight, and also a preference for welfare and job creation programs that could aid the underclass. The conceptualization, label, sympathies, and policy preferences constituted a pronounced ideological construct, with "ideology" being understood not as duplicitous falsehood but rather a normative set of ideas beneficial to selected groups and interests. At its peak, the power of the "underclass" as an ideological construct was not to be underestimated.

The ideological notion of an "underclass" made its presence felt in law, a discourse in which ideology is frequently evident. In particular, certain courts acted to counter exclusionary zoning, a practice especially common in the new, outlying suburbs. While an end to exclusionary zoning could not in itself have ended the impoverishment of the underclass, the phenomenon of exclusionary zoning is nevertheless particularly disconcerting. When suburbs zone in ways that keep the underclass out, these suburbs in effect consign the underclass to rundown, center-city neighborhoods with high crime rates, drug problems, and deficient social capital. Exclusionary zoning physically and symbolically suggests members of the underclass are neither part of nor welcome in the American mainstream.

Unfortunately, as the twentieth century drew to a close, attention to the "underclass" declined precipitously. The urban poor did not disappear and, if anything, continued to grow in numbers and as a percentage of the population. The urban poor also remained concentrated in the decaying cores of America's increasingly postindustrial cities. Yet the notion of an "underclass" was first turned against the urban poor, and, then, by the start of the twenty-first century, notions of the "underclass" virtually vanished from policy-making and political discourse. Journalists, sociologists, and politicians came increasingly to blame the urban poor for their own poverty, and programs providing the urban poor with the entitlements and jobs necessary to raise their social standing gradually fell by the wayside. The courts largely abandoned their efforts to put a stop to the practice of exclusionary zoning related to class.

The rise and fall of the "underclass" as an emergent ideological construct and as a prompt for legal change was neither simple nor one-directional. The dominant ideology, after all, manifests itself in complex ways, and the very complexity obscures ideology to some extent and thereby enhances its effectiveness. That being said, a dominant ideology usually tends toward the preservation of the status quo. Power moved to minimize the clout of "underclass" ideology, turning the notion in a negative direction by using it to deplore the urban poor. Power then dropped the construct altogether. As Eva Cherniavsky has observed, "power operates to *fix* social and political relations and to *suture* individuals and collectives to what will therefore appear—if the 'fix' holds—as the natural or given contours of their identities, communities, nations, or worlds."[1]

## Discovering the Underclass

Urban poverty is hardly new in the United States, but perceptions and understandings of it have changed over time. In the earliest decades of the Republic and especially after the Financial Panic of 1819, evangelical reformers worried about the growing number of "paupers" in American cities and built poorhouses and facilities in which the paupers' characters might be improved.[2] In the middle decades of the nineteenth century, more secular reformers singled out the urban poor as both the cause and victim of social disorder, and Charles Loring Brace's Children's Aid Society actually transported thousands of perceived "street urchins" to farms and villages in the Midwest.[3] In the final decades of the nineteenth century and early decades of the twentieth century, a massive immigration from Europe contributed to both a growth in the number of poor Americans "and the widespread panic about poverty that would grip the nation."[4]

Concern about the urban poor continued into the post-World War II era. Starting in the 1960s and then extending into the 1970s, commentators began referring to the urban poor as an "underclass." The renowned Swedish economist Gunnar Myrdal, for example, wrote as early as 1962 of the American "under-class," hyphenating the term in the process.[5] This group had become recognizable, Myrdal thought, just as the last batches of immigrants from southern and eastern Europe and their descendants once and for all became integrated in American society. In Myrdal's conceptualization, the "under-class" consisted of "unemployed and, gradually,

1 Eva Cherniavsky, *Neocitizenship and Critique*, Social Text, Summer 2009, at 1, 2.
2 Paul Boyer, *Urban Masses and Moral Order in America, 1820–1920*, at 87 (1978).
3 *See id.* at 85–6.
4 David Wagner, *Ordinary People: In and Out of Poverty in the Gilded Age* 25 (2008).
5 Gunnar Myrdal, *Challenge to Affluence* 34 (1962).

unemployable and underemployed persons and families at the bottom of society."[6] The line between the working class and the "under-class," he warned, had become almost "a caste line, since the children in this class tend to become as poorly endowed as their parents."[7]

Myrdal's scholarship seems not to have caused the surge in commentary on the "underclass" in the late 1970s and immediately thereafter, but at that point in time large numbers of journalists, sociologists, and politicians began to speak of the urban poor as an "underclass." These groups did not agree on a precise definition of "underclass" or on what to do about the urban poor's problems. However, they did agree that United States, and especially its largest cities, had become the home of a large, semi-permanent "underclass," and that "a devastating gulf" existed "between the underclass and mainstream life."[8]

The journalists, sociologists, and politicians who spoke so passionately about the "underclass" during the 1970s and 1980s can be thought of in a non-pejorative way as "ideologues," that is, expounders and promoters of normative systems of thought that might relate to public affairs. This is perhaps most obviously the case with politicians, and, indeed, ideology is clearly manifest in politics. However, many individuals wearing many hats—law enforcement officials, ministers, professors, film directors, artists, and others—sometimes speak and write ideologically. "Ideology" consists of a set of images, ideas, beliefs, and even logic; and "ideologues" create and communicate the set. The journalists, sociologists, and politicians who emphasized the notion of an "underclass" and related attitudes and policies were adding to the existing ideological range. As noted at the outset, the "underclass" as an ideological construct was new and emergent.

Among the various groups of commentators that came to discuss the underclass, journalists stood first in line. The initial extended journalistic treatment of the underclass appeared as a cover story in the August 29, 1977, issue of *Time,* the nation's leading newsweekly.[9] The article, in keeping with *Time's* policies at the time, did not sport the name of an individual author and most likely was group-written. Focusing on the residents of American ghettos, the article stressed these individuals' lack of jobs, weak family structures, and tendency toward crime and violence. The article said the underclass lived in "a different world, a place of pock-marked streets, gutted tenements and broken hopes."[10] Lest *Time's* huge middle-class readership have difficulty imagining this sector of the population, the magazine's editors included gripping visual imagery along with the written text. The sizable picture spread featured children playing on rubble, defiant teenagers

6 *Id.*

7 *Id.* at 38.

8 *See* J. David Greenstone, *Culture, Responsibility, and the Underclass, in* The Urban Underclass 405 (Christopher Jencks & Paul E. Peterson eds., 1991).

9 *The American Underclass—Destitute and Desperate in the Land of Plenty*, Time, Aug. 29, 1977, at 17.

10 *Id.* at 23.

staring menacingly into the camera, and an elderly woman sitting on a battered garbage can.

Comparable articles followed in the early 1980s, the most notable being a three-part series by Ken Auletta in the *New Yorker*.[11] Like many of his journalistic brethren, Auletta assumed most members of the underclass were members of minority groups, but the underclass is not defined by race. Recent immigrants, regardless of their country or continent of origin, might become members of the underclass. Caucasians also belong to the underclass, although journalists tended to overlook them because poor Caucasians are not as concentrated in distinct urban neighborhoods as are minority members of the underclass.

Poverty and a tenuous relationship to the labor market define the underclass, and it is in this sense quite different than the "working class" or proletariat, which is central and favored in Marxian theory. For Marx, it seemed likely that exploited industrial workers would seize control from the bourgeoisie and lead the way to socialism and eventually communism. The social configuration in Marxian theory that most closely resembles the underclass is the "lumpen proletariat," a group Marx took to consist primarily of vagabonds and petty criminals.[12] Marx hardly thought the lumpen proletariat would assist the proletariat in its struggle for liberation.[13]

Struck by the flowering of journalistic treatments of the underclass, Herbert J. Gans used a Lexis database to survey three newsmagazines *(Newsweek, Time,* and *U.S. News and World Report)* and three major daily newspapers *(Chicago Tribune, Los Angeles Times,* and *New York Times)*. His study showed clearly the increase in references to and commentaries on the underclass by journalists. There was a huge increase during the early 1980s vis-à-vis the late 1970s and another comparable increase in the late 1980s vis-à-vis the early 1980s.[14]

With the underclass being recognized and discussed in so many magazines and newspapers, it is not surprising that academic sociologists began scrutinizing the apparent class formation. The most prominent and respected of the sociologists to address the subject of the underclass was William Julius Wilson. He sought to place the phenomenon of an American underclass in historical context. The underclass, he argued, had emerged largely because of post-World War II deindustrialization and the changes in the American labor market. As industry closed down or moved to foreign countries, access to good jobs came to depend increasingly on

---

11 Auletta's articles appeared on Nov. 16, 23, and 30, 1981, and were then collected in Ken Auletta, *The Underclass* (1982; revised ed., 1999).

12 *See* Karl Marx, *The Eighteenth Brumaire of Louis Bonaparte, in* Marx & Engels: Basic Writings on Politics and Philosophy 320, 343–4 (Lewis S. Feuer ed., 1959).

13 Marx described the lumpen proletariat as "social scum, that passively rotting mass thrown off by the lowest layers of old society." Karl Marx, *Manifesto of the Communist Party, in* Marx & Engels, *supra* note 12, at 18.

14 Herbert J. Gans, *The War Against the Poor: The Underclass and Antipoverty Policy* 37 (1995).

educational criteria. Poorly educated urban Americans found their employment options limited and, in some cases, nonexistent. In Wilson's words, the underclass was "the very bottom of the economic hierarchy and not only includes those lower-class workers whose income falls below the poverty level but also the more or less permanent welfare recipients, the long-term unemployed, and those who have officially dropped out of the labor market."[15]

While Wilson's emphasis was chiefly on the economic reasons for the emergence of the underclass, he also insisted that problems of underclass joblessness were "reinforced by an increasing social isolation in impoverished neighborhoods."[16] Wilson, in other words, invoked a spatial element; he was aware of where the members of the underclass lived. He noted that starting in the 1970s middle-class families had moved out of the center-city neighborhoods and that the number of such neighborhoods with poverty rates above 40 percent had strikingly increased.[17] These neighborhoods were not only physically run-down, but also deficient in social safeguards and supports. In this extremely debilitating environment, members of the underclass might experience frustration and boredom, and social pathologies including but not limited to drug use, prostitution, and criminal behavior might result.[18]

Law contributed to the spatial aspect of the problem as suburban governments increasingly used zoning ordinances to exclude the underclass from the suburbs. These ordinances, of course, do not refer to the underclass or the poor. References of this sort would make the ordinances vulnerable to legal challenges, not to mention registering as politically problematic. However, the poor can be excluded through various indirect techniques, such as zoning for non-residential uses only, requiring minimum lot sizes or square footage, and restricting the number of bedrooms. These techniques are neither secret nor particularly crafty. Authors of standard zoning guides outline them for the uninformed.[19]

Before long, politicians and elected officials were also deploring the development of an underclass in the midst of American prosperity. President Jimmy Carter, for example, created a commission in 1979 to consider challenges for the 1980s, and a sub-committee of the commission published a report that focused in large part on the underclass.[20] The report bemoaned contemporary

---

15 William Julius Wilson, *The Declining Significance of Race: Blacks and Changing American Institutions* 156 (1980).

16 William Julius Wilson, *The Underclass: Issues, Perspectives, and Public Policy, in* The Ghetto Underclass: Social Science Perspectives 20 (William Julius Wilson ed., 1993).

17 *See id.* at 12–13.

18 *See id.*

19 *See* 3 Patricia E. Salkin, *American Law of Zoning* §§ 22–17 (5th ed. 2008); Peter Salsich & Timothy J. Tryniecki, *Land Use Regulation* 379–82 (2d ed. 2003).

20 *See* President's Commission for a National Agenda for the Eighties, *Report of the Panel on Policies and Prospects for Metropolitan and Nonmetropolitan America: Urban America in the Eighties* 16–23 (1980).

cities' inability to "generate diffuse social and economic well-being" for the underclass as American cities had for earlier waves of immigrants.[21] Traditional economic opportunities in industry and manufacturing, the report noted, migrated out of the cities, leaving the underclass behind and "increasingly distressed."[22] Furthermore, the report somberly added, "the condition of a sizeable portion of the underclass is relatively permanent … . Avenues of escape are shrinking, unreliable, and inadequate."[23]

Not to be outdone by a commission established by the executive branch, the US Congress referred to the underclass routinely in its debates and deliberations during the 1980s. The term "underclass" as a referent for a certain socioeconomic sector of the population, in other words, became standard in lawmakers' discussions. According to Herbert J. Gans, for the years 1985–93 the average annual usage of "underclass" in the *Congressional Record* was 40.3.[24]

Of particular interest are the formal Congressional hearings on the underclass held in May 1989 by the Joint Economic Committee,[25] whose membership consisted of ten members of the House of Representatives and another ten members from the Senate. Representative David. R. Obey of Wisconsin chaired the hearings. When the Committee convened, Obey announced the goal to review the plight "of what has been described by many as America's underclass."[26] Many Americans, Obey thought, "are unaware of the real face of economic deprivation, but highly visible manifestations of the tragedy of the underclass, like soaring teenage pregnancies, drug murders, [and] chaotic schools, have alerted the [n]ation as a whole to the fact that the problem affects us all."[27]

The Joint Economic Committee heard testimony and took formal statements from experts on the underclass, including Professor Lawrence M. Mead of New York University's Department of Politics and Professor Elijah Anderson of the University of Pennsylvania's Department of Sociology. Mead was especially sensitive to the way the "isolation of the inner-city poor" in inner-city neighborhoods cut the underclass off from the mainstream economy.[28] Anderson pointed out that the best employment opportunities for poorly educated members of the underclass were low-skilled service jobs as waitpersons and cooks in fast-food restaurants or as cleaning and security workers in malls and office parks.

---

21 *Id.* at 17.

22 *Id.*

23 *Id.*

24 *See* Gans, *supra* note 14, at 46.

25 *See* The Underclass: Hearing Before the Joint Economic Comm., 101st Cong. (1989).

26 *Id.* at 1.

27 *Id.*

28 *Id.* at 23.

Unfortunately, most of these jobs "are located many miles from the inner-city, out of range of so many young black people."[29]

While commission reports from the executive branch and Congressional hearings provided important insights regarding the "underclass," the courts were most prepared to act regarding the problems of the "underclass," especially those related to exclusionary zoning. One might understandably assume in this regard that the federal courts would invoke federal constitutional law in an attempt to stop exclusionary zoning by suburban governments, but, in a string of important zoning decisions from the early 1970s, the federal courts in effect disabled themselves as legal actors in this area.[30] Instead, the state courts proved more willing and able to address the ways suburban governments used zoning laws and other legal devices to exclude the underclass and thereby consign them to run-down areas of the center-cities.

Courts in New Jersey were the most active in attempting to thwart exclusionary zoning practices designed to keep the poor and working class from taking up residence in selected communities. Starting in the mid-1970s and continuing through the mid-1980s, the NAACP and other parties sued the Township of Mount Laurel, with appeals of lower-court decisions reaching the New Jersey Supreme Court on two occasions. The Township of Mount Laurel is exactly the kind of outlying suburban community most likely to engage in exclusionary zoning. It is located on the eastern edge of the sprawling metropolitan area that includes Philadelphia and its suburbs to the west of the Delaware River in Pennsylvania and Camden, Cherry Hill, and other municipalities to the east of the Delaware River in New Jersey. Philadelphia and Camden in particular are home to substantial underclass populations. Some members of these populations might have liked to move to outlying parts of the growing metropolitan area in order to be near low-skilled service jobs and, more generally, to escape their center-city neighborhoods. Outlying suburbs such as the Township of Mount Laurel, meanwhile, were prepared to zone in ways that excluded the urban poor. As subsequently became clear, members of the Supreme Court of New Jersey were especially concerned with exclusionary zoning by outlying suburbs unwilling to accommodate the poor and working class in expanding metropolitan areas.

In 1975, before concern with an "underclass" had become pronounced, the first decision of the New Jersey Supreme Court set the stage for the aggressive judicial law-making of the 1980s.[31] The Court concluded that the Township of Mount Laurel excluded low and moderate-income people by, in effect, over-zoning for industry in the remaining large swaths of undeveloped land in the Township. The Court quoted with approval the trial court's statement that the Township of Mount Laurel "through its zoning ordinances has exhibited economic discrimination in that the

29 *Id.* at 43.

30 *See* David Ray Papke, *Keeping the Underclass in Its Place: Zoning, the Poor, and Residential Segregation*, 41 Urban Lawyer 787, 797–804 (2009).

31 *S. Burlington Cnty. NAACP v. Twp. of Mount Laurel*, 336 A.2d 713 (N.J. 1975).

poor have been deprived of adequate housing and the opportunity to secure the construction of subsidized housing."[32] Like other outlying suburbs, the Township of Mount Laurel "in effect builds a wall around itself to keep out those people or entities not adding favorably to the tax base."[33] In reaching this conclusion, the Court was appreciative of one of zoning's oldest secrets: zoning is about not merely land uses and building types, but also people and classes of people. Citing the New Jersey Constitution's promise that state citizens possessed the "natural and unalienable" right "of acquiring, possessing, and protecting property,"[34] the Court invalidated the Township of Mount Laurel's zoning ordinance to the extent it failed to "make realistically possible the opportunity for an appropriate variety and choice of housing for all categories of people who may desire to live there, ... including all those of low or moderate income."[35] The Township of Mount Laurel, in the court's view, had violated the obligation of New Jersey municipalities located in or near metropolitan areas to take on their "fair share of the present and prospective regional need" to house the poor and those of modest means.[36]

Eight years later, the New Jersey Supreme Court revisited and reaffirmed matters in a decision commonly known as *Mount Laurel II*.[37] By this point in time, public concern with the "underclass" had heightened, and ideological sensitivities and concerns clearly played a role in the Court's decision. The Justices' ideological preferences did not derive simply from their party affiliations, as the decision on appeal was unanimous. Ideology also did not manifest as variable perceptions of facts, a pattern one scholar has underscored in selected cases.[38] Instead, members of the Court seemed more generally to have taken to heart the concerns and "logic" of the "underclass" construct as emergent ideology. This ideology is controlling in *Mount Laurel II*.

In more specific terms, the Court was detectably irritated by the Township of Mount Laurel's piddling efforts to abide by the Court' s earlier demands:

> The *Mount Laurel* case itself threatens to become infamous. After all this time, ten years after the trial court's initial order invalidating its zoning ordinance, Mount Laurel remains afflicted with a blatantly exclusionary ordinance. Papered over with studies, rationalized by hired experts, the ordinance at its core is true to nothing but Mount Laurel's determination to exclude the poor.[39]

---

32 *Id.* at 723.

33 *Id.*

34 N.J. Const. art. I, § 1.

35 *See S. Burlington Cnty. NAACP*, 336 A.2d at 731–2.

36 *Id.* at 732.

37 *S. Burlington Cnty. NAACP v. Twp. of Mount Laurel*, 456 A.2d 390 (N.J. 1983).

38 *See* Dan M. Kahan, *"Ideology in" or "Cultural Cognition of" Judging: What Difference Does It Make?* 92 Marq. L. Rev. 413 (2009).

39 *S. Burlington Cnty. NAACP*, 456 A.2d at 410.

The Court was also irritated that other New Jersey suburbs had failed to take on anything resembling their "fair share" of housing for the poor, and the Court in fact combined its review of the Mount Laurel ordinance with reviews of ordinances from five other New Jersey municipalities.[40] Resentful of the suburbs' intransigence, the Court paused to imagine what the state would look like if such action continued:

> [P]oor people forever zoned out of substantial areas of the state, not because housing could not be built for them but because they are not wanted; poor people forced to live in urban slums forever not because suburbia, developing rural areas, fully developed residential sections, seashore resorts, and other attractive locations could not accommodate them, but simply because they are not wanted.[41]

In what two commentators characterized as "an exercise of judicial activism rarely seen,"[42] the Court in *Mount Laurel II* tried both to stop the suburban resistance to *Mount Laurel I* and also to get municipalities and developers in metropolitan areas to actually build inexpensive, multi-family housing that members of the underclass might afford to rent. The Court warned suburbs that "numberless" projections would not suffice and that the number of "fair share" housing units needed immediately and in the future had to be provided.[43] The Court went so far as to list the kinds of "inclusionary zoning" steps that should be taken: density bonuses for developers who provide for low and moderate-income families, mandatory set-asides for low and moderate-income housing, over-zoning for low and moderate-income housing, and acceptance of mobile homes and mobile home parks.[44] The Court's call for the inclusion of mobile homes merits emphasis. Mobile homes constitute one of the most viable rental housing options for the underclass, but many suburbs do all they can to keep out mobile homes.[45] The opposition to mobile homes relates in part to the housing itself and also in larger part to the type of people thought most likely to live in mobile home parks. Since at least the 1950s people who live in mobile homes have been called trailer trash, and mobile home parks have struck the members of the middle and upper classes "as a new kind of slum."[46] The Supreme Court of New Jersey sought to counter this kind of biased thinking.[47]

---

40 They were the Townships of Mahwah, Franklin, Chester, and Clinton and the Borough of Carteret. *Id.*

41 *Id.* at 415.

42 William B. Stoebuck & Dale A. Whitman, *The Law of Property* 633 (3d ed. 2000).

43 *S. Burlington Cnty. NAACP*, 456 A.2d at 419.

44 *Id.* at 419.

45 *See* Alan D. Walls, *Wheel Estate: The Rise and Decline of Mobile Homes* v (1997).

46 *Id.* at 173.

47 *See S. Burlington Cnty. NAACP*, 456 A.2d at 450–51.

The efforts of the New Jersey Supreme Court enabled only the tiniest percentage of the underclass to escape run-down, center-city neighborhoods, but the era's more important development was its enhanced appreciation of the plight of the urban poor. Journalists, sociologists, and politicians had taken to calling the group the "underclass." This conceptualization and the concomitant sympathies and policy preferences can be thought of as an emergent ideological construct, and it had the potential to engender sympathy among policymakers and jurists. Legal discourse is always open to ideological input. In particular, the notion of the "underclass" contributed to the sense that it was unjust for suburbs to exclude the urban poor, to consign them to the dangerous inner-city, and generally to block their access to the mainstream of American socioeconomic life.

## Abandoning the Underclass

As noted earlier, the process by which conceptualizations, labels, attitudes, and policy preferences emerge and become or fail to become part of the dominant ideology is complicated. The notion of an "underclass" appeared in the late-1970s and seemed during the 1980s to energize efforts to end exclusionary zoning, and also perhaps to contribute to other varieties of legal change. But even as the notion of an "underclass" gained momentum, spokesmen for middle and upper-class class interests began developing their own unsympathetic understandings of the underclass and its plight. Leaders of both major political parties took to blaming the urban poor for their poverty and for the physical decay and deficient social capital in the center-city neighborhoods where they had to live. By the end of the twentieth century, the conceptualization of the urban poor as an "underclass" disappeared from political discourse.

The journalists who had originally reported on the "underclass" were sympathetic. A caption under a picture in the 1977 *Time* article of a baby, teenaged mother, and young grandmother for example, read "Discrimination's Sad Testament."[48] However, the 1980s saw a pronounced downturn in the economy, and the time became right for scapegoating. Conservative journalists began to blame the underclass for sapping resources and, more generally, for refusing to embody traditional American beliefs in hard work, thrift, and a sort of secular puritanism.

The most prominent conservative journalist to report on the underclass was Myron Magnet, who authored, among other pieces, a widely read 1987 article in *Fortune*.[49] Magnet was not content to think of the underclass as the most needy sector of the population. He instead cast underclass communities as "urban knots that threaten to become enclaves of permanent poverty and vice."[50] What primarily distinguishes members of the underclass, Magnet asserted, "is not so much their

48 *The American Underclass*, *supra* note 9, at 34.
49 Myron Magnet, *America's Underclass: What To Do?* Fortune, May 11, 1987 at 13.
50 *Id.* at 13.

poverty or race as their behavior—their chronic lawlessness, drug use, out-of-wedlock births, non-work, welfare dependency, and school failure. 'Underclass' describes a state of mind and a way of life. It is at least as much a cultural as an economic condition."[51]

The sociological literature also changed its orientation. William Julius Wilson's scholarly work was such an impressive accomplishment that many sociologists continued on the trail he had blazed,[52] but during the 1980s sociologists who did not share Wilson's politics and approaches also began to write on the "underclass." The conservative sociologist Christopher Jencks, for example, asked if the notion of an "underclass" helped policy-makers understand the variety of changes experienced by the urban poor:

> Everyone who stops to think recognizes that the world is untidy in this sense. We use class labels precisely because we want to make the world seem tidier than it is. The purpose of labels is to draw attention to the differences between classes. But by emphasizing differences between classes, such labels inevitably encourage us to forget about the much larger differences that exist *within* classes.[53]

The sociologist Herbert J. Gans, a more progressive academic than Jencks, expressed concern "about the harm being done by the word 'underclass' as a new label for condemning the poor as undeserving."[54] Labels such as the "underclass," Gans warned, "focus on behavior that hides the poverty causing it, and substitutes as its cause moral or cultural or genetic failures."[55]

Eventually the criticism from his peers influenced Wilson himself. In 1990, in his presidential address to the American Sociological Association, Wilson announced that he was giving up on the term "underclass."[56] Fearing that the term had become a pejorative way of talking about inner-city blacks, he suggested using the phrase "ghetto poor" instead.[57] Wilson was a friend of the urban poor, but his alternative phrase seemed unlikely to inspire any solidarity or lead to more aggressive political demands by the urban poor.

In the political realm, a sea change occurred following the election of Ronald Reagan to the Presidency in the fall of 1980. His Omnibus Budget Reconciliation

---

51 *Id.*

52 For a review of major sociological treatments of the "underclass," *see* John Welshman, *Underclass—A History of the Excluded, 1880–2000,* at 138–55 (2006).

53 Christopher Jencks, *Rethinking Social Policy: Race, Poverty, and the Underclass* 201–02 (1992).

54 Gans, *supra* note 14, at xi.

55 *Id.* at 59.

56 *See* Alice O'Connor, *Poverty Knowledge: Social Science, Social Policy, and the Poor in Twentieth-Century U.S. History* 272 (2001).

57 For a discussion of Wilson's disavowal of the term "underclass," *see* Bill E. Larson, *Meditations on Integration, in* The Underclass Question 6 (Bill E. Lawson ed., 1992).

Act of 1981[58] slashed federal antipoverty funding and restricted eligibility for assorted federal programs. The goal seemed to be an elimination of aid for all but the "truly needy."[59] In the opinion of some, the Reagan Administration's so-called "War on Drugs," which provided funding primarily for prisons and law enforcement, in effect replaced what Democrats had in the 1960s called the "War on Poverty."[60] In addition, the Reagan Administration's willingness to turn to conservative think tanks for guidance regarding social policy ultimately played a major role in how politicians and policy-makers conceptualized and labeled the urban poor.[61] Think tanks such as the Heritage Foundation, Manhattan Institute, American Enterprise Institute, and Hudson Institute did not perceive a semi-permanent and growing "underclass" that needed government benefits and job programs to escape poverty.

The most important individual thinker during the Reagan-Bush years was Charles Murray. One scholar has characterized Murray's *Losing Ground*[62] as "arguably the most influential book in social policy published in America in the 1980s."[63] Using analytic research to buoy his claims, Murray insisted that the fortunes of the poor had deteriorated in recent decades due to government policies. "The first effect of the new rules," he said, "was to make it profitable for the poor to behave in the short term in ways that were destructive in the long term."[64] Especially harmful, in Murray's opinion, were government programs and handouts: "We tried to provide more for the poor and produced more poor instead. We tried to remove the barriers to escape from poverty, and inadvertently built a trap."[65] Murray argued in a vein likely to appeal to blue-collar workers—many of whom would become so-called "Reagan Democrats"—that it was unfair to workers and laid-off workers to provide welfare for those who would not seek employment.[66] In Murray's often charged language, the latter were "drones."[67]

What should be done about the situation? Murray invoked one of the greatest staples of the dominant ideology: individual achievement according to merit. This was "hardly a new ideal in American thought," he acknowledged, but "the ideal itself has never lapsed."[68]

58 Omnibus Reconciliation Act of 1981, P.L. 97–35, 95 Stat. 357–933 (1981).
59 *See* O'Connor, *supra* note 56, at 242.
60 *See* Helene Slessarev, *The Betrayal of the Urban Poor* 11 (1997).
61 *See* O'Connor, *supra* note 56, at 2, 44, 242.
62 Charles Murray, *Losing Ground: American Social Policy, 1950–80* (1984).
63 Welshman, *supra* note 52, at 134.
64 Murray, *supra* note 62, at 9.
65 *Id.*
66 *See id.* at 198.
67 *Id.*
68 *Id.* at 233.

> Some people are better than others. They deserve more of society's rewards, of which money is only one small part. A principled function of social policy is to make sure they have the opportunity to reap those rewards. Government cannot identify the worthy, but it can protect a society in which the worthy can identify themselves.[69]

Murray thought American society was very good at reinforcing the investment of an individual in himself, but it had failed to reinforce this for the poor.[70] Instead of welfare payments and special benefits, the poor needed the freedom to act on their own. "It is time to get out of their way."[71] Alice O'Connor describes *Losing Ground* as "not just a critique of Great Society programs but an attack on the idea that big government liberalism could help the poor at all."[72]

It is tempting to associate this line of thought with Reaganite Republicans, but by the early 1990s many Democrats were thinking in the same way. Bill Clinton himself came to accept the notions of individual responsibility among the poor, the market as a distributor of social good, and the need to crack down on welfare cheaters. In his Presidential campaign of 1992, Clinton suggested that there should be a "new covenant" between the government and the poor and that, as part of this covenant, welfare should be available only to those who play by the "rules of the game."[73] After his election, Clinton carried through on his campaign promise to "end welfare as we know it."[74] Congress voted to replace the familiar Aid to Families with Dependent Children (AFDC) welfare entitlement with the more restricted and limited Temporary Assistance for Needy Families (TANF) program, and Clinton eagerly signed so-called "welfare reform" into law. Realizing that "welfare reform" had become a bipartisan demand, three high-ranking Department of Health and Human Services officials resigned in protest over Clinton's statements and actions.[75]

Nobody felt the changes more than those in the actual underclass, and Clinton himself seemed to appreciate this as he continued to speak of the "underclass." However, the attitudes and policies related to the urban poor had changed. In accepting the nomination at the Democratic National Convention in 1996, for example, Clinton spoke of building a bridge to the twenty-first century for the poor. Acknowledging, as had so many others, that the urban poor were contained and concentrated in the depressed center-cities, he said the "bridge" could perhaps

---

69 *Id.* at 234.

70 *See id.* at 234–5.

71 *Id.* at 235.

72 O'Connor, *supra* note 56, at 249.

73 *See* William A. Kelso, *Poverty and the Underclass: Changing Perceptions of the Poor in America* 180–1 (1994).

74 *See* Richard Delgado, *The Myth of Upward Mobility*, 68 U. Pitt. L. Rev. 879, 908 (2007).

75 *See* O'Connor, *supra* note 56, at 5.

end the poor's "exile" and "isolation."[76] However, Clinton added the hope that his approach "ends the permanent underclass."[77] Just how this would happen without welfare entitlements and job programs was unclear. Clinton and his party seemed to have accepted the idea that members of the underclass need only roll up their sleeves and get to work.

Given the ideological shift among journalists and sociologists and in the Congress and the White House, judicial efforts to end exclusionary zoning not surprisingly ground to a halt. The practice of exclusionary zoning was aimed at perpetuating the concentration of the underclass in urban center-cities. It should have been troubling to courts on the east and west coasts and in the rapidly de-industrializing Midwest that growing generations of the poor were packed into the center-cities and that many newer, outlying suburbs were doing all they could to keep out the poor. But alas, few courts rose to the challenge as did the New Jersey courts of the early 1980s.

The two states that are most frequently praised in the secondary literature for their concern with exclusionary zoning are New York and Pennsylvania. New York has unambiguous case law requiring that a zoning ordinance be struck down if it was enacted with an exclusionary purpose or if it showed a lack of regard for regional housing needs and had an unjustifiable exclusionary effect.[78] However, the New York courts have also held that the challenges of an exclusionary zoning ordinance must show the ordinance was *the* reason for the inadequate development of inexpensive rental housing. The claim can be dismissed if rising housing costs or economic stagnation was also a factor.[79] This places an almost impossible burden on the plaintiff and makes the core New York doctrine ineffective in fighting exclusionary zoning.[80]

In Pennsylvania, the Supreme Court appeared to accept something resembling a "fair share" approach, but in the opinion of commentators the state's approach is fatally flawed because the law revolves around land uses rather than classes of people and what they can pay for housing.[81] The Pennsylvania Supreme Court has recognized "a clear distinction between restrictions in use of property and the exclusion of classes of people" and insisted "only the former is the proper

---

76 PBS Newshour, "President Bill Clinton—Acceptance Speech," Aug. 29, 1996, http://www.pbs.org/newshour/bb/politics/july–dec96/clinton_08-29.html?print (last visited Dec. 20, 2012). .

77 *Id.*

78 *Robert E. Kurzius Inc. v. Inc. Vill. of Upper Brookville*, 414 N.E.2d 680, 684 (N.Y. 1980).

79 *See Suffolk Housing Services v. Town of Brookhaven*, 511 N.E. 2d 67, 70 (N.Y. 1987).

80 *See* Henry A. Span, *How the Courts Should Fight Exclusionary Zoning*, 32 Seton Hall L. Rev. 1 (2001).

81 *See* Katrin C. Rowan, *Anti-Exclusionary Zoning in Pennsylvania: A Weapon for Developers, A Loss for Low-Income Pennsylvanians*, 80 Temp. L. Rev. 1271, 1272 (2007).

subject of the analysis we synthesized."[82] Furthermore, under Pennsylvania law a developer may demonstrate that zoning is exclusionary under the existing doctrine and build single family homes rather than the inexpensive multi-family rental housing that was originally proposed. The practice is apparently common and known in Pennsylvania as "sue and switch."[83]

Courts in other states have done even less in recent years to address exclusionary zoning. As a result, exclusionary zoning techniques—large minimum lots and floor areas, limits on multi-family housing, bans on mobile homes—"continue to be major obstacles to affordable housing today."[84] Indeed, minimum lot sizes continue to grow, "with ten-, twenty-, and even forty-acre lots in new ranchette subdivisions … . If these trends continue, then an increasing share of our urban regions will be off limits to Americans who cannot afford a big house on a big lot."[85]

Perhaps the saddest testimony to courts' inability or unwillingness to act aggressively to end exclusionary zoning comes from Mount Laurel Township itself. "Overall, the zoning pattern of Mount Laurel [was] neither more nor less exclusionary than that of most suburban communities,"[86] but by the 1980s Mount Laurel had become a symbol for the type of suburban community progressive courts had to confront. The Supreme Court of New Jersey had done just that, but as the twenty-first century dawned, Mount Laurel lacked diversity. The Township's minority population was 14.3 percent of its whole population, while New Jersey's minority population was 34 percent of the whole. Only 16 percent of Mount Laurel's housing units were rental units compared to 34 percent for all of New Jersey.[87]

Suburban exclusionary zoning, of course, was not the only reason the poor remained in the center-city. Lacking assets, the poor have virtually no access to suburban housing markets, and many of those who somehow scraped together a down payment and obtained a high-rate mortgage have in recent years faced foreclosure. But still, exclusionary zoning and the refusal of the appellate courts to eliminate or at least to limit the use of exclusionary zoning was the most distinctly "legal" factor in the poor's continued concentration in decaying center-cities.

The ideological winds have changed direction. Journalists, sociologists, and politicians grew less enamored with the "underclass" construct and the attitudes and policies it inspired. The courts—sponges of sorts for ideology—looked the other way when allegations and demonstrations of exclusionary zoning geared

82 *BAC, Inc. v. Bd. of Supervisors of Millcreek Twp.*, 633 A.2d 144, 147 (Pa. 1993).

83 *See* Rowan, *supra* note 81, at 1290–91.

84 Brian R. Lerman, *Mandatory Inclusionary Zoning—The Answer to the Affordable Housing Problem*, 33 B.C. Envtl. Aff. L. Rev. 383, 386–7 (2006).

85 Robert L. Liberty, *Abolishing Exclusionary Zoning: A Natural Policy Alliance for Environmentalists and Affordable Housing Advocates*, 30 B.C. Envtl. Aff. L. Rev. 581, 584 (2003).

86 *Id.* at 581 n.1.

87 *Id.* at 597.

to class came before them. What had seemed in the late 1970s and early 1980s to be an emergent ideological thrust was overwhelmed by a traditional, dominant ideology.

## Conclusion

It is too late to revive the ideological notion of an "underclass" and its concomitant sympathies and preferred policies. As the historian E. P. Thompson emphasized in his legendary *The Making of the English Working Class,* class "is an *historical* phenomenon … . Consciousness of class arises in the same way in different times and places, but never in *just* the same way."[88] Consciousness of a class also declines and disappears in different ways in different eras and societies, and when the consciousness of a class disappears, it is unlikely to reappear.

Consciousness of the "underclass" as an ideological formation first emerged in the late 1970s, built power during the 1980s, and then dramatically shifted during the Clinton Presidency, when the majority of policy-makers and social commentators came to accept and reassert the idea that members of the "underclass" were responsible for their own individual situations. In the early years of the twenty-first century the "underclass" construct virtually disappeared. Yet even if the ideological struggle related to the "underclass" is for all intents and purposes over, more general lessons are nevertheless available about the nature of ideology, the ways ideology might shift over time, and the importance of ideology in the legal discourse.

For starters, the rise and fall of the "underclass" as an ideological construct reminds us that certain abstracted, normative notions have greater ideological potential than others. While the notion of an "underclass" proved to have limited staying power, the actual term "underclass," which implied an unfamiliar netherworld, did have clout initially. Some have suggested that the term did help "to capture an intensity of poverty."[89] Writing of the use of the notion in the United Kingdom, Fred Robinson and Nicky Gregson said:

> There is no doubt that a careful use of the underclass as a term and a concept can be very effective. It can serve to highlight key problems: the fact of increasing polarization; the entrapment of the poorest and the absence of routes for upward social mobility; and the increased concentration of the poorest, the most disadvantaged, in a residualised rental housing sector.[90]

---

88 E.P. Thompson, *The Making of the English Working Class* 9, 10 (1966).

89 Carey Oppenheim & Lisa Harker, *Poverty: The Facts* 17 (3d ed. 1996).

90 Fred Robinson & Nicky Gregson, *The "Underclass"—A Class Apart?* 34 Critical Social Policy 38, 49 (1992).

Even a conservative commentator such as Charles Murray acknowledged that the notion of an "underclass" was eye-catching: "[c]ertainly, any report which purports to be about an 'underclass' rather than boring, old-fashioned, poverty is likely to receive greater media attention."[91]

As the large number of journalists, sociologists, and politicians who gravitated to the notion of an "underclass" during the 1980s confirms, the term and the discussion it invited had substantial ideological potential. The attraction of an ideological construct promoting the interests of the weak for bourgeois spokesmen and theorists is consequential. The weak and powerless, after all, need sympathy and support from the more powerful in order to have any hope to advance an emancipating, egalitarian program. The ideological construct of the "underclass," at least initially, appealed to members of the middle and upper classes in ways other notions did not.

In addition, the notion of the "underclass" had the potential to direct and energize the urban poor themselves. Writing of critically minded social groups in the dawning period of industrial capitalism prior to the appearance of socialist politics and modern labor activism, E.J. Hobsbawm observed that these groups in general could not mount a focused expression for their needs and aspirations.[92] The urban poor in the United States during the final decades of the twentieth century lived in a largely post-industrial as opposed to pre-industrial setting, but they too could have benefitted from a focused self-impression. According to Helene Slessarev, the urban poor are politically disabled in part because of their sense of powerlessness,[93] and a shared sense of being members of the "underclass" could conceivably have helped the urban poor break free of disabling attitudes.

Something resembling a "class consciousness" is perhaps more than we might expect among the urban poor. As noted earlier, the underclass is not the same as the working class, which is so central in Marxian and leftist thought. Affiliation with the working class largely derives from experiences within the realm of industrial production, and "[c]lass-consciousness is the way in which these experiences are handled in cultural terms; embodied in traditions, value-systems, ideas and institutional forms."[94] The experiences of the urban poor, by contrast, are shaped less by relations within industrial production and more by marginality in the labor market, containment within deteriorating urban neighborhoods, and problems associated with drugs, violence, crime, and severe health hazards. Rather than a "class-consciousness," a generalized sense of collectivity through shared denial is more likely. The "underclass" construct might have helped in this regard. Wilson's

91 Institute of Economic Affairs, *Charles Murray and the Underclass* 9–10 (Ruth Lister ed., 1996).

92 *See* E.J. Hobsbawm, *Primitive Rebels: Studies in Archaic Forms of Social Movements in the 19th and 20th Centuries* 10 (1965).

93 *See* Slessarev, *supra* note 60, at 12.

94 Thompson, *supra* note 88, at 10.

substitute notion of the "ghetto poor" holds little promise in this regard, and the phrase "urban poor" is equally uninspiring.

Decidedly fluid and permeable, the legal discourse is always open to ideology, be it emergent constructs related to the "underclass" or countless other possibilities. Delineations, comparisons, and conclusions are mainstays in the legal discourse, and as the influence of the "underclass" construct in the decisions of the Supreme Court of New Jersey illustrate, ideology can influence thought processes in both courtroom arguments and judicial decisions. And, indeed, the dominant ideology, which turned the notion of an "underclass" into something negative and then rejected it completely, also played its role in the legal discourse.

Why did the ideological notion of the "underclass" disappear? On one level, the alternative emphasis on individual responsibility, even for those trapped in post-industrial urban poverty, reflects a resurgence of the dominant ideology's traditional emphasis on the individual. Most Americans tend to believe that poverty results from a lack of effort, and this attitudinal predisposition overwhelmed a structural analysis emphasizing weak schools, poor housing, and especially a shortage of meaningful jobs.[95] Surely this ideological proclivity is well established in the legal discourse. As the legal historian Lawrence Friedman once observed, "If there is a single leitmotif of modern law, whether civil rights law, commercial law, family law, or the law of landlord and tenant, it is an extreme emphasis on the *individual,* and on individual choice and consent; the whole system turns on this point."[96] Once members of the urban poor are taken to be responsible for their own plight, we can hardly expect courts to speak out forcefully against attempts to keep the urban poor out of the suburbs *and* in the decrepit inner-cities.

On a more abstracted level, the eliding of the ideological notion of the "underclass" by the dominant ideology illustrates the uses of ideology by power. The "underclass" as an ideological construct was, after all, critically minded. It was a critique of claims and assumptions that social life is fair and just. When the construct was dropped, the urban poor lost a conceptualization and a label that had attracted support from the middle and upper classes. The notion of an "underclass" might also have contributed to political self-awareness for the urban poor and strengthened the group's demands for an end to their debilitating oppression, but that possibility also disappeared. In the present, the underclass continues to exist, but we are very unlikely to see it as such.

---

95 Studies have shown Europeans, by contrast, favor structural explanations for poverty; they are less inclined to point to personal weaknesses and shortcomings. *See* William Julius Wilson, *When Work Disappears: The World of the New Urban Poor* 95, 159–61 (1996).

96 Lawrence M. Friedman, *Law, Lawyers, and Popular Culture*, 98 Yale L. J. 1579, 1585 (1989).

# Chapter 9
# Governmental Marks: What Souvenirs Say About Speech and Sovereignty

Malla Pollack

Words have power. The ability to name a social group, especially one from which exit is difficult, confers enormous power over the group's members. A polity is such a social group, a social group partly defined by citizenship in a government-institution. Using the term "polity" in its broadest sense, this chapter discusses words and phrases which name the polity or evoke its persona, that is, "governmental marks." A mark or trademark[1] is an artificial persona created and controlled by the mark-holder. Legally classifying words as marks commodifies them, increasing the namer's power in two ways: it gives the words monetary value and provides the mark-holder with the legal right to prevent others from manipulating the words' meaning.

To prevent money from debasing the other metrics of value invested in the group's identity, such words, and such group's human members, need to be freed from the putative mark-holder's control. This chapter suggests refusing mark status to such words both in order to prioritize people over property and institutions (such as governments), and for a number of less-abstract policy reasons.

The concept of liberal[2] representative government is that government does what citizens tell it to do, while refraining (despite possible majority support) from some types of actions which overly intrude upon individuals' autonomy. This sketch assumes counter-factually that communication operates in only one direction: individuals with set goals speak to government; government listens. Both prongs of this picture are unrealistic. Individuals' goals are malleable. Governments are extremely loquacious.[3]

1 Technically, a "trademark" is a mark for a product; a "service mark" is a mark for a service. 15 U.S.C. § 1127. The difference between trademarks and service marks is legally irrelevant except for registration matters. *See* 3 Louis Altman & Malla Pollack, *Callmann on Unfair Competition, Trademarks and Monopolies* § 17A:9 (4th ed. 2012) [hereinafter Callmann]. "Mark" and "trademark" are often used interchangeably in situations, such as this chapter, in which the distinction between service marks and trademarks is not at issue.

2 "Liberal" is used in this chapter to refer to the concept of limited, citizen-serving government as discussed, for example, in John Stuart Mill, *On Liberty* (1859).

3 *See generally* Mark G. Yudof, *When Government Speaks* (1983).

This chapter discusses one type of talk broadcast by the government-as-institution neglected by the growing government speech literature—marketing.[4] The chapter explores the practices and professional literature on destination marketing through three interwoven strands of commentary: free speech, citizen-sovereignty, and trademark law. Viewed in conjunction, these perspectives demonstrate that governmental marks are problematic. The government of liberal-republican theory does not "own" or "control" its persona; sovereign citizens do. Furthermore, the group may not vote to limit any individual citizen's right to speak—especially about the government. Therefore, governmental marks should not be off-limits to any speaker, commercial or otherwise.

I am not proposing a ban on government's use of governmental marks. Such a suggestion would be unrealistic and, perhaps, counterproductive. My suggestion is that governmental marks not be treated as marks. Absent actual fraud or actual confusion, everyone should be able to use these designations.

Note, however, that not all marks used by governmental entities are "governmental marks." The Florida Sunshine Tree® represents citrus fruit, not the polity.[5] Nor is the government the only entity with pretensions to exclusive control of "governmental marks." For example, General Motors has aggressively, and to a large degree successfully, asserted common-law rights in the over-all look (trade dress) of the Hummer.[6] But the US military, not GM, is the source of the trade dress's consumer appeal. GMs' Hummer-brand SUVs are descendants of

---

4 The few other articles discussing government marks are largely descriptive. *See* 1 J. Thomas McCarthy, *McCarthy on Trademarks and Unfair Competition* § 9:7.50 (4th ed. 2012); William C. Garvert, *Government Trademarks*, 20 Idea 335 (1979); Sharon K. Sandeen, *Preserving the Public Trust in State-owned Intellectual Property: A Recommendation for Legislative Action*, 32 McGeorge L. Rev. 385 (2001). One student recognized both the possibility that the LAPD might use a mark to pressure movie producers regarding film content and the primacy of revenue in the LAPD's desire to register its putative marks with the USPTO. *See* M. Fowler, Note, *To Protect and ... to Profit: the Trademarking of the LAPD as an Example of Expanding Intellectual Property Rights*, 74 S. Cal. L. Rev. 1623 (2001).

5 *See* Registration 72373340 ("A PRODUCT OF THE FLORIDA SUNSHINE TREE" & design, certifying citrus fruit or products made from citrus fruit which was grown both in Florida and under "specified standards"); Registration 0932033 ("THE FLORIDA SUNSHINE TREE" with no stylistic limitation, certifying same); Registration 1559414 ("FRESH FROM THE FLORIDA SUNSHINE TREE" & design, certifying same).

6 *See General Motors Corp. v. Lanard Toys, Inc.*, 468 F.3d 405 (6th Cir. 2006) (affirming final judgment for GM in trade dress case), *cert. denied*, 552 U.S. 819 (2007); *AM General Corp. v. Daimler-Chrysler Corp.*, 311 F.3d 796 (7th Cir. 2002) (affirming denial of preliminary injunction that Daimler-Chrysler had requested against GM, regarding part of the Hummer trade dress); *General Motors Corp. v. Let's Make A Deal*, 223 F. Supp.2d 1183 (D. Nev. 2002) (issuing preliminary injunction against sale of car kits allegedly likely to cause confusion with GM's HUMMER trade dress). *But see General Motors Corp. v. Urban Gorilla*, LLC, 500 F.3d 1222 (10th Cir. 2007) (affirming denial of GM's motion for a preliminary injunction against manufacturer of kits allegedly resembling Hummers).

the military HUMVEES manufactured by AM General LLC for the US Army.[7] GM's marketing campaigns for its more luxurious, civilian versions of the original military vehicle purposefully evoke the earlier design's military machismo.[8] The absurdity of a privately held business owning the look and reputation of a US Army military vehicle was thrown into high relief by G.M.'s 2009 announcement of its plan to sell the Hummer brand to a Chinese firm.[9]

## Government Marketing

Advertising works. Firms spend large sums designing and distributing advertisements because advertisements sell. Advertising's icons also migrate into everyday speech. A well-conceived and executed advertising campaign creates or reinforces a personality for the product or service advertised. The mark serves as short-hand for the personality.[10] Consumers' relationships with a strong brand are largely emotional.[11] Current American trademark law gives the mark-holder an extraordinary level of control over this contrived personality, control beyond that needed to prevent consumer-confusion.

Many putative mark-holders are not private entities. Since the mid-1990s, cities, states, and countries[12] have stampeded into aggressive self-marketing.[13] Additionally, the various branches of the US military have launched licensing

---

7 *See Daimler-Chrysler Corp.*, 311 F.3d at 808–11; *see also Lanard Toys, Inc.*, 468 F.3d at 410–11 (on question regarding functionality doctrine).

8 *See* Joint Appendix at 1990–94, *Lanard*, 468 F.3d 405 (6th Cir. 2006).

9 The deal later collapsed. *See* Soyoung Kim & David Bailey, *GM To Shut Down Hummer After China Deal Fizzles,* Reuters (Feb. 24, 2010), http://www.reuters.com/article/2010/02/24/us-gm-hummer-idUSTRE61N5XE20100224 (last visited Dec. 23, 2012) (reporting both original deal and deal's collapse).

10 "In sum, the firm's selection, maintenance, and control over its personas—advertising's "who"—is essential." Barbara Stern, *Integrated Communication: The Company "Voice" and the Advertising Persona, in* Integrated Communication 87, 100 (Esther Thorson & Jeri Moore eds., 1996); *see also id.* at 87–102 (explaining need for construction of a singular persona).

11 *See, e.g.,* Kenneth E. Clow & Donald Baack, *Integrated Advertising, Promotion and Marketing Communications* 216–18 (2d ed. 2004); Keith Dinnie, *Nation Branding* 64 (2008); *see also* Mark Bartholomew, *Advertising and the Transformation of Trademark Law*, 38 N. M. L. Rev. 1, 4 (2008).

12 *See* Dinnie, *supra* note 11, at 53, 59, 134, 156–7, 184, 202, 233, 240 (providing numerous slogans recently used in nation-branding campaigns).

13 *See* Simon Anholt, *Competitive Identity: The New Brand Management for Nations, Cities and Regions* xi–xii (2007) (reporting that when he began writing about "*nation branding*" in 1996, his "conversations on the subject were largely theoretical, and mainly with marketing academics" while now "every place on earth wants to do something to manage its international reputation").

campaigns.[14] Certainly, local politicians have long worked at attracting both tourists and new businesses to their communities, but something important has changed. Governments are now willing to sue local merchants for selling tourist merchandise bearing government-claimed marks, even when the so-called marks pre-date organized government advertising[15] or are merely the initials of the local police or fire department.[16] This is brand management as if a city were manufacturing a box of cornflakes. Even Simon Anholt, the guru of nation-branding,[17] recognizes the oddity of such behavior:

> [T]he product doesn't come out of a factory, but is the very homeland of the people trying to market it (where they and their parents and grandparents were born, raised, schooled and trained), and [the persons marketing the brand] are public servants rather than marketing professionals, and [this] brand management is merged with foreign policy, public diplomacy, tourism [and] trade promotion.[18]

Anholt gives mouth-service to the tensions, but concludes that a skilled executive could orchestrate an effective campaign without undermining liberal government.[19] I disagree. To grasp the impact of my argument, the reader needs to recognize the scope of symbols that constitute marks.

---

14 *See infra* text accompanying notes 136–40.

15 *See R&R Partners, Inc. v. Tovar*, 447 F. Supp. 2d 1141 (D. Nev. 2006).

16 For example, after 9/11 the government of the City of New York started an aggressive effort to internalize profit from the newly enhanced reputation of the New York City Police and Fire Departments, including sending "hundreds of cease and desist letters" which were "served by hand on vendors and retailers in New York City and by mail and email on retailers and internet sellers throughout the U.S. and other countries." *Complaint* ¶20, *City of New York v. Albert Elovitz, Inc.*, 04-cv-2787 (S.D.N.Y. Apr. 12, 2004)*; see also id.* ¶¶ 21, 22, 41 (other enforcement actions).

17 *See* Dick Martin, *Rebuilding Brand America* 258 (2007) (describing Anholt as "the acknowledged master of place branding and a member of Business for Diplomatic Action's advisory council.").

18 Anholt, *supra* note 13, at 72; *see also id.* at 75 ("the people are the brand").

19 *See id.* at 40. Similarly Dinnie emphasizes ethical considerations and the need to involve multiple stakeholders. *See* Dinnie, *supra* note 11, at 163–79. Nevertheless, Dinnie sees the failure of Britain's nation rebranding initiative in the early 1990s as a failure by the organizers effectively to communicate the benefits of the initiative to key stakeholders. *See id.* at 30. The fully ethical response should be (in my mind) accepting that the public has rejected the proposal.

## Governmental Marks

The United States flag is a mark.[20] Federal law defines a mark as "any word, name, symbol, or device, or any combination thereof" used by any person or entity "to identify and distinguish" corresponding goods or services, or the origin of goods or services.[21] While not usually described as a mark, the flag of the United States is undoubtedly the strongest symbol used to identify and distinguish all related to the country.[22] "The very purpose of a national flag is to serve as a symbol of our country; it is, one might say 'the one visible manifestation of two hundred years of nationhood.'"[23]

---

20 The Lanham Act recognizes this by baring registration of matter which "[c]onsists of or comprises the flag ... of the United States." 15 U.S.C. § 1052(b). The nation-branding literature agrees. Dinnie, for example, explains the importance of basing a nation-brand on the nation's already existing "symbols," "imagery," and "iconography," of which the nation's flag is the "most obvious element." Dinnie, *supra* note 11, at 63, 69.

Lack of registration is not, by itself, a legal bar to using a symbol—even to using a symbol as a mark. *See generally* 4A Callmann, *supra* note 1, § 26:104.

21 15 U.S.C. § 1127. A "brand" is often defined in almost identical language. *See* Dinnie, *supra* note 11, at 14. Brands, like marks' secondary meaning, are recognized as existing in mind of the audience. *See id.* at 14–15. Putative marks which are neither the generic name for the goods or services involved nor merely descriptive of such goods or services are classified as "inherently distinctive" and, therefore, treated as marks as soon as they are used in commerce by their holder. *See generally* 3 Callmann, *supra* note 1, §§ 18:2; 18:11; 18:15;20:17. Marks which are classified as "descriptive" are only protected as marks if they acquire "secondary meaning," which means that the public considers them to primarily refer to the source of the relevant goods or services. *See generally id.* §§ 20:27–20:31; *infra* text accompanying note 88.

22 Using the flag of a country creates an association or endorsement relationship, similar to that created by the logos of sports teams. The logo or flag symbol does not indicate the manufacturer of the physical object on which it appears. *See generally*, 3A Callmann, *supra* note 1, § 22:10. Currently sports teams obtain licensing revenue from such goods. However, such merchandising is a relatively recent phenomenon. *See, e.g.*, *Boston Prof'l Hockey Ass'n, v. Dallas Cap & Emblem Mfg., Inc.*, 510 F.2d 1004, 1008 (5th Cir. 1975) (holding that professional team had right to prevent unauthorized sale of cloth patch decorated with its logo even though consumers were not confused regarding identity of patch's manufacturer). Government entities are beginning to request revenue-generating control over "their" symbols, as sports teams began to do in the 1970s. Sports teams, however, are privately owned entities. Representative governments are not.

Statutory provisions preventing registration of government symbols (such as the flag) by private entities, *see, e.g.,* 15 U.S.C. § 1052(b), merely require an entity manufacturing a good with such a symbol not to pose as a government agent. This is similar to Dallas Cap's use of a disclaimer on its packages of team logo-patches. The court, however, rejected a disclaimer as a sufficient remedy. *See Boston Prof'l Hockey*, 510 F.2d at 1013. Lack of registration is not, by itself, a legal bar to using a symbol—not even to using the symbol as a mark. *See generally* 4 Callmann, *supra* note 1, § 26:104.

23 *Texas v. Johnson*, 491 U.S. 397, 405 (1989) (citation omitted).

In *Texas v. Johnson*[24] the Supreme Court held that the First Amendment prevents the government from barring communicative use of the flag for political protest, even when the mode of communication involves burning or mutilating the flag. In a subsequent case involving a federal statute, the Court rejected the government's asserted interest in "'protect[ing] the physical integrity of the flag under all circumstances' in order to safeguard the flag's identity 'as the unique and unalloyed symbol of the Nation.'"[25] The Court mentioned no constitutional problem with the government adopting and publicizing the flag, but rejected any government attempt to prevent others from using this symbol for disparate meanings.

This holding, however, has barely affected outcomes in cases characterized as trademark disputes. It should have. Consider *R&R Partners, Inc. v. Tovar*,[26] a case involving Las Vegas, Nevada. The Las Vegas Convention and Visitors Authority (LVCVA), a city agency that encourages tourism, launched an exceptionally successful campaign based on the slogan WHAT HAPPENS HERE STAYS HERE (WHHSH). Tovar, a private firm dealing in souvenir merchandise, started selling t-shirts and other merchandise decorated with the phrase "What happens in Vegas stays in Vegas" (WHIVSIV).[27] The City government sued and obtained a summary judgment holding Tovar had violated LVCVA's mark rights in WHHSH. Key to the court's conclusion was a survey "indicating that one out of three participants believed that Defendants' shirts were associated with the City of Las Vegas."[28] This use of the survey takes a standard trademark tool and blindly subsumes within it an (I hope obviously) incorrect political claim: the government entity known as the City of Las Vegas *owns the right to decide who may associate with (that is, in trademark doctrine has the right to control the reputation of)* the place/community/society/tourist-destination known as the "City of Las Vegas."[29] The court's error is treating the multi-faceted "City of Las Vegas" as a product akin to a Las Vegas (brand) toaster and, perhaps even worse, treating the government of Las Vegas as the manufacturer/distributor of the product, hence, the entity entitled to trademark control of the product's reputation.

---

24 *Id.*

25 *United States v. Eichman*, 496 U.S. 310, 315 (1990) (quoting Government's brief).

26 447 F. Supp. 2d 1141 (D. Nev. 2006).

27 Please note that this article deals with trademark, which protects only indicia of origin. Copyright, not trademark, protects creativity (authorship). *See Dastar Corp. v. Twentieth Century Fox Film Corp.*, 539 U.S. 23, 33–4 (2003). The words and phrases discussed in this chapter are not copyrightable subject matter. *See, e.g., Higgins v. Keuffel*, 140 U.S. 428, 431(1891) (name of plaintiff's product, "water-proof drawing ink," is not copyrightable).

28 *Tovar*, 447 F. Supp.2d at 1154. R&R Partners, Inc. was LVCVA's advertising agency. At the time of the suit, Tovar held a federal registration of its slogan; LVCVA did not (though it later obtained federal registrations).

29 To clarify, the court was not basing its conclusion on any belief that actual or potential tourists were aware that a city agency had paid an advertising agency to create the WHHSH publicity.

## Applying Free Speech Doctrine to Governmental Marks

Governmental marks resemble government speech because speakers use marks to present their chosen public image. Governmental marks resemble regulation of private parties' speech by the government because the essence of mark ownership is the right to stifle others' use of the mark. Recognizing governmental marks expands the power of government to undercut classic First Amendment protections of speech. My proposal is to classify governmental marks as ineligible for mark status, thereby allowing all speakers (including the government) to speak, while preventing any speaker from stifling other would-be-speakers.

### *Governmental Marks as Government Speech*

The flag burning cases were correctly decided because they were analyzed as speech cases, not trademark cases. The majority in *Johnson* focused on the protestors' free speech rights against the government. The dissenters saw the speech embodied in the flag itself, but they wanted this symbol protected from the meaning-changes desired by the protestors. Neither side mentioned that the flag was a mark. However, free speech doctrine has changed. Were the current Supreme Court to accept a governmental marks case for clarification of its free speech aspects, the outcome is not predictable.

The problem with current free speech doctrine is the Court's willingness to shield government actions from court review by deeming them "government speech," as opposed to government regulation of private persons' speech. In *Rust v. Sullivan,* [30] doctors working for clinics receiving government funding sued over agency regulations preventing doctors from discussing the possibility of abortion with patients. The Court refused to recognize either the doctors' or patients' viewpoints regarding their relationship; instead, the Court declared that in this venue the doctor was merely the government's own mouthpiece.[31] In a more mundane dispute, the Court upheld federal government power to require industry-targeted assessments used to support advertising, despite the plaintiffs' disagreement with the message broadcast.[32]

---

30 500 U.S. 173 (1991).

31 The government speech classification was not completely clear in the original opinion, but was clarified in later cases. *See Legal Services Corp. v. Velazquez*, 531 U.S. 533, 540–41 (2001); *Rosenberger v. Rector & Visitors of Univ. of Va.*, 515 U.S. 819, 833(1995).

32 *Johanns v. Livestock Mktg. Ass'n*, 544 U.S. 550 (2005); *see also ACLU v. Bredesen*, 441 F.3d 370 (6th Cir. 2006) (holding license plate to be government speech), *distinguishing Wooley v. Maynard*, 430 U.S. 705 (1977) (holding slogan on license plate to be compelled speech); *Eugene Evans v. City of Berkeley*, 194 P.3d 394 (Cal. 2006) (holding that city may refuse to allow Boy Scout troop to use city-subsidized marina because troop would not unequivocally pledge not to discriminate on basis of sexual orientation), *distinguishing Boy Scouts of America v. Dale*, 530 U.S. 640 (2000) (upholding BSOC's right to oust gay scout leader despite state anti-discrimination statute).

Flag-decorated souvenir mugs offered for sale to tourists as they finish a guided tour of the White House might be characterized as government speech; by distributing the mugs, the government is touting its own point of view on patriotism. The Court has already accepted government speech lacking a clear message.[33] Combining this characterization with lower protection for individuals' commercial speech,[34] and with the general applicability and common-law origin of trademark doctrine,[35] one could argue for a government right against commercial sellers of souvenir merchandise decorated with the government's marks. The flag burning cases expressly did not reach commercial use of the United States flag.[36] The Court had no need to do so because the government had not sued someone selling flags or flag-decorated mugs.

Several cases might support the government's right to curb mark-infringers. Before the modern era of free speech jurisprudence, the Court upheld a Nebraska state statute that defined as a misdemeanor "selling, exposing for sale, or having in possession for sale, any article of merchandise upon which shall have been printed or placed, for purposes of advertisement, a representation of the flag of the United States."[37] The Court affirmed Halter's conviction for selling beer in bottles decorated with the American flag. However, Halter had not raised any First Amendment issues.[38]

---

33 Justice Alito elaborated on the complexity of determining the meaning of a Ten Commandments' monument, characterizing the monument as government speech. *See Pleasant Grove City v. Summum*, 444 U.S. 460, 476 (2009). *Compare* Spense v. Washington, 418 U.S. 405, 410–11 (1974) (holding that display of upside-down flag marked with peace symbol was "speech" for purposes of the First Amendment because "[a]n intent to convey a particularized message was present, and in the surrounding circumstances the likelihood was great that the message would be understood by those who viewed it"), *with Johanns v. Livestock Mktg. Ass'n*, 544 U.S. 550, 561n.5 (2005) (ruling "Beef. Its what's for dinner" is government speech despite tension with other government-messages).

34 *But see Sorrell v. IMS Health Inc.*, 131 S.Ct. 2653 (2011) (using heightened scrutiny for a regulation of commercial speech); *id.* at 2677 ("neither of these categories—'content-based' nor 'speaker-based'—has ever before justified greater scrutiny when regulatory activity affects commercial speech"; objecting to majority's use of heightened scrutiny) (Justice Breyer, dissenting).

35 *Compare Cohen v. Cowles Media Co.*, 501 U.S. 663, 669 (1991) ("generally applicable laws do not offend the First Amendment simply because their enforcement against the press has incidental effects on its ability to gather and report the news," listing the right of publicity as such a generally applicable law), *with New York Times v. Sullivan*, 376 U.S. 254 (1964) (enforcing constitutional limitation on civil actions for libel).

36 *United States v. Eichman*, 496 U.S. 310, 315 n.4 (1990).

37 *Halter v. Nebraska*, 205 U.S. 34, 38 (1907).

38 *See also Robart v. State*, 82 P.3d 787 (Alaska Ct. App.), *cert. denied*, 543 U.S. 940 (2004). Despite a First Amendment argument, the court upheld Robart's conviction for violating a statute against commercial use of the state seal without permission. Robart had included the seal in a medallion.

The Supreme Court rejected a free speech attack on a statute empowering the United States Olympic Committee (USOC) to block even non-confusing, promotional uses of the word "Olympic" in *San Francisco Arts & Athletics, Inc. v. U.S. Olympic Commission* [39] (the *Gay Olympics* case). The Court saw no First Amendment problem because adequate substitute words existed, and the limitations reached little except "commercial speech," then receiving scant First Amendment protection.[40] Amazingly, the Court concluded that Congress could "reasonably" have decided that the commercial and promotional value of "Olympic" was the product of the USOC's efforts, despite the historical basis on which the USOC had built.[41] The holding may have a far reach: the Court was willing to imply the key congressional finding, it deferred to this questionable and merely implied conclusion, it ignored free speech issues in this merchandising situation, even though the objective was to raise funds to change the public image of a politically charged group, and it used a one-actor-takes-all approach to cultural meaning. The Court might rule that (at least as regards souvenirs), Congress could reasonably decide, for example, that the Executive Department had created the promotional power of the President's official seal.[42]

In sum, current free speech case law foreshadows possible court blindness to the free speech problems with governmental marks.

### *Governmental Marks as Regulation of Citizens' Speech*

I reject the characterization of governmental marks as government speech. So should the courts. Extending the government speech doctrine to this extent would prevent, for the first time, a person from sending a message, as opposed to allowing government monopoly of a limited, rivalrous resource used by the government to send its chosen message.[43] Nothing in *Pleasant Grove City v.*

39 483 U.S. 522 (1987) (holding constitutional the Amateur Sports Act).

40 *See id.* at 536. The Court also presumed that Congress had found that "most commercial uses of the Olympic words and symbols are likely to be confusing." *Id.* at 539. The Supreme Court's last substantive opinion on commercial speech seemed to provide it an increased level of protection. *See Sorrell,* 131 S. Ct. 2653.

41 *See U.S. Olympic Comm.*, 483 U.S. at 532–3.

42 If the Court is willing to go this far, I would expect it to also see no problem with Congress allowing the Patent and Trademark Office to make similar judgments related to registration of marks. *See* 15 U.S.C. § 1052. Additionally, per federal statute, anyone who "knowingly manufactures, reproduces, sells, or purchases for resale, either separately or appended to any article manufactured" the seal of the President, the Vice President, the House of Representatives, the Senate, or the Congress" (except on objects for official use by the federal government or as allowed by federal regulation) is subject to criminal liability. No likelihood of confusion or intent to deceive is required. *See* 18 U.S.C. § 713(b)-(e).

43 The limitations of park land were central to the Court's decision in *Summum. See Summum*, 129 S. Ct. at 1138.

*Summum*[44] prevented placement of the rejected monument in non-government physical space or prevented holding a church meeting in the park at issue; nothing in *Johanns v. Livestock Marketing Association*[45] prevented the plaintiffs from launching a counter-advertising campaign about differences between types of beef; nothing in *Rust* blocked the plaintiffs from supporting abortion in distinct venues;[46] nothing in *FAIR v. Rumsfeld*[47] prevented the law schools from putting up posters attacking "don't ask don't tell." In contrast, the court in *R&R Partners, Inc. v. Tovar*[48] enjoined defendant's sale of t-shirts with competing messages, even though the shirts' existence impacted the city's own message only to the extent that it competed for listeners' attention in the market place as a whole.

Unlicensed sales of coffee mugs decorated with an American flag should be protected as speech. Someone who uses such a mug is expressing her patriotism. Someone who buys such a mug or offers one for sale may also be expressing an opinion; or may merely be recognizing the desire of the mug's future end-user to express her beliefs. The argument builds on the Court's existing holdings protecting the right to use the flag for anti-government speech.[49]

First, the right to use the flag to make negative statements about the government-as-institution is hollow absent the ability to obtain a flag. Therefore, government-as-institution should not have the right to block flag-venders from selling flags, despite the commercial nature of selling. Otherwise protest is functionally limited to people able to sew their own flags.[50] This position is undercut by the *Gay Olympics* case.[51] Leaving aside any criticism of the opinion,[52] the *Gay Olympics* case is easily distinguishable. The majority held that the USOC was not a state

44 555 U.S. 460 (2009).

45 544 U.S. 550 (2005).

46 "The Secretary's regulations do not force the Title X grantee to give up abortion-related speech; they merely require that the grantee keep such activities separate and distinct from Title X activities." *Rust v. Sullivan,* 500 U.S. 173,196 (1991).

47 547 U.S. 47 (2006).

48 447 F. Supp.2d 1141 (D. Nev. 2006).

49 *See United States v. Eichman,* 496 U.S. 310 (1990); *Texas v. Johnson,* 491 U.S. 397 (1989); *Spense v. Washington,* 418 U.S. 405, 410–11 (1974); *Street v. New York,* 394 U.S. 576 (1969).

50 *But see* Jack M. Balkin, *The Future of Free Speech in a Digital Age,* 36 Pepp. L. Rev. 427, 440–41 (2009) ("The great tension in twentieth century free speech theory was the increasing protection of the formal freedom to speak against the background of technologies of mass broadcast that reserved practical freedom for a relative few."), *objecting to* Alexander Meiklejohn, *Political Freedom: The Constitutional Powers of the People* 26 (1960) (asserting that First Amendment centers on expression of all points of view, not expression by all people).

51 *San Francisco Arts & Athletics, Inc. v. U.S. Olympic Comm.*, 483 U.S. 522 (1987).

52 *But see, e.g.,* Keith Aoki, *Authors, Inventors and Trademark Owners: Private Intellectual Property and the Public Domain,* 18 Columbia-VLA J.L. & Arts 191, 235–64 (1994) (criticizing case); Michael Madow, *Private Ownership of Public Image: Popular*

actor;[53] presumably, a court could, therefore, hold that the persona of the USOC is not "governmental" in my sense.[54]

Second, the Court has recognized First Amendment speech in mundane objects, including some standard items sold by souvenir shops, most importantly, slogan-emblazoned T-shirts.[55] The Court has protected the speech elements of automobile license plates,[56] hardly distinguishable in speech usage from souvenir license-plate holders.[57] Such speech transcends the commercial speech category, even though it is part of a product obtained from a commercial source. As the Ninth Circuit said of another inexpensive object, the souvenir mug "is not advertising the product; it is the product. It is sold for a profit, but that does not make it commercial speech for First Amendment purposes."[58]

Third, viewpoint discrimination is one of the most disfavored types of government speech regulation.[59] The government cannot block the sale of mugs

---

*Culture and Publicity Rights*, 81 Cal. L. Rev. 127, 142–3 (1993) (criticizing case); Malla Pollack, *A Right to Know?*, 17 Cardozo Arts & Ent. L.J. 47, 84–6 (1999) (criticizing case).

53 *See U.S. Olympic Comm*, 483 U.S. at 543–8.

54 *Cf. Delano Farms Co. v. California Table Grape Com'n*, 586 F.3d 1219, 1225–6 (9th Cir. 2009) (holding that same analysis governs whether an entity is part of the government when considering whether its regulation of others' speech is limited by the First Amendment and when considering whether its own speech is immune from First Amendment limitations pursuant to the government speech doctrine).

55 *See Cohen v. California*, 403 U.S. 15 (1971) (protecting "Fuck the Draft" t-shirt worn inside state court house).

56 *Wooley v. Maynard*, 430 U.S. 705 (1977) (holding that state may not force car-owner to display license plate motto, "Live Free or Die"); *see also, e.g., Sons of Confederate Veterans,, Inc. v. Atwater*, 2011 WL 1233091, at *1 (M.D. Fla. Mar. 30, 2011) ("Florida's specialty license plate program implicates private speech rights, and ... is unconstitutional to the extent it grants the Florida Legislature discretion to decline approval of an application for a specialty license plate based on the sponsor's viewpoint.").

57 Of course, the major legal distinction between license plates and license plate holders is that state governments legally require use of the former, but not the latter. My point, however, is that both use automobiles as speech platforms. The difference in volition supports my argument. *Accord* Joseph Blocher, *Government Property and Government Speech,* 52 Wm. & Mary L. Rev. 1413, 1436, 1479 (2011) (arguing that "possession [of physical property] enables expression only when it is volitional, or at least is perceived to be. In other words, my possession of something is generally unexpressive if I had no choice (and/or I am generally understood to have had no choice) but to accept it"; therefore, "[t] he unavoidable implication is that the expression emanating from specialty license plates is both governmental and private.").

58 *Hilton v. Hallmark Cards*, 580 F.3d 874, 885 n.7 (9th Cir. 2009) (holding that Hallmark® greeting card is not commercial speech and thus merits greater protection).

59 "Viewpoint discrimination is thus an egregious form of content discrimination. The government must abstain from regulating speech when the specific motivating ideology or the opinion or perspective of the speaker is the rationale for the restriction." *Rosenberger v. Rector & Visitors of Univ. of Va.*, 515 U.S. 819, 829 (1995).

picturing a flag burning.[60] Therefore, allowing the government to block the sale of a mug only if decorated with an *unblemished* flag constitutes viewpoint discrimination.[61] Buying a souvenir mug with the presidential seal is a statement of political support; buying a mug with an elephant smashing the presidential seal is a statement of political disagreement with a president from the Democratic Party.[62] Basic free speech doctrine requires identical legal treatment of the protest and non-protest mugs.

However, several counter-arguments require further discussion. First, the souvenir mug many not qualify as speech; merely buying or drinking from a souvenir mug decorated with the presidential seal might not provide a sufficiently clear message.[63] However, several recent Supreme Court cases recognized expressive activity in situations in which the content was no less amorphous. The *Summum* majority opinion had no problem with the jumble of possible messages related to the monument at issue; it was still held to be government speech.[64] In *Johanns* the Court accepted "Beef. It's What's for Dinner" as "government speech" despite its vagueness both inherently and in light of the government's simultaneous advocacy that Americans eat less animal protein.[65] Additionally, recent expressive association cases have empowered speech-analysis of the low-key signification of cultural attitudes. Chief Justice Rehnquist, writing for the majority in *Boy Scouts of America v. Dale*[66], characterized "the time spent with the youth members" by "the scoutmasters and assistant scoutmasters" as purposefully "inculcat[ing] them

60 *See LightHawk, the Environmental Air Force v. Robertson*, 812 F. Supp. 1095 (W.D. Wash. 1993) (holding that government's purported mark-rights in Smokey the Bear are insufficient to outweigh public's legitimate interest in using Smokey Bear in political-protest poster).

61 *Accord R.A.V. v. City of St. Paul*, 505 U.S. 377, 383–4 (1992) (even the most disfavored "areas of speech can [not] ... be made the vehicles for content discrimination unrelated to their distinctively proscribable content. Thus, the government may proscribe libel; but it may not make the further content discrimination of proscribing only libel critical of the government.").

62 *See also* Lisa P. Ramsey, *Increasing First Amendment Scrutiny of Trademark Law*, 61 SMU L. Rev. 381, 396–7 (2008) (defining merchandise marked with the names or slogans of political groups as outside "commercial speech.").

63 *Spense v. Washington*, 418 U.S. 405, 410–11 (1974)(holding that display of upside-down flag marked with peace symbol was "speech" for purposes of the First Amendment because "[a]n intent to convey a particularized message was present, and in the surrounding circumstances the likelihood was great that the message would be understood by those who viewed it.").

64 *See Pleasant Grove City v. Summum*, 555 U.S, 460, 476 (2009).

65 *See id.* (dealing with a free speech claim by characterizing Ten-Commandments monument as government speech without a clear message); *Johanns v. Livestock Mktg. Ass'n*, 544 U.S. 550, 561 n.5 (2005) (ruling "Beef. Its what's for dinner" is government speech despite tension with other government-messages).

66 *Boy Scouts of Am. v. Dale*, 530 U.S. 640 (2000).

with the Boy Scouts' values—both expressively and by example."[67] Rehnquist did not classify such diffuse signification (through knot-tying lessons, camping trips, and hiking) as non-communicative for purposes of the First Amendment. As Justice O'Connor stated in an earlier concurring opinion, "[i]t is easy enough to identify expressive words or conduct that are strident, contentious, or divisive, but protected expression may also take the form of quiet persuasion, inculcation of traditional values, instruction of the young, and community service."[68]

Market transactions for licensed merchandise support the speech—import of the mugs and other souvenirs at issue. When a government entity licenses the insignia of the New York Police Department for use on t—shirts, caps, toy cars, and pencils, it charges the manufacturer.[69] The manufacturer can afford this charge because retail customers have demonstrated willingness to pay a premium for having such an everyday object proclaim an emotional tie to New York City's Finest. What else is this but expression? Since the entity with which the consumer wishes to associate is a government entity, the expression is by definition political.[70] As the freedom-of-expressive association cases demonstrate, expression does not have to be strident. A flag cigarette box on the living room table and NYPD pencils in the study are entitled to expressive legal status. The flag is not the only politically expressive mark in the United States, just the one with the loudest voice.

Second, perhaps the government's claim to marks is not stifling speech; it is merely insisting on a license fee for use of certain expressive symbols. However, this distinction seems blocked by the line of cases forbidding taxes targeting newspapers.[71] One could proclaim that slogans propagated by marketing specialists or tourist emporia are too trivial for First Amendment protection.[72] But basic free

---

67 *Id.* at 649–50 (2000) (classifying such behavior as "expressive activity").

68 *Roberts v. United States Jaycees*, 468 U.S. 609, 636 (1984).

69 *NYPD Licensing,* New York City Police Foundation, http://www.nycpolicefoundation.org/netcommunity//Page.aspx?pid=629. The federal government recruits potential licensees of various symbols by promising public willingness to pay more for merchandise because of its communicative power. *See* http://www.symbols.gov (providing product and licensing materials for marks such as "Smokey Bear" and "Woodsey Owl").

70 NYC & Company is the organization that handles all such licensing for the City of New York. *See* http://www.nycandcompany.org/licensing ("The NYC & Company licensing division is the central licensing authority and exclusive worldwide licensing agent for the City of New York") (last visited Jan. 2, 2013).

71 *See, e.g., Arkansas Writers' Project, Inc. v. Ragland,* 481 U.S. 221 (1987) (holding tax unconstitutional); *Minneapolis Star & Tribune Co. v. Minnesota Comm'r of Revenue*, 460 U.S. 575 (1983) (holding tax unconstitutional). *But see Leathers v. Medlock*, 499 U.S. 439 (1991) (holding tax constitutional).

72 *Cf. Fair v. Rumsfield*, 547 U.S. 47, 62 (2006) ("Compelling a law school that sends scheduling e-mails for other recruiters to send one for a military recruiter is simply not the same as forcing a student to pledge allegiance, or forcing a Jehovah's Witness to display the motto "Live Free or Die," and it trivializes the freedom protected in *Barnette*

speech concerns require that each member of the public have the individual right to decide what symbolic materials are trivial or significant, without government fettering.[73]

Third, the government is the voice of the people. The people as a group have no way to coordinate their responses to situations except through the government. Following the procedure in the people-created Constitution, the people elect representatives.[74] With their delegated power, the representatives choose other appropriate agents to assist in conducting the people's joint political business. To function, the government needs the power to decide limits on public claims of association with various aspects of the government. The government acts appropriately in creating these limits because it is the people's constitutionally chosen agent.

This argument has two flaws. First, the minor flaw: the argument does not address the trademark problem with governmental marks. This problem is minor because the government, as republican sovereign, could enact statutes giving control of governmental marks to the relevant government entities without the standard trademark requirement that the government entity be publically recognized as the relevant "unique source."

The major flaw derives from the liberal nature of the republic. As discussed above, the limits on governmental marks come from two such sources, the First Amendment and the status of each natural person as part of the sovereign. Repeat: *each* natural person must be treated as part of the sovereign; the sovereign is not merely the institutionalized "summation" of persons' positions incorporated into the government-as-institution.

The United States is not a single, biological being composed of citizen-cells. The United States is a republic. Each citizen's vote counts toward obtaining a bundled commodity—a named individual as an office holder. If this individual does not intend (or is not allowed) to run for another term, the individual lacks even the leash of popular disapproval at the polls. Even if the individual does intend to stand for re-election, the public's control over the official's actions is

---

and *Wooley* to suggest that it is."). *But see Cohen v. California*, 405 U.S. 15, 15 (1971) (opening the opinion regarding a t-shirt motto with "[t]his case may seem at first blush too inconsequential to find its way into our books, but the issue it presents is of no small constitutional significance.").

73 Cf. *West Va. St. Bd. of Educ. v. Barnette*, 319 U.S. 624, 642 (1943) ("If there is any fixed star in our constitutional constellation, it is that no official, high or petty, can prescribe what shall be orthodox in politics, nationalism, religion, or other matters of opinion or force citizens to confess by word or act their faith therein.").

74 *See* Dinnie, I note 11, at 169–70 (asserting that the head of state has the "legitimacy of a democratic mandate" to control nation-branding, but only marketing professionals have the needed expertise; therefore, arguing in favor of public-private sector structures.). *But see generally* A. Michael Froomkin, *Reinventing the Government Corporation*, 1995 U. Ill. Rev. 543 (discussing control problems with such public-private entities); Paul R. Verkuil, *Outsourcing Sovereignty* (2007) (same).

quite limited. Leaving aside the myriad problems with the mechanics of vote-counting, the corporate nature of the press, the impact of monetary donations, the limited power of one vote among so many, and the tactical approaches of campaign managers, voters have very limited choices. Each voter can only choose between available candidates. Functionally, availability in most races graces only candidates of the two major parties; a minor party candidate rarely has any realistic chance of election. Consider the plight of a voter who is pro-choice and anti-Afghan war when major party candidate *A* (who is anti-choice and pro-Afghan war) runs against major party candidate *B* (who is anti-choice and anti-Afghan war). The voter can vote against the war in Afghanistan but is muzzled regarding choice. Even if the proffered major-party candidates represent distinct sides on all of the citizen's top issues, the voter is not sufficiently empowered. Because the top issues determine the voter's election-day choice, elected officials have virtual carte blanche on everything else.

Serious respect both for each citizen's autonomy and for each citizen's ownership of national sovereignty supports extreme caution in deeming any position taken by the government-institution to be the *unique* voice of the sovereign people speaking through an empowered agent. Notice the limits of this claim. It does not prevent government action based on less than unanimous consent. It does not prevent government speechmaking based on less than unanimous consent. It does not prevent the government-as-institution from speaking in favor of specific policy choices. It does, however, prevent the government-as-institution from closing down competing statements made in the name of the group by the group's individual members. This comports with the Supreme Court's caution that "fundamental rights may not be submitted to vote; they depend on the outcome of no elections."[75] Therefore, while the government-as-institution is entitled to "market" itself by creating self-chosen personas, it is not entitled to *exclusive control* of such personas. Characterizing such personas is core political speech, regardless of the media used. Lack of mark rights by the government in governmental marks is an aspect of respect for the multitude of autonomous individuals holding ultimate sovereignty.

But perhaps some non-sovereign aspect of government supports standard mark-rights over governmental marks. My claim about the relationship between persons and a liberal, republican government requires that the government be acting as a government, that is, a sovereign. Government entities within the United States, both federal and state, have a large number of court-distinguished faces. When a government entity is regulating, it is operating as a sovereign and must stay within the Constitution's limits on sovereign authority. But a government-

75 *Santa Fe Indep. School Dist. v. Doe*, 530 U.S. 290, 304–305 (2000); *see also Board of Regents v. Southworth*, 529 U.S. 217, 235 (2000) ("To the extent the referendum substitutes majority determinations for viewpoint neutrality it would undermine the constitutional protection the program requires. The whole theory of viewpoint neutrality is that minority views are treated with the same respect as are majority views.").

institution is also an employer with a right to discipline employees in ways it would not be allowed to discipline citizens.[76] It operates bricks and mortar offices performing government functions; it may prevent these locations from disturbance by unauthorized trespassers.[77] Furthermore, it may act in the marketplace by selling physical goods.[78] Presumably, if the government operated a flag-factory, it would not be required to distribute its products for free.[79]

The Supreme Court has never addressed whether the government acting in any of its non-sovereign roles may refuse to allow citizens to speak or to sell speech-goods to other citizens. The government's ends in controlling expressive content would be to protect the government's reputation or simply to earn fees for use of the expression. However, existing case law, although involving distinguishable factual situations and legal theories, points to the unconstitutionality of both goals.[80]

76 *See, e.g., Garcetti v Carbellos*, 547 U.S. 410 (2006).

77 The government, "no less than a private owner of property, has power to preserve the property under its control for the use to which it is lawfully dedicated." *Adderley v. Florida*, 385 U.S. 39, 47 (1966) (upholding conviction for trespassing on grounds of state jail).

78 *See, e.g., Reeves, Inc. v. Stake*, 447 U.S. 429 (1980) (resident-preference policy of state operated cement plant is within market-participation exception to the dormant commerce clause). A number of cases deal with mark disputes where one side is a government-run enterprise. *See, e.g., City of Philadelphia v. EMI Earthmate*, 72 U.S.P.Q.2d 12761 (E.D. Pa. 2004)(dispute over whether city(which manufacturers product) or defendant (which distributes product) has rights to the product's brand name); *see also Saratoga Vichy Spring Co., Inc. v. Lehman*, 625 F.2d 1037 (2d Cir. 1980); *Zipee Corp. v. U.S. Postal Service*, 140 F. Supp. 2d 1084 (D. Or. 2000).

79 Since 1937, the government has been selling flags which have been flown (briefly) over the Capitol Building through the office of the Architect of the Capitol. *See* http://www.capitolflags.gov.

80 Recently, a federal court held that a county ordinance purporting to bar all private uses of the county's official seal was unconstitutional as applied to a news-blog which used the seal to signal material regarding that county. *Rothamel v. Fluvanna Cnty.*, 810 F. Supp. 2d 771, 784–5 (W.D. Va. 2011):

> The County states that Rothamel has no more right to display the County seal than he does to drive the County's automobile. Equating the appropriation of physical government property with the use of a likeness County's automobile. .... While the County is correct that Rothamel does not have the right to take possession of a physical seal owned by the County, the County cannot control all privately-owned images or representations of the seal simply by declaring an interest in managing its own property. The First Amendment requires a more specific and substantial interest in restricting speech than the broad desire to safeguard government property. The County asserts that the central issue of this case is "the extent to which the County can protect its own property from misuse." The only form of misuse of the likeness of the seal identified by the parties, however, is its display in such a manner as to imply County sponsorship or approval of a private message with which the County has not agreed to be associated. As I

The cases involving non-sovereign government action all turn on the consumable, rivalrous nature of objects and places. Marks, including the flag, are symbols, not objects or physical locations. Flag objects are rivalrous and consumable; the flag symbol is neither. Therefore, government "ownership" rights over tangible personal and real property are irrelevant to the current issue.[81] My burning thousands of flags does not prevent the government from flying thousands of flags on government buildings.[82] The government's purported interest in exclusive control of a symbol reduces to a government desire to control how the public perceives the government. Thus, the government's claim echoes the Sedition Act of 1789,[83] which the Court has repeatedly described as unconstitutional.[84] The relatively bland speech implicit in non-protest flag-mugs does not change this outcome. The First Amendment disallows "subtle" as well as blunderbuss censorship.[85]

---

stated above, this ordinance is not particularly adapted to preventing deceptive displays of the seal's image."

81 *But see Texas v. Johnson*, 491 U.S. 397, 438–9 (1989) (Stevens, J., dissenting) ("Respondent was prosecuted because of the method he chose to express his dissatisfaction with those policies. Had he chosen to spray-paint—or perhaps convey with a motion picture projector—his message of dissatisfaction on the facade of the Lincoln Memorial, there would be no question about the power of the Government to prohibit his means of expression. The prohibition would be supported by the legitimate interest in preserving the quality of an important national asset. Though the asset at stake in this case is intangible, given its unique value, the same interest supports a prohibition on the desecration of the American flag.").

82 *Accord Citizens United v. Fed. Election Comm'n*, 130 S. Ct. 876, 899 ( 2010) ("The Court has upheld a narrow class of speech restrictions that operate to the disadvantage of certain persons, but these rulings were based on an interest in allowing governmental entities to perform their functions. The corporate independent expenditures at issue in this case, however, would not interfere with governmental functions, so these cases are inapposite.").

83 Sedition Act of 1798, ch. 74, 1 Stat. 596 § 2 (July 14, 1798).

84 "Although the Sedition Act was never tested in this Court, [footnote omitted] the attack upon its validity has carried the day in the court of history ... . The invalidity of the Act has also been assumed by Justices of this Court. [Citations omitted.] These views reflect a broad consensus that the Act, because of the restraint it imposed upon criticism of government and public officials, was inconsistent with the First Amendment." *NY Times v. Sullivan*, 376 U.S. 254, 276 (1964). *See also Republican Party of Minnesota v. White*, 536 U.S. 765, 794–5 (2002) (Kennedy, J., concurring); *Lee v. Weisman*, 505 U.S. 577, 626 (1992) (Souter, J., concurring); *Columbia Broadcasting Sys. v. Democratic National Comm.*, 412 U.S. 94, 156–7 (1973) (Douglas, J., concurring).

85 "Government has no business in collating, dispensing, and enforcing, subtly or otherwise, any set of ideas on the press. Beliefs, proposals for change, clamor for controls, protests against any governmental regime are protected by the First Amendment against governmental ban or control." *Columbia Broadcasting Sys.*, 412 U.S. at 156–7 (Douglas, J., concurring).

The government's only remaining claim to mark-exclusivity rests on its right to collect revenue for some subset of its services, which the government may seek to classify as non-sovereign.[86] This argument has force to the extent that the service is non-governmental, but such a conclusion places the mark outside the governmental marks category. At core, the issue is the scope of the "governmental marks" category—a different, though very difficult question.

In sum, private speakers' use of putative governmental marks should receive full free speech protection both when they use the "marks" in protest and when they buy "marked" mundane merchandise from private vendors at prices that do not include government license fees.

## Governmental Marks Are Not Marks

To be protected as a mark, matter must function as an indicium of origin: it must designate one (and only one) "source" for the good or service at issue.

I claim that the name (or nick-name[87]) of a city or country is the indicium of origin of more than the government of that city or country; that is, the word or phrase does not indicate an exclusive source. Because it does not refer to a unique source, the name-phrase is not a mark capable of exclusive appropriation by a mark holder. This claim builds on trademark law's long-standing refusal to give anyone exclusive control over a geographically descriptive designation. To some degree my claim is factual: many putative governmental marks can be empirically demonstrated not to have such unique referents. However, for policy reasons, even if the population could be induced to believe that one needs government permission to sell mugs decorated with American flags, the courts should not

86 The government, as sovereign, for the sole purpose of raising additional revenue from its non-sovereign endeavors (such as selling mugs), could not pass limits on private parties' speech. *Accord Clear Channel Outdoor, Inc. v. City of New York*, 594 F.3d 94, 105 n.12 (2d Cir. 2010) (rejecting argument that New York City's zoning regulations on billboards are unconstitutional because the City is using a crack-down on privately owned billboards to increase revenue obtained by government-agencies from rental of billboard space on government-agency owned land and street furniture, because the facts do not demonstrate this type of discriminatory enforcement by the government; "[t]here is also no basis for a finding that the City's Zoning Resolution impermissibly favors government speech over private speech."). However, in the case of governmental marks, the government is not asking that its property be afforded more legal protection than is afforded the same type of property when held by private persons. On the contrary, this article is arguing that "governmental marks" not be given the standard quasi-property rights allowed to "marks."

87 More than one geographic location, furthermore, may claim the same nick-name. For example, the government tourist agency of one location sued a private merchant using the nick-name "surf-city" to refer to a different location. *See Settlement Agreement and Stipulation for Dismissal, Flotsam of California, Inc. v. Huntington Beach Conf. & Visitors' Bureau*, Civ. 06-07028 (N.D. Cal. Jan. 2008).

protect such government exclusivity. As a matter of law, the flag's design should be within the public domain.

The background to this claim is established trademark doctrine regarding geographically descriptive marks. A geographic word or phrase is classified as "descriptive," therefore, only subject to exclusive appropriation when the entity claiming mark-rights proves that the existence of "secondary meaning," that is, that the public primarily recognizes the putative-mark as a reference to the putative mark-holder, as opposed to a reference to a location.[88] Furthermore, such exclusive mark rights are never fully exclusive. Anyone may still use the geographic designation in its original descriptive sense.[89] If confusion is likely, the defendant business is rarely ordered to stop using the geographic term; instead it is required to modify its promotional practices to clarify that it is not associated with the mark holder by, for example, including a disclaimer on its labels.[90]

Trademark case law (with no excursions to the Constitution) has limited both governmental and private ownership of territorial marks. A government's sovereign jurisdiction over location x does not automatically create government-held mark rights over the name of x;[91] even sovereign jurisdiction *plus* owning the real estate involved may be insufficient.[92] Coining a place-designation does not give mark rights in the new term to the neologism's creator.[93]

Next, as an empirical matter, many (if not most) putative governmental marks do not fulfill the basic criteria for being a mark. As an empirical matter, the public

---

88 *See* 3 Callmann, *supra* note 1, §§ 18:59; 20:32.

89 *See American Waltham Watch Co. v. U.S. Watch Co.*, 53 N.E. 141 (Mass. 1899) (Oliver Wendell Holmes). Cf. Daniels, *Note: The Branding of America; The Rise of Geographic Trademarks and the Need for a Strong Fair Use Defense*, 94 Iowa L. Rev. 1703 (2009) (arguing that public rights in geographic terms can be best protecting by strengthening the fair use defense to trademark infringement, that is, the defense that the term is being used for its original descriptive meaning).

90 *See* 4 Callmann, *supra* note 1, § 23:57.50.

91 *See City of Coral Gables v. Rosenthal*, 141 So. 2d 632 (Fla. Dist. Ct. App. 1962) (city lacks standing to object to business' use of name "Coral Gables Convalescent Home"; dicta that geographic name may not be exclusively appropriated); *City of Indian Hills v. Indian Hills Dev. Co.*, 219 S.W.2d 776 (Ky. 1949) (geographic name may not be exclusively appropriated).

92 *See Dept. of Parks & Recreation v. Bazaar del Mundo Inc.*, 448 F.3d 1118 (9th Cir. 2006).

93 *See OBX-Stock Inc. v. Bicast, Inc.*, 558 F.3d 334 (4th Cir. 2009) ( James Douglas, plaintiff's founder, coined "OBX" as a reference to the Outer Banks of North Carolina; since "OBX" was generic or geographically descriptive and without secondary meaning, plaintiff had no rights in it as a mark). Creation may also be insufficient to found copyright over the neologism. *See Hayden v. Chalfant Press, Inc.*, 281 F.2d 543, 547 (9th Cir. 1960) (holding that "once appellant had christened a geographic location" and placed that name on a copyrighted map, the name could be reused "with impunity" because the names are not "a part of the protected portion of the copyright.").

does not recognize each of them as a reference to one, unique source. The Las Vegas case is a good example.

Consider the sentence: "Las Vegas boosts tourism." This sentence could mean that the government of the City of Las Vegas takes actions to increase tourism. It could also mean that the Las Vegas chapters of the Lions and the Rotary Clubs have joined forces to fund some type of activity, or that an unincorporated association of businessmen had done so, and so forth and so on.

Someone who pronounces the phrase "Las Vegas" may be using it as a noun or an adjective and may be referring to any of the following:

- a geographic location ("I drove to Las Vegas.");
- a market area ("J&J ran this advertisement in Las Vegas.");
- an unorganized group of people ("Las Vegas businessmen support tourism.");
- an attitude ("His work habits are so Las Vegas.");
- a type of style ("That pink dress is so Las Vegas.");
- a type of business ("It's in Atlantic City but it's a Las Vegas casino.");
- a society ("Let's discuss the religious history of Las Vegas."); or
- some combination of these (and probably more).

Let us look more closely at the record in *Tovar*.[94] The *Tovar* court ruled for the LVCVA largely because one-third of persons responding to a survey perceived t-shirts reading "What Happens In Vegas Stays In Vegas" to be "associated with the City of Las Vegas." My first point is that the "City of Las Vegas" is not synonymous with the government of the City of Las Vegas.[95] Furthermore, the survey proved only that a third of respondents believed the t-shirts were "associated with" Las Vegas. In context, respondents may merely have believed that the t-shirts *promoted* Las Vegas. Such a belief is not equivalent to perceiving the slogan as an indication of the t-shirt's *commercial source;* a fortiori, the survey does not demonstrate that the slogan indicates any *unique* commercial source (that is, functions as a mark); a fortiori, the survey does not demonstrate that any appreciable group of respondents believed that the t-shirt originated with any subset of the *government* of the City of Las Vegas. The court seems to have assumed all of these unproven conclusions.

Looking past the court's opinion to the record evidence does not solve the problem. The survey expert declared that "27.4 percent of the Test Group and 0.0 percent of the Control Group thought the t-shirt was put out by either the city of Las Vegas or some official entity representing the city such as a Tourism Board

94 *R&R Partners, Inc. v. Tovar*, 447 F. Supp. 2d 1141 (D. Nev. 2006).

95 *See In re* Kimpton Hotel & Restaurant Gp., 55 U.S.P.Q.2d 1154, 1157–8 (TTAB 2000) (affirming refusal to register "Hotel Monaco"; finding applicant's survey not to be probative because it did not distinguish between affiliation with the government of Monaco and origin in the geographical location known as Monaco).

or the Chamber of Commerce."[96] The participants had been asked "If you have an opinion, who do you think puts out this T-shirt?"[97] "Put out" strikes me as rather unclear in the circumstances (though it is a common phrase in trademark surveys[98]). A city is not a sports team or a t-shirt manufacturer, neither is a tourism board or a chamber of commerce. The remaining survey questions did not clarify "put out." Any survey respondent who named an entity as having "put out" the t-shirt was asked for a reason for their belief and then was finished with the interview. Respondents with no opinion regarding who had "put out" the shirt were asked about the possibility that someone had "authorized or given permission" for the shirt. Those respondents who had no opinion regarding authorization or permission were asked about the possibility that someone had "sponsored or endorsed" the shirt.[99] The participants were thus given three chances to support plaintiff's claim of likelihood of confusion.

Even more unsettling, the expert's submission does not include any list of the respondents' verbatim replies.[100] Instead, the expert supplied a chart which, under the heading "Thought to be Put out By," lumps 27.4 percent under the caption "LV/ city of/COC/tourism." A total of 8 percent of respondents attributed authorization or sponsorship (per question sets two and three) to the slightly different conglomeration of "Las Vegas/City of/ Tourism Board/COC."[101] Adding together all reported allegedly-pro-plaintiff responses provides a total of 35.4 percent.

The report itself is not consistent regarding headings. In the authorization chart, "Tourism" has been replaced by "Tourism Board." Those respondents who said "tourism" without board may not have been referring to an organized entity at all, let alone a government agency of some kind. Even "Tourism Board" might refer to a non-governmental entity. The report does not specify how many respondents said "Las Vegas" and how many said "City of Las Vegas." The former is much less likely to refer to the government of the city. Additionally, even, the response "City of Las Vegas" is ambiguous. Furthermore, the Chamber of Commerce is not a government entity—either nationally[102] or in Las Vegas. The Las Vegas

---

96 Kenneth Hollander, *A Study of Likelihood of Confusion as to the Origin, Source, Association, or Sponsorship of Dorothy Tovar's Use of "What Happens In Vegas Stays In Vegas"* 12, Exhibit G to *Declaration of Yoshiko Inoue in Support of Plaintiffs' Motion for Summary Judgment Against Defendant Dorothy Tovar* (Sept. 15, 2006), Tovar, 447 F. Supp. 2d 1141. The Control Group was shown a t-shirt with the slogan "Have A Nice Day."

97 Hollander, *supra* note 96, at 9.

98 *See* Jerre B. Swan, *Likelihood of Confusion Studies and the Straitened Scope of Squirt*, 98 Trademark Rep. 739, 742 (2008).

99 A positive response to any of these questions was followed up by the query "Why do you think that?" *See* Hollander, *supra* note 96, at 9.

100 This omission violates accepted best-practices for such surveys. *See* 3 Callmann, *supra* note 1, § 20:30; 3A id. § 21:9; McCarthy, *supra* note 4, § 32:181.50.

101 *See* Hollander, *supra* note 96, at 16.

102 "The US Chamber of Commerce is the world's largest business organization representing the interests of more than 3 million businesses of all sizes, sectors, and

Chamber of Commerce is a membership association of businesses which lobbies government on behalf of business interests.[103]

The *Tovar* study was intended to prove likelihood of confusion; the court incorrectly assumed that the phrase functioned as a mark. The court did not require proof of secondary meaning. It should have done so. As discussed above, the name of a geographical location is considered "descriptive" in trademark doctrine; an entity cannot obtain mark rights in a "descriptive" term unless it develops "secondary meaning." Secondary meaning exists when a substantial section of the relevant audience believes the purported mark is an identifier for a *unique* source. In a survey intended to evidence secondary meaning, courts generally require higher positive response levels than demanded in likelihood of confusion surveys. Furthermore, the response level required increases in direct proportion to the purported mark's descriptiveness. Recognition by 35.4 percent of respondents is almost always too low to prove secondary meaning. Some courts have refused to find secondary meaning despite recognition rates over 80 percent.[104] The *Tovar* survey does not purport to reach a generally-acceptable level.[105] Furthermore, since more than one entity is lumped together in the survey results, this report does not prove any recognition-level for any individual entity.

In my opinion, the only fact strongly evidenced by the *Tovar* survey is that roughly one third of the test group saw the t-shirt as a promotion of Las Vegas—which merely demonstrates that they could read the words on the t-shirt.[106]

In sum, neither "Las Vegas" nor "What Happens in Vegas Stays in Vegas" is an indicium of origin referring to some single, unique, even if unknown, originating entity; neither phrase is a mark.

---

regions." http://www.uschamber.com/about (last visited January 2, 2013).

103 *See* http://www.lvchamber.com/about.

104 *See* 3 Callmann, *supra* note 1, § 20:30.

105 The *Tovar* opinion implies that the slogan is an inherently distinctive mark, that is, a mark which is protectable without proof of secondary meaning. Plaintiff submitted the survey to show likelihood of confusion, not secondary meaning. Courts are quite inconsistent regarding the percentage needed for a survey to support confusion, rates from 6 percent to 90 percent have been accepted. Rates as high as 25 percent have been held to prove that confusion is *not likely*. *See* 3A Callmann, *supra* note 1, § 21:9.

106 *See* Hollander, *supra* note 96, at 13. This page reports the reasons given by respondents for their answer to the who "put out" the shirt inquiry. A large percentage of the persons whose response to the first question was coded into "LV/city of/COC/tourism" or into "Other LV mentions" are coded as responding to the "because of" inquiry with something coded as "Slogan/ad for city." The percentages to the follow question are given as percentages of the total test group and add up to 27.0 percent. *Id.* "Reading" questions are disfavored in trademark surveys. *See, e.g., Franklin Resources, Inc. v. Franklin Credit Management Corp.*, 988 F. Supp. 322. 335 (S.D.N.Y. 1997).

## Governmental Marks Should Not Be Recognized As Marks

If the only problems with governmental marks were factual ambiguities of the type just discussed, not all governmental marks would self-destruct. The Seal of the Office of President of the United States, for example, does not seem susceptible to multiple overlapping meanings, or at least not the bewildering array possible with "the United States of America." Furthermore, in some cases presenting the problem, one might be able to construct a survey separating out the disparate possible meanings. In a subset of that subset, one might have a sufficiently high percentage of respondents in agreement for a court to enforce one entity's mark rights in the material at issue.

Additionally, public perception that a good is associated with or sponsored by an entity changes over time. As putative mark holders become more aggressive in asserting claimed rights, even though no lawsuits continue to final judgment, the set of alternative goods shrinks. This tendency is exacerbated by the usual risk-averse nature of potential defendants. The tendency to risk-aversion rises when the putative mark holder has deep pockets. The public, therefore, observes the absence of unlicensed goods, and reasonably assumes that any marked merchandise is licensed. In sum, mark claimants foster the likelihood of confusion; bellowing about doubtful rights may create the rights originally asserted without justification.[107]

Government entities should not be allowed to enforce exclusive rights in putative-governmental marks regardless of public perception. This policy claim is not based on trademark doctrine alone. It is based on a claim about the complex relationship between individuals and a liberal, republican government. One could paraphrase Lincoln's Gettysburg Address;[108] the United States constitutes government of the people, by the people, and for the people. Therefore, I (one of the people) am part of the United States; therefore, no mere trademark claim should be capable of ousting me from my right to employ the label "United States" for my own use. Absent fraud, I have a right not to be excluded from self-description of my "origin" or "association" with the "United States of America." The contrary position, allowing governmental marks, empowers the mark-holder both to manipulate and use sovereign citizens.

### *Empowering Citizens to Choose Their Own Affiliations*

This right to chose one's own affiliations with the polity is a necessary corollary to free speech's intersections with the right of expressive association and with the concept that the people are the ultimate sovereign. Free speech rights cannot

---

107 *See, e.g.*, Mark McKenna, *Trademark Use and the Problem of Source*, 2009 U. Ill. L. Rev. 773, 776 (2009) (discussing instability of mark-rights due to instability of public perception).

108 Abraham Lincoln, *The Gettysburg Address, reprinted in* Garry Willis, Lincoln at Gettysburg 263 (Touchstone 1992).

be limited by majority vote;[109] association is a free speech right;[110] therefore, this right to claim association cannot be limited by government. Natural persons determine for themselves their emotional ties to the United States in general or to its separable aspects. The government does not have the power to order anyone to self-associate (or not self-associate) with, for example, the armed forces of the United States; that emotional tie is not subsumed within the government's physical power to draft people into the army or to refuse to allow persons to enlist.

Consider the decision of the Trademark Trial and Appeal Board (TTAB) to refuse registration of a design mark for the Association of the United States Army (AUSA).[111] The TTAB found that the mark in the application was likely to be confused with two marks already registered to the U S Army. AUSA is a private, non-profit educational organization that has operated since 1950.[112] The AUSA's declared mission is to "represent every American Soldier by—Being the voice for all components of America's Army;—Fostering public support of the Army's role in national security; [and]—Providing professional education and information programs."[113]

My objection is not to the TTAB's refusal to allow the registration.[114] I object to the TTAB.'s allowing the Army the power to prevent others from associating themselves with the Army.[115] In my view, the AUSA *is* an association "affiliated" with the US Army. It is an association of people who have chosen to affiliate

109 "One's right to life, liberty, and property, to free speech, a free press, freedom of worship and assembly, and other fundamental rights may not be submitted to vote; they depend on the outcome of no Elections." *W. Va. State Bd. of Educ. v. Barnette*, 319 U.S. 624, 638 (1943).

110 *See Roberts v. United States Jaycees*, 468 U.S. 609, 618–19 (1984) (collecting cases going back to 1923).

111 *In re* Ass'n of U.S. Army, 85 U.S.P.Q.2d 1264 (TTAB 2007) (affirming the examining attorney's refusal of the application). The application was for a complex design with the words "ASSOCIATION OF THE UNITED STATES ARMY." The TTAB is a tribunal of administrative law judges which decides certain registration disputes. *See* 15 U.S.C. § 1067. The proceeding was ex parte: the applicant's appeal from the USPTO trademark examiner's refusal to register the mark. The US Army was not a party. *See generally* 4A Callmann, *supra* note 1, §§ 26:61 to 26:100 (discussing ex parte and inter partes procedures involving federal mark registrations). However, branches of the US military have filed inter partes proceedings objecting to others' registrations or applications to register marks. *See infra* note 137. Refusal of registration does not prevent the AUSA from making use of the mark. Such an injunction may only be issued after a judicial branch decision regarding infringement. *See* 4A Callmann, *supra* note 1, § 26:104.

112 Association of the United States Army, http://www.ausa.org/about (last visited Jan. 2, 2013).

113 *Id.*

114 Governmental marks should not be registrable by anyone. *See infra* Section VI. The USPTO's refusal to allow registration does not prevent AUSA from using the mark; to stop use, the Army would need to win an infringement suit. *See* 15 U.S.C. §§ 1067, 1116.

115 *Ass'n of the U.S. Army*, 85 U.S.P.Q.2d, at 1269.

themselves with the army, by advocating for members of the Army and their families. The members of AUSA should not need the Army's permission to either support the Army or advertise that they do so.

Neither am I in favor of the military attempting to influence civilians' attitudes. The United States Air Force (USAF) invested over $800,000 to formulate a modern, unified theme to project its identity to current members, potential recruits, and the general public.[116] The USAF exhorts the public that "[t]he best way for consumers to support the US Air Force when they're purchasing merchandise is to only buy from companies holding an official license."[117] Those who might use USAF symbols without permission are warned about potential legal penalties.[118] I would prefer to divorce supporting the troops from buying merchandise. I would like to support the troops by making sure that the United States only goes to war with good cause, never fights to prop-up dictators, and always provides the best care for injured service-persons.[119]

*Undercutting Manipulation of Citizens' Attitudes*

Focus again on the two basic premises of liberal, republican government: sovereign primacy of citizens and limitations on the group's control over any natural person. Marketing literature demonstrates my point that any government-held exclusive right to control governmental marks subverts these foundations of political legitimacy. According to Simon Anholt, premier practitioner of Nation Branding (a/k/a Competitive Identity):

> [T]he first and most important component of my national [Competitive Identity (CI)] strategy is creating a spirit of benign nationalism amongst the populace, notwithstanding its cultural, social, ethnic, linguistic, economic, political, territorial and historical divisions.[120]

Anholt teaches that CI works when government has "a good, clear, believable and positive idea of what their country really is, what it stands for and where

116 *See* A.J. Bosker, *Air Force Identity, Symbol In Transition* (Nov. 19,2008), http://www.trademark.af.mil/news/story.asp?id=123124738.

117 "*Official license holders*," at Air Force Trademark & Licensing Program, http://www.trademark.af.mil.

118 "Failure to obtain a license or approval would be grounds for the seizure of all non-approved merchandise bearing USAF marks. It could also result in jail time and numerous fines if convicted." What if you do not get a license?, in Frequently Asked Questions 10, at Air Force Trademark & Licensing Program, http://www.trademark.af.mil.

119 *See infra* text accompanying notes 136–40 (discussing US military's mark enforcement activities).

120 Anholt, *supra* note 13, at 16. Anholt claims that he is concerned about the ethics of CI, especially if practiced on a superficial level. *See id.*, at 22–3 (arguing for ethics and deep change).

it's going, and manage[s] to coordinate" the six "natural channels" that influence others' perceptions of the country.[121] These channels are the country's tourism promotion; its export brands (which he recognizes are probably privately owned); the government's foreign and domestic policy; solicitations for foreign investment, students, talent, and expansions of foreign companies; cultural exports and exchange; *and the behavior of the country's people*, both as reported and as witnessed by visitors or hosts during foreign travel.[122]

Anholt is preaching integrated marketing: entity-wide, univocal support of the persona chosen by top management. Promoting such behavior by the representative government of a large, diverse country is a perversion. Government brand management involves officials manipulating *citizens' attitudes*,[123] rejecting the theory that government follows citizens' extrinsically chosen goals. Experts warn managers of nation-brands that "[t]he population's own perceptions of the nation brand are a powerful driver of the external image."[124] Therefore, "countries ... need to start educating children to be better informed, more enthusiastic and prouder advocates of their own nations."[125] One reason a country might choose

---

121 *Id.* at 26.

122 *Id.* at 25–6.

123 Successful companies "live their brand." . . .

> As in any successful political or marketing campaign, if the messages and actions the United States *does* control are grounded in consistent brand values, over time "living the brand" will win out. Of course, that requires a level of strategic agreement and concerted action that few countries can muster except in times of war. America had such a moment in the days immediately after the attacks of September 11, but it dissolved ...
>
> [T]he search for Brand America needs to be the product of a rigorous debate between key players in the public and private sectors ... .
>
> [E]fforts to counter anti-Americanism need to involve the American public ... . Just as companies have to "live their brand" to be credible and relevant, the people of the United States need to understand and reflect Brand America—[which Martin defines as] the combination of liberty and respect for others—in all their dealings with the people of the world.

Martin, *supra* note 17, at 244, 245, 258.

124 Anholt, *supra* note 13, at 56.

125 *See id.* at 107. For example, the International Marketing Council of South Africa [hereinafter "the Council"] was created in August 2000; it formulated the "essence" of the nation brand as "South Africa: Alive with Possibility." "When this was adopted by all [involved groups], South Africans from all sectors of its society were engaged to live up to the brand Promise: 'Alive with Possibility.' To this end, The Council continuously seeks the cooperation of government departments, public entities, the private sector non-governmental entities and the media." Yvonne Johnston, *Country Case Insight—South Africa, in* Dinnie, *supra* note 11. The Council, the entity "responsible" for the "mother-brand" performed two major operations: international efforts and domestic efforts. Under the domestic portfolio, the Council "[d]eveloped campaigns ensuring that South Africans live[d] up to the brand promise." Therefore, "[an extensive campaign was undertaken to

consciously to create and promote a nation-brand is to "enhance nation building" by "nourishing confidence, pride, harmony, ambition, [and] national resolve."[126] Remember that political decisions are at least partially emotional and are manipulable through use of shared symbols, such as the flag.[127]

Before dismissing government advertising programs as trivial influences, consider the demonstrated effectiveness of some internal branding programs, programs aimed at aligning employees' self-image with the success of their firm. Such programs have resulted in employees over-investing in their firms' stock for emotional reasons, even when the investment strategy clearly was irrational.[128] Such programs "by manipulating employees' identities to align them with the corporate brand, [may give] employers ... a more comprehensive level of control [over their workers, a/k/a corporate citizens] and standardization [of workers/ corporate citizen's behavior] than was possible with direct supervision and traditional management strategies."[129]

Even if a marketer's end-goal is an external audience, internal effects will result. Marketing research confirms that much of the long-term benefit of advertising campaigns stems from their effect on firm insiders.[130] For countries, this means citizens. Repeated empirical studies show that the direct effects of marketing tactics on consumers are often shallow and almost invariably short-lived. However, marketing actions generally result in higher net sales impact than can be explained by direct effects on consumers. The difference in both amount and lasting impact is "striking."[131] This difference is attributable to the

---

ensure South Africans not only fe[lt] proud to be South Africans but live[d] up to the brand promise," using "[m]ass media advertising, [p]ublic relations," and "[b]rand ambassadors." *Id.* at 9. As part of its domestic portfolio, the Council conducted a national perception audit, *see id.* at 9–10, and decided that it needed to "continue with efforts to sell South Africa to South Africans." *Id.* at 11.

126 Dinnie, *supra* note 11, at 17 (discussing P. Temporal).

127 *See* Brent T. White, *Ritual, Emotion, and Political Belief,* 43 Georgia L. Rev. 447, 495–509 (2009) (explaining theory of symbolic politics).

128 *See* Marion G. Crain, *Managing Identity: Buying into the Brand at Work,* 95 Iowa L. Rev. 1179 (2010).

129 *Id.* at 1208. While many of the specific practices used in in-house branding efforts are unavailable to government tourism agencies, their subjects have already been pre-disposed to nationalism.

130 *See also* Clow & Baack, *supra* note 11, at 404 (discussing importance of repeatedly communicating the firm's brand-strategy to employees). "[A] major factor in the success of the New Zealand nation-branding strategy was that the brand resonated as strongly for the people of New Zealand as it had been seen to motivate its prospective buyers." Dinnie, I note 11, at 28. Egypt's attempts to convince foreign-businesses that it is a good place to do business require "full ownership, support, and awareness of the message on a public and business level locally." *Id.* at 40.

131 *See* Koen H. Pauwels, How Dynamic Consumer Response, Dynamic Competitor Response and Expanded Company Action Shape Longterm Marketing Effectiveness,

"cross support" of the marketing actions by other persons inside the company. Sales people become more enthusiastic; managers outside marketing rev-up their activity. This insider synergy has led to the current triumph of the Integrated Marketing Communications (IMC) framework.[132] Anholt is preaching IMC when he strongly recommends message coordination among not only numerous government spokespersons, but also among those governmental speakers and businesses promoting themselves abroad.

Some governments have created campaigns precisely to mobilize their citizenry behind the marketing play. New York City followed that strategy in promoting JUST ASK THE LOCALS™.[133]

> If the domestic population and other domestic stakeholders are not aware of the images and reputations that are being projected of their own country, they cannot be expected to "live the brand." The result can be a gap between reality and the projected image, which will create dissonance when tourists, foreign investors and so on discover that the nation's projected image is not rooted in reality. There needs to be internal buy-in to the nation-brand by both the public sector ... and also by the private sector companies in their behavior with foreign companies ...
>
> Loyalty is an important component of brand equity. In the context of nation-brands, programs need to be put in place to enhance loyalty levels among a very diverse range of "customers," including the country's own citizens.[134]

This phenomenon is potently illustrated by the recent trademark-control efforts of branches of the US military. In addition to the licensing efforts of the various service-academies[135] (which might be considered no more dangerous than the licensing activities of other colleges), the Army, Air Force, Navy, and Marine

---

http://ssrn.com/abstract=405123.

132 *See id.* at 28–30.

133 TM symbol courtesy of NYC & Company. *See* NYC & Company, 2007 Annual Report 30, 35, 44 (2008) [hereinafter 2007 AR]; NYC & Company, 2008 Annual Report 26, 30, 46 (2009), both available at http://www.nycgo.com.

134 Dinnie, *supra* note 11, at 70.

135 According to a government-filing, the Naval Academy has been obtaining over $200,000 per year from licensing its marks for use on merchandise since 1994; the Air Force Academy has acquired some $2.5 million since 1991; the US Coast Guard Academy earned $10,500 in 1991. *See* Statement of Facts in Support of [US's] Motion for Summary Judgment ¶¶ 100; 123; 151, *United States v. Branch Licensing Group*, No. 2:09-cv-02629-HRH (D. Ar. 2009) (referenced document filed Sept. 9, 2011).

Corps are now actively licensing and policing[136] "their" trademarks.[137] These programs, suggested by a public relations consultant, originally aimed to increase voluntary enrollment after the end of the draft.[138] Presumably, recruitment lagged because potential soldiers, sailors, and marines had an insufficiently positive view of the armed services and an insufficiently military view of desirable citizen involvement in government. While teaching patriotism might be necessary to the

136 While discussion of specific these specific cases is beyond the scope of this chapter, my investigations located two law suits and several inter partes proceedings in the USPTO involving marks claimed by the US military. *See Branch Licensing Group*, No. 2:09-cv-02629-HRH (default judgment against the firm defendant for failure to obtain suitable counsel was entered by the court on Aug, 10, 2011, Dkt. No. 67; the two remaining defendants proceeded pro se, per Dkt. Nos. 63 & 64 entered July 7, 2011; as of Sept. 15, 2011, a motion for summary judgment against these two defendants was pending); *U.S. v. AFIP Labs, et al.*, D. Md. (No. RWT-09-2908) (ended by Consent Decree entered Jan. 19, 2010, on file with author). As of Aug. 15, 2011, oppositions were pending against registration of the marks "MARINEADE" and "NAVYADE," both for sports drinks. The US Marine Corps brought a petition to cancel the registration for "MARINE CORPS TIMES" for newspapers but withdrew its petition with prejudice due to a settlement. (Files available at upsto.gov) Additionally, the US Marine Corps submitted Letters of Protest against applications for registration of the marks "Marine Brand," "Marine Brand Crunches," "Marine Sharpshooter," "Marine Ops," and "Leatherneck." *See* email from Jessica O'Haver, Director Marine Corps Trademark Licensing Office (Aug. 25, 2011) (on file with author); *see generally,* 4A Callmann, *supra* note 1, at § 26:60 (explaining Letters of Protest). According to the USPTO database, as of Dec. 23, 2012, the applicants had abandoned their applications to register each of Marine Brand, Marine Brand Crunch, Marine Ops, and Leatherneck; Marine Sharpshooter had been rejected on the ground that the mark falsely suggested a connection with the US Marines, but the applicant was still within the time limit for filing an appeal from that decision. Also as of Dec. 23, 2012, the Department of the Navy had withdrawn without prejudice its oppositions to Navyade and Marineade. While the applicant for Navyade and Marineade had submitted specimens of the marks' use in commerce, the U.S.P.T.O had rejected both specimens. The applicant, however, had not yet missed the deadline for submitting substitute specimens. *See generally* Trademark Manual of Examining Procedure §§ 904-904.07(b) (Oct. 2012), http://tmep.uspto.gov/RDMS/detail/manual/TMEP/Oct2012/d1e2.xml (providing regulations regarding specimens of use).

137 *See* Email from David L. Noakes, Public Affairs Policy, Office of the Assistant Sec'y of Defense (Public Affairs) to author (July 26, 2011) (on file with author); *see also* telephone interview with Scott Chafin, attorney with US Army (Aug. 2, 2011) (notes on file with author); telephone interview with April Rowden, Air Force licensing program (July 13, 2011) (notes on file with author); O'Haver, *supra* note 136; email from Geoffrey McNutt, Associate Counsel (Trademark/Copyright), Office of Counsel of the Office of Naval Research (Sept. 8, 2011) (on file with author).

138 *See* Telephone interview with Chafin, *supra* note 137.

survival of the nation state, danger lurks in either militarizing or dogmatizing such lessons.[139]

### *Undercutting Use of Citizens as Means*

Fundamental to treating a human being with respect is approaching that person as a member of the kingdom of ends.[140] Liberal republicanism requires the government-as-institution to respect each citizen-sovereign.[141] Providing the government-as-institution with mark-holder control over governmental marks is incompatible with this goal. Consider the implied status of individuals living inside a nation when the government-as-institution uses "its" trademarks aggressively to enhance the nation-brand. In relation to exported products, citizens become props

139 *See generally* Martha C. Nussbaum, *Teaching Patriotism: Love and Critical Freedom, Univ. of Chicago Public Law and Legal Theory* (July 2011), http://ssrn.com/abstract=1898313; *see also id.* at 14 ("we must insist that the truly patriotic attitude is one that repudiates orthodoxy and coercive pressure and celebrates liberties of speech and conscience ... . [We] need to cultivate the critical faculties early and continuously, and to show admiration for them, insisting that critical freedom, not herdlike obedience, is the mark of the true patriot.").

140 Immanuel Kant, *Fundamental Principles of the Metaphysic of Morals*, available at <http://www.gutenberg.org/dirs/etext04/ikfpm10.txt>. Kant taught that since each human was a moral agent, each person was intrinsically valuable. Therefore, morality required each of us to treat every other human with the respect due to a member of the "kingdom of ends" as opposed to merely using other people as tools (means) to reach our own goals (ends). This exhortation requires "treat[ing] people as ends in themselves and never as means only." Joseph Raz, *The Morality of Freedom* 145 (1988); *see also, e.g.*, Elizabeth Anderson, *Value in Ethics and Economics* 8–11(1993) (discussing different methods of valuation); Charles Taylor, *Philosophy and the Human Sciences* 231–2 (1996) ("[I]n fundamental ethical matters, everyone ought to count, and all ought to count in the same way.").

141 "We inhabit, reproduce, and reconstruct culture by living in it, using it, adding to it, building on it, and altering it through our use of it. A democratic culture is not democratic because people get to vote on what culture should be like. It is democratic because people get to participate in the production of culture through mutual communication and mutual influence. Democratic culture invokes a participatory idea of democracy." Jack M. Balkin, *The Future of Free Expression in a Digital Age*, 36 Pepp. L. Rev. 427, 438 (2009).

to support the economic growth of companies internationally associated with the country,[142] even if these firms are no longer supportive of the local population.[143]

Tourism, this century's growth industry,[144] is even more disrespectful of residents. To tourism, a city or nation is a "destination" to be marketed. Marketing success is tied to the ability to supply customers with the promised product, which includes the behavior of persons encountered at the destination. Destinations exist along a spectrum running from the "traditional 'open' destination" where "visitors and residents mingle" without centralized control to "the enclosed destination" whose "value" lies in "the total control of product design, investment and management, organized to deliver the satisfactions that targeted customer segments seek." The enclosed model aims to maximize profits through "fully engineered destinations in which all aspects are under one management control."[145] Therefore, from an economic perspective, "[c]ompared with the traditional 'open' visitor destinations model, enclosed resorts have a massive advantage."[146] Disneyland®, Sandals,® and Club Mediterannée® employees are superior replacements for annoyingly independent residents precisely because the management can standardize their appearance and behavior.

Nation-branding campaigns, therefore, may try to teach the residents[147] to imitate the behavior of resort-employees. Germany provides a striking example. Brand-Germany jumped in value after hosting soccer's 2006 World Cup, which displayed to the global audience "fun-loving and friendly" Germans, rather than the expected efficient but "dour and humorless" Germans. The welcoming natives were influenced by an organized marketing campaign spreading the theme "Du bist Dutschland" (that is, "You are Germany").[148]

---

142 "[A] survey released by Global Market Insite ... showed that almost 80 percent of consumers surveyed abroad distrusted the US government, 50 percent distrusted US companies, and 20 percent said that they 'consciously avoid American brands' as a result." Martin, *supra* note 17, at 60. Therefore, Martin argues to business leaders that they need to fix "brand America" for the sake of their firms' prosperity. *See id.* at 1, 55–6, 85. Cf. Dinnie, *supra* note 11, at 46 ("[T]he nation-brand identity of Germany has been largely built upon the global success of brands such as BMW, Mercedes and Daimler.").

143 *See* Robert Reich, *The Work of Nations* 243 (1992) (explaining the death of the "national champion" corporation whose fate was entwined with that of its native country).

144 *See* Victor T.C. Middleton & Jackie Clarke, *Marketing Travel and Tourism* 3–16 (3d ed. 2001).

145 *Id.* at 465.

146 *Id.* at 466.

147 *See, e.g.,* Martin, *supra* note 17, at 25; Middleton & Clarke, *supra* note 144, at 94–5 (recommending "two-way communication through strong public relations" with "the residents of a destination community" in order to "foster positive attitudes and behavior." ).

148 *See* Gianfranco Walsch & Klaus-Peter Wiedmann, *Branding Germany, in* Dinnie, *supra* note 11, at 154, 154–8.

Anholt's "benign nationalism"[149] seems an odd characterization of programs in which the government chooses a slogan for your country and charges you for the privilege of demonstrating your benign nationalism by purchasing a coffee mug with that slogan. Perhaps the federal government could decide to claim exclusive mark rights in "God Bless America!™" and, to protect the country's assets,[150] sue any firm that dares offer non-licensed mugs asking any divinity's help for your country. Cease and desist letters go out to the purveyors of mugs reading "God Bless America!,"[151] as well as "Allah Bless America," "Thor Bless America," "Buddha Smiles On America," "Does God Bless America?," "Haliburton Bless America," and "God Bless America With Cheap Gas."[152]

Am I projecting my nightmare vision onto well-meaning marketing professionals? I don't think so. Contrast my earlier discussion of free-speech rights in the national flag,[153] in which open-use is a positive characteristic, with a marketing-expert's dismay at such uncontrolled use of the same symbol:

---

149 *See* Anholt, *supra* note 13, at 16. *But see* Dinnie, *supra* note 11, at 251 ("Coordinating bodies need to be established that *do not impose obligations on the nation-brand stakeholders,* but which identify potential synergies between the different stakeholders and act as a catalyst to help realize these synergies.") (emphasis added).

150 *See* 2007 Annual Report, *supra* note 133, at 6 ("NYC & Company is responsible for positioning and promoting NYC as an aspirational global brand ... . As the brand steward, ... We will continue to manage the City's assets with a disciplined approach toward the brand, ensuring return on investment.").

151 A search of the database of the USPTO in July of 2011 produced four live registrations for marks including the words "God Bless America." Two were for these words without any design element or stylistic restraint. Reg. No. 1759844 (for music publication, seemingly held by the entity holding copyright in the song of the same title); Reg. No. 2917898 (for fireworks). Two included design components. Reg. No. 2872206 (for t-shirts and sweat shirts); Reg. No. 3897798 (for "God Bless America 365" and design for an on-line directory service providing information about attractions in the USA). The search produced no matches for any of the other hypothetical marks mentioned in this paragraph.

More than one entity may use the same words in a mark, provided that other factors do not produce a likelihood of confusion. Determining whether a likelihood of confusion exists in any specific situation is very fact intensive. *See generally* 3A Callmann, *supra* note 1, at ch. 21. Determinations of likelihood of confusion for purposes of federal registration turn on the contents of the registration(s) and application(s) at issue while infringement suits look at likelihood of confusion in actual market conditions. *See* 4A Callmann, *supra* note 1, § 26:57.50.

152 The Las Vegas governmental agency handling its slogan "WHAT HAPPENS HERE STAYS HERE®" sent cease and desist letters over WHAT HAPPENS IN CANCUN, WHAT HAPPENS IN NEW ORLEANS, and a brewery slogan, WHAT'S BREWED HERE STAYS HERE. Eric Goldman, *What Happens in Nastygrams ...* , Technology & Marketing Law Blog (July 2, 2005, 4:02 PM), http://blog.ericgoldman.org.

153 *See supra* text accompanying notes 20 to 38. .

> The visual manifestations of national identity are familiar to all—flags, for example, are probably the most potent visual expression of national identity. Their recognition levels result in designs of a country's flag being used as a visual shorthand by products that wish to highlight their country of origin (COO). One problem that can arise from this is that any brand from a given country is free to use a design of the flag in its packaging or other forms of marketing communications, and this makes it difficult if not impossible for nations to ensure that only high quality products and brands use the flag in their branding.[154]

Marketing goals are in inescapable tension with free speech. In sum, the ideal of a liberal, republican government is inconsistent with the government-as-institution wielding mark-holder power over governmental marks.

### *Governance Problems Aggravated by Governmental Marks*

One of the major uses of governmental marks is earning money through the sale of licensed souvenir merchandise. In common with all non-tax means of provisioning government, this creates significant problems with citizen control of government. It undermines transparency and accountability; it provides perverse incentives that encourage principal/agent failure. As with local building codes, a government agency may choose a vendor which intends to obtain payment directly from the public *because* the cost does not come out of the agency's limited budget, even though the overall cost to the public is *higher*.[155]

First, taxes are the historically proven way to control government. The power of the purse was Parliament's trump card against Charles I of England. At the time Parliament's power was relatively minimal, but a vote was necessary to use one major source of income, the "subsidy," a nation-wide tax vaguely equivalent to a general tax on all privately held wealth. Without this limited power over the purse, the King of England might still rule as well as reign. Charles I managed to govern for eleven years without Parliament. However, when suddenly faced with simultaneous rebellion in Scotland and Ireland, Charles I called Parliament into session for the sole purpose of voting the subsidy. Instead, Parliament fought for legal reforms. Thus began the English Civil War, which started England on the road to Parliamentary supremacy.[156]

The use of non-tax funds is especially problematic regarding the military. Fear of a standing army was sufficiently high during formation of the United States that

---

154 Dinnie, *supra* note 11, at 113–14.

155 *See* Malla Pollack, *Purveyance and Power*, 30 Sw. L. Rev. 1, 119–37 (2000) (discussing case involving copyright protection for private-written building code)

156 *See generally* Conrad Russell, *The Fall of the British Monarchies* (1991) (revisionist account); Samuel R. Gardiner, *History of England from the Accession of James I to the Outbreak of the Civil War, 1603–1642* (1903) (classic account).

the Constitution prohibits legislation funding the armed forces for more than two years.[157] Nevertheless, the Departments of Defense and Homeland Security are rolling out major trademark licensing programs.[158] While the statutory authority bars licensing fees that "exceed by more than a nominal amount the amount needed to recover" the Departments' licensing costs, the Departments may use excess money for "morale, welfare, and recreation activities."[159] While the Air Force's primary motive, as with the other services, is image control, it does list revenue as one of its goals.[160] How much money is involved? For fiscal year 2007, the Army's licensing income was about $1,277,000, including a one-time payment of $1.25 million for a ten-year license for a video-game; the Air Force's receipts totaled approximately $32,000.[161] In fiscal 2008, the Army obtained $777,000; the Air Force $52,000.[162] For fiscal 2009, the Army's income was $632,000; Air Force $105,000; Navy just under $263,000.[163] The 2010 fiscal year's figures are Army $1,002,780; Navy $391,658; Air Force $193,000.[164] The Navy's licensing income in 2011 was $315,723; the Air Force's $270,000; the Army received over

---

157 *See* U.S. Const. Art. I, sec. 8, cl. 12 ("Congress shall have the power ... To raise and support Armies, but no Appropriation of Money to that Use shall be for a longer Term than two Years.").

158 *See* website of the Air Force Trademark & Licensing Program, http://www.trademark.af.mil; *see also* US Marine Corp Job Announcement Number 43-09 for a trademark attorney to work on *inter alia* "the Marine Corps' recently established Trademark Licensing Program Office" (on file with author).

159 10 U.S.C. § 2260(c)(2),(d)(2). This money is not spent on airplanes or munitions; it helps support amenities for members of the armed forces (such as bowling alleys and PXs). Congress appropriates very limited funds for these amenities. Their command unit is largely self-supporting. *See* Chafin, *supra* note 137. While I could not obtain complete figures, the Army licensing program forwarded approximately $700,000 to this command during the 2010 fiscal year. *See id.* The Navy licensing program has provided funds for similar services: approximately $213,000 in fiscal 2009, and about $250,000 in fiscal 2010. *See* McNutt, *supra* note 137. The Air Force sent its equivalent unit $31,000 in fiscal 2010 (from 2008 income) and $94,000 in fiscal 2011 (from 2009 income). *See* email from April Rowden, Air Force Public Affairs (Sept. 14, 2011). However, Congress could use the licensing income as a reason to stop its limited appropriation for this aspect of the military, freeing those funds for other uses.

160 *See Why does the U.S. Air Force have a licensing program?*, http://www.trademark.af.mil/questions/topic.asp?id=1474 (last visited Jan. 2, 2013). The other website-supplied reasons are giving the Air Force "control over its logos and marks" in order to ensure the "quality and consistency" of licensed merchandise, and creating "a cooperative and positive working relationship with the manufacturers and retailers who work with the Air Force." *Id.*

161 *See* email from James Chafin, Army attorney (Aug. 17, 2011); Rowden, *supra* note 159.

162 *See* Chafin, *supra* note 161; Rowden, *supra* note 159.

163 *See* Chafin, *supra* note 161; Rowden, *supra* note 159; McNutt, *supra* note 137.

164 *See* Chafin, *supra* note 161; Rowden, *supra* note 159; McNutt, *supra* note 137.

$1.5 million.[165] The Marine Corps collected approximately $960,000 in royalties from August 2010 through August 2011.[166] Because these licensing programs are relatively new, most of the collected funds are being used to operate the licensing programs themselves.[167] Taxes are wonderful precisely because no one likes to pay them. Funding government through taxes creates public control as well as accountability and transparency. Levying taxes requires detailed, public discussion both of where the money will come from and how it will be spent. Priorities are visible. John Q and Jill R Public may be watching.

Now consider non-tax income. This comes from selling mugs decorated with the Great Seal of the United States,[168] commemorative stamps and other post-office-themed products,[169] and museum reproductions.[170] It comes from criminal forfeitures.[171] It comes from fees for services.[172] It can be tied to government, but not completely of it, such as various types of government corporations[173] and "official" yet private foundations.[174] When government is funded from non-tax income, the public loses control over the relative priorities among government projects. The public does not get to choose the amount of income received by the government entity involved. Finding out how much is involved and how that

---

165 *See* Chafin, *supra* note 161; Rowden, *supra* note 159; McNutt, *supra* note 137.

166 *See* email from Jessica C. O'Haver, Director, USMC Trademark Licensing Office (Aug. 3, 2011) (on file with author). As of that date, the program had not yet transferred any funds to the Corps morale services. *See id.*

167 *See* Chafin, *supra* note 161; Rowden, *supra* note 159; McNutt, *supra* note 137; O'Haver, *supra* note 166.

168 An extremely large number of buying opportunities are available through the Federal Government's online portal at http://firstgov.gov; choose "for visitors to the US", then "more on line services", then "buy from government," then "Government Stores – Souvenirs, Books, and Gifts."

169 The United States Postal Service's online store, http:/www.usps.gov, sells much more than stamps. It also offers framed reproductions of stamp-art, jewelry, decorative objects, games, tote-bags, recordings, and books. *See id.* at "For Fun."

170 The Smithson Institution's gift items are largely such reproductions. The proceeds are used to support the museums and the National Zoological Park. *See* "about us" at the Smithsonian Institution Store, http:/wwwsimthsonianstore.com/custserv/about.jsp.

171 "For some localities, forfeitures have become a major revenue source for local police and prosecutors." Les Picker, *Forfeiture Laws, Policing Incentives, and Local Budgets* (National Bureau of Economic Research), http://www.nber.org/digest/oct04/w10484.html .

172 For example, the United States Patent and Trademark Office charges fees for filings related to patents and to mark registrations. *See* http://www.uspto.gov.

173 *See generally* Froomkin, *supra* note 74 (explaining protean nature of the government corporation). *See also* Paul R. Verkuil, *Outsourcing Sovereignty* 171 (2007) (outsourcing raises "enormous issues of legitimacy and accountability").

174 *See* NYPD Foundation's self-description, at http://www.nypolicefuondation.org/about/asp; FDNY Foundation's self-description at http://fdnyfoundation.com.

income is allocated may be almost impossible. If a project requires a subsidy, this can be hidden outside of the budget.[175]

A non-tax source of income may lessen public pressure to fund an activity, even if it is not being funded sufficiently. "Earmarked funds" may substitute for budget funds, instead of supplementing them. Without any public decision to defund, changes in market conditions can drastically reduce a dedicated project's income, precipitously lowering the resources available.[176] Some lotteries intended to help states' public education systems have had such unintended consequences.[177]

Even if the original decision to allocate non-tax income to a project is highly visible to the public, later changes to the operation of the money-pipeline may escape scrutiny. The changes may seriously skew incentives away from what the legislature intended and what the public in general believes was approved. For example, the Comprehensive Drug Abuse Prevention and Control Act of 1970 gave federal and local police power to seize drug-related assets through civil forfeiture. Congress thought this would give local police greater incentives to seize drugs. However, "local governments ... capture a significant fraction of the seizures that the police make by reducing their other allocations to policing ... . The police ... respond to the real net incentives for seizures ... not simply the incentives set out in [the federal] statute."[178] Thus the incentive for police seizures is less than intended by the federal government because the police departments do not receive the full amount provided by forfeitures.

Outside income can cause serious changes in agents' incentives and behavior.[179] In 2008, the National Academy (NA), a private non-profit entity governed by artists, sold two paintings to "shore up its finances and enable it to show more

175 *See* Froomkin, *supra* note 74, at 596.

176 *See* Randy Bobbitt, *Lottery Wars* 32 (2007) (stating that California public education system lost needed services when lottery produced $176 million less than projected in 1990).

177 *See id.* at 31–2 (reporting decline of school funds as a percentage of state budgets after introduction of lotteries in some states and refusal of state citizens to approve other types of school funding despite insufficiency of lottery revenue in some states); Donald W. Gribbin & Jonathan J. Bean, *Adoption of State Lotteries in the United States, with a Closer Look at Illinois,* 10 Independent Review 351, 360–61 (2005); Michael Heberling, *State Lotteries,* 6 *Independent Review* 597, 602–603 (2009); A. Maureen Thompson & David L. Silvernail, *Selected Fiscal Issues Briefs* 11–12 (Maine Education Policy Research Inst. Jan. 2000).

178 *See* Picker, *supra* note 171.

179 *Accord Tumey v. Ohio*, 273 U.S. 510, 523 (1927) ("[I]t certainly violates the Fourteenth Amendment and deprives a defendant in a criminal case of due process of law to subject his liberty or property to the judgment of a court, the judge of which has a direct, personal, substantial pecuniary interest in reaching a conclusion against him in his case," holding unconstitutional a state statute paying judges and police officials from moneys collected from persons convicted of violating statutes prohibiting manufacture and distribution of alcohol.)

of its holdings on a consistent basis." The Association of Art Museum Directors responded by "asking its members to cease lending artworks to the academy and [to cease] collaborating with it on exhibitions." According to the Association's official statement, the NA "is now breaching one of the most basic and important" principles of the museum world "by treating its collection as a financial asset, rather than the cornerstone of research, exhibition and public programming, a record of human creativity held in trust for people now and in the future."[180]

Public criticism may not suffice to correct changes in the behavior of agents. The Smithsonian Institution, for example, entered into a contract with the for-profit cable network Showtime® to form a joint venture, which acquired a right of first refusal for commercial documentaries based on the Smithsonian's collection. Academics and documentarians, major users of the Smithsonian, expressed sufficient outrage, prompting Congress to hold a hearing. Nevertheless, the contract is still in effect.[181] Furthermore, the public is unlikely to learn about most agent detours or to be able to raise sufficient public protest to catch the attention, let alone the votes, of legislators.

Even pure agents who manage an entity's putative intellectual property may be misled into acting as if the entity's goals were the same as those of a for-profit corporation: growth of assets and profits. For example, New York City has developed an extensive licensing program for its putative marks. The most profitable are those of the Fire and Police Departments, seemingly because of their remarkable heroism on September 11, 2001. In support of this licensing program, the City has taken a number of actions that seem more suitable for a business in competition with other city-located businesses. One would expect the City to support all businesses located within its jurisdiction. For example, the City operates an aggressive, on-going effort to prevent the sale of unlicensed souvenir items using the city's putative marks.[182] Such behavior is hardly supportive of retailers trying to obtain less-expensive or more varied merchandise. Additionally, this

---

180 Randy Kennedy, *National Academy Sells Two Hudson River School Paintings to Bolster Its Finances*, N.Y. Times, Dec. 6, 2008.

181 *See, e.g.*, Edward Wyatt, *Smithsonian-Showtime TV Deal Raises Concerns*, N.Y. Times, Mar. 31, 2006). The Smithsonian-Showtime contract was not cancelled. *See Statement on the GAO Report on the Smithsonian's Contract with Showtime from Sheila Burke, Deputy Secretary and Chief Operating Officer*, Smithsonian Institution News, Dec. 14, 2006, http://www.si.edu. The Smithsonian's 2008 fiscal year reports do not provide any financial details about the resulting joint venture, Smithsonian Networds. *See Management's Discussion with and Analysis FY 2008; Detailed Performance Data Report for FY 2008; Financial Statements with Independent Auditor's Report FY 2008,* all available at http://www.si/edu/about/policies/default.asp.

182 *See* Telephone Interview by author with Gerry Singleton, Office of Corporation Counsel, City of New York (July 29, 2008); *see also* Michael A. Cardozo, *City Files Suit Against Illegal Seller of Merchandise Bearing Police and Fire Dept. Logos* (Press Release; NYC Law Dept., Office of the Corporation Counsel, n.d.), http://nyc.gov/html/law/home.html.

presumably took many hours of work by police or other investigative employees. Did anyone ask the city's population whether these resources should have been spent on more nefarious illicit activity? The City threatened and filed a number of legal actions. Would the city's legal resources have been better spent deterring other threats to the City?

The use of government resources to prevent unlicensed souvenirs raises the question of whether the government should be in the souvenir business at all. While I can understand the military's desire to advertise in pursuit of voluntary enlistees,[183] that goal does not support blocking competition in Air Force coffee-mugs or Navy ashtrays.

Vending mugs and t-shirts is hardly a traditional or core government function. No government sensitivity to due process, justice for all, equal access, or free speech is required to distribute plush toys, statuettes, coffee mugs, and plastic versions of firemen's helmets. I failed to locate any reports of market failure in the souvenir industry that might have required government intervention. If competition helps the economy, creates jobs, and leads to better products available for purchase at lower prices, why is the government shutting down competitors in the souvenir business? Shutting down unlicensed merchandise is even odder when the government entity does not vend such goods, as happened in *Tovar*.[184] New York City even insisted that a franchise chain of police-themed pizzeria-delicatessens refrain from opening any restaurants in the tri-state area.[185] The City government is not a food vendor. Nor does it have any sovereign interest in the food sources of New Jersey and Connecticut. Why not let tourists and residents decide if they like their restaurant bills written on "Summons Violations" and their take-out orders delivered in mock-police cars?[186] Furthermore, the citizens of New York City do not have direct control of the City's marketing programs. These are run by a private organization, which receives massive public funding, but largely limits its promotional efforts and expert research to entities which pay membership fees—less than 2000 of the city's multitudinous business taxpayers.[187] Nor do the

183 *See* telephone interview with Chafin, *supra* note 137.

184 *R&R Partners, Inc. v. Tovar*, 447 F. Supp. 2d 1141 (D. Nev. 2006). The LVCVA "tr[ies] desperately" to prevent its registered marks ('ONLY VEGAS with design' and 'WHAT HAPPENS HERE STAYS HERE') from appearing on souvenir merchandise; that would "dilute" the value of the "asset." The city government gets no revenue from licensing the marks. Telephone interview with Luke Pushnig, Legal Counsel to the LVCVA (July 22, 2008).

185 *See* Jeffrey D. Friedlander, *Safeguarding the City's Intellectual Property*, New York L.J., Aug. 18, 2008, referring to *City of New York v. New York Pizzeria Delicatessen, Inc.*, No. 05 CV 2754 (S.D.N.Y.) (stipulated settlement entered by court May 7, 2008).

186 Complaint ¶ 42 at 9, *New York Pizzeria Delicatessen*, No. 05 CV 2754 (relying on defendant's press release).

187 *See* NYC & Company, Annual Reports of 2007, 2008, and 2009, http://gonyc.com (choose "About Us" at bottom of home page).

citizens of New York have direct control over the spending of the licensing fees earned from the City's marks; most are controlled by private foundations.[188]

Additionally, a government-entity's self-identification as a mark holder does not help create the "benign nationalism" recommended by the world's expert on Nation Branding.[189] Think of the counter-productive emotional impact of the US Army's filing a legal action against a non-profit association that had boosted the Army without charge for 50 years.[190] Having grown up in New York City as the child of a small-business owner, I have some experience with the difficulty of running any business (especially a small one) within its borders. Yet NYC's government repaid local merchants with lawsuits for daring to sell merchandise promoting the City's Fire and Police Departments. This assault on an already-beleaguered constituency seems counter-productive.

In sum, governance theory and experience counsel against allowing government-institutions mark-rights in governmental marks.

## Concluding Proposal

Putative governmental marks should not receive the legal protection of mark status. Such matter should be treated as unownable following current legal refusal of mark-status for the name of any type of merchandise. [191] Governmental marks should neither be registrable nor enforceable through lawsuits invoking trademark doctrine. The public, however, should be protected from fraud and deception. Therefore, on proof of fraud, in the tort sense of that word, the plaintiff should receive a fraud remedy. For example, if the Association of the United States Army took delivery of tanks paid for by the US Army, it should be liable.

Additionally, on proof by clear and convincing evidence[192] of a significant history of actual confusion caused by the mark-use, the defendant should be

---

188 *See* Interview of Gerry Singleton, NYC Corporate Counsel, Division of Affirmative Litigation (July 29, 2008) (on file with author); *see also About Us*, http://www.nycpolicefoundation.org/about.aps; FDNY Foundation, *Supporting the Critical Life-Saving Work of the New York City Fire Department*, http://fdnyfoundation.com.

189 *See* Anholt, *supra* note 13, at 16.

190 *In re Ass'n of United States Army*, 85 U.S.P.Q.2d 1264 (TTAB 2007), discussed in detail, *supra,* text accompanying notes 111–13. The US Army was not a party to that proceeding.

191 The name of a type of merchandise is classified as "generic." Generic terms are legally incapable of being or becoming marks—for example no one may claim exclusive rights in "laundry detergent," as opposed to, for example, Tide.® *See, e.g.*, 3 Callmann, *supra* note 1, §§ 18:1 to 18:3; McCarthy, *supra* note 4,

192 Clear and convincing evidence is the standard in trademark law for disfavored claims, such as fraud on the Patent and Trademark Office. *See In re Bose*, 580 F.3d 1240 (Fed. Cir. 2009) (insisting that subjective intent is required and rejecting TTAB's flirtation with a lower standard of proof).

required to use a disclaimer.[193] The causal connection between the putative mark and the actual confusion should not be assumed without hard proof. Actual confusion should be relevant only at the point of transaction, congruent with false advertising doctrine. Monetary relief should be limited to cases of actual fraud and awarded under the rules applicable to fraud cases.

Furthermore, "governmental marks" should be construed broadly. The set should include any word, phrase, symbol, device, slogan, or some combination thereof that invokes the ethos of the polity in its broadest sense. Therefore, the group would include most, if not all, slogans used by any entity, technically governmental or not, to promote tourism to a geographic location. Trademark doctrine does not support allowing one entity to obtain ownership over another's persona or identity. Private entities should not be allowed to control governmental marks.[194]

Governmental mark status should be a basis for opposing an application for registration. It should also be a basis for cancelling a registration at any time. Standing to oppose an application or to petition and to cancel an existing registration should be broad. Because no entity should enjoy exclusive rights to a governmental mark, mere economic interest may not provide a sufficient incentive for a possible competitor to sue; even if the plaintiff wins, the plaintiff does not gain exclusivity. Furthermore, the harm involved in one entity's appropriation of a governmental mark is not merely economic. Therefore, any member of the polity should have standing.[195] Because such putative marks infringe rights of the public, neither incontestible status nor laches should be allowed to interfere in any proceeding regarding the governmental nature of a putative mark.[196] While

---

193 *Accord United States v. Washington Mint, LLC*, 115 F. Supp. 2d 1089, 1107 (D. Minn. 2000) (judgment for plaintiff, but limiting relief to use of a more prominent disclaimer).

194 For example, a private alliance ran a major campaign promoting, among other things, relocation of educated, young-persons to Des Moines, using the slogan "Whatever You're Doing; Do More of It in Des Moines." *See* Stuart Eliot, *On Advertising*, N. Y. Times, Oct. 22, 2007. While not registered, under current doctrine, the private group seemingly has common law mark rights in the slogan. Under my proposal, it does not.

195 This suggestion follows the standing approach regarding attacks on marks which allegedly are immoral or scandalous, or are disparaging of a group of natural persons. *Ritchie v. Simpson*, 170 F.3d 1092 1023, 1024–5 (Fed. Cir. 1999) (holding that even a member of the general public has standing to oppose a mark as immoral or scandalous); *Harjo v. Pro-Football Inc.*, 45 U.S.P.Q.2d 1789 (TTAB 1998) (holding that any member of an allegedly disparaged group has standing to petition for cancellation of the offending mark).

196 *Cf. Jarrow Formulas, Inc. v. Nutrition Now, Inc.*, 304 F.3d 829, 841 (9th Cir. 2002) (stating that in some cases public interest will prevent acceptance of laches defense, especially if confusion is inevitable and raises safety concerns). *But see Pro Football, Inc. v. Harjo*, 565 F.3d 880 (D.C. Cir.) (affirming laches-based dismissal of petition to cancel registration of "REDSKINS" for a football team on ground that mark disparages Native Americans), *cert. denied,* 130 S. Ct. 631 (2009).

not necessary, the system might benefit from an USPTO-maintained list of words, phrases, symbols, devices, and combinations thereof that are not available as marks due to their governmental nature. "Governmental marks" should be treated as signs whose meaning floats freely through the air wafted by common use.[197]

197 *Cf. International News Service v. Associated Press*, 248 U.S. 215, 250 ("The general rule of law is, that the noblest of human productions-knowledge, truths ascertained, conceptions, and ideas-become, after voluntary communication to others, free as the air to common use.") (Brandeis, J. dissenting); Yochai Benkler, *Free as the Air to Common Use: First Amendment Constraints on Enclosure of the Public Domain*, 74 N.Y.U. L. Rev. 354 (1999) (arguing for a vibrant public domain).

# PART V
# The Shaping of Private Law

# Chapter 10
# Adverse Possession and Sovereignty[1]

Larissa Katz

There are two quite different ways to assert the relationship of owners to their property. Either we emphasize the status of the thing as my property ("Blackacre is my property") or we can emphasize my status as owner ("I am the owner of Blackacre"). To understand the relationship of owner to property fully, we need to make sense of both perspectives.[2] Ownership, I will argue here, is best understood as an office—a unique position of authority over the owned thing—rather than merely as a set of rights over the thing.[3] The central organizing principle of ownership is the positive account of the owner's authority to set the agenda for the thing, rather than the negative account of what the owner may prevent others from doing with the thing.

This account of ownership as an office is crucial to a proper understanding of the common law of adverse possession. For many years scholars have puzzled over why the law should reward thieves, as it seems to do.[4] Why should the law grant property rights to someone who has acted as owner of the thing, adversely to the rights of the true owner? Many US jurisdictions, driven by moral disapprobation of land "thieves," have moved toward a theory of adverse possession based on mistaken possession. And in the UK, the approach to adverse possession sidesteps the moral issue by focusing instead on a narrow technical account of what exactly

1 This is adapted from Larissa Katz, *The Moral Paradox of Adverse Possession: Sovereignty and Revolution in Property Law*, 55 McGill L.J. 47 (2010)

2 For a conception of ownership as an organizing idea, *see* Jeremy Waldron, *The Right to Private Property* (1991); Larissa Katz, *Exclusion and Exclusivity in Property Law*, 58 U. Toronto L.J. 275 (2008) [hereinafter Katz, *Exclusion and Exclusivity*]. For controversy as to what ownership means, *see* Bruce A. Ackerman, *Private Property and the Constitution* (1977); Katz, *Exclusion and Exclusivity*; J.E. Penner, *The 'Bundle of Rights' Picture of Property*, 43 UCLA L. Rev. 711 (1996). For the English lawyer's perspective on the idea of ownership with respect to land, *see* Kent McNeil, *Common Law Aboriginal Title* (1989).

3 I develop this conception of ownership in previous work. *See* Katz, *Exclusion and Exclusivity*, *supra* note 2; Larissa Katz, *A Principle of Abuse of Right*, 122 Yale L.J. 1444 (2013) [hereinafter Katz, *Abuse of Right*].

4 For a defense of rewarding land "thieves," see Lee Anne Fennell, *Efficient Trespass: The Case for 'Bad Faith' Adverse Possession*, 100 Nw. U. L. Rev. 1037, 1053–9 (2006) [hereinafter Fennell, *Efficient Trespass*].

happens when squatters succeed.[5] Many UK courts now think of true owners and adverse possessors as different only in degree rather than in kind; the adverse possessor gains the full rights of ownership because the owner's rights are extinguished after a time and the adverse possessor has the next-strongest claim over the thing. But these, I believe, are deep and troubling developments in the law. Instead, we should keep hold of an older idea of adverse possession that is still alive in Canada (and which used to dominate in Australia and the UK as well).[6] According to this view, an adverse possessor is entitled to claim title in property when he has effectively dispossessed the true owner as the occupant of the office of owner. So it is entirely appropriate that courts should require that the adverse possessor had the intent to act as the (unique) owner of the property and therefore that he acted as though the true owner had no rights over the property. I call this the "inconsistent use" test.[7]

This chapter proposes a new understanding of the law and morality of adverse possession based on a view of the adverse possessor, not as a land thief nor as a deserving laborer, but rather as someone akin to the leader of a bloodless *coup d'état*.[8] A successful adverse possessor assumes the mantle of ownership for much the same reason that a successful *coup d'état* produces a government whose authority to rule is undiminished by the initial illegality of its path to power. Social order requires that someone wield ownership authority in the former case, and public authority in the latter. Adverse possession solves the moral problem of agenda-less objects just as the recognition of the existing government (whatever its origins) solves the moral problem of state-less people.

The relationship between adverse possession and the legitimacy of post-revolution government is mostly one of analogy. But it is also something more than this because ownership is also a part of the larger system of public authority.

---

5 *See Cheshire and Burn's Modern Law of Real Property* (E.H. Burn & J. Cartwright eds., 17th ed. 2006) [hereinafter *Cheshire & Burn*] (relativity of title).

6 For a Canadian case, *see e.g.*, *Keefer v. Arillotta* (1976), 13 O.R. 2d 680 (Can. Ont. C.A.); Bruce Ziff, *Principles of Property Law* 128–31(4th ed. 2006).

7 Some have interpreted this test to make adverse possession difficult to establish, reflecting the same moral concerns that motivate some US jurisdictions to require good faith—a concern with land "theft." *See e.g.*, *Keefer*, 13 O.R. 2d 680; *Fletcher v. Storoschuk* (1981), 35 O.R. 2d 722 (Can. Ont. C.A.). As a result, there is one strand of case law that is increasingly unwilling to allow deliberate squatters to prevail under any circumstances. *See infra* note 77 and accompanying text. This is mistaken, I will argue.

8 I will use "*coup d'état*" and "revolution" interchangeably, although by *coup d'état* I mean a special kind of revolution—one in which a powerful elite takes over the government without necessarily acting in the name of the people and without dismantling, but rather taking over, the existing institutions. *See also infra* note 101 (distinguishing the adverse possessor from the conscientious revolutionary who claims to represent the will of the people and who seeks not just to oust the current office holder but to introduce a new order). I am grateful to Arthur Ripstein for suggesting that the analogy of adverse possession to revolution is more accurately described as an analogy to a *coup d'état*.

It is part of the way that the state orders society. Of all the ways that the state relies on owners, the most important is the owner's function of setting the agenda for an object and so setting a framework that organizes the uses others can make of it.[9] Insofar as the social order is in part constituted by owners, the state needs to ensure that owners are doing the agenda setting promised by the state, or else face a breakdown in the social order. The adverse possessor, having asserted effective authority over the object and displaced the original owner, assumes an indispensable role in both the property system and the larger system of public authority.

Part I of this chapter provides an overview of the three models of adverse possession, which rely upon strikingly different conceptions of ownership and possession. Part II develops the analogy between adverse possession and a successful *coup d'état* in order to explain the morality of adverse possession.

## Part I: Three Models of Adverse Possession

### *A Proceduralist Model*

The first model, recently adopted in England,[10] emphasizes the non-adversarial and procedural nature of adverse possession. On this view, the adverse possessor succeeds where she possesses and intends, in the ordinary sense, to possess the land for the requisite time period. The dispossession of the true owner is simply the result of sufficient acts of possession by the adverse possessor rather than any intentional ouster of the true owner.[11] Nothing more is needed: no intent to own, and no "hostility" or conflict with the owner.[12] As a result, an owner can

9 *See infra* note 97 and accompanying text. This explains what Henry Maine called the "presumption ... that *everything ought to have an owner,*" characteristic of modern property systems. Henry Maine, *Ancient Law* 249 (1963) (1861) (emphasis in original). There are many other reasons why a society may not tolerate vacancies, related to the obligations that the state imposes on owners. *See, e.g.*, Eduardo Peñalver, *The Illusory Right to Abandon*, 109 Mich. L. Rev. 191 (2010). For a different take on the service that owners provide the state *see* Larissa Katz, *Governing through Owners: How and Why Formal Private Property Rights Enhance State Power,* 160 U. Pa. L. Rev. 2029 (2012) [hereinafter Katz, *Governing*].

10 Australia has also recently adopted this approach. *See, e.g.*, Adrian J. Bradbrook, Susan V. MacCallum & Anthony P. Moore, *Australian Real Property Law* 688–94 (4th ed. 2007); Martin Dixon, *Modern Land Law* 501–503, 510 (6th ed. 2009).

11 *J.A. Pye (Oxford) Ltd. v. Graham,* [2002] UKHL 30, [2003] 1 A.C. 419, [38] (appeal taken from Eng.)

12 For cases rejecting an intent to own and emphasis on owner's future plans, *see Powell v. McFarlane* (1979), 38 P. & C.R. 452 (Eng. Ch.D.); *Laing and Laing v. Moran and Moran,* [1952] O.R. 215 (Can. Ont. C.A.); *J.A. Pye,* [2002] UKHL 30; *Beaulane Properties Limited v. Palmer*, [2005] EWHC 817, [2005] 4 All E.R. 461 (Ch.).

inadvertently lose title to her land even in circumstances where she has not abandoned or forgotten about it.[13] The squatter does not engineer a takeover of the owner's position and does not acquire a *new* ownership right at the end of the day.[14] When the original owner's right to re-enter is extinguished, the squatter by default is left with a right to possess the land that is better than anyone else's.[15] Adverse possession merely sets out the process by which the owner's rights are extinguished but does not carve out new rights for the possessor.[16]

This model of adverse possession rests on a particular understanding of ownership and its place in the common law. It fits with the old feudal view that the English common law does not have a concept of ultimate ownership of land.[17] Instead of ownership, the law recognizes a hierarchy of rights to possess that are, relative to one another, either stronger or weaker.[18] To *own* is just to wield a right to possess that is good against other persons asserting claims.[19] Even though the squatter is a trespasser, the law will protect him from dispossession by anyone

---

13 The "new" position on adverse possession raises the possibility of a conflict with the Protocol to the Convention for the Protection of Human Rights and Fundamental Freedoms, Mar. 20 1952, 213 U.N.T.S. 262 [hereinafter Convention], which protects against disproportionate interference with property rights. *See Beaulane Properties*, [2005] EWHC 817(Ch.) (finding a violation of Article 1 of the Convention). *But see* J.*A. Pye (Oxford) Ltd. v. United Kingdom*, no. 44302/02, 2007-III Eur. Ct. H.R. (Grand Chamber) (finding no such violation).

14 Frederick Pollock & Robert Samuel Wright, *An Essay on Possession in the Common Law* 91 (1888); Mark Wonnacott, *Possession of Land* 162 (2006); Brian Bucknall, *Case Comment, Teis v. Ancaster: Knowledge, the Lack of Knowledge and the Running of a Possessory Title Period* (1998) 13 R.P.R. 3d 68, 68 (Can.); *See also* Percy Bordwell, *Disseisin and Adverse Possession*, 33 Yale L.J. 1, 7 (1923).

15 For this interpretation, *see e.g.*, John M. Lightwood, *A Treatise on Possession of Land* 153 (1894).

16 Thus, in an action by the owners in *J.A. Pye (Oxford)*, no. 44302/02, 2007-III Eur. Ct. H.R. in the European Court of Human Rights, the lawyers for the government resisted any claim that the state had expropriated or taken the rights of the true owner and transferred them to the adverse possessor.

17 *See generally infra* note 24 and accompanying text.

18 Pollock & Wright, *supra* note 14, at 93 (the adverse possessor has a "right in the nature of property which is valid against every one who cannot show a prior and better right."). The notion of ultimate ownership slipped into the common law through the availability of the *jus tertii* defense in limited circumstances—that is, if the defendant did not forcibly dispossess the plaintiff, she can raise the existence of a third party's better title to defeat the plaintiff's action to eject. *See* 7 Sir William Holdsworth, *A History of English Law* 65–8 (2d ed. 1966), cited in McNeil, *supra* note 2, at 50.

19 Any loss of rights by the owner, on this view, is due to the owner's own inaction, not to a "taking" by the state or another. *See J.A. Pye (Oxford)*, no. 44302/02, 2007-III E.C.H.R. at para. 65.

other than the true owner.[20] What is more, third parties cannot challenge his right on the grounds that someone other than he is the true owner.[21]

The emphasis on relativity of title to explain the owner's position suggests a parity between the position of the adverse possessor (as holder of a right to possess good against the whole world except someone with a superior right to possess) and the position of the owner (as holder of a right to possess that is good against the whole world including the possessor).[22] It suggests that the difference between owner and possessor is one of degree rather than of kind. This apparent symmetry between the positions of the possessor and owner, on this model, accounts for why the squatter need not aim to take over from the owner or intend to acquire a position other than the one she occupies already. A right to possess is all the possessor has to start with and all that she or anyone can have at the end of the day.

The proceduralist model fails to acknowledge the essential differences in the *nature* of the owner's and the squatter's rights, in keeping with the view that English law, unlike civilian law, gets by without the idea of ownership.[23] The perception that our system of property works without the concept of ownership is the product of property law's roots in feudalism. The feudal origins of English property law produced a system of estates, in which the legal rights in land were always held of someone higher up the feudal chain and ultimately held of the Crown. As Professor J.W. Harris wrote, "[s]ince what is conveyed is always an estate in the land, it has been widely assumed that 'ownership' of land, as such, is not a conception internal to English land law."[24] But it would be a mistake to conclude that Anglo-American

---

20 Even the owner is limited in what she can do to regain possession: the owner has the right to enter and repossess her land only before the statutory period expires and only without violence. *See* 2 *Anger and Honsberger Law of Real Property* 1497 (A.H. Oosterhoff & W.B. Rayner eds., 2d ed. 1985). *See also* Thomas W. Merrill & Henry E. Smith, *Property: Principles and Policies* 198 (2007); Jesse Dukeminier & James E. Krier, *Property* 125–6 (5th ed. 2002). The owner cannot force the squatter but, if she meets resistance, must bring an action to eject. *See Anger & Honsberger Law of Real Property* (Anne Warner La Forest ed., 3d ed. 2008) (the right to enter and retake possession independent of court action but any violence might amount to assault). *See also Powell v. McFarlane* (1979), 38 P. & C.R. 452, 476 (Eng. Ch.D.): "Until the possession of land has actually passed to the trespasser, the owner may exercise the remedy of self-help against him. Once possession has actually passed to the trespasser, this remedy is not available to the owner … "

21 Ziff, *supra* note 6, at 139–40 (discussing the *jus tertii* defense); Merrill & Smith, *supra* note 20, at 226–7; Dukeminier & Krier, *supra* note 20, at 110.

22 This emphasis on relativity of title is motivated by the view that ownership is not really a legal concept, and that all anyone can have is a right to possession. *See infra* note 24.

23 *See* Larissa Katz, *The Concept of Ownership and the Relativity of Title*, 2 Jurisprudence 191 (2011) (arguing that the rights of owners and possessors are different in kind.)

24 J.W. Harris, *Property and Justice* 69 (1996). *See also* Bernard Rudden, *Notes Towards a Grammar of Property*, 1980 Conv. & Prop. Law. 325, 325; A.D. Hargreaves, *Modern Real Property*, 19 Mod. L. Rev. 14 (1956). *See also Cheshire & Burn*, *supra* note 5,

law has not produced a robust concept of ownership, albeit one that we need to glean from a wide array of property rules and doctrines.[25] It is of course true that the idea of ownership in the common law is rarely defined or directly discussed in property jurisprudence.[26] But this on its own should not lead us to overlook the concept of ownership within our legal system. As I discuss elsewhere, the concept of ownership in Anglo-American property law emerges from the way in which various property doctrines, taken together, establish and preserve the special position of the owner as the agenda-setting authority.[27] Harris similarly locates the concept of ownership in the common law, arguing that ownership is quite simply an *incident* of legal estates in land.[28] As earlier property writers like H. W. Challis wrote, "[a fee simple] confers, and since the beginning of legal history it always has conferred, the lawful right to exercise over, upon, and in respect to, the land, every act of ownership which can enter into the imagination ... and, for all practical purposes [the right] of ownership."[29] This is what Professor Baker meant when he wrote, "by the thirteenth century the tenant was in reality the owner of the land."[30] The Crown by that point had created the safeguards that enabled tenants to exercise agenda-setting authority with respect to the land without interference by their overlords.[31]

---

at 114–15; Dixon, *supra* note 10, at 501; McNeil, *supra* note 2, at 8–9; William L. Prosser, *Handbook of the Law of Torts* 68 (3rd ed. 1964) (noting early English common law blurred the conceptual distinction between ownership and possession).

25 *See* Harris, *supra* note 24, at 69–72 (arguing that the idea of ownership of land is internal to the common law and has been so since at least the medieval period). *See also* 2 Sir Frederick Pollock & Frederic William Maitland, *The History of English Law: Before the Time of Edward I*, at 6 (2d ed. 1959) (noting that medieval jurists like Bracton "ascribed to the tenant in demesne ownership and nothing less than ownership."). Holdsworth, on narrower doctrinal grounds, thought that modern property law does contain the idea of ownership. His argument was that the law permits a qualified *jus tertii* defense, a limited appeal to the existence of a true owner in circumstances where the defendant did not forcibly dispossess the plaintiff. For a discussion, *see* McNeil, *supra* note 2, at 50–51.

26 An important exception is in the context of US takings cases, where the US Supreme Court has struggled to define property rights coherently. *See* Michael A. Heller, *The Boundaries of Property*, 108 Yale L.J. 1163, 1202–17 (1999).

27 *See* Katz, *Exclusion and Exclusivity*, *supra* note 2, at 290.

28 Harris, *supra* note 24, at 70–71.

29 *See Challis's Law of Real Property: Chiefly in Relation to Conveyancing* 218 (Charles Sweet ed., 3d ed. 1911).

30 J.H. Baker, *An Introduction to English Legal History* 237 (4th ed. 2002). *See* Harris, *supra* note 24, at 70; Pollock & Maitland, *supra* note 25.

31 Civilians, facing a similar challenge, came up with the distinction between *dominium directum* and *dominium utile* to explain ownership in the context of feudalism. *See* Robert Feenstra, Dominium *and* ius in re aliena*: The Origins of a Civil Law Distinction*, *in* New Perspectives in the Roman Law of Property: Essays for Barry Nicholas 111, 112–13 (Peter Birks ed., 1989).

The recent English approach to adverse possession side-steps the moral paradox by emphasizing the relativity of title. There is, on this view, no usurpation—no "private taking"—but simply the natural defeasibility of the owner's right to possess when he fails to take action, thus leaving the adverse possessor's right to possess that much stronger.[32] On the English view, we do not have a thief one minute and an owner the next, but rather someone whom the law recognizes as having a right to possess before the statutory period expires, and an even stronger right to possess thereafter. With respect to the owner himself, the squatter maintains a right to possess until the owner extinguishes it by re-entry.[33] And vis-à-vis the rest of the world, the law not only treats the squatter as having a right to possess, but forbids mention of the better right of the true owner in a dispute with a third party.[34]

### *A Legal Moralist Model*

Modern American approaches to adverse possession reveal a much greater concern with the *effect* of adverse possession in tran2sforming squatters into owners.[35]

32 This was the view of English law of adverse possession taken by the Grand Chamber of the European Court of Human Rights in *J.A. Pye (Oxford) Ltd. v. United Kingdom*, no. 44302/02, 2007-III Eur. Ct. H.R. (Grand Chamber) (the effect of adverse possession is not a deprivation of possession but rather a regularizing of title). Contrast this view of adverse possession with the common view, in the American context, that adverse possession is a kind of "takings" or transfer of rights by the state from one person to the next. *See, e.g.*, Fennell, *Efficient Trespass*, *supra* note 4, at 1055 ("Background governmental power, not any acquisitive thoughts in the mind of the new owner, dispossesses the original owner."); Richard A. Epstein, *One Step Beyond Nozick's Minimal State: The Role of Forced Exchanges in Political Theory*, 22 Soc. Phil. & Pol'y 286, 305–307 (2005) (statutes of limitations produce forced exchanges, but are justified because they also produce Pareto improvements).

33 There is a debate about whether the adverse possessor has a right to possess depending on material fact of possession or a form of seisin that continues until the disseisee terminates it by re-entry. *See* McNeil, *supra* note 2, at 50–51 (discussing Holdsworth).

34 For a discussion of the *jus tertii* defense, *see* McNeil, *supra* note 2, at 50–51. *See also* Pollock & Wright, *supra* note 14, at 91. It is not unwaveringly the case that the common law forbids a defense based on the better right of a third party. Where the defendant has not forcibly dispossessed the plaintiff (for instance, the latter's right to possess is not founded on actual possession), the defendant can defeat the plaintiff's claim by raising a *jus tertii* defense. Holdsworth took this as evidence that the modern common law has an idea of (absolute) ownership that is distinct from (relative) possession. McNeil, *supra* note 2, at 50–51.

35 *See* Bordwell, *supra* note 14, at 12–13 (emphasizing the acquisition of new rights by the squatter.) This is so notwithstanding the fact that the law of adverse possession in the US is grounded in statutes of limitation that, as in England, technically produce this effect by extinguishing the original owner's ability to bring an action to eject the squatter. Many US scholars of property law have (quite rightly, as I will argue below) decried this characterization of adverse possession and have argued in favor of the proceduralist, non-

Adverse possession in American case law and commentary is commonly described as a form of private "taking" or land theft, with the apparently anomalous result that the law through adverse possession sanctions theft.[36] This perceived shift in the law's attitude to the squatter has led American courts and commentators increasingly to view the law of adverse possession primarily as a tool to correct the mistakes of good faith squatters:[37] deliberate squatters are morally undeserving of the disproportionate reward that adverse possession is seen to deliver.[38] This has had an impact on the evolution of adverse possession doctrine. Few US jurisdictions require that squatters deliberately challenge the title of the original owner in order to succeed, and some have gone so far as to limit the availability of adverse possession to good faith squatters.[39]

Historically, this was not the case. There was a time, particularly when the West was being settled, when it was seen as socially beneficial to encourage land-hungry locals to take over from absentee paper title holders.[40] As a result, many US jurisdictions historically either did not inquire into the mental state of the

adversarial approach that I have described above. *See, e.g.*, Henry W. Ballantine, *Title by Adverse Possession*, 32 Harv. L. Rev. 135, 141–2 (1918). *See also* Dukeminier & Krier, *supra* note 20.

36 See, e.g., Ballantine, *supra* note 35, at 141(identifying and then disagreeing with the view that adverse possession amounts to the statutory confiscation of property or a "parliamentary taking"); Jeffrey Evans Stake, *The Uneasy Case for Adverse Possession*, 89 Geo. L.J. 2419, 2420 (2001) ("The doctrine effects a transfer of state-sanctioned rights in land from owners to nonowners without the consent of the owner"). *See also* Fennell, *Efficient Trespass*, *supra* note 4, at 1039 n.9.

37 Fennell, *Efficient Trespass*, *supra* note 4; R.H. Helmholz, *Adverse Possession and Subjective Intent*, 61 Wash. U.L.Q. 331, 332–3 (1983) (showing the negative reaction of judges to deliberate squatters, even in jurisdictions where good faith is not required); Thomas W. Merrill & Henry E. Smith, *The Morality of Property*, 48 Wm. & Mary L. Rev. 1849, 1876 (2007).

38 *See* Thomas W. Merrill, *Property Rules, Liability Rules, and Adverse Possession*, 79 Nw. U. L. Rev. 1122 (1985) (arguing for a liability rule protection for owners in the case of bad faith squatters to reduce the size of the reward).

39 *See* Dukeminier & Krier, *supra* note 20, at 127; Fennell, *Efficient Trespass*, *supra* note 4, at 1047 (describing "bad faith" requirements for adverse possession as a minority approach that is increasingly losing favor and describing the dominant objective approach).

40 Eduardo M. Peñalver & Sonia K. Katyal, *Property Outlaws*, 155 U. Pa. L. Rev. 1095, 1106–07, 1109 (2007). A supporting rationale was that a squatter grows attached to the land she possesses and comes to consider it her own. *See* Oliver Wendell Holmes, Jr., *The Common Law* (2005) (1881); Lightwood, *supra* note 15, at 152–3 (noting a policy to "withhold[] from one who has slept upon his right ... [rather] than to take away from the other what he has long been allowed to consider as his own, and on the faith of which the plans in life, habits, and expenses of himself and his family may have been unalterably formed and established ..."). Of course, attitudes toward adverse possession are cyclical. Henry Maine wrote in 1861 that "[p]rescriptions were viewed by the modern lawyers, first with repugnance, afterwards with reluctant approval." (Maine, *supra* note 9, at 276).

squatter or even required that squatters have a hostile intent in order to prevail.[41] Over time, as unsettled land became increasingly scarce, deliberate squatting came to be seen in a different light, namely, as an attack on the security of ownership and as morally reprehensible.[42] The deliberate squatter came to be cast in the judicial imagination as a land thief to whom protection is offered only reluctantly, with a utilitarian's eye to the larger ills avoided by doing so.[43] On this view, the apparent windfall enjoyed by a deliberate squatter who is transformed into the owner is justified, if at all, on the basis that adverse possession prompts lazy owners to use their land or sell it off, roots out stale claims resting upon old evidence so that title searches are simpler and less costly, and respects the expectations of third parties who have relied on appearances of ownership.[44]

American instrumentalism held the moral paradox of adverse possession at bay for some time. So long as adverse possession was seen to perform important services, such as rooting out stale claims, third party reliance, or the improved efficiency of land use, Amercian courts suffered windfalls to "land thieves."[45] Recently, however, American commentators have suggested that many of the supposed benefits of adverse possession are either not sufficiently valuable to offset the costs of rewarding theft, or better achieved through other legal mechanisms.[46]

---

41 *See* Peñalver & Katyal, *supra* note 40, at 1110–11 (explaining how the doctrinal developments supporting bad faith adverse possession were one way in which the courts sided with squatters against absentee landlords in the West). The common law approach in the state of Maine is the best example of this approach: adverse possessors had to show a hostile intent, and good faith squatters were thus often disqualified if they could not show an intent to own what was not theirs. *See also* Dukeminier & Krier, *supra* note 20, at 142–4; Fennell, *Efficient Trespass*, *supra* note 4, at 1039 n.9; Margaret Jane Radin, *Time, Possession, and Alienation*, 64 Wash. U. L.Q. 739 (1986).

42 *See, e.g.*, Merrill & Smith, *supra* note 37, at 1876 (adverse possessors are seen as bad people according to the simple moral code that underlies property law). For the views of property scholars on the morality of deliberate squatting, *see* Fennell, *Efficient Trespass*, *supra* note 4 at 1048 (citing Richard Epstein, Thomas Merrill, Richard Helmholz, Richard Posner and others on the immorality of deliberate squatting).

43 Richard A. Epstein, *Past and Future: The Temporal Dimension in the Law of Property*, 64 Wash. U.L.Q. 667, 679–80, 685 (1986); Stake, *supra* note 36, at 2433 (noting a cost of the doctrine of adverse possession is that it "creates an opportunity to steal land, a behavior we do not want to encourage"). *See also Walls v. Grohman*, 337 S.E.2d 556, 562 (N.C. 1985) ("We have concluded that a rule which requires the adverse possessor to be a thief in order for his possession of the property to be 'adverse' is not reasonable …") (cited in Fennell, *Efficient Trespass*, *supra* note 4, at 1040 n.11).

44 Merrill, *supra* note 38, at 1128–33. *See also* Dixon, *supra* note 10, at 502.

45 The idea that adverse possession is inconsistent with the idea of ownership rights and yet justified for instrumental reasons is an old one, and one to which Hegel and others felt obliged to respond. *See* G.W.F. Hegel, *Elements of the Philosophy of Right* 94 (Allen W. Wood ed., H.B. Nisbet trans., 1991) (1820).

46 *Cf.* Fennell, *Efficient Trespass*, *supra* note 4, at 1084 (arguing that while the conventional utilitarian arguments in favor of adverse possession are not convincing, it is

For instance, as Professor Fennell has argued, the interests of third parties are adequately protected by tort actions for detrimental reliance, and land registries and recording systems now preserve evidence of title and so ensure the marketability of title previously threatened by old claims.[47] Others point out that it is no longer self-evident that adverse possession leads to more efficient uses of land, because our society no longer straightforwardly prefers development and active uses of land over conservation and passive uses.[48] Not being able to locate the benefits of adverse possession for deliberate squatters in utilitarian terms, American courts and commentators have become increasingly responsive to what they see as the moral paradox of adverse possession.[49] As a result, judicial practice increasingly favors inadvertent or good faith squatters even in jurisdictions where adverse intent is formally no bar to a successful claim based on adverse possession.[50]

### *An Inconsistent Use Model*

The third approach, like the legal moralist model and unlike the proceduralist model, acknowledges that turning squatters into owners works a radical transformation. At the same time it avoids collapsing into a moral paradox. Although this approach is not perfectly articulated in any jurisdiction, its crucial component—the inconsistent use test—was once found throughout the common law world.[51] According to the inconsistent use test, adverse possession is successful only when the possessor has used the land in a manner inconsistent with the original owner's agenda for it.[52]

---

efficient to allow deliberate squatters to acquire property rights through adverse possession in some circumstances).

47 *See id.* at 1063–4 (articulating other areas of law that protect against detrimental reliance, etc.). *See also* Stake, *supra* note 36.

48 *See generally* Abraham Bell, *Private Takings*, 76 U. Chi. L. Rev. 517 (2009).

49 Fennell's response is that there *are* benefits of deliberate adverse possession that have gone unnoticed. *See* Fennell, *Efficient Trespass*, *supra* note 4, at 1073–6. On Fennell's functionalist approach, we bracket questions about the morality of adverse possession so long as there are efficiency-based reasons for adverse possession.

50 Helmholz, *supra* note 37, at 332–3; Fennell, *Efficient Trespass*, *supra* note 4, at 1046.

51 *Leigh v. Jack*, (1879) 5 Exch. Div. 264 (Eng.). For cases in England following *Leigh v. Jack* see, e.g., *Littledale v. Liverpool Coll.*, [1900] 1 Ch. 19 (Eng. C.A.); *Williams Bros. Direct Supply Stores Ltd. v. Raftery*, [1957] 3 W.L.R. 931 (Eng. C.A.). This approach started to fall out of favor in England in the 1970s and is no longer the law there. *See Powell v. McFarlane* (1979), 38 P. & C.R. 452 (Eng. Ch.D.); *Buckinghamshire County Council v. Moran*, [1989] 3 W.L.R. 152 (Eng.) (also endorsing Slade J.'s approach in *Powell*, (1979), 38 P. & C.R. 452); *J.A. Pye (Oxford) Ltd. v. Graham*, [2002] UKHL 30, [2003] 1 A.C. 419 [38] (appeal taken from Eng.); Martin Dockray, *Adverse Possession and Intention-I*, Conv. & Prop. Law. (N.S.) 256, 257 (1982).

52 *Tecbuild Ltd. v. Chamberlain* (1969), 20 P. & C.R. 633, 643 (U.K. C.A.) (distinguishing between an "intent to exclude the true owner" and "an intent merely to

The inconsistent use test requires the squatter to show that she has in effect ousted and intended to oust the true owner.[53] A friendly or amicable relationship between the adverse possessor and the owner will tend to rule out adverse possession.[54] The inconsistent use test thus preserves a wide scope for the owner to pursue the ends of her choosing insofar as she is immune from all but the most direct and confrontational challenge to her authority. The effect of the inconsistent use test is that an owner is quite secure in her position even if her plans for the land do not include present uses of it, so long as the possessor does not make use of the land in a manner that is inconsistent with her plans for it. Possession is not adverse where it does not defeat the owner's plans for the property.

The inconsistent use test construes adverse possession as a bid to oust the owner from his position of authority.[55] The squatter's acts of possession are sufficient for this purpose only when they are inconsistent with the owner's intended use and so pose a true challenge to the owner's position. This understanding of "possession" may be at odds with the current English view of the ordinary meaning of the word, but it has deep roots. There are some similarities between the kind of possession required to defeat ownership on the inconsistent use test, and the idea of possession found in Roman law. On the Roman law conception, possession means roughly to "[sit] in power" or to "hold in the manner of an owner."[56] Thus, the Romans distinguished between detention, which is occupation without the intention to own, and possession.[57] Possession, on the Roman view, requires both acts of possession and intention, collectively known as *animus possidendi*. If possession means to

---

derive some enjoyment from the land wholly consistent with such use as the true owner might wish to make of it.").

53 *Keefer v. Arillotta* (1976), 13 O.R. 2d 680, 692 (Can. Ont. C.A.).

54 *Id.*; *St. Clair Beach Estates Ltd. v. MacDonald* (1974), 5 O.R. 2d 482 (Can. Ont. H.C.J.). But note the mutual and unilateral mistake cases in Ontario, which create a different set of requirements responding to the befuddled neighbor paradigm of adverse possession. *See, e.g.*, *Teis v. Ancaster (Town of)* (1997), [1998] 35 O.R. 3d 216 (Can. Ont. C.A.); *Key v. Latsky* (2006), 39 R.P.R. 4th 160 (Can. Ont. C.A.); *Wood v. Gateway of Uxbridge Props.* (1990), 75 O.R. 2d 769 (Can. Ont. Gen. Div.).

55 *Fletcher v. Storoschuk* (1981), 35 O.R. 2d 722 (Can. Ont. C.A.).

56 For the distinction between ownership and possession, *see* Barry Nicholas, *An Introduction to Roman Law* 105, 107–108 (1962). Relativity of title still matters in that possession is protected by the fact that a person who has possession has an action against a dispossessor *Id.* at 108. Romans understood possession to mean "the holding of a thing in the manner of an owner, the exclusive holding of a thing." *Id.* at 111. Nicholas explains the etymology of the word "possession" and notes that the literal translation could be "sitting in power." *Id.* at 111 n.1. Thus, the lessee "does not *hold in the manner of an owner*. His holding acknowledges the superior right of the lender. Conversely if ... he ceases to acknowledge that right and attempts to hold adversely to the lender, he then acquires possession." *Id.* at 111 (emphasis added).

57 *Id.* at 111. *See also* Maine, *supra* note 9, at 281 (possession signifies "physical detention coupled with the intention to hold the thing detained as one's own.").

hold in the manner of owner, then it follows that *animus possidendi* means the intent to own for oneself.[58] This understanding of possession complicates the position of deliberate squatters. For a deliberate possessor to "sit in power" or to "hold in the manner of owner," he must in effect set out to displace the existing owner. Perhaps to avoid encouraging intentional ouster, Roman law limited the availability of adverse possession to good faith squatters.[59] The inconsistent use test takes the same bold understanding of what it means to possess but omits the moral safeguards against ouster by "bad faith" squatters as found in Roman law.[60] On the inconsistent use approach, adverse possession is not restricted to good faith squatters but, on the contrary, is most readily achieved by deliberate squatters who challenge the owner's claim of authority.

The inconsistent use approach suggests that there is a distinction in kind (and not just in degree of exigibility) between a possessor and an owner. The key to understanding the distinction between owner and mere squatter is to understand the role of possession in establishing and maintaining their respective rights. Ownership does not depend on physical possession.[61] A person can own without ever having taken possession of the land in a physical sense. Actual possession, by contrast, *is* the underlying material manifestation of the squatter's right to possess.[62] This is not to say that ownership is a matter purely of formal right. The owner's position also depends on a material manifestation. But the material fact on which ownership depends is not actual possession, but rather the effective authority to control the agenda.[63]

---

58 For a discussion of German jurists' interpretation of the act and intention requirements in the Roman law of possession *see* Oliver Radley-Gardner, *Civilized Squatting*, 25 Oxford J. Legal Stud. 727, 734–9 (2005).

59 Justinian's Institutes 2.6 (Peter Birks & Grant McLeod trans., 1987). This excludes those who have an *animus furandi* but enables good faith purchasers who assert ownership over land they believe to be their own, but who are mistaken as to the validity of their title, to prevail in some circumstances. *See also* Maine, *supra* note 9, at 238 (stating that good faith is required for usucaption, in keeping with the view that the function of adverse possession was to cure defects in title).

60 *See* discussion *infra* Part II.

61 *See, e.g.*, Bordwell, *supra* note 14, at 2 ("It is common knowledge that the owner of land does not cease to have legal possession by his moving off the land and allowing it to lie idle.").

62 For the Roman law distinction between ownership and possession see Nicholas, *supra* note 56, at 115 (possession is a fact in the sense that there is and must be a material manifestation of it, whereas ownership is "not a fact but a right. Ownership exists whether or not there is any material manifestation of it ...").

63 *See* Katz, *Exclusion and Exclusivity*, *supra* note 2, at Part III (arguing that ownership is a special position of agenda-setting authority). This is true of all forms of ownership, including a commons. *See* Larissa Katz, *Red Tape and Gridlock*, 23 Can. J.L. & Jurisprudence 99, 108–110 (2010) (distinguishing between use-rights and an ownership stake in the commons and citing Elinor Ostrom's example of irrigation systems, where

Because the underlying material manifestation of ownership is not ordinary possession but rather effective authority, mere acts of possession by a squatter that are not otherwise inconsistent with the owner's plans do not present a sufficient challenge to the owner's position. In order to take over as owner, an adverse possessor must not only exclusively occupy the land but must also defeat the owner's agenda, which may or may not itself involve a physical presence on the land.[64] Thus, on this approach, an adverse possessor ousts the owner from her position of authority not by "merely squatting" but by taking possession in the manner of an owner and establishing that the original owner lacks effective authority. What this approach requires of the adverse possessor is both the intent to own and the acts of ownership.[65] The possessor, to meet the inconsistent use test, must aim to take over from the true owner and to step into her shoes. It is not enough for him simply to intend to carry on in his own shoes as possessor, as it is on the current English approach.[66]

The importance of effective authority to the owner's position continues the analogy between ownership and sovereignty.[67] Just as a ruler's position primarily rests on authority and not coercion, the owner's position rests on authority and not the brute fact of possession.[68] Ownership does not normally require that an owner actively possess the land; what it means to take charge as owner is to exercise the

owners of "dry land" have rights to use water but are not co-owners of the water insofar as they are not represented in the decision-making process about how it is used and allocated).

64 The obvious weight given to an owner's agenda-setting function, as opposed to the owner's present use and occupation of the property, generated some of the criticism we see of the inconsistent use test that I discuss below. *See Bradford Investments (1963) Ltd. v. Fama*, [2006] 77 O.R. (3d) 127 (2005),(discussing the concern that the inconsistent use test insulates investors from adverse possession).

65 *Hughes v. Griffin*, [1969] 1 All E.R. 460 at 464 (C.A.); *Booker v. Palmer*, [1942] 2 All E.R. 674 at 677 (C.A.) (holding that the trespasser must intend to become an owner, and cannot become an owner without intending to); *Ricard v. Williams*, 20 U.S. 59 (1822) (where possession under a lease that turned out to be void cannot ripen into title under adverse possession because possession must be adverse; there is a distinction between mere squatting and possession *qua* owner, with an intent to own).

66 On this view, adverse possession is acquisitive. *See, e.g.*, Feenstra, *supra* note 31, at 121. The adverse possessor does not derive her right from the former owner, as would be the case in a transfer of rights by sale or gift, but rather acquires a new right. *See, e.g.*, Harold Potter, *The Modern Law of Real Property and Chattels Real* 606 (1929) (squatter does not take "the estate of the former owner; on the contrary, he acquires a new estate.").

67 Katz, *Exclusion and Exclusivity*, *supra* note 2, at 278.

68 The expression "possession is nine-tenths of the law," refers to a presumption that a possessor is also the owner, which, as an evidentiary matter, helps to sort out title in the absence of land title systems. *See Cambridge Idioms Dictionary* (2d ed. 2006) "possession is nine-tenths of the law." This expression does not, however, refer to the importance of possession itself to the concept of ownership.

authority to set the agenda for a resource.[69] Authority, however, must be effective or its very legitimacy will be undermined.[70] This is true of a sovereign but also of an owner. Ordinarily, an owner's authority to set the agenda for her land will be effective even in the absence of physical acts of possession. Where others accept her as owner, they accept also that her plans for the future use of the land, as well as her present uses, deserve deference.[71]

But this is not to say that possession in the ordinary sense has no role to play in preserving ownership. The role of possession in preserving agenda-setting authority is analogous to the importance of coercion to preserving the state's effective authority. Generally, the state exercises its power by making laws that people have reason to obey. The state's power is primarily a function of its authority and not of its coercive force.[72] But where people disobey the law and so challenge the state's authority, the state will need to resort to coercion to bolster the effectiveness of its authority.[73] Similarly, where others disregard an owner's authority by challenging his agenda through inconsistent use, an owner may have to resort to actual possession to remain in power with respect to his land.[74]

The inconsistent use test is typically applied in resolving a contest between a deliberate squatter and an owner-occupier. There has been some confusion in the case law about how to extend this approach when the adverse possessor acts in good faith. The good faith squatter honestly but mistakenly believes that he owns the property and so is unaware of the existence of a true owner. Some courts have found the inconsistent use test difficult to apply in these cases. The good faith squatter cannot intend to oust the owner and assert authority in her stead if he is unaware of the owner's existence. And in cases of mutual mistake where the owner is unaware of the trespass, the good faith squatter cannot have been said to have acted inconsistently with the true owner's agenda because the true owner would not, in that case, have been in a position to form one. The obstacles that the inconsistent use test presents for the good faith squatter are hard to explain if we see adverse possession through the lens of legal moralism, which demands that there be some connection between the reward of ownership through adverse possession and the individual desert of the squatter. As a result, jurisdictions that

69 Insofar as it is possible to abandon land, an owner abandons where she fails to take charge. Thus, where she forgets about the land or simply fails to form any plans for it, she stands to lose her property to a squatter. This would amount, in the context of adverse possession, to a discontinuance of possession by the owner. *See* Peñalver, *supra* note 9, at 211 n.77; McNeil, *supra* note 2, at 70–71.

70 Joseph Raz, *The Authority of Law: Essays on Law and Morality* 9, 28 (1979).

71 Waldron, *supra* note 2.

72 *See* Leslie Green, *The Authority of the State* 71–5 (1988).

73 *See* Raz, *supra* note 70, at 86.

74 An owner can bring an action to eject within the statutory time period rather than actually repossessing the land herself, which is just to say that she has the option of calling on the state to exercise its coercive powers on her behalf. *Keefer v. Arillotta* (1976), 13 O.R. 2d 680, 692 (Can. Ont. C.A.).

have adopted the inconsistent use test in the context of deliberate squatters have subjected good faith squatters to a much less rigorous test for adverse possession than deliberate squatters.[75]

There is, however, a way of extending the inconsistent use test in the context of the good faith squatter that neither disqualifies her in every case nor treats her good faith as a count in her favor. An approach based on inconsistent use need not be read as requiring that a squatter oust the owner in every case. The inconsistent use test simply resolves, as between two contenders, the question of who in fact has authority. The inadvertent squatter should be able to succeed in the limited circumstances where adverse possession can proceed *without* ouster because the true owner does not claim authority over the land but rather has discontinued possession.[76] This is one way to resolve cases of mutual mistake, where the true owner fails to claim agenda-setting authority because she is unaware that she is in fact the owner.[77] Where the owner has no intended use of the land because she does not know it is hers, she has, in a sense, vacated the position, leaving it open to the inadvertent squatter to assume the position in her place.[78] This analysis would apply equally in cases where the owner is unilaterally mistaken about her rights: by failing to exercise her authority, she has created a vacancy that may be exploited by either a knowing or inadvertent squatter.

Where, however, the owner has not discontinued use, a squatter must establish that he has ousted the owner and has effective authority. In cases of unilateral mistake, where a good faith squatter believes he is the owner but where the true owner continues to exercise effective authority over the land, the squatter has not taken over the position of owner. It is true enough that the good faith squatter in cases of unilateral mistake will find it next to impossible to satisfy the inconsistent use test. But this is problematic only if we think that there ought to be some connection between the virtue of the squatter and the reward of adverse possession. It is precisely this kind of legal moralism that I challenge in the discussion that follows, where I will argue that it is not on the merits of the use or the user that

75 The standard for good faith squatters is an intent to exclude the whole world, including the true owner. *See Teis v. Ancaster (Town of)* (1997), [1998] 35 O.R. 3d 216, 225–6 (Can. Ont. C.A.)

76 *Rains v. Buxton*, (1880) 14 Ch. D. 537, 539–40 (dispossession "is where a person comes in and drives out the others from possession" and discontinuance is where "the person in possession goes out and is followed into possession by other persons").

77 This appears to have been the thinking in *Mueller v. Lee* (2007), 59 R.P.R. 4th 199, para. 26 (Can. Ont. Sup. Ct. J.). It is easier for a squatter to prevail in cases of mutual mistake because the owner who is not aware of her rights lacks *animus possidendi*.

78 In this regard, we can distinguish the inconsistent use test from the implied permission test, advocated by Lord Denning but abolished by statute. *Wallis's Cayton Bay Holiday Camp Ltd. v. Shell-Mex*, [1974] 3 W.L.R. 387 (Eng.) is the case in which Lord Denning tried to resurrect the implied permission test. Under the implied permission test, adverse possession is impossible if the landowner has no plans for the land. The squatter is deemed to possess with the permission of the owner in that case.

adverse possession is justified, but rather on the imperative in any property system to guard against vacancies in the position of owner.

The inconsistent use approach avoids the conceptual blandness of the English approach but risks being mired in the moral paradox to which the American approach is so sensitive. As we have seen, there is a current model in English law that distinguishes between owners and possessors not in kind, but in degree, primarily in terms of the exigibility of the right (exigible against all others in the case of the owner, and against all but those with a superior right to possess in the case of the possessor).[79] The inconsistent use test, by contrast, sets up a much sharper distinction between owners and possessors. At the same time, it presents a startling shift in the law's attitude toward the adverse possessor pre- and post-limitation period from a mere possessor (with no legal right to oust the owner) to owner with full protection.

## Part II: Revolution and Rehabilitation

On what grounds can we justify the transformation of squatters into owners? To understand the moral significance of adverse possession, we need to begin with the proper analogy. Much of the moral analysis of adverse possession has proceeded by analogizing adverse possessors to land thieves. This is the wrong analogy. What distinguishes theft or robbery from adverse possession? Consider the characteristic modus operandi of the thief: the thief achieves his goals—permanent control of someone else's property—either by force or by stealth.[80] The thief's method tells us something about the character of his claim to the object. The thief takes physical possession of the object with intent to deprive the owner permanently of possession without making a counterclaim of authority. The thief does not enter into a contest for legitimate authority over the object, but rather, as his resort to force or secrecy reveals, asserts control *in spite of* his recognition of the owner's superior authority. What is significant about this is that the thief is not inviting an evaluation of a competing claim to authority nor is he demanding to be judged the owner as a result of his actions. Insofar as the thief controls the object, his aim is to dupe society into thinking he is the owner, which is quite different from trying to elicit a judgment that he is in fact the owner.

Contrast the character of the thief's claims with the character of the adverse possessor's claims. The adverse possessor demands public recognition of her authority as owner, which she achieves only where she manifestly has authority over the land in place of the original owner. Thus, adverse possession is successful

---

79 *See* Harris, *supra* note 24, at 81–4 (ownership and possession as concepts in the common law). *See also* McNeil, *supra* note 2, at 74–7.

80 George P. Fletcher, *Rethinking Criminal Law* 38 (1978) (defining the core of theft, common law larceny, as "a forcible or stealthful taking").

only where it is peaceful, open and notorious.[81] Stealth or force undermines the adverse possessor's claims because by sneaking or forcibly removing the original owner, she in effect reveals that she lacks effective authority.

The character of an adverse possessor's claim is much more like that of a new government following a *coup d'état* than that of a thief. An adverse possessor does not merely circumvent the authority of the original owner but rather displaces it by asserting his own claim to authority. The adverse possessor claims exclusive and supreme authority, as does a new government, whatever its origins. This explains the public nature of an adverse possessor's authority. His claim amounts to a challenge to the owner's position of authority through the assertion of his own authority, which is necessarily a public act. The nature of an adverse possessor's claim as a public assertion of authority also explains why an offer to purchase land or other written acknowledgment of the true owner's status has the effect that the squatter's possession, up until the acknowledgment or offer, is deemed to be possession on behalf of the owner.[82] The significance of such a written acknowledgment is not that it reveals the squatter's awareness of the original owner's claims and so his bad faith. Of course, a deliberate squatter knows that someone else has paper title to the land in question, just as the leader of a *coup d'état* knows that there is a government with a right to rule (perhaps because it was democratically elected). Rather, an acknowledgment or offer to purchase is significant because it amounts to acceptance of the true owner's claims to legitimate authority inconsistent with the possessor's own public assertions of authority (made notwithstanding the owner's formal title).[83]

The analogy between adverse possession and a *coup d'état* helps to clarify the significance of the retroactive nature of the claim that the squatter makes. An adverse possessor and the leader of a *coup d'état* undergo a transformation once they succeed in displacing the existing authority. The adverse possessor becomes owner, and the leaders of a *coup d'état* become the new government. This transformation is retroactive: just as a new government's legitimacy is immune from challenge on the ground that it came to power illegally, so too is an owner immune from challenge on the ground that she once was an adverse possessor.[84]

81 *See Teis v. Ancaster (Town of)* (1997), [1998] 35 O.R. 3d 216, 221 (Can. Ont. C.A.) ("Possession must be open and notorious, not clandestine, for two reasons. First, open possession shows that the claimant is using the property as an owner might."); *Sherren v. Pearson*, [1887] 14 S.C.R. 581, 585 (Can.); *Powell v. McFarlane* (1979), 38 P. & C.R. 452, 478 (Eng. Ch.D.); Dukeminier & Krier, *supra* note 20, at 139–44; Carol M. Rose, *Possession as the Origin of Property*, 52 U. Chi. L. Rev. 73, 79–80 (1985).

82 *See* Merrill & Smith, *supra* note 20; Oosterhoff & Rayner, *supra* note 20; Ziff, *supra* note 6, at 128 (noting the effect of an offer to purchase on adverse possession).

83 La Forest, *supra* note 20, at 1542–6. *See also* Matthew Noah Smith, *Rethinking Sovereignty, Rethinking Revolution*, 36 Phil. & Publ. Aff. 405, 408 (2008) (describing revolution as necessarily a public spectacle).

84 For the doctrine of "relation back" in adverse possession, *see* Dukeminier & Krier, *supra* note 20, at 128–9. *See also* Fennell, *Efficient Trespass*, *supra* note 4, at 1051 n.65,

We retroactively construe the squatter as the owner from the outset just as we construe the leaders of the *coup* as the government from the moment they acquired effective authority.[85] The difficulty in ascertaining the original owner's and the former government's loss of authority (but also the importance of so doing) explains why there is a time lag in the law's validation of the squatter's and the new government's authority.[86] The squatter must establish that the owner lacks effective authority on day one but then must still wait out the statutory time period before the law recognizes that she has taken over from the original owner. This period is necessary to determine whether the original owner has in fact failed to exert effective authority from day one. The loss of authority cannot be, as Hart put it, "verified or falsified ... in short spaces of time."[87] It is difficult to pin down precisely when de facto authority actually ceases to exist simply because authority survives *some* resistance or interruption.[88]

The retroactive nature of adverse possession confirms that ownership authority is conclusive and not provisional. The adverse possessor's de facto authority does not compete with the owner's de jure authority during the statutory period. Rather, as we confirm after the waiting period, there was all along but a single person whose decisions about the object were authoritative. The retroactive nature of adverse possession also explains why the successful squatter, like the leaders of a successful *coup d'état*, cannot be held to account for wrongdoing. The adverse possessor is recognized as owner from day one even though, had he not succeeded, he would have been liable for trespass, just as the leaders of a failed *coup d'état* would have been liable for treason.[89]

---

1054. The legal claim that an adverse possessor's or the new government's law is the law of the land has a close analog in Kant's view that there is a moral duty not to inquire into the pedigree of a state. Christine M. Korsgaard, *Taking the Law into Our Own Hands: Kant on the Right to Revolution, in* Reclaiming the History of Ethics: Essays for John Rawls 297, 306–7 (Andrews Reath, Barbara Herman & Christine M. Korsgaard eds., 1997).

85 H.L.A. Hart, *The Concept of Law* 118 (2d ed. 1994).

86 Property theorists have long been puzzled by the importance of the lapse of time to the success of a squatter's claim. *See, e.g.*, Maine, *supra* note 9, at 212 ("[W]hy it was that lapse of time created a sentiment of respect for his possession ... are questions really deserving the profoundest examination."). My account shows why it is not the adverse possessor's reliance established over a long period of possession, nor the expectations of third parties so much as systemic reasons that explain the time requirement. *See supra* notes 44 and 47 and accompanying text (discussing reliance as a rationale for adverse possession).

87 Hart, *supra* note 86, at 118.

88 *Id. See also* Arthur Ripstein, *Force and Freedom: Kant's Legal and Political Philosophy* 387 (2009).

89 Thus, a former adverse possessor (one who has succeeded in taking over as owner) is immune from any claims by the ex-owner for rents or damages arising from her pre–limitation period trespass. *Beaulane Properties Ltd. v. Palmer*, [2005] EWHC 817 (Ch.). *See also* Limitations Act, R.S.O. 1990, c. L-15, § 5(1) (Can.) (explaining the owner's right is deemed to have arisen from the moment of dispossession by the squatter). When this

### *Justifying Adverse Possession*

What justifies adverse possession on this approach? At first glance, the analogy of adverse possession to a *coup d'état* appears to raise as many moral worries as the analogy of adverse possession to land theft. The positivist's answer—that the adverse possessor, like the new ruler, in fact wields authority—does not seem to provide an answer to why we ought to recognize the adverse possessor's (or the new ruler's) claims to authority. There are, however, good justificatory reasons for the attention that the law pays to facts on the ground in the case of adverse possession, just as there are good justificatory reasons for recognizing the new government's post-revolution rule.

Let me start by explaining the positivist's claim that a new government has legitimate authority in spite of the wrongfulness of its route to power and in spite of the existence of another organization with the right to rule but without effective authority. The existence of authority is not purely a question of law but also one of fact. Of course, international law or the law of a given nation may recognize or validate a new government's assertion of authority, but this has no effect on the new government's status in relation to its people. Hart made this point when he argued that an English law declaring Tsarist laws to be the law of Russia would in no way change the fact that the Communist Party was the government of Russia.[90] It simply would mean that, in cases decided by English law that bear on Russian events, English courts would apply Tsarist law. We cannot resolve the question of whether a legal system continues to exist purely as a question of law.[91]

There are also moral reasons for recognizing the fact of the matter when a new government claims authority (and has effective authority). The moral quality of our relations with others depends on our ability to work out collectively what justice requires and to implement policies that reflect these collective decisions.[92] Seen in one way, the state provides an indispensable moral service: it provides authoritative solutions to coordination problems that otherwise would lead to disagreement and factionalism.[93] The state acts as a moral guide, helping us to

right is extinguished, the squatter is not liable for rent or damages from the moment of dispossession onwards, even though she is liable before the statutory period expires. In the United States, this is known as the doctrine of "relation back." Dukeminier & Krier, *supra* note 20, at 128–9.

90 Hart, *supra* note 86.

91 *But see* Smith, *supra* note 84 (arguing that there is the possibility of decentralized authority).

92 Some have attributed a similar view to Kant. *See, e.g.*, Jeremy Waldron, *Kant's Legal Positivism*, 109 Harv. L. Rev. 1535, 1540 (1996) (arguing that there is a "need for a single, determinate community position on the matter—one whose enforcement is consistent with the integrity and univocality of justice.").

93 This is the Razian view that the legitimacy of the state rests on its contribution to solving the problems presented by disagreement about how social actors ought to coordinate and cooperate. Raz, *supra* note 70, at 50–52. *See also* Jeremy Waldron, *Kant's Theory of the*

achieve what we have reason to do better than if we acted alone.[94] It does so in part by providing good answers to common problems (for instance when the government regulates dangerous substances) but even more importantly, it does so simply by providing a single answer when we might, in exercising our individual practical reasoning, come up with many reasonable but diverging answers. A state of nature is marked by a plurality of opinion, with no authority that can provide a final answer. It is only a state that speaks for all of us that can close the debate on how to conduct our common affairs. To deny the authority of the new government is to deprive ourselves of this mechanism for coordination and, in effect, to thrust everyone back into a state of nature.

Adverse possession can be justified on analogous grounds. Adverse possession solves the moral problem of agenda-less objects just as the recognition of a new government post-revolution solves the moral problem of a lawless people. The moral significance of adverse possession thus plays the role of ensuring that ownership serves its primary function.[95] The owner's primary function in a system of property is to take charge of an object by setting the agenda for it. Within the constraints set by the government's own agenda, owners have the authority to ignore the interests and opinions of others and to set what they think is a worthwhile agenda for the object in light of their own interests. The exclusive agenda-setting authority of owners does not require that others exclude themselves entirely from an object but rather that they act in harmony with the owner's agenda or at least the agenda that the law imputes to her.[96] Ownership resolves conflicts not by keeping everyone except the owner out, but rather by ensuring that others defer to the owner's decisions.[97] The effect of ownership is to provide a hierarchical structure for decision making about a thing. The owner, within the constraints set by government, makes the ultimate decisions about the agenda for an object and others must fall in line.

Ownership thus avoids the potential for conflict among users that exists when there is no one clearly in charge of an object. If the original owner were to lack effective authority and the adverse possessor were denied de jure authority, there would be no authoritative resolution to questions about use with respect to that object. The function of ownership to coordinate uses of an object would be unfulfilled. When there is a vacancy in the position of owner (because there is no one with effective authority), we are thrust back into a mini "state of nature" in

---

*State*, *in* Toward Perpetual Peace and Other Writings on Politics, Peace, and History 179, 192 (Pauline Kleingeld ed., 2006) (the coordination aspect of Raz's normal justification thesis for authority is "also the key to the Kantian theory of the state").

94 Raz, *supra* note 70, at 24–5.

95 It is not just the law of adverse possession that accomplishes this. The law of abandonment also restricts the ability of an owner to divest herself of responsibility for land. *See* Peñalver, *supra* note 9.

96 Katz, *Exclusion and Exclusivity*, *supra* note 2, at 278.

97 For a fuller development of this point, *see id.*

our relations with respect to that object. The law of adverse possession is just one way of ensuring that there is always someone in charge in the eyes of the law, and thus no destabilizing vacancies. This is why the law validates the adverse possessor's claims only where the owner can be shown actually to have lost effective authority. This is also why the owner defeats the squatter's claims by showing that he continues to be in charge of an object. Ultimately, the law's most pressing concern is not *who* is owner but rather that the office of owner is filled.[98]

*Imperfect States, Imperfect Owners*

The legitimacy of adverse possession, on this account, is not tied to the relative merits of the agenda that an adverse possessor sets for the object any more than the legitimacy of a government depends on the merits of its directives.[99] The aim of adverse possession is not to ensure that the most deserving user of the object owns it any more than a system of property generally guarantees that any particular owner has the best moral claim to own that particular thing. The morally relevant aspects of a squatter's claim concern not the abuses of the original owner or her failure to set a sufficiently valuable agenda, but rather the original owner's failure to occupy fully the role of owner.

I thus make no attempt to vindicate the adverse possessor on the basis of her moral standing as a conscientious revolutionary, one who stands outside the legal system to resist the bad exercise of authority by others. There are cases outside the law of adverse possession where squatters or others who challenge the owner's authority do so in the manner of a revolutionary.[100] These are property outlaws: for example, civil rights leaders organizing sit-ins in segregated restaurants,[101] squatters taking

98 A similar point explains the importance of the rule against perpetuities. *See id.* at 306. There are other benefits to guarding against vacancies in the property system. I discuss elsewhere the advantages to the state in having a system of private ownership in place such as the power that a state that defines property rights has to press owners into its service. *See* Katz, *Governing*, *supra* note 9.

99 *See* Raz, *supra* note 70, at 31–2 (authority does not depend on perfectly guiding our action in all cases).

100 *See, e.g.*, Peñalver & Katyal, *supra* note 40, at 1170–72 (2007) (justifying resistance to the formal property system). Lee Fennell points out the difficulties in distinguishing between "good" and "bad" outlaws in Lee A. Fennell, *Order With Outlaws?*, 156 PENNumbra (2007), http://www.pennumbra.com/responses/12-2007/Fennell.pdf. *See also* Korsgaard, *supra* note 85, at 320 (notwithstanding the absence of a right to revolt, the conscientious revolutionary is justified by her success on the grounds that she has in fact "promoted the cause of justice on earth.").

101 *Bell v. Maryland*, 378 U.S. 226 (1964); *Lombard v. Louisiana*, 373 U.S. 267 (1963); *Gober v. City of Birmingham*, 373 U.S. 374 (1963); *Avent v. North Carolina*, 373 U.S. 375 (1963); *Shuttlesworth v. City of Birmingham*, 373 U.S. 262 (1963); *Garner v. Louisiana*, 368 U.S. 157 (1961).

over vacant public housing en masse in London,[102] and environmentalists chaining themselves to trees in British Columbia.[103] The demands of a property outlaw, like those of the revolutionary, are not just to be put in the place of the owner but rather are for institutional change—change to what can be owned privately, change to how we define the scope of an owner's authority, and change to how entitlements are distributed. In the case of the property outlaw, the attack goes much deeper than a disagreement about the use to which the current owner puts the land. It is an attack on the very institutions that support the owner's authority to do as she does. The property outlaw appeals to moral reasons to justify her attack on the system of property much as the conscientious revolutionary does for her attack on the system of governance.

The property outlaw, however, is not the paradigmatic case of the adverse possessor, and we need not justify adverse possession on similar moral grounds. We do not throw the original owner over for the adverse possessor on the grounds that the latter will do a better job any more than we reject the authority of the state on the grounds that it has not provided perfect guidance in all cases. Whether or not we allow for the possibility of revolutionaries to assert their own opinions of what is just and right, it would be much harder to make the case for the moral standing of a non-owner to act on her extralegal judgment about the quality of an individual owner's tenure and his own suitability as a replacement. One reason is that this extralegal stance would undermine the function of a property system, which is to provide the assurances that allow a person to set the agenda for an object of property *without* attending to the interests and opinions of others.[104] It would be quite another matter if a system of property were meant to guarantee the best possible agenda for a resource or to direct objects to their highest-value uses.[105] The conscientious adverse possessor might then declare that he is morally justified in helping along the ends that justify the system of property, assuming that he can get a judge or some other official to agree that his agenda for the land represents a more valuable use than that of the original owner. Owners who have exercised their authority poorly, that is, by failing to select the highest-value use of land, ought not to be (and in law are not treated as) more vulnerable to adverse possessors than those who have exercised their authority well. The adverse possessor thus looks very little like the conscientious revolutionary on my account and much more like the leader of a *coup d'état*, whose reasons for

102 *Southwark London Borough Council v. Williams* (1970), [1971] 2 W.L.R. 467 (C.A.).

103 *MacMillan Bloedel Ltd. v. Simpson* (1994), 92 B.C.L.R.2d 1 (C.A.).

104 There are of course important constraints on the exercise of this authority, the most important of which is the principle of abuse of right. An owner exercises her authority abusively where she selects her agenda for a reason other than her subjective determination of the best use of the object in light of her interests. *See* Katz, *Abuse of Right*, *supra* note 3.

105 *See* Katz, *Red Tape and Gridlock*, *supra* note 63, at 119–20.

assuming power may well be opaque to those from whom he demands recognition as the new government.

## Conclusion

In an "inconsistent use" model of adverse possession, we have both the conceptual basis for distinguishing between owners and adverse possessors (lacking in the recent English approach to adverse possession) and the theoretical basis for overcoming the moral paradox of deliberate adverse possession (missing from the consensus American view). Rather than land theft, adverse possession is more akin to a bloodless *coup d'état*, in which a new ruler ousts the old office holder and steps into her place. Just as the leaders of a successful *coup d'état* turn into a new government that has authority over its subjects, so too is a successful adverse possessor retroactively transformed into an owner and immunized on this basis from liability for her initially wrongful invasion of another's land. The rehabilitation of the adverse possessor avoids vacancies in the property system just as the rehabilitation of the new ruler following a *coup d'état* maintains the possibility of political authority and civil society.

# Chapter 11
# The Semi-Sovereign Corporation

Daniel J.H. Greenwood

Corporations are commonly called "property," as if they were things that can be owned, bought, sold and controlled under the ordinary laws of property. This metaphor is false. Certainly,, corporations own property. That is one of the most ancient prerogatives of the legal form. But the right to own property does not make the organization itself property.[1] This is manifestly false. Undoubtedly, property law can usefully be thought of as conveying a limited form of sovereignty.[2] Corporate law even more clearly creates a form of sovereignty. But viewing the organizational law of corporations as a branch of property law serves only to obfuscate (the leading alternative, pretending that directors are agents of shareholders, is even less revealing). Corporations are the legal manifestations of organizations: firms, cities, or non-profits. Thus, even more than ordinary property law, corporate law is about relationships of power between people. Moreover, the largest of our corporations are inherently public, influencing the lives of employees, customers, suppliers and investors across the world. Our most important institutions should no more be governed by property law than the state itself.

More prosaically, corporate law as we know it simply does not grant corporate participants anything resembling the standard bundle of property rights to exclude, control, sell, and destroy.[3] Nor does it hold them to the associated responsibilities of owners for the consequences of their actions: the most famous incident of corporate privilege is the shield of so-called "limited liability," which relieves shareholders of any liability for corporate obligations.

On the contrary, corporate law carefully excludes investors and employees alike from the rights of ownership. Instead, it creates a decision-making body—

1 Similarly, transferable shares of for-profit corporations clearly are property: share owners may buy, sell, or destroy their shares at will with little consideration of the interests of others. But shareholders do not own corporate property. A shareholder of Microsoft, for example, who sought to exclude non-shareholder employees from the Microsoft headquarters would be quickly led away by forces of the state, men in blue, if not white coats.

2 *See* Morris R. Cohen, *Property and Sovereignty*, 13 Cornell L. Q. 8, 29 (1927).

3 The law insists that the shareholder maintain a formal separation between personal and corporate assets: the core of "piercing the veil" doctrine is that shareholders that treat the corporation's property as their own will be held personally liable for corporate obligations, as if the corporation really were shareholder property or its decision-makers mere agents of the shareholders. *See, e.g.*, *Berkey v. Third Ave. Ry. Co.*, 244 N.Y. 84 (1926).

the board of directors or trustees—that is explicitly barred from acting as the firm's owner.[4] Far from owners, board members are legally required to act as fiduciaries for the entity itself, exercising independent judgment to act in the interests of the firm as they perceive it, regardless of their own interests or desires. Meanwhile, other corporate participants, even if they have the right to buy and sell their interests in the firm (as do share and bond owners of a publicly traded business corporation), have only the most limited rights to determine firm policies or control firm assets.[5]

The corporation-as-property metaphor suggests that even the largest multinational business corporations, however critical to social welfare, are somehow analogous to a private home—the sanctuary of an individual owner, protecting him or her from the pressing obligations of social life. But corporations are not private homes. Neither shareholders nor managers of publicly traded corporations have anything resembling full ownership rights, and shareholders—which are mainly institutions themselves—have little claim to the protected sphere of autonomous action that is so crucial to the standard defences of private property.

Liberal democracies successfully eliminated the claims of kings that the state ought to be seen as a sort of property owned by its elite (even Locke contended that only the "investors"—real estate taxpayers—had a claim to the vote). Some of our corporate theorists, in contrast, seem to be working to replace the liberal project with the political theory of the Sun King.

## Self-Governing Institutions

Corporations ought to be understood as semi-sovereigns: self-governing institutions to which we have granted a high degree of autonomy from ordinary democratic processes. Corporate law is primarily constitutional law, determining how internal decision-making will be organized and decision-makers appointed. The fiduciary duties of directors and their agents serve (with varying degrees of success) to restrain corporate officers from treating their offices as personal property, while the limitations on judicial review of the business judgment rule function as a direct parallel to comity, protecting internal corporate processes from review by other sovereigns.

Recognizing the public nature of our multi-national corporations will clarify the enormous democratic and republican deficits in their governance. We ought to view them with the same awe and skepticism with which we see the state itself:

4 Employees of government institutions often do have property-like rights to their offices, structured by civil service laws or the due process clause under influence of Charles Reich's *New Property* principles. *See* Charles A. Reich, *The New Property*, 73 Yale L.J. 733, 767 (1964).

5 Del. Code Ann. tit. 8, § 101 (West 2012); *Wilkes v. Springside Nursing Home, Inc.*, 353 N.E.2d 657 (Mass. 1976).

as institutions vital to civilization and prosperity, but always threatening to depart from their appropriate role as our servants to, instead, pursue power and mastery.

Nonetheless, American law usually classifies corporations as private—entities that need to be protected from government, not government-like power structures from which we need to be protected. Accordingly, the Supreme Court and legislatures grant our publicly traded transnational corporations personal rights such as speech[6] and privacy,[7] but we do not have a structure of fundamental rights against them.[8]

Corporate law has no equivalent to the public doctrine of settled expectations—within the corporation, paradoxically, property rights are few and far between. In particular, employees usually have little or no enforceable claim to the product of their labor, the perquisites of office or status, due process or even equality under law. On the contrary, they may be terminated at any time for no reason or any reason not barred by the anti-discrimination laws. As agents, they must obey the orders of their superiors and lack the basic right protected by property, that of a sphere of privacy in which an individual's will is supreme, or the fundamental liberal right of freedom of thought and speech. To say what you believe at work, if you believe something different from what your corporate superiors wish, will get you fired—and not only will the state not enforce a right of freedom of thought, but it will deem the firing "for cause" and deny you unemployment insurance. Employee workspaces—including private spaces such as desk drawers or email accounts—are subject to employer monitoring without notice, consent or process.

In short, our corporate law fails to reflect the liberal rights associated with limited government.

Moreover, we have yet to achieve basic republican principles in corporate governance. Corporate power is routinely centralized with no countervailing powers or checks and balances. Montesquieu's theory of power checking power

---

6 *Pierce v. Soc'y of Sisters*, 268 U.S. 510 (1925) (allowing a corporation to a assert First Amendment claim without discussion of its standing); *First Nat'l Bank v. Bellotti*, 435 U.S. 765 (1978) (overturning state legislation limiting use of corporate money to influence referendum on the ground that corporate expenditures are "free speech" protected against majoritarian law); *Citizens United v. Fed. Election Comm'n*, 558 U.S. 310 (2010) (extending *Bellotti* to protect corporate expenditures to influence federal elections). For a fuller, if now incomplete, listing of corporate constitutional rights, *see* Carl J. Mayer, *Personalizing the Impersonal: Corporations and the Bill of Rights*, 41 Hastings L.J. 577, 664–5 (1990). The Court has extended virtually the entire Bill of Rights to corporations, with only one explicit exception: the right against self-incrimination. (No corporation has yet litigated the newly-invented personal right to bear arms under the Second Amendment.)

7 *See, e.g.*, *Silverthorne Lumber Co. v. United States*, 251 U.S. 385 (1920) (limiting the majority's right to supervise corporations by creating a corporate right to freedom from inspection under the Fourth Amendment).

8 *The Civil Rights Cases*, 109 U.S. 3 (1883) (inventing the State Action Doctrine to hold that the Fourteenth Amendment protects citizens against violations of equal protection and due process only if the invader is the "state," not a corporation created by the state).

has no corporate law equivalent. Indeed, the chief executive is usually also the chairman of the legislative-like board, in a sort of parliamentary system without parties, citizen voting or judiciary. Unlike citizens, corporate customers and employees lack any governance rights, rights to dissent or criticize, and even any right to avoid expulsion from the community. Ordinary civil service norms, from neutral decision-making to Freedom of Information sunshine provisions, do not apply even to the largest and most bureaucratic firms, while the rule of law, in the sense of ordered regularity, applies only until the board or its delegates decide that it should not.

Indeed, contemporary corporate governance law ignores not only the basic claims of liberal political theory but even the most limited demands of pre-modern political theory. Every medieval theorist understood that the difference between a king and a tyrant is that a legitimate king acts in the public interest for the public good. Corporate law, in contrast, is clear that corporations are free to determine collective policies entirely without regard to the interests or values of their employees, customers and the citizens of the nations that create them. Those corporate participants and dependants have no more voice in the corporate "legislature" than medieval serfs had in theirs; the courts, meanwhile, generally cloak corporate board decisions in the protection of the business judgment rule. Pointedly, in the one circumstance where courts limit board discretion—when the company is up for sale—the judicial rule is that the board may not respond to the needs of such corporate participant at all. Instead, once the company is in so-called "Revlon Mode," its officeholders must ignore all interests and voices in the corporate entity, acting solely to maximize share price.[9]

Since Aristotle, we have recognized that the core of justice is treating equals equally. Our large corporations, however, institutionalize a very different principle: to those who have much, much will be given. They routinely favor the powerful or connected, interpreting competitive principles to allow treating people according to their usefulness to the firm. In corporate law, the law of one price has no place; firms routinely offer discounts to favored customers, pay employees different rates for similar work; and hire or promote officers or appoint directors because of their personal connections. In the public sphere, we'd generally consider this egregious corruption; in the corporate world it is simply "the moral[ity] of the marketplace."[10]

Moreover, within the limits of the punitive sanctions granted them—expulsion, defaming, and ostracizing—corporations are free to discipline customers and employees with no semblance of due process. The elaborate networks of anonymous informers and files of inaccurate information in our credit reporting

---

9 *Revlon, Inc. v. MacAndrews & Forbes Holdings, Inc.*, 506 A.2d 173 (Del. 1986).

10 Quoting, slightly out of context, Justice Cardozo's opinion in *Meinhard v. Salmon*, 164 N.E. 545, 546 (N.Y. 1928), which holds fiduciaries to a higher standard. Corporate decision-makers owe no fiduciary duty to citizens of the countries in which they operate, nor to corporate employees nor, ordinarily, customers.

system would put any police state to shame.[11] Even the oldest commandment of good government—that judges should accept no payments from the litigants[12]—does not apply to corporate adjudicators, who routinely view themselves as having no duty at all towards either truth, social norms or those whose fates they determine.[13]

Finally, in a democratic age, corporate law defies the most fundamental principles of democracy.[14] First, of course, those most affected by corporate governance are excluded entirely: in ordinary business corporations, employees are routinely denied the vote, and even when their pension funds own voting shares, Federal pension law often requires fund fiduciaries to act in the hypothetical interests of imaginary future pensioners even if those conflict with the actual opinions, values, or interests of the living employees.[15]

---

11 *See* Scott Thurm, *Next Frontier in Credit Scores: Predicting Personal Behavior*, Wall St. J. (Oct. 27, 2011), http://online.wsj.com/article/SB10001424052970203687504576655182086300912.html (reporting on credit bureaus attempts to find new users for their predictions).

12 *See, e.g.*, *Exodus* 23:8; *Deuteronomy* 16:18–19. Plato is similarly clear on this basic point. Plato, *Laws* XII (R.G. Bury trans. 1926) (360 B.C.E.) (proposing death penalty for anyone who accepts a gift for serving the country). Hammurabi, in contrast, provides Draconian punishments for bribing witnesses and for judges who change their verdict, but does not mention bribing the judge in advance. *Code of Hammurabi* 4–5 (L.W. King ed. 2004) (1780 B.C.E.).

13 *See, e.g.*, *Kamin v. Am. Express Co.*, 383 N.Y.S.2d 807 (Sup. Ct. 1976), *aff'd*, 387 N.Y.S.2d 993 (App. Div. 1976) (holding that failing to collect amounts due from DNC was not a violation of fiduciary duty); Richard White, *Railroaded: The Transcontinentals and the Making of Modern America* 353 (2011) (describing Charles Francis Adams' view, as President of Union Pacific, that his "duty to his stockholders" required bribery of Federal officials).

14 It is perfectly legal to organize a democratic corporation, which we would call an "employee coop." However, employee coops are rare, in part because existing law creates enormous financial incentives for incumbents to, instead, allocate future gains to themselves. *See also*, Henry Hansmann, Ownership of the Firm, 4 J.L. Econ. & Org. 267 (1988) (describing reasons why capital ordinarily hires labor rather than the other way around). Some corporations appear to be operated in the interests of elite employees even when the formal organizational rules suggest otherwise: consider, for example, investment banks such as JP MorganChase or Goldman Sachs that pay out most of their economic profit as salary, or high-tech firms like Microsoft that give executives huge stock distributions. Under current corporate law, these issues are delegated to the corporation's incumbent decision-makers with no equivalent to the limits constitutional principles place on political office-holders.

15 *See* ERISA, 29 U.S.C. § 1104(a)(1)(A)(i) (providing that ERISA trustee must manage fund solely for the purpose of providing retirement benefits). For further discussion, *see* Daniel J.H. Greenwood, *Fictional Shareholders: For Whom Are Corporate Managers Trustees, Revisited*, 69 S. Cal. L. Rev. 1021, 1069 n.106 (1996).

In the for-profit sector, corporations usually have elected boards. Corporate elections, however, bear little resemblance to democracy. Generally, corporations allocate votes on the distinctly anti-democratic rule of one share one vote, as if shares rather than human beings were the citizens of the community. Worse still, shares (and therefore the votes they command) are routinely saleable, with no imputation of corruption to those who simply buy elections. Thus, rule is not by the people but by economic incumbents: past economic success or luck gives wealth-holders the ability to translate money into power, and, therefore, into more money.

Moreover, in practice, plutocracy usually takes a back seat to bureaucracy. Publicly traded shares are largely voted by institutional investors that are themselves corporations or similar institutions. As a result, share voting often functions quite similarly to the bureaucratic hierarchy within the firm: professionals or fiduciaries supervise other other professionals or fiduciaries.

Even this limited legislative answerability is far from universal or expected. Most corporate boards are self-perpetuating in all but crisis circumstances. First, most corporate elections are uncontested, so the board's incumbents, via its nomination committee, in effect appoint their own successors. Even should an outsider contest an election, incumbents are permitted to use corporate funds to wage their campaign, while insurgents must fund themselves. As a result, contested share elections occur, in practice, only when an outsider buys up a majority or close to a majority of the votes. But since the judicial approval of the "poison pill" (which creates enormous financial penalties for such purchases without prior board approval), even this tactic requires the consent of the incumbent directors.[16]

Moreover, it is not uncommon to find Articles of Incorporation designed to ensure that outside shareholders have no authority even in extremis. It is perfectly legal (and routine) to allocate a block of shares controlling a majority of votes to a particular shareholder, which may itself be a corporation, trust or other entity, and thus ensure that control is perpetually exercised by the incumbents and their chosen successors. Alternatively, corporations may allocate votes differently than dividend rights, making it easier for incumbents to retain control while attracting outside funds. Google's two founders, for example, have extra voting rights for

16 Only once has an outsider dared to trigger a poison pill without prior consent of the incumbent board or a court order. *See, e.g., Moran v. Household Int'l, Inc.*, 500 A.2d 1346, 1352 (Del. 1985); Arthur Fleischer, Jr. & Alexander R. Sussman, *Takeover Defense* § 5.04[D][2], at 5-58 to -59 (6th ed. 2002). While the Delaware courts have ordered boards to lift the barrier created by the poison pill when they deemed the pill's use inappropriate, *see, e.g., City Capital Assocs. v. Interco Inc.*, 551 A.2d 787 (Del. Ch. 1988), since *Unitrin, Inc. v. American General Corp.*, 651 A.2d 1361, 1367 (Del. 1995), the bar for judicial intervention has been set quite high. On the effectiveness of the pill, *see, e.g.,* Guhan Subramanian, *Bargaining in the Shadow of Takeover Defenses*, 113 Yale L.J. 621, 627 (2003).

their shares that guarantee that they can always outvote all other shares.[17] Moreover, it is perfectly permissible, and common in the not-for-profit sector, to create a corporation in which the board—the legislative body—is entirely and permanently self-perpetuating (without regard even to the rule against perpetuities).

Classical liberal thought sharply distinguishes between private and public, civil society and the state. The state exists to restrain citizens from a Hobbesian war of all against all and, more generally, to limit the violence and coercion of private power. However, as Hobbes' own work exemplifies, a state powerful enough to restrain private violence and bullying is itself a frightening concentration of potentially dangerous power. Thus, liberty requires a careful balance: a state powerful enough to restrain private power, yet restrained enough to prevent it from becoming itself a tool of oppression. Hobbes proposed the core of the liberal solution: the laws should be "as Hedges are set, not to stop Travellers, but to keep them in the way," that is, preventing overreaching and abusive behavior—but not restricting people to particular roads or, especially, particular destinations.[18]

Without a doubt,, the distinction between state and private coercion is generally problematic.[19] State violence stands behind the corporate, property, contract and criminal law that define private hierarchy and enforce private power relations. Illegitimate private coercion is not always distinguishable from (and rarely preferable to) state oppression. Indeed, as the article that inspires this collection makes clear, significant property owners are at least as much public officials as most constitutionally recognized state actors.[20]

Nonetheless, our political rhetoric tends to sharply distinguish between public and private coercion (and the Supreme Court's constitutional jurisprudence is defined by this distinction, restricting itself only exclusively to state action, with only the undeveloped exceptions of the Thirteenth Amendment bar on badges of slavery and the Article I, Section 9 ban on titles of nobility). In both law and politics, contemporary Americans are far more likely to claim rights against the state than against purportedly private persons such as oppressive corporate property owners, monopolists, rentiers, polluters, corrupters of public officials or other villains of the rhetoric of other places and other eras.

Since the great corporate law transformation at the beginning of the twentieth century, for-profit business corporations have grown to dominate large sectors of the economy and our culture. Today, neither violence nor unjust overweening power is a state monopoly (if they ever were). Prisons have been privatized, corporate police forces are larger than municipal ones, cities offer "rent-a-cop" programs to large firms, and the military itself has largely been outsourced to Halliburton and

17 Google is by no means unique. For example, The New York Times, Hershey's and Campbell's Soup each have had provisions designed to assure that the founding family or its designees can always outvote publicly traded shares.

18 Thomas Hobbes, *Leviathan* 239–40 (Richard Tuck ed., 1991) (1651).

19 *Shelley v. Kraemer*, 334 U.S. 1 (1948).

20 Cohen, *supra* note 2, at 26.

other "private" actors. Private prisons, a judicial system increasingly delegated to arbitration, ever increasing corporate tracking of our purchasing, entertainment and political activities and preferences,[21] entirely private credit rating services and internal company discipline and security make a mockery of any claim that the state retains a monopoly on the legitimate use of violence or social control.

Instead, we are reverting to a system of feudal polynomoi, in which the democratically elected government is only a small part of the regulatory and coercive apparatus. As the state diminishes and our largest economic entities expand, the public-private dichotomy is increasingly dysfunctional, concealing potentially unjust power relations and distracting us from needed reform.

Public corporations are, under current law, private. Government agencies, however limited their scope or goals, are public, even when, as in the case of the Federal Reserve, they are controlled by private actors themselves beholden to the profit motive. Two sets of bureaucratic power structures barely distinguishable in their processes or influence are treated as if they were radically different. The result is that we have speech and privacy rights against a local school board, but US law grants our employers an unquestioned right to probe the contents of our desks and email accounts. Our freedom of information rights to a transparent government are so much stronger than the autonomy or privacy or academic freedom rights of government employee that political operatives can use them to examine the emails of a state university professor who has criticized them,[22] but Google and Koch Industries have privacy rights that prevent us from knowing how they plans to change, or endanger, our lives or political system. The City Assessor needs to have a reason and a process before raising my taxes, but my access to medical care is dependent solely on the whims and market power of my employer.

Our major corporations share many of the characteristics of sovereigns. They should share the responsibilities as well.

---

21 *Compare* Charles Duhigg, *How Companies Learn Your Secrets*, N.Y. Times Magazine, Feb. 15, 2012, http://www.nytimes.com/2012/02/19/magazine/shopping-habits.html (describing elaborate data analysis efforts of Target and other corporations), *with* George Orwell, *1984* (1949) (describing less accurate, if more malevolent, data collection by a fictional state).

22 For descriptions of politically motivated demands for disclosure of faculty emails, *see* Outside Legal Counsel, *Filing FOIA Requests for Professors' Emails* (March 30, 2011), http://www.olcplc.com/public/media?1301490262 and Professional Staff Congress, City University of New York, *FOIA, Academic Freedom and the Use of University Email and Computer Resources* (Apr. 12, 2011), http://www.psc-cuny.org/our-rights/foia-academic-freedom-and-use-university-email-and-computer-resources. This kind of invasion of the professor's work product violates the spirit, if not necessarily the rules, of tenure and academic freedom meant to protect individual academics from exactly this type of political pressure.

**Quasi-Sovereigns: "Worms in the entrayles of the state"**

Cohen points out that property law always conveys a form of sovereignty—control over other people and not just things. Corporate law is even explicitly a branch of public, political, law. Property still retains aspects of its origins in medieval status law. Corporate law remains centrally the law organizing a coercive governance structure. The central right of a corporate board is the right—normally absent from contractual, private, relationships—to bind dissidents without their actual consent. The entire corporation must follow the rules set down by the accredited governing powers. (Locke, following Socrates, attempted to justify coercive governmental powers by a theory of tacit consent—subjects may be said to have consented to the law if they do not emigrate. But tacit consent is not actual consent as it is understood in private law, which always requires more than merely failing to flee. Corporate law, like public law, has theories of tacit consent but does not depend on actual consent. In a modern corporation, many participants may exit freely—although not shareholders, which may only transfer their rights and obligations, not abandon them. But this is at most a right of emigration, which does not vitiate the general principle: corporate boards bind all corporate participants regardless of consent. Corporate law is, thus, fundamentally non-contractual, public rather than private.)

In the beginning, everyone understood that corporations were somewhat sovereign. The ancient corporations—the Church, the Knights Templar and the Knights Hospitallers of St. John (which at various times from the First Crusade to the French Revolution controlled Jerusalem, Acre, Tripoli, Rhodes, and Malta as well as many fortresses elsewhere), the Universities, the City of London, later the British East India Company and the Massachusetts Bay Company—were "corporations" precisely because they were corporate and corporeal. A corporation acted as a single body, by making law for their members.

Right of clergy, the students' right to be tried by the law of the University (and to carry their national student law with them even as they studied abroad), the City's right to self-regulate: these law-making governance rights were the essence of the beast. Hobbes famously contended that corporations are a threat to the state's monopoly on lawmaking, "as it were many lesser Common-wealths in the bowels of a greater, like wormes in the entrayles of a naturall man."[23] This

23 Hobbes, *supra* note 18, at 230. "Another infirmity of a Common-wealth, is the immoderate greatnesse of a Town, when it is able to furnish out of its own Circuit, the number, and expence of a great Army: As also the great number of Corporations; which are as it were many lesser Common-wealths in the bowels of a greater, like wormes in the entrayles of a naturall man." *Id. Compare* Mark J. Roe, *Strong Managers, Weak Owners: The Political Roots of American Corporate Finance* (1994) (describing early anti-trust and banking law as motivated by fear of corporate political power), *with* Howard Zinn, *A People's History of the United States: 1492–Present* 261, 264–85 (Harper Perennial 1995) (1980) (describing anti-monopoly popular movements), *and* Herbert Hovenkamp,

view was not unusual—not only was it a common view in the centralizing states of the early modern period, it continued to be a mainstream American rhetorical trope into the twentieth century

These early corporations did not distinguish clearly between business and politics.[24] Between the beginning of the seventeenth century and the Revolution, France created seventy-five "Colonization Companies," with charters granting not only monopoly trading rights but also "political powers."[25] Similarly, while some of the American colonies were founded with land grants,[26] others famously begin with charters creating bodies "corporate and politic": the Plymouth Council,[27] the Massachusetts Bay Company,[28] Connecticut,[29] the Treasurer and Company of Adventurers and Planters of the City of London, for the first Colony in Virginia[30] and the Hudson Bay Company (in Canada).[31]

The original charters for both the London Company (to settle Virginia) and the Plymouth Company (to settle New England) made these corporations more state-like than today's American states: each gave the respective company the right to control immigration, issue coins, fortify and defend the territory and impose

*Enterprise and American Law 1836–1937* 131–49 (1991) (summarizing academic debate regarding political forces behind railroad regulation).

24 As late as 1801, there were only eight manufacturing corporations in America. Philip Blumberg, *The Multinational Challenge To Corporation Law* 6 (1993).

25 M.F. Lindley, *The Acquisition and Government of Backward Territory in International Law* 92 (1926).

26 For land grants, see, for example, Charter to Sir Walter Raleigh (1584) and Charter of Carolina (1665). These charters take the form of deeds of land to an owner.

27 Charter of the Plymouth Council (1620). *Cf.* William Bradford, &c. Surrender of the Patent of Plymouth Colony to the Freeman, March 2d, 1640, *available at* http://avalon.law.yale.edu/17th_century/mass05.asp (original patentees transfer to the "Freemen of this Corporacon of New Plymouth all that ther right and title power authorytie priviledges immunities and freedomes graunted in the said Letters Patents.").

28 "And them by the name of the Governor and Company of the Mattachusetts Bay in Newe England, one bodie politique and corporate in deede, fact, and name." Charter of the Colony of The Massachusetts Bay in New England (1628), *reprinted in* 1 Records of Massachusetts 10 (Nathaniel B. Shurtleff ed., AMS Press 1968) (1853).

29 "We have thought fit, and at the humble Petition of the Persons aforesaid, and are graciously Pleased to create and make them a Body Politicly and Corporate, with the Powers and Privileges herein after mentioned." Charter of Connecticut (1662).

30 *See* Joseph S. Davis, *Essays in the Earlier History of American Corporations Numbers I-III*, at 32 (1917) ("This company was frankly a business corporation ... organized on the model of the East India Company.")

31 Lindley, *supra* note 25, at 95–6, states that the 1670 Hudson Bay Company charter explicitly granted it "legislative and judicial powers over all the inhabitants of the lands ceded it" as well as the right to have an army and a navy, make war and peace, and so on, all under the sovereignty of the King "as of our Manor of East Greenwich in our county of Kent in free and common Soccage." The Company sold its territories to the Crown in 1869.

customs duties[32]—rights of sovereignty that American states gave up no later than 1789. But these seem to have been less extraordinary derogations of the King's authority than simple consequences of the basic conceptualization of the new colonies as business corporations sharing characteristics with that other corporate estate, the aristocracy.

The most dramatic example, perhaps, is the British East India Company. Organized as a for-profit corporation paying dividends to its shareholders, the East India Company made its profits from the tea and opium trade with China and trade with and tax revenues from India. Early on, it claimed the right to build forts and cities, to make peace and war, enter into treaties and govern and tax the inhabitants of regions it conquered—all independent of Parliament (as its charter stemmed from the Crown) and on equal terms with the non-European governments (and rival European trading companies).[33]

Indeed, its attorneys went so far as to assert sovereign immunity. In the case of *Nabob of Arcot v. East India Company*,[34] stemming from a demand by the Nabob for an accounting of his revenues, the Company argued:

> A bill on this subject cannot be entertained by this court; transactions between sovereign princes ... cannot be liable to any municipal jurisdiction. No law can apply between them, but the law of nations. These are such transactions: for, by the charters and acts of parliament, the East India Company **are constituted a sovereign power,** or at least are the delegates of the sovereign power of this country . ... Your Lordship will not entertain a suit that cannot be executed by common means. ... [T]he East India Company ... are under the absolute authority of the Board of Controul, and cannot act but under their direction. Suppose their orders and those of the Court should be contradictory, what a situation the Company would be in![35]

32 Lindley, *supra* note 25, at 93

33 The East India Company obtained the right to make war in 1661 and 1683, the right to coin money in 1677, conquered Bengal in 1757 and after 1765 directly controlled the taxation of Bengal, Behar and Orissa as a nominal subordinate of the Moghul Emperor. From 1767, the charters also expressly note that the Company exercised these seemingly sovereign powers "for the Crown." *Id.* at 94–5.

34 *Nabob of Arcot v. East India Co.*, 29 Eng. Rep. 544 (Ch. 1791), discussed in Antony Anghie, *Finding the Peripheries: Sovereignty and Colonialism in Nineteenth-Century International Law*, 40 Harv. Int'l L.J. 1, 37 (1999). According to the case report, the Nabob had assigned these revenues to the Company in payment of debts, but contended that the Company had taken more than it was entitled to. Burke has an elaborate discussion of the origins of the debt, which he sees as part of the deep corruption of the Company. Edmund Burke, *Speech on the Nabob of Arcot's Debts*, *in* 3 The Writings and Speeches of the Right Honourable Edmund Burke 26–35 (J.F. Taylor ed., 1901).

35 *Nabob of Arcot v. East India Co.* (1791) 29 Eng. Rep. 544, 545–6 (Ch.), 3 Bro. C.C. 292, 294–5.

The argument is ambivalent regarding whether the Company is itself a sovereign or rather a delegate of the sovereign of England, reflecting the confused effects of Pitt's India Act of 1785. For the first 185 years of its history, the East India Company had been a private, profit-maximizing monopolistic corporation; Pitt's act put the Company under the control of a quango-style "superintending" board including governmental officials, transforming it into a sort of regulated industry.[36]

But the Company's argument is crystal clear in its insistence on radical autonomy. Its lawyers insist without hesitation that the Company makes its own rules, using its own internal mechanisms, and no one outside—not even a British court—is entitled to restrain it (except by the law of nations, here meaning mainly force of arms). Only its own "Board of Controul," not a court, may tell it how to behave.

To be sure, the other side contests the claim that the East India Company is a sovereign state (on the ground that its existence depends on an Act of Parliament, which could have been said of the Canadian state as well). Nonetheless, it too accepts the basic view of corporations as quasi-sovereign by their nature—referring to Lord Baltimore as a "dependent sovereign."[37] In reply, the Company makes the ambiguity more explicit:

> They do not refer to the mixed nature of the Company, which though, here, considered as a trading Company, is, there, in the character of a sovereign power. ... [N]o instance is produced of one sovereign power bringing an action against another sovereign power.[38]

The duality of the great trading corporations as business enterprises and semi-sovereigns continued to be recognized for centuries. Even as late as 1901, a British treatise considers them sufficiently sovereign to be subjects of international law, largely because of their treaty making power.[39] Of course, it would be another half century before most countries received that status.[40]

Nor was the official governing role of the trading corporation a brief moment in corporate history. The Hudson Bay Company governed much of what is now Canada from 1670 to 1869, when it sold its colonies to the crown.[41] The British South Africa Company did not turn over its most explicitly governmental

36 John Keay, *The Honourable Company* 390–91 (1991).

37 *Id.*, referring to *Penn v. Lord Baltimore*, 1 Vesey Sr. 444 (Eng. 1750).

38 *Nabob of Arcot v. East India Co.* (1791) 29 Eng. Rep. 544, 548 (Ch.), 3 Bro. C.C. 292, 299–300.

39 Hannis Taylor, *A Treatise on International Public Law* § 222 (1901).

40 Anghie, *supra* note 34, at 76–7 (noting that colonies and most non-European indigenous governments were not considered sufficiently sovereign to be deemed legal persons in international law).

41 Lindley, *supra* note 25, at 95–6.

functions until 1923; the British North Borneo Company, formed in 1881 to be a sort of vassal state nominally under the Sultan of Borneo, continued under its original charter even later.[42] Moreover, the combination of business and politics is not restricted to these clearly political corporations. All corporations were viewed as quasi-sovereigns.

As the early British corporations treatise author Kyd put it in 1793, a corporation is a "body politic" or a "political person" created "for the maintenance and regulation of some particular object of public policy."[43] In the special charter era, the right to be a "body politic" was a key part of the grant of corporate status, even for corporations that later Americans would classify as private, as in, for example, the Charter of Dartmouth College,[44] the Incorporation of Harvard College (1650),[45] and the charter of the College of William and Mary (1693).[46] Indeed, the courts held that the words "body politic" were essential for a statutory grant to create the basic corporate right of legal personality (that is, the right to deemed a single actor regardless of changes in the affiliated human beings).[47]

---

42 *Id.* at 100, 103, 106.

43 1 Stewart Kyd, *A Treatise on the Law of Corporations* 13, 14, 28 (Garland Publishing 1978) (1793).

44 The Dartmouth College charter uses language that echoes a grant of property right: "we have willed, given, granted, constituted and ordained, and by this our present charter, of our special grace, certain knowledge and mere motion, with the advice aforesaid, do, for us, our heirs and successors for ever, will, give, grant, constitute and ordain." But the right the King grants and ordains is political existence, not possession of property: "that there shall be in the said Dartmouth College, from henceforth and for ever, **a body politic** consisting of trustees of said Dartmouth College." Tr. of *Dartmouth Coll. v. Woodward*, 17 U.S. 518, 524–6 (1819) (emphasis added).

45 3 Records of Massachusetts, *supra* note 28, at 195. The articles create a corporation consisting of the President, five fellows and a treasurer, and declare that "said president & fellowes, for the time beinge, shall for euer hereafter in name & fact be **one body polliticke & corporate** in law, to all intents & purposes, and shall haue ppetuall succession, & shalbe called by the name of President & Fellowes of Harvard Colledge ... and by that name they ... may purchase & acquire to themselves ..." The 1672 charter repeats the "body pollitick & corporate in lawe" language, if with slightly different spelling. 4 *Id.* at 536.

46 *See Royal Charter*, College of William and Mary (1693), http://scrc.swem.wm.edu/wiki/index.php/Royal_Charter. *Compare id.* para. V, *with id.* para. IX:

"And we give and grant to them, or the major part of them, by these our letters patents, a continual succession, to be continued in the way and manner hereafter specified; as also full and absolute liberty, power and authority, of making, enacting, framing and establishing such and so many rules, laws, statutes, orders and injunctions, for the good and wholesome government of the said college." *Id.* para. IX.

47 *See* Davis, *supra* note 30, at 23. Legal personality is a set of rights to act as a single body. In the earliest charters, the package always includes the right to have a corporate seal, to hold property, enter into contracts, and sue and be sued in the corporate name, and to have corporate decision-making processes bind the entire firm including dissenters. Each of the rights, of course, has always been subject to restrictions; in the earlier charters, the

Kyd and his contemporaries meant "body politic" quite seriously: A corporation was an institution entitled to make "orders," adjudicate violations and impose "penalties" and "fines" on dissident or disobedient members.[48] Thus, even charters for obviously non-political institutions, such as Dartmouth College, explicitly provided for "law making," much the same as a municipality's would.[49]

In short, a corporation was a derogation of sovereignty, an authorization for a group of people to form a mini-government. The William and Mary Charter recognizes the potential conflict quite clearly, explicitly subordinating the college's "laws, statutes and injunctions" to the king's and the colony's, as if it were a subordinate state agency.

Now we can see why corporate charters caused such anxiety to Hobbes, the great advocate for a unified state and abolition of the medieval corporations. Corporations were a sort of commonwealth, just as the Hobbesian commonwealth itself is a corporation to pursue the common interests of its members. The same anxiety explains why the early United States restricted them to clearly public purposes: education, banks, transportation and large manufacturing enterprises.[50]

A century later, the economy had radically changed. In the mid-nineteenth century, our important corporations were railroads, and while they were commonly viewed as part of a great national enterprise, they were unquestionably operated for the private enrichment of a handful of insiders as much as to promote the national interest.[51] Nonetheless, even as corporate lawyers began their great

---

restrictions were far stricter than is the current norm. Thus, for example, corporate charters normally set a maximum and sometimes a minimum capitalization to limit the degree to which an immortal organization could accumulate property. Charters routinely limited the scope of the firm's activities and thus the contracts it could enter into. Moreover, before the second half of the nineteenth century, investors and firm "members" were nearly always deemed guarantors of firm obligations—while the firm was primarily liable for its contracts (and, after some controversy, torts), if it was unable to meet its obligations, investors or members could be compelled to add capital (with varying limits) to the firm.

48 Thus, for example, in 1648, the General Court of Massachusetts Bay authorized the "shewmakers" and the "cowpers" (coopers) to incorporate for three years, to control quality. The two grants are almost word for word identical. The assembled shoemakers or coopers and their elected officers "shall have power to **make orders** for the well governing of their company," and "shall have **power to heare & determine all offences** against any of their said orders" 2 Records of Massachusetts, *supra* note 28, at 249–51.

49 Harvard's charter similarly authorizes "the president & fellowes, or major part of them, ... to make from time to time such orders and by lawes for the better ordring & cariing on the worke of the colledge as they shall thinke fitt; provided they, the said orders, be allowed by the overseers." *Id.* (The requirement of prior approval by the overseers was removed in 1657, 4 *Id.* at 316.). The 1672 charter refers not to bylaws, but "orders and lawes". 4 *Id.* at 536.

50 *See supra* note 21 and accompanying text.

51 *Compare* White, *supra* note 13 (describing how insiders became fabulously wealthy while railroads failed to generate economic returns or provide an effective or useful service) *with* Burke, *supra* note 34 (describing how insiders of the East India Company

campaign to win private status and private rights for their patrons, the metaphor analogizing corporations to commonwealths remained strong. Angell and Ames, in the standard mid-nineteenth-century hornbook, refer to the power to make by-laws as "legislative": by-laws must be "considered as private statutes for the government of the corporate body."[52]

Similarly, mid-century courts were clearly aware that the right to make rules binding on the entire corporation contravenes ordinary private law norms. Then, as now, corporate law allowed a board to impose rules on all "members," [53]—shareholders, employees and others subject to its jurisdiction—without individual consent or, in most cases, even voting rights.[54] In sharp contrast, ordinary contract and property norms bind only those who have individually consented to the specific norm, while tort law binds because the norms are traditional or legislatively imposed by the sovereign authority of the people as a whole. Accordingly, the core board right to bind without actual consent is, as the nineteenth century courts regularly note, a "limited legislative power" or "a power of qualified legislation."[55]

Because corporations were viewed as fundamentally delegations of sovereign power, the issue of the competence of municipal courts to resolve issues involving corporations remained controversial through the nineteenth century. After all, comity generally precludes a court in one jurisdiction from judging the sovereign acts of another government. Corporations, as expressions of sovereignty, seemed to be entitled to similar deference. Thus, in 1843, Angell and Ames devote six pages to establishing the apparently controversial position that a foreign corporation may be sued if jurisdiction can be obtained by seizing its property.[56]

---

profited even as the institution did not, and with little connection to success or failure in the corporations' purported economic or social goals).

52 Joseph Angell & Samuel Ames, *Treatise on the law of Private Corporations Aggregate* 65 (2d ed., Boston, C.C. Little & J. Brown 1843).

53 The early term "members" has no precise analogue in modern business corporations, which are not membership organizations.

54 In modern business corporation law, the board's power to make rules binding on employees is derived from general principles of agency law (principals have inherent power to direct their agents). The board has little formal power to bind shareholder or other investors, but it does have plenary, undelegated power to operate the corporation, commit corporate assets, and initiate changes in corporate governance, including, in most states, enacting corporate bylaws. *See, e.g.*, Del. Code Ann. tit. 8, § 101 (West 2012). Other corporate actions, including mergers and amendments to the articles of incorporation, may be initiated only by the board but require consent of a majority of the voting shares. *See, e.g.*, *Smith v. Van Gorkum*, 488 A.2d 858 (Del. 1985), *overruled by Gantler v. Stephens*, 965 A.2d 695 (Del. 2009) (declaring board's duty to determine whether to enter into merger non-delegable).

55 *See, e.g.*, *Tuttle v. Walton*, 1 Ga. 43, 45, 51 (1849).

56 Angell & Ames, *supra* note 52, at 336–42. *Cf. Howell v. Chicago & N.W. R.R.*, 51 Barb. 378, 379 (N.Y. Gen. Term 1868) ("Previous to the Code [noted in next footnote], foreign corporations were not the subject of litigation in the courts of this state, except

It went without saying that mere in personam jurisdiction was impossible—to the courts, corporations looked too much like the sovereigns that created them. In the end, legislative intervention was required. In New York, an 1849 act of the legislature finally reversed the common law rule and allowed foreign corporations to be sued.[57]

But even after that statutory innovation, courts worried whether exercising jurisdiction over a corporation created by another state for "visitation"—that is to "examin[e] into the affairs of a corporation"[58]— might be an infringement of comity, an invasion of the respect due to a fellow sovereign, and beyond the domestic court's subject matter jurisdiction.[59]

As a 1904 New York court put it:

> If the illegal acts of the directors or of the corporation offended solely against the majesty of the state to which it owed its life—in other words, constituted only public wrongs—the proposition is probably correct, for we are not compelled to, nor should we, entertain actions simply to redress the outraged dignity of foreign governments.[60]

But I am not concerned here with the niceties of jurisdiction, but rather with a way of thinking about the corporation. The jurisdictional problem—the doctrinal origin of the modern choice of law rule known as the "internal affairs doctrine"—arises only because even ordinary business corporations seemed, like the British East India Company, to be sort of sovereign.

---

when proceeded against by the attachment of their property for the collection of a debt or the redress of a wrong.").

57 N.Y. Bus. Corp. Law § 1314 (McKinney 2013), derived from a 1920 amendment to the Gen. Corp. Law in turn derived from Code Civ. Proc. 1780, enacted in 1849 and amended in 1880. The original text appears in N.Y. Laws 1849, ch. 107 (authorizing suits "against any corporations created by or under the laws of any other state, government or country, for the recovery of any debt or damages").

58 *State* ex rel. *Weede v. Iowa Southern Utilities Co. of Delaware*, 2 N.W.2d 372, 388 (Iowa 1942) (exercising jurisdiction over and applying Iowa law to Delaware corporation).

59 These early concerns about comity and jurisdiction eventually evolved into the modern common law choice of law doctrine known as the "internal affairs doctrine." In the modern version, courts assume jurisdiction over foreign corporations, even for matters that nineteenth century lawyers would have considered "visitation," but they apply the law of the incorporating state even when ordinary choice of law principles would counsel otherwise. This doctrine, which allows American corporations to evade any state-level attempts to reform corporate law by simply changing allegiance, is hard to justify on policy or democratic terms. However, it has a certain internal logic as a historical remnant of deference to the state that created the corporation, even if the incorporating state's involvement and interest is, today, basically a fiction.

60 *Miller v. Quincy*, 72 N.E. 116, 118 (N.Y. 1904).

Sovereignty and the deference due a sovereign continued to permeate corporate law even at the end of the nineteenth century. The Eighth Circuit in 1893 justified judicial deference to corporate boards (the doctrine that today is called the business judgment rule). Today, this doctrine is considered completely independent of the internal affairs doctrine, but the court's language suggests that both originated in the same sense of comity:

> Corporations are in a certain sense legislative bodies. They have a legislative power when the directors or shareholders are duly convened that is fully adequate to settle all questions affecting their business interests or policy, and they should be left to dispose of all questions of that nature without applying to the courts for relief.[61]

Modern courts have offered various explanations of the business judgment rule: shareholders seek risk-taking boards and therefore should be happy to accept the risk of breach of fiduciary duty by directors (although not employees),[62] or judicial review will drive directors and officers (D&O) insurance rates up, presumably because directors routinely violate the law, or it is unfair for some unexplained reason to hold directors to the ordinary standards of care that apply to all other professionals. The turn-of-the-century court had a justification explanation far more tightly connected to the actual doctrine and not dependent on finding some reason why directors are different from all other corporate actors or professional fiduciaries. In the older view, courts should decline to review board decisions or should be extremely deferential to them—the essence of the modern business judgment rule—for a simple, clear, rationale dating back to Montesquieu's division of powers or the international law system's notion of sovereignty. Coordinate branches must defer to one another. Courts should not be overly quick to reverse decisions of foreign states, or legislatures, or administrative agencies, or juries—or corporate boards. The board is given a constitutional stature of an independent state.

The notion that a corporation was a mini-state was once as commonplace as Hobbes' metaphor of the state as an artificial person, a body-corporate, remains today. Hobbes himself, for all his emphasis on the unlimited power of the single sovereign in his system, notes that subordinate "bodies politique" are quite common and that they have the power to make law over their subjects.[63]

61 *Republican Mountain Silver Mines v. Brown*, 58 F. 644 (8th Cir. 1893).

62 *Joy v. North*, 692 F.2d 880 (2d Cir. 1982).

63 "And that which is said here, of the Rights of an Assembly, for the government of a Province, or a Colony, is applicable also to an Assembly for the Government of a Town, an University, or a College, or a Church, or for any other Government over the persons of men." Hobbes, *supra* note 18, at 159–60.

## Death of Self-Government

This way of thinking—the corporation as a mini-state, either delegated from the supreme sovereign or coexisting with it in a semi-feudal or federal balance of powers—has disappeared from the academic discussion of corporations and almost as completely from the cases.

Modern metaphors overwhelmingly describe corporate purposes and actions as private, not public. The terms we use describe the corporation not as political governance but a form of property or contract or agency or trust—a series of metaphors inconsistent in almost every respect but their mutual emphasis on privacy and market and their de-emphasis of the necessarily coercive nature of powerful bureaucracies.[64] Scholars describe shareholders as "owners" or "principals" rather than "voters" or "investors" and then puzzle about why shareholders have none of the rights or responsibilities of ownership or principals and directors aren't trustees for them.

The drive to see corporations as private and consensual is so powerful that even the corporation's relationship with its shareholders is often characterized by agency or property metaphors—although either, if taken seriously, would threaten entity (limited) liability and, indeed, corporate personality. After all, if shareholders were either owners or principals of the firm, ordinary property and agency rules would make them fully liable for its obligations. Indeed, ordinary property and agency doctrines would make the firm itself a common law conspiracy in restraint of trade: a corporation, after all, is above all else a convenient way for a group of investors to negotiate collectively, even while other factors of production, such as employees or retail customers, are required to do so individually.

The ideological function of this shift in metaphor is clear: it resolves, or at least elides, a major problem in the democratic legitimacy of the corporation. As a self-governing entity, business corporations are a sort of cross between herren-democracy and straight out plutocracy—neither obviously legitimate in the modern age. Only a small part of the relevant electorate was given the vote: shareholders but not bondholders, investors of money but not investors of time or effort; freely transferable publicly traded shares with cheap risk spreading but not employees with genuine commitments and unavoidable exposure to the firm's success or failure; potentially exploitable or locked-in shareholders, but not equally or more exploitable bond investors, long term employees, pension beneficiaries, customers or suppliers. In a generally democratic age, restricting the vote in this way is a problem for any political forum.

We have no satisfactory theory justifying disenfranchising all participants other than shares. Some economic theorists have suggested that shareholders

64 Daniel J.H. Greenwood, *Introduction to the Metaphors of Corporate Law*, 4 Seattle J. Soc. Just. 273 (2005).

are more vulnerable than other corporate participants,[65] but this is obviously false. Shareholders are highly mobile, fully diversified providers of a fungible commodity. If any corporate participant can rely on market forces for protection, this would be it. Employees, customers and suppliers, in contrast, are likely (as Oliver Williamson has emphasized) to have firm-specific investments subject to monopoly expropriation.

A related claim is that shareholders are the "residual risk bearers" in the firm and therefore most interested in its results at the margin;[66] this claim seems to rely on a failure to understand the relevant law and willful disregard of the actual practices. The actual law is that, to the extent that a corporation generates economic gains—that is, its product could be sold for more than its inputs must be paid—directors are free to allocate those gains to any corporate participant. The business judgment rule precludes litigants from second-guessing corporate decisions to lower prices (thereby giving surplus to customers, as economic theory suggests will happen in competitive markets), to increase wages or employment or executive bonuses,[67] or to reinvest in the business.[68] On the upside, then, shareholders have little formal claim to corporate surplus. Conversely, on the downside, shareholders are entirely protected from sharing in corporate losses: the most fundamental rule of modern corporate law is that the corporation and its creditors may never demand additional funds from shareholders. Moreover, there is no empirical evidence that shareholders are the marginal recipients in fact: corporations are much more likely to vary employment than dividends, suggesting that the real residual risk bearers are employees.

Others have suggested that shareholders "deserve" the vote because they are most aligned with corporate interests. This also seems false. Although corporate interests are often casually assumed to mean shareholder interests, even the most casual student of the American economy can quickly identify instances where shareholders profited even as the company suffered, starting with the great railroad fortunes and ending with the last round of private equity "going-private" transactions. Sometimes advocates contend that corporate interests should be defined to mean shareholder interests, but that results in incoherence: shareholders, particular modern diversified portfolio investors that also hold derivatives and

65 *See, e.g.*, Oliver E. Williamson, *The Economic Institutions of Capitalism* (1998); Henry Hansmann, *The Ownership of Enterprise* (2000).

66 *See, e.g.*, *The Anatomy of Corporate Law* (Reinier Kraakman et al eds. 2004).

67 In an earlier age, John Kenneth Galbraith assumed that most corporate surplus went to unionized employees and middle managers. John Kenneth Galbraith, *The New Industrial State* (1967). After several decades in which shareholders took the bulk of the surplus, it is increasingly clear that top managers are becoming the chief beneficiaries. *See, e.g.*, In re *Walt Disney Co. Derivative Litigation*, 906 A.2d 27 (Del. 2006).

68 *See, e.g.*, Merton H. Miller & Franco Modigliani, *Dividend Policy, Growth, and the Valuation of Shares*, 34 J. Bus. 411 (1961) (justifying reinvestment on the ground that under narrow theoretical conditions, shareholders would be indifferent between reinvestment and dividend payouts).

related instruments, have no unified, a priori, interest. A shareholder that holds a competitor, has shorted the stock, or seeks to purchase the company on the cheap, may have a strong interest in the stock price dropping or the company doing poorly; shareholders that specialize in trading may care more about movements in the stock price rather than the underlying company.[69] A portfolio shareholder that has diversified away all company specific risk is specifically avoiding any commitment to the company's particular interests.

Even leaving aside the limitations on the voting population, corporate law defies basic democratic norms. The standard voting rule is not "one person one vote" but the wealth-based "one share one vote"—as if the corporate "citizens" were not the shareholders but the shares themselves—in defiance of the most elementary rule of democracy. Shares and their associated votes are freely saleable, so corporate governance is quite literally for sale, without any suspicion of corruption. Moreover, the issues on which voters may opine are sharply restricted. Indeed, the basic corporate law principle that the directors, not the shareholders, manage the company, is generally understood to require that directors ignore the will of the shareholders. They must, instead, exercise independent business judgment in the interests of the company,[70] much as George III's parliament "virtually represented" the American colonies or Burke asserted his obligation as a statesman to substitute his judgment for his constituents' in the pre-democratic United Kingdom. This reduces even the voters to subjects rather than citizens: corporate governance may be "for" shares but it is definitely not "by" or "of" them.

At the beginning of the American era, these limited understandings of citizenship and voting might have been within the realm of republican theory. After all, most Americans had no vote and many were explicitly excluded from citizenship.[71] Moreover, the business corporations of the day generally had "members" who were more than today's algorithm-powered computerized rapid-fire stock traders profiting at the expense of other traders in a zero-sum game.

---

69 *See* Greenwood, *supra* note 15, at 1028; Henry T.C. Hu & Bernard Black, *The New Vote Buying: Empty Voting and Hidden (Morphable) Ownership*, 79 S. Cal. L. Rev. 811 (2006).

70 Del. Code Ann. tit. 8, § 101 (West 2012). *See also Smith v. Van Gorkum*, 488 A.2d 858 (Del. 1985), *overruled by Gantler v. Stephens*, 965 A.2d 695 (Del. 2009) (finding directors personally liable for breach of duty where board allowed shareholders to vote on whether to accept a facially attractive buy-out offer). If the shareholders have any comparative advantage as decision-makers at all, it must be in deciding whether to hold or sell stock, which is, after all, the decision professional investors are paid to make. By refusing to allow a board of directors to refer this decision to the shareholders, the Delaware Supreme Court made the strongest possible statement of the limited role of shareholders in corporate decision-making.

71 *Dred Scott v. Sandford*, 60 U.S. 393 (1856) (holding that no African-American was a citizen of the United States), *superseded by constitutional amendment*, U.S. Const. amend. XIV.

But we have long since abandoned the notions of virtual representation or restricting the franchise based on wealth. Today, in a generally democratic age, there is something deeply distasteful about restricting the vote in a political forum only to (some of) those who have invested hard cash rather than blood and sweat—and no possible justification for allocating votes on any important issue on the basis of dollars rather than head count. As a result, any description of the modern business corporation that seeks to legitimize current law must begin by deflecting attention from its fundamental form and original sin.

Moreover, the mid-nineteenth century rise of the all-powerful board gives a self-governing corporation aspects of Quesnay's "legal despotism": a unitary executive, lacking any balance of powers, with virtually unlimited power. Quesnay defended absolute monarchy on the ground that the monarch, as the sole owner of all the land in the country, would internalize all the proceeds of economic activity and therefore maximize it.[72] The board nominally elected by timeless, diversified investment funds makes the same claim to universality: shares, as the purported recipient of the firm's marginal product, have the strongest incentive to maximize the firm's financial well-being; the board acts in their name as the legal despot.[73]

All of this makes corporate governance hard to defend as compatible with modern democracy. Were we to return to metaphors of the corporation as polity or quasi-legislature, the state it would bring to mind would be Saudi Arabia, or perhaps the former Soviet Union under the kleptocrats, or various dictatorships of the right or left. If this is a government, it is one that treats most of its subjects as helots to be exploited, not part of the common good.

Its pretenses to consent of the governed are at best Lockean "tacit consent," that is., that in a market economy, those who are sufficiently unhappy with the corporation's leaders can sever ties with it, with all the usual limitations to that argument.[74] But free exit does not exist. A core reason companies incorporate is precisely to avoid the free exit of partnership; institutional continuity is essential to induce people to commit to and trust the firm. Individual shareholders (and bondholders during the pendency of the bond) can transfer their rights to another, but have no right to withdraw capital from the corporation. Employees with firm-specific investments in skills, relationships, family location, insurance or seniority;

---

72 *See* Bernard E. Harcourt, *The Illusion of Free Markets: Punishment and the Myth of Natural Order* 94 (2011) (describing Qesnay's defense of absolute monarchy as the only way to align the interests of the governed and the governors).

73 *See, e.g.*, Greenwood, *supra* note 15, Williamson, *supra* note 65 (claiming, implausibly, that shareholders are the most vulnerable participants in the firm and therefore require the special protection of a vote). *But see* Armen A. Alchian & Harold Demsetz, *Production, Information Costs, and Economic Organization*, 62 Am. Econ. Rev. 777 (1972) (claiming, implausibly and contrary to law, that no coercion or exercise of power can occur inside a firm because corporations are entirely contractual).

74 *See, e.g.*, John Locke, *The Second Treatise on Government* (J.W. Gough ed. 1966); Plato, *Apology of Socrates* (Michael C. Stokes trans. 1997); Albert O. Hirschman, *Exit, Voice & Loyalty* (1970).

retirees with firm-specific pensions or medical care; suppliers or customers in bilateral monopolies or otherwise tied to the particular firm—all these persons in relationship with the firm have only limited "exit" options and their "tacit consent" is similarly atrophied.[75] The right to exit is no more a guarantee of sound corporate governance than the right to emigrate makes for decent political governments, and for much the same reason.

Similarly, corporate law's rejection of the basic principle of division of power flies in the face of three centuries of political theory. The unitary executive, despite some recent attempts to rehabilitate it, remains as unappealing as the absolute monarchy from which it is descended. The claims of monarch and corporate autarchy are equally implausible: absolute power corrupts absolutely in the corporate as well as the political sector, and just as we know that dictators and monarchs regularly get rich while impoverishing their nations, it only takes the most casual glance at the modern world to understand that shareholders and CEOs often find ways to gain even as the firm, and its other participants—employees, bondholders, customers and suppliers—suffer.[76] Indeed, the entire ecosystem of the leveraged buyout and private equity firms is based largely on this premise. Often it is far easier to transfer value than create it.[77]

For these reasons, corporate spokesmen have long since abandoned the public metaphors of corporate law. Portraying your institution as standing in the proud tradition of Saudi Arabia monarchs, or even the English Parliament of the rotten borough era, lacks a certain public appeal. The modern alternative requires a good deal of sleight of hand to maintain a coherent façade. Still, Adam Smith made real, an amalgam of property, trust, contract and agency, in which shareholders are entitled to exploit because they own, even though they must be protected because they lack the normal attributes of ownership, and directors must serve them as agents even though they are not their agents, has at least some claim to legitimacy in a market democracy. We call shareholders owners of publicly traded corporations not because they are but because they are not.

## Corporation as Semi-Sovereign

But the demise of the public metaphor does not mean that the underlying insights of the older view are less true. On the contrary, our public corporations are more state-like than ever.

---

75 *See generally* Williamson, *supra* note 65.

76 For a theoretical account, *see* Greenwood, *supra* note 15.

77 *See generally* Daniel J.H. Greenwood, *Enronitis: Why Good Corporations Go Bad*, 2004 Colum. Bus. L. Rev. 773; Daniel J.H. Greenwood, *The Dividend Puzzle: Are Shares Entitled to the Residual?*, 32 J. Corp. L. 103 (2006). For a sampling of the many empirical accounts, *see* White, *supra* note 13.

Hannah Arendt famously criticized the rights of man by pointing out that when men and women were stripped of their rights as citizens and members of a national people—they turned out to have no rights at all. The rights of men were meaningful only as rights of citizens. The eternal "Rights of Man, which by themselves were supposed to be independent of citizenship and nationality ... proved to be unenforceable ... whenever people appeared who were no longer citizens of any sovereign state."[78]

Thinking of corporations as quasi-sovereign—to some degree taking on aspects of the states that create them, and to some degree as independent states or at least sub-state governmental entities themselves—helps frame a series of issues. Arendt suggests the first: whether corporate affiliation isn't today taking on some of the importance of national affiliation. It is my job, not my citizenship, that gives me basic social security rights, including access to medical care, pension benefits, and parental support such as maternity leaves and assistance in financing increasingly unaffordable education for my children. Without a corporate affiliation, consumer-unfriendly computer systems might prove virtually unnavigable. It's the right corporate affiliation, even more than the right passport, that allows you to work in the country you prefer. Corporate positions even allow people to bring some of their law with them, like the medieval university students—drinking in Saudi Arabia, for example, or taxation in the United States. Even for the classic liberal rights, corporate affiliation is as critical as citizenship. As an academic, my freedom to speak is made meaningful by my corporate affiliation—independent scholars are perhaps not as badly off as the stateless, but still, neither libraries nor Westlaw nor even serious reads of submissions to the journals are readily available without the correct institutional backing.

One could multiply examples. The proposition that large private institutions have taken over many functions of the unified state, in a revised return to the feudal notion of multiple estates, is not likely to be controversial. But if corporate relations are this important, the mere right to exit is not enough. We must begin to assert the basic rights of citizenship against our corporate governors—the right not to be exiled, the right to criticize, basic privacy rights. Perhaps even property rights of the Charles Reich variety[79]—rights to retain a position, to exclude the boss from private desk space or email, or to a personal sphere of opinion or practice protected from the corporate authority's claims to religion or political conformity.

Most fundamentally, though, we need political rather than property rights. We must establish the political right to have our good considered a part of the common good. Benefits to citizens are not costs to the nation but its purpose; similarly, we

78 Hannah Arendt, 2 *Origins of Totalitarianism* 173 (1951). *See also id.* at 174, 176. "[W]hoever is no longer caught in it [the system of citizenship] finds himself out of legality altogether (thus during the last war stateless people were invariably in a worse position than enemy aliens) ... [The stateless have no] place in the world which makes opinions significant and actions effective."

79 *See generally* Charles Reich, *supra* note 4.

need to end the self-colonization of corporations, created by our law, that treat us as mere tools to advance the goals of the real oldest established permanent floating crap game in New York—a traveling pool of international capital mediated through layers of private profit-maximizers.

More controversial might be the extent to which these are privileges of affiliation with corporations, as opposed to large institutions generally; after all, Bechtel, large law partnerships and major universities provide these privileges as well as the exchange-traded firms.[80] Business corporations remain our preeminent large corporations, so focus on them would be warranted even if other institutions posed essentially similar issues.

But more to the point, the peculiar governance of business corporations in fact makes them somewhat different than other large institutions: alone of all our governance structures they are directed to slavishly follow the market regardless of whether its directives make sense.[81] They alone function as agents for a legal construct, with no internal moderating principle or countervailing force.[82] They alone have no institutionalized mechanism for constituents, unbound by fiduciary duties to the institution itself, to restrain the institution when its goals conflict with more important ones: profit is good, but it can conflict with more important values as well. Thus, as power is devolved to these institutions, publicly traded corporations should cause us special worry. They distinctively lack the restraints and balances that mark intelligent government.

Let me nod towards a few other implications that must be held for future discussion.

### *Shareholders as Fundamental Rights Beneficiaries*

One of the more interesting aspects of the corporate metaphor is the ambiguity regarding the corporation's borders and subjects. In this chapter, I've mostly assumed that the corporation primarily affects its employees and that they are, therefore, the closest analogy to the subjects of a state. But corporate law often ignores employees, acting as if the investors, or at least the equity investors, were the key constituency of the firm. Corporate "democracy" as it is usually discussed in the literature refers not to human control over corporations seen as quasi-governments, but rather to the system of voting proportional to dollar investment in equity that is formally the ultimate control mechanism over our corporations. Whatever that is, it isn't democracy.

80 Thanks to Neil Cohen for urging me focus on this.

81 Directed at least by the Wall Street Journal and a handful of cases, such as *Dodge v. Ford Motor Co.*, 170 N.W. 668 (Mich. 1919). Other cases are more reticent about demanding that corporations pursue profit at all costs. *See, e.g.*, *Paramount Commc'ns, Inc. v. Time, Inc.*, 571 A.2d 1140 (Del. 1989).

82 *See* Greenwood, *supra* note 15, at 1023–5.

But considering the shares as corporate subjects does raise some interesting issues.

If we consider the shareholder role as a rough analogue to citizens in the quasi-sovereign corporation, we see that shares have a far more effective international rights regime than we've managed to create for real people.

And one that doesn't depend on nationality in the classic sense at all.

First, shareholders, or more properly the role of shareholding (not the full people who invest) have achieved the stateless Rights of Man that Arendt saw as unenforceable and empty. The shares traded in the New York Stock Exchange are owned in large part by institutions. Pushing through the institutions to find the human ultimate beneficiaries is difficult, and sometimes conceptually unclear (who are the human beneficiaries of a university endowment?). But many estimates suggest (as the macro numbers do as well) that a large and growing portion of the investment is foreign, or, more interesting still, of hidden formal citizenship. Shares are not human, but they are stateless.

Shares, regardless of citizenship or locale of their ultimate human owners or beneficiaries (if any) do have effective legal protection of their rights inside the corporation. Without exaggerating the degree to which shares control the firm, the fact remains that corporations are generally run in their interest—and, most relevantly for the nationality point, shares held by foreigners (and even non-human institutions) are normally treated indistinguishably from those held by Americans.

Moreover corporate law and the stock market makes real the right to exit in a way that the refugees have never had. Arendt emphasizes that even the right to emigrate, when it existed, wasn't worth much without a commensurate right to immigrate. In the world of share-citizenry, the situation is quite different. Not only may investors sell the stock of a company that mistreats them, but they are free to buy the stock of other companies. Stock investors need not remain stateless, unaffiliated with any corporation, unprotected by any system of internal lawmaking.

### *Corporations as Actors*

The same, of course, is true of our corporations themselves. They too have rights today that are effectively protected without regard to nationality.

Indeed, it is increasingly difficult to intelligibly assign nationality to the largest corporations. Is Chrysler German or American? What would be the relevant test? Should those of us who long boycotted VW now add PT Cruisers to the list?

With hitherto unimaginable economic power and often physical power to match, corporations are independent players to a far greater extent than most of the members of the United Nations. They are not subordinate governmental units—if indeed they even have nationality. Nonetheless, modern law grants corporations rights of comity greater than the human rights of citizens.

Corporations may freely choose their own constitutive law under the "internal affairs doctrine," thus disempowering most local attempts to control their processes. Their decision-makers are largely free of judicial interference under the "business judgment doctrine." Agency law creates a legal default rule that the corporation's hierarchs have absolute control over all subordinates, who are supposed to set aside their own interests and views during the workday. Courts routinely hold that corporate employees forfeit ordinary rights of citizenship while at work, including freedom from searches or monitoring and freedom of conscience. Corporate bureaucrats are entitled to freedom from routine open government laws under judicial extensions of the Bill of Rights. They are allowed to spend corporate assets to influence the very regulators and lawmakers who are supposed to ensure that corporate assets are only used for socially useful purposes—and under Supreme Court doctrine, this corruption of the political and economic system is "free speech" entitled to Constitutional protection.

Since the earliest years of the Republic, the Supreme Court has consistently created fundamental rights for corporations even in the face of clear constitutional language to the contrary, and has done so with alacrity notably lacking with respect to actual Americans.[83] Thus, even before it denied citizenship to African-Americans, the Court decided that corporations could invoke diversity jurisdiction to access the Federal courts despite the Constitution's limitation of this privilege to "citizens."[84] After the Civil War, the Court thought it obvious that the Fourteenth

83 *Santa Clara Cnty. v. S. Pac. R.R.*, 118 U.S. 394, 396 (1886) (extending the Fourteenth Amendment guarantees of equal protection and due process to railroads). *Santa Clara* long predates the death of Jim Crow, which excluded African-Americans from basic equality. *See, e.g.*, *Plessy v. Ferguson*, 163 U.S. 537 (1896), *overruled by Brown v. Bd. of Educ.*, 347 U.S. 483 (1954), or the repeal of the Married Women's Property Acts, which denied women fundamental property and contract rights. Even today, the Supreme Court treats corporations with a solicitude it refuses to actual American citizens: under current doctrine, a state legislature may discriminate in favor of every interest group, corporate or otherwise, except African-Americans. *See Williamson v. Lee Optical*, 348 U.S. 483 (1955); *Regents of Univ. of Cal. v. Bakke*, 438 U.S. 265 (1978); *Gratz v. Bollinger*, 539 U.S. 244 (2003); *Meredith v. Jefferson Cnty. Bd. of Educ.*, 547 U.S. 1178 (2006); *Ricci v. DeStefano*, 557 U.S. 557 (2009).

84 *See Bank of the United States v. Deveaux*, 9 U.S. (5 Cranch) 61, 86 (1809), *overruled by Louisville, Cincinnati, & Charleston R.R. v. Letson*, 43 U.S. (2 How.) 497, (1844) (holding that corporation is "certainly not a citizen and, consequently, cannot sue or be sued in the courts of the United States" but then extending diversity jurisdiction nonetheless by ignoring the separate legal personality of corporation). This fiction, however, would have disallowed diversity jurisdiction for virtually all corporations (either they don't have members or the members are likely to defeat diversity). Rather than apply the clear language of the Constitution, the Court instead created new legal fictions to reach the same result. *See Louisville, Cincinnati,& Charleston R.R. v. Letson*, 43 U.S. (2 How.) 497, 558 (1844) (overruling *Deveaux* and holding that corporations will be fictionally "deemed" citizens for diversity purposes); *Marshall v. Balt. & Ohio R.R.*, 57 U.S. (16 How.) 314 (1853) (overruling *Letson* and holding that a corporation's shareholders will be deemed to be citizens of the corporation's state of incorporation regardless of reality). The Congress has limited this fictional expansion of the Constitution slightly by statute. *See* 28 U.S.C.

Amendment's equal protection and due process clauses should apply to corporations with no support from language, history or structure, it had far more trouble finding that equal protection required treating women or African-Americans or Chinese-Americans or Japanese-Americans as full members of the polity.[85]

In short, we've allowed business corporations to assert rights to protection from their own and other governments, protection against ombudsmen, protection against political decisions to reallocate the social resources they control, protection against investigations into how they operate their internal affairs, and protection against demands that they serve the interests of those they exploit.

*Corporations as Nation States*

Travel as an executive of a major multinational and you bring with you an international regime of protection stronger, in many respects, than the national one that comes with your passport. American executives in trouble spots can expect security forces in their defense, quick evacuation, medical care not available to the locals, even exemption from petty local rules such as Saudi Arabian bans on liquor or sexual discrimination. Try that as a tourist.

Passports themselves are readily available to those with the right corporate connections. I myself worked comfortably in London for six months as a representative of my employer, something simply unavailable to me as a naked bearer of the Rights of Man or even the rights of Americans. More prosaically, even for those not in the elite, and particularly for Americans, our health care, our

---

§ 1332 (2012) (stating that a corporation is also a citizen, for diversity purposes only, of its principal state of business). As a consequence, corporations have a privilege denied to actual citizens: they may manufacture diversity by simply filing the papers necessary to reincorporate in a diverse state. *Compare Black & White Taxicab & Transfer Co. v. Brown & Yellow Taxicab & Transfer Co.*, 276 U.S. 518 (1928) (allowing corporation to reincorporate to create diversity), *with Morris v. Gilmer*, 129 U.S. 315 (1889) (holding that a human being must actually change his or her domicile to create diversity). Curiously, the Court continues to follow *Deveaux* with regard to unincorporated associations.

85 *Santa Clara Cnty. v. S. Pac. R.R.*, 118 U.S. 394 (1886) (allowing, in an unreasoned opinion, railroad corporations to assert a right to equal protection to void state legislation). It is, of course, quite contrary to usual American legal interpretative methods to read one word as switching meanings twice in two paragraphs (only human persons "born or naturalized" are counted for apportionment). Nor has anyone ever coherently claimed that the Civil War was fought to free business corporations. *See, e.g.*, Morton J. Horwitz, Santa Clara *Revisited: The Development of Corporate Theory*, 88 W. Va. L. Rev. 173 (1985). Extending Fourteenth Amendment rights to corporations, of course, limits the rights of the citizens and people whom the Amendment was meant to protect, since it reduces our ability to protect ourselves from corporate incompetence or overbearing. *Cf.* Ronald Dworkin, *Life's Dominion* (1993) (arguing that a state may not classify a fetus as a person without infringing on the competing rights of pregnant women).

ability to pay our mortgages and our credit cards, our pensions, all depend on our corporate affiliation.

Conversely, violations of our human rights are at least as likely from the corporations we work for as from our states. Corporations can dismiss us without a hearing; the state cannot. Corporations can search our desks without explanation or warning, or read our mail, or even prevent us from using our computers. As suppliers rather than employers, it is corporations, not our governments, that have decided that it is permissible to clog our computers with cookies.

Need I go on? If I could choose between being a lifetime employee of a major world corporation and having a passport, it seems clear to me that taking corporate protection would be more worthwhile. And if I had the choice of having protection against the City of Salt Lake's possible future depredations and those of my health insurance company, I'd much prefer rights against the latter. In the last election, many of our states banned gay marriage. But the effects on real people's real lives will be far greater if many of our major corporations decide to continue to give benefits.

Isn't it time we began to see our largest and most powerful bureaucratic actors as the public entities they are?

# Chapter 12

# Status, Contract, Identity, and Sovereignty: What the Romans Have to Tell Us About Family Property

David S. Rosettenstein

In an era of ever increasing global mobility, a significant challenge for those working in the family law arena is to forge an appropriate vision for the distribution of assets on divorce. The root of the problem is that in some jurisdictions family lawyers have become comfortable with protocols that depart from the traditional approaches adopted by property lawyers for identifying proprietary interests. While classic determinants may identify ownership rights during the subsistence of a marriage, at least in the United States, all bets are off once the marriage comes to an end. At one end of the spectrum are the status-imposed regimes of community property and equitable distribution. At the other lies a universe notionally regulated by contract.[1] Nowhere does title to property absolutely control the consequences for assets acquired during the marriage, although in some jurisdictions unique acquisition pathways, such as claims deriving from gift, devise, or descent, provide a well fortified defensive position.[2]

The justification for a departure from the proprietary approach, at least in the Anglo-American tradition, is the idea that the state is a third party at the distribution table. It alone is the ultimate arbiter of appropriate outcomes, both to guard its own interests and the interests of the principals in the soon-to-be-dissolved nuclear family.[3] Historically, this unique blend of sovereign self-dealing and paternalism led to resistance to the idea that the parties themselves could dictate outcomes by

1 *See, e.g.*, Brian Bix, *Bargaining in the Shadow of Love: The Enforcement of Premarital Agreements and How We Think About Marriage*, 40 Wm. & Mary L. Rev. 145 (1998).

2 *See, e.g.*, *N. J. Stat. Ann.* § 2A:34–23(h) (West 2009) (legislation aimed at ensuring that on divorce "family derived" assets are preserved for the source family).

3 Bix, *supra* note 1, at 172–3. Bix sees the historical perspective as one that includes a wealthy family as an additional principal. The contemporary reliance on prenuptial agreements involves other goals, linked either to an individual spouse or the state: (1) ensuring that children from a prior marriage retain certain family wealth, despite possible claims by the new spouse; (2) assuring that the economically weaker spouse-to-be will have adequate economic protection after divorce; (3) attempting to make any eventual divorce simpler and less contentious; and (4) assuring that certain family heirlooms or family wealth

agreement.[4] That resistance has faded, but even under the contemporary regime in which a majority of states in America accept the idea that property division on divorce is amenable to regulation by agreement, the sovereign has kept its thumb on the scale. Between analyses of the fairness of the process by which prenuptial agreements are entered into and of unconscionability imposed with reference to the time the agreement was executed or comes to be enforced, in no instance can the executing parties know for certain that their arrangements will be enforced.[5] In short, as between spouses, on divorce, neither title nor contract absolutely controls the allocation of assets.

While the above vignette may be depressing enough for conventional property lawyers, the situation becomes more confusing conceptually once one injects an international component into the analysis. European civil law systems may dictate spousal ownership rights both during the marriage and on its termination, or like the modern US system they may leave open a shift in ownership from formal title during the marriage to contingent entitlement on its termination. Additionally, civil law systems, through complex statutory shares structures, give a hint of the proverbial eight hundred pound gorilla lurking in the wings in the form of a world that contemplates that the ownership interests at stake may be as much those of the couple's respective families as they are of the individuals themselves.[6] Indeed, in this respect civil law systems are but the tip of the iceberg. Other cultures and traditions adopt as their key motivation the reinforcement, directly or derivatively, of the position of the family. The social objective is to protect the family's financial infrastructure.[7] This chapter sheds light on this global universe by spotlighting

---

stay within a family upon divorce. *Id.* at 150. The last item is the only one truly reflecting the concerns of the "family" as the Romans might recognize it.

4 Bix, *supra* note 1, at 151, 158.

5 *See* Unif. Premarital Agreement Act, 9C U.L.A. § 6 (2001). As of 2012, 22 states have adopted the Act.

6 *See, e g.,* Code civil [C. civ.] art. 914 (Fr.) (Act No. 72–3 of 3 Jan. 1972, protecting interests of ascendants in up to one half of a deceased's estate). French inheritance law was reformed by the *loi* of June 23, 2006, which removed the *reserve* in favor of ascendants who now can only inherit by bequest from the testator out of the disposable portion of the estate. *See* John Bell, Sophie Boyron & Simon Whittaker, *Principles of French Law* 262 (2d ed. 2008). For a detailed insight into the tension between the competing claims of family entitlements and testamentary autonomy in France, Germany, and the United States *see* Jens Beckert, *Inherited Wealth* 21–80 (Thomas Dunlap trans., 2008).

7 Of course the concept of a "family" in this context also is cultural. Thus, among the Bedouin of the Sinai and Negev deserts a man's primary financial obligation is to his clan by virtue of a system of collective responsibility. Clinton Bailey, *Bedouin Law From Sinai and the Negev* 60–100 (2009). If the wife is from another clan, on divorce she has to look to the resources of her clan. *Id.* at 77. But care is required in the analysis. It is possible to argue that such a system does not support the family in the narrow sense. Rather, it is part of a system requiring owners to internalize the social costs of using their property and in the process to adjust their behavior appropriately. *See* Raj Bhala, *Understanding Islamic*

the legal doctrine associated with the Roman law concept of *dos* (think "dowry" for time being; this is a rough and potentially misleading approximation). In so doing, we acknowledge that the boundaries of the historical evolution of Roman jurisprudence are more or less known, while our present juridical universe is currently at some indeterminate point in its development.

In America, property law doctrine did not crumble due to an attack from the outside. Rather the property regime for the most part caused its own irrelevancy to the process of distribution of assets on divorce. A rigid adherence to title-based principles produced intolerable outcomes in a world where families classically had one breadwinner and one house-spouse and where managerial competency was gender determined. The husband tended to be the sole title holder (certainly as to assets beyond the matrimonial home), and on divorce he reaped the rewards of title.[8] These rules and practices operated in an American social context of the nuclear family, which decoupled wives from their birth families. The overall combination of social and property law practices produced a post-divorce scenario in which former wives, not infrequently with children in their care, were left in straitened circumstances. Alimony awards (assuming there was one in the context of a fault-based divorce system) were unable to ameliorate the imbalance.[9] Accordingly, the state, driven both by concerns for the resulting burden on taxpayers,[10] and perhaps by a measure of compassion, intervened to force property distributions premised on notions of equity.[11] The property consequences of marriage shifted from the realm of property law to one of status-derived outcomes.

Unfortunately, the outer limits of equity are arbitrary. And arbitrariness breeds insecurity, especially when coupled with a world in which serial monogamy is a

---

*Law* 494–95 (2011). But on death Sharia law does seek to safeguard the interests of a broad range of family members. *Id.* at 1111, 1127–63.

8 *See Principles of the Law of Family Dissolution: Analysis and Recommendations* 647, 648 (2002) [hereinafter *Principles*].

9 *Id.* at 809–10.

10 In modern family law in America, this tax burden proposition is almost axiomatic, even if not necessarily rational, or underpinned by coherent theory, or implemented by logical rules. *See Principles*, *supra* note 8, at 25, 424789, 794. In this regard, and in many other contexts, the world currently is wrestling with issues relating to inter-generational financial obligations, both public and private. Interestingly enough, the European tradition, which is much more closely linked to Roman roots, increasingly is torn between concepts of private wealth and public burdens. See 14th Conference of International Society of Family Law, "*Generation solidarities*," http://www.law2.byu.edu/isfl/2011lyonconf/XIVe%20 CONGRES%20-%20programme%20-%20%20Projet%20_eng_.pdf

11 Community property systems, which nowadays are touted as paradigm vehicles for achieving gender equity, actually started life as a mechanism geared to protecting one spouse's separate property (and hence the property interests of that spouse's broader family) from the claims of the other spouse. *See The Visigothic Code* (Forum Judicum) 126–7, 642–3, 654 (S.P. Scott trans. & ed. 1910).

common practice and marriage for a lifetime is known to be an illusory datum.[12] While England for centuries has sought the security and certainty of property law embedded in a trust structure,[13] America has sought solace in contract, specifically prenuptial agreements.[14] Interestingly, these different techniques suggest different visions of entitlement—in the English case almost literally. In America, the vision of fortune is personal. The American dream after all is not one of inheritance from one's family, although the phenomenon of inherited wealth is not unknown.[15] In England, the vision is of the landed gentry whose entailed interests and other title-based claims ensured social certainty, if not material security, from generation to generation.[16] In England, to the visionaries of legal doctrine, the roots of personal identity are family identity, but not family identity alone. It is family identity conceptually rooted to the land. But, not just any land. The anchor of the identity was the family estate,[17] or at very least the region of the country where the family might claim an affiliation, albeit attenuated, was situated. Even if penury resulted in title to the landed estate ending up in the hands of the National Trust, the identity of the family estate, and the associated family, was thereby preserved in perpetuity.

In America, liquidation is the consequence of impoverishment, and even extends to the "family compound." Indeed the same fate may befall the compound when the title linkage to family members becomes too attenuated. The property owes its identity to the family members rather than vice versa. When attenuated

12 As of 2004, 22.9 percent of the US population over the age of 15 had been divorced once, 13.2 percent of the population had been married twice, and 3.1 percent of the population had been married three or more times. Since 25.8 percent of the population never married, the prospects for those who do are not too promising. US Census Bureau, *Number, Timing and Duration of Marriages and Divorces: 2004* (Table 3).

13 Rhys Williams, *Drugs peer faces blow to inheritance: Blenheim trustees move to tie up estate,* The Independent, Mar. 17, 1994, http://www.independent.co.uk/news/uk/drugs-peer-faces-blow-to-inheritance-blenheim-trustees-move-to-tie-up-estate-1429555.html (effort to put the business of affairs of Blenheim Palace into a trust to prevent them falling under the control of the Duke of Malborough's eldest son, Lord Blandford, who ordinarily would succeed to the estate on the death of his father). *See also* Beckert, *supra* note 6, at 69.

14 Bix *supra* note 1, at 153, 173. America has more easily accepted prenuptial regulation of the consequences of marriage ending by death rather than by divorce. This author speculates that one of the reasons was a concern to protect family property—apart from the argument that, unlike divorce, death is not seen as a subversion of the institution of marriage. In the American tradition, to the extent that there is a concern to protect *family property*, it is better described as a concern to protect *family wealth.*

15 Beckert, *supra* note 6, at 78. This author, citing various sources, estimates that in the United States between 600 and 900 billion dollars is transferred between generations annually. *Id.* at 14.

16 Beckert, *supra* note 6, at 69.

17 Primogeniture was, after all, designed to ensure the integrity of the real estate as it devolved.

linkage causes loss of identity the property comes on the market.[18] The benchmark in America is the bottom line division of wealth, not the allocation of specific assets. In this context all assets are seen as fungible rather than unique. Accordingly, it is less problematic for the state to dictate bottom line results as the consequence of marital status. Specifically, these are bottom line results with respect to the individual relicts of the dismantled nuclear family. They are not bottom line results with respect to "source" families. The emergence of prenuptial agreement treatments reflects an effort in the face of instability to produce security, not just as to resource preservation in the bottom line sense, but even more specifically as part of an effort to secure the integrity and continuity of assets and wealth as a source of family stability in an unstable world.[19]

## The Roman Construct

### *Background*

The Roman model was neither the English model nor the American model. The Romans had an interest in wealth as such and certainly real-estate as such. But, while Roman families did establish links to specific real estate, identity was premised on membership in a wealthy family, not ownership of the estate. Wealth without birth would not do. However, the converse also was true. And, the state's interest was omnipresent as well. Its objective, however, was the viability of the family, rather than the fairness or adequacy of specific material outcomes. The institution of *dos* gives us some insight as to how the Romans went about establishing their priorities. But first some background.

Classical Rome offers an interesting location for an analysis because operationally it evolved from a localized city to a multi-continental empire. Rome moved to peoples and cultures, and people and cultures moved to Rome. In the process, Roman law mutated from the law of a city-state to the law of the

18 A tension between family and the market is inevitable. Thus, Caroline Kennedy inherited her father's cottage in the "Kennedy compound" in Hyannis Port, but then sold it to her uncle, Edward, as she wished to vacation elsewhere, and he wanted to keep the property in the family.

19 *Radmacher v. Granatino,* [2010] UKSC 42 Eng.), is a nice example of this. A wealthy French woman married a German in England. The wife's family induced the couple to enter into a prenuptial agreement to ensure that none of her current or future wealth derived from her family would end up in the hands of her husband. The arrangement raised choice of law issues: which matrimonial property regime and controlling law would govern? The French family's efforts failed because of English law's reluctance to recognize the enforceability of prenuptial agreements. Presently England is considering a change in this law. *See* Law Commission, *Matrimonial Property, Needs and Agreements* (supplementary consultation paper published in 2012), http://lawcommission.justice.gov.uk/areas/marital-property-agreements.htm

known world. But this evolution did not flow directly from conquest and treaty. Rather conquest and treaty provided the opportunity for evolution. Potentially, the increasingly sophisticated Roman legal regime was available for imposition, adoption, or rejection. And everywhere there were families in various stages of social and legal recognition.[20] Additionally, Roman law provides us with perspectives unknown to Anglo-American jurisprudence, but which are not uncommon in other parts of today's world.

*The Role of the Family in Classical Rome*

Roman law begins life as a rigid formulaic system available only to Roman citizens. Its roots lay in the interests of the patricians,[21] who were various citizens of enhanced status. With the passage of time, the law assimilated the interests of the landed plebians,[22] who originally were inhabitants of conquered towns. The plebians in time became a group with the rights of citizens, including notably for our purposes the right to enter into legally recognized marriages. Moreover, these plebians obtained the right to hold property. But unlike the roots of patrician ownership of land, the plebian's property right was not based in clan (*gens*) membership,[23] even though when the outsiders gained citizenship status they were assigned to membership of a particular clan.[24] The patrician land ownership structure envisaged collective family ownership. In contrast, the premise of plebeian ownership was linkage of the asset and the individual. Still, with these foundations, whether land ownership flowed from the clan or existed discretely, the significance of family ties and the resulting link to land remained strong. Its potency was demonstrated when Servius Tullius, who ruled from 578 to 535 BC, reorganized the political structure of Rome, he grounded that reorganization on land ownership.[25] In due course (445 BC), plebians could even marry patricians.[26]

20 Rudolph Sohm, *The Institutes* 110 (James Crawford Ledlie trans., 3d ed. 1970) (1907). Sohm points out that when Roman citizenship ultimately became available to all Imperial communities in 212 AD), this effectively "laid the axe unto the root of every other law in the Empire." But the new citizens of the Empire really received a Roman law mutated and undergoing mutation by centuries of exposure to these other legal regimes. *Id.* at 114–16.

21 Technically, although the issue is somewhat obscure, the patricians in very early Rome probably were the elders of the clans composing the state. The patricians as a class were the descendants of these individuals. *Patricii* has been loosely, but informatively, translated as "father's sons." *Id.* at 34, 38.

22 *Id.* at 44.

23 *Id.* at 40.

24 *Id.* at 38.

25 *Id.* at 40–1.

26 *Id.* at 42 n.16.

Of course, who actually married whom involved an interplay among occupational prestige, power, legal status, and birth.[27]

So now patricians and plebians alike, as citizens, set about conquering the world, taking their common legal system, the *ius civile,* with them. In this process small landowners disappeared into a vassal-like relationship with the proprietors of *latifundia,*[28] who alongside a major merchant class now became the wielders of power within the state.[29] Socially, the upper classes needed their links to the land because engaging in mere trading (*mercatura)* was unacceptable to maintain a person's class standing. On the other hand, a person preserved his virtue if his commercial activity merely extended those activities traditionally identified with the "agricultural" sphere. In contemporary terms, we might see such a Roman as a "wheeler-dealer," that is, a trader on a grand scale (*magna et copiosa*), especially if he invested the trading profits in land-related pursuits.[30] At its height, the Roman Empire functioned as a cash economy,[31] but as the Empire waned, the *latifundia* went into self-sustaining economic isolation, leading to the imposition of the same economic regime on the cities. Then the state's economy depended on exchanges in kind.[32] But in the interim there was a thriving economy rooted by real and social necessity in the land, even as the interstices of the economy were solidly filled by routine commercial activities of a diverse nature.[33]

The keystone to Rome's political and economic success was its families. And a person's proprietary interests were subservient to the structure of that individual's family. As one author put it:

> A person's property [under Roman Law] is affected *in its entirety* both by the position he occupies in his family, and by its devolution on his death. Not only does the family affect the property of the individual during his life, but to the family is due the fact that, even after his death, his property continues to exist as a living whole.[34]

27 *See* P.R. C. Weaver, *Social Mobility in the Early Roman Empire: The Evidence of The Imperial Freedmen and Slaves, in* Studies in Ancient Society 121, 125 (M.I. Finley ed., 1974).

28 Literally, "broad estates." These were large landholdings worked by cheap labor, often slaves. The system of ownership spread throughout the Roman Empire as conquered land was exploited. *See* Sohm, *supra* note 20, at 45.

29 *Id.* at 45.

30 John D'Arms, *Commerce and Social Standing in Ancient Rome* 5–7, 23–5 (1981). At very least, status required classifying such persons as *negotiatores* rather than mere *mercatores*.

31 *Id.* at 149.

32 Sohm, *supra* note 20, at 45 & 45 n.4.

33 *See generally* D'Arms, *supra* note 30.

34 Sohm, *supra* note 20, at 159.

The relationship between family and property is critical because throughout the empire society was stratified based on family and wealth. The sons of senators were expected to end up as one of the six hundred or so senators, but to do so, apart from winning an election, the candidate had to be worth a million sesterces. The next down the rung, the *equites*, had to muster four hundred thousand sesterces before elevation to the class by the emperor. The next layer was composed of decurions, the top one hundred men in each city, who in terms relative to their city were well off, even if not absolutely so.[35] Social mobility existed, but was checked by some re-stratification over the centuries. The pace of upward mobility "must have been the slow climb of family over generations, not the rocketing climb of individuals."[36] Whatever the source of family wealth, the preferred investment was land.[37] In the nature of things real estate is less susceptible to accidental or malicious destruction; thus, it functions as a more appealing asset in troubled times. Indeed, the reason for the enactment of the *lex Claudia* (218 BC), which limited the capacity of ships owned by senators, may have been to prevent the sudden impoverishment of members of the ruling class.[38] Loss of property meant loss of status and political extinction.[39]

So, wealth mattered. But there were strings attached. Just any wealth would not do. There were only three socially acceptable methods by which an aristocrat could accumulate wealth—inheritance, *dos*, and government office.[40]

35 Keith Hopkins, *Elite Mobility in the Roman Empire*, *in* Studies in Ancient Society 103, 103 (M.I. Finley ed., 1974).

36 *Id.* at 117.

37 *Id.* at 104. This fact must have played a role in the legal constraints imposed on a husband alienating or encumbering land contained in the *dos*, or otherwise belonging to the wife. This protected her family's interest in the preferred investment class. *See infra* text accompanying note 99.

38 D'Arms, *supra* note 38, at 31–4. In reality, although the law remained in force for two hundred and fifty years, the upper reaches of Roman society found ways to exploit commercial opportunities, either directly or indirectly through the use of associates, through the broad umbrellas of *familia*, *clientela*, and *amicitia*. *Id.* at 39–47, 154. Who had to be included in these relationships evolved with the political structure of Rome. With an emperor at the helm, the relevant groups needed to include the emperor's favorites. *Id.* at 151–2.

39 Peter Garnsey, *Legal Privilege in the Roman Empire*, *in* Studies in Ancient Society 141, 147 (M.I. Finley ed., 1974).

40 Hopkins, *supra* note 35, at 118. One author has pointed out that the challenge for those seeking to preserve their social status was finding ways to exploit the economic opportunities available to them as members of a privileged class, while preserving a set of values that we might characterize as "non-economic." D'Arms, *supra* note 30, at 49. A senator should not, and sometimes could not, engage in *negotia*. An equestrian could. *Id.* at 61, 160. Family behavior among Roman aristocracy has displayed the same goals as other aristocracies through the ages: biological reproduction, transmission and extension of patrimony, and the diversification and expansion of symbolic capital. Mireille Corbier, *Divorce and Adoption as Roman Familial Strategies*, *in* Marriage, Divorce, and Children

These constraints were enormously important. To get political power, and not infrequently government office, the individual had to have both birth and wealth. Marriage and the associated *dos* could provide both the wealth and a suitable family connection—if not for the current generation, then at least for those following. We will now focus our attention on the topic of *dos*.

### *The Nature of* Dos *and its Relationship to Family Structure*

*Dos* was an essential ingredient of Roman marriages from the earliest days of the Republic. Basically, it was a contractual arrangement between the bride's *paterfamilias* or a third party[41] and the intended groom (or his *paterfamilias*).[42] The *paterfamilias* was the legal head of a Roman family. This *familia proprio iure* comprises all those individuals who were legally under the power of the *paterfamilias*. Technically, marriage and blood ties were irrelevant. The *paterfamilias* had power over all the issue of those who were in his power.[43] Among the plethora of powers of the *paterfamilias* was the ability to marry off, or prevent the marriage of, those in his power. He could regulate their divorce or give them in adoption. At first, the power tended to be absolute, but later practice recognized the wishes of dependents in some contexts.[44] Originally, the *paterfamiliae* arranged marriages in which the power over the wife was transferred to the husband's power structure (that is, there was a marriage *in manu*[45]). When the law developed to include a requirement of the bride and groom's consent, the requirement of the consent of any *paterfamilias* did not go away.[46] Indeed, in due course the groom's father would have to consent even if he was not at that time the groom's *paterfamilias*, because there was the possibility that on the death of a more removed *paterfamilias* the actual father would become the *paterfamilias* not just of the groom, but also of any issue of the marriage.[47] In short, the individual who possibly would have not just the power, but also the responsibility of a *paterfamilias*, was given the ability to limit his exposure.

---

in Ancient Rome 47 (Beryl Rawson ed., 1996). The ready availability of divorce in Rome presented a special opportunity in the achievement of these goals. *Id.*

41 Technically, *dos* provided by anyone who is not a paternal ascendant of the woman is treated as *dos* from a "third party" and is termed "adventitious." This technical classification included cases in which a woman *sui iuris* provided her own *dos*. As a social matter *dos* for a poor woman might be provided by wealthy relatives, friends, or patrons. *See* Bruce W. Frier & Thomas A.J. McGinn, *A Casebook on Roman Family Law* 75–6 (2004).

42 Sohm, *supra* note 20, at 465–6.

43 J.A.C. Thomas, *Textbook of Roman Law* 411–12 (1976).

44 *Id.* at 420.

45 *See infra* text accompanying notes 58–65.

46 After all, among the Roman aristocracy the purpose of marriage was familial alliance, not sex. Corbier, *supra* note 40, at 51.

47 Thomas, *supra* note 43, at 420–21.

On the death of the *paterfamilias* those immediately under his power became *sui juris*.[48] They became *paterfamiliae* in their own right—well almost: On the death of a woman's *paterfamilias* she became *sui juris*, but always remained under the guardianship of another male.[49]

Sovereign power concerns were reflected in blanket prohibitions, such as those restricting civil marriages to those between two Roman citizens and between a citizen and some specially privileged inhabitants of the Italian peninsula living close to Rome and other foreigners.[50] The roots of this rule probably were only technical. A valid marriage required the ability to rely on the *ius civilis*, which was only available to Roman citizens. Later issues of social prejudice came to the fore. The integrity of the underlying social structure was protected by various provisions in force at different times; for example those prohibiting marriages between members of the senatorial class and plebians, freemen or freewomen, and even actors.[51] Extension of marriage restrictions, however, has a negative impact on the Roman population. In time the state so needed a "citizen" population that it made the right to marry generally available after the *Constituio Antoniniana* in 212 AD.[52] Overall, the sovereign's primary objective seems to have been class-based procreation.[53]

Originally a dependant *(filius)* had no proprietary capacity,[54] but beginning with the Empire it was possible for the dependant to acquire a *peculium* which, depending on its character, might become the *paterfamilias*'s property on the death of the *filius*. However, in due course, the *peculium* could become the *filius*'s alone, free of any right of succession by the *paterfamilias*, if it came to the *filius* on the death of a mother. This rule was subsequently extended to other acquisitions by the *filius* not derived from the *paterfamilias*. Ordinarily the income from the *peculium* was the *paterfamilias*'s, and if the *filius* was emancipated by the *paterfamilias* the *paterfamilias* kept a significant portion of the capital. Otherwise, the *paterfamilias* could not alienate or appropriate the capital, and on the *paterfamilias*'s death the *peculium* went to the dependant *filius*.[55] On marriage, the wife if she was *sui juris*

48 *Id.* at 413.

49 *Id.* at 447, 463–5; Sohm, *supra* note 20, at 490–92.

50 Thomas, *supra* note 43, at 421.

51 *Id.* at 422. The sovereign's need for an undistracted soldier required, until about 220 AD, that a soldier on service could not marry. Similarly, the integrity of the provincial administration led to the prohibition of high officials in that administration (and their sons) from marrying women of the province. The duty to the state should not be subverted by a competing loyalty. *Id.* at 423.

52 *Id.* at 421.

53 The significance of social status is nicely demonstrated by the elaborate rules regulating whether a woman retained the designation as *clarissima* (translatable as most famous, illustrious, or eminent) after divorcing a person of that rank. Frier & McGinn, *supra* note 41, at 97.

54 Sohm, *supra* note 20, at 177, 484.

55 *Id.* at 485; Thomas, *supra* note 43, at 416–17.

(that is, not under the power of a *paterfamilias*), kept her own property, unless she married *in manu*, an arrangement discussed in the next paragraph; otherwise she remained subject to the constraints of her family. Inter-spousal gifts were banned.[56] Marriage alone did not confer a right of intestate succession, and only later did the law recognize that spouses owed each other limited duties of mutual support.[57] This framework aimed to preserve the integrity of the family's property arrangements. The principal function of the marriage was to forge power relationships among individuals and over property.

Older Roman marriage law involved marriages *in manu*. In these situations, the wife moved from the power structure of her family to the power structure of the husband's family. He or his *paterfamilias* became her *paterfamilias*.[58] In the early years, the *in manu* structure probably was an element of all Roman marriages.[59] Such property as the wife previously owned, or acquired later by means such as inheritance, transferred to the husband's *paterfamilias,* or her husband, as the case might be.[60] But, unlike a wife not married *in manu*, she acquired a right of intestate succession to her husband.[61] Over time a number of forces undermined this basically simple arrangement. On the one hand, the formal loss of power to an "alien' family became unacceptable to well-born women.[62] After all, when her original *pater* died, an unmarried woman would be *sui iuris*—essentially her own legal person. Why relinquish this prospect for one where she might be in the power of her husband for a protracted period? Moreover, the women who stayed in their original family found their autonomy increasing. Until the time of Hadrian, a woman still in her original family had no authority to execute a will. The traditional objective was that on her death her assets should revert to her *agnates*, that is, those family members who were or would have been subject to the "power" of a common male ancestor. This process might be subverted if she had the testamentary capacity to will property to others. Tutelage, at least in the form of the nearest agnate's *tutela legitima*, was the legal construct by which the

56 Thomas, *supra* note 43, at 424.

57 *Id.* at 424–5.

58 Sohm, *supra* note 20, at 459–60; Thomas, *supra* note 43, at 446–7.

59 Thomas, *supra* note 43, at 446. After all, a marriage *in manu* might emerge from the parties acting as husband and wife, that is, if he enjoyed the rights and performed the duties of a husband. After one year, *usus* conferred that status on him, even after a forcible abduction of the woman. Sohm, *supra* note 20, at 517–18. Technically, *manus* was theoretically separate from the marriage itself, but the power transfer normally occurred synchronously with it. Susan Treggiari, *Divorce Roman style: How Easy and how Frequent was it?*, in Marriage, Divorce, and Children in Ancient Rome 31 (Beryl Rawson ed., 1991).

60 *Tituli ex Corpore Ulpiani* (*Ulpiani Regularum Epitome*) (*Ulp. Reg.*) 19.18–19. The precise boundaries of the transfer of property are unclear. In some instances various assets seem amenable to treatment as *dos*, but in others not. *See* Jane F. Gardner, *Women in Roman Law & Society* 71 (1986).

61 Sohm, *supra* note 20, at 509.

62 Thomas, *supra* note 43, at 447.

guardian was given the means to protect his contingent expectancy.[63] But in due course Roman law came up with a mechanism for enabling a woman to exchange a traditional guardian for a powerless one.[64] Essentially then, we see parallel processes at work in which, over time, a woman acquired more autonomy within her agnatic family and more independence from her husband. So not surprisingly, by the late Republic marriage *in manu* had become unpopular, and by the time of Gaius (c. 150 AD) the concept disappeared.[65] With wives now able to preserve their relative autonomy outside of the husband's family, what became of the *dos*?

*Dos* was a property contribution made by a bride, or others acting on her behalf, pursuant to a marriage contract.[66] In one vision of things it was her contribution to the upkeep of the household.[67] This purpose was advanced when a significant component of the *dos* consisted of real estate. The normally steady returns from such assets furnished a more secure foundation on which to maintain the household, contrasted, say, with the returns on trading operations.[68] One public policy justification, or perhaps rationalization, for the existence of the *dos* structure was that it facilitated the procreation of children and thereby the necessary

63 *Id.* at 454. Technically, even if a woman was *sui iuris*, that is, she had the right to manage her own property, she lacked the power to engage in certain juristic acts without the assistance of a guardian. One of these activities was the execution of a will. Sohm, *supra* note 20, at 490. In certain instances a married woman producing sufficient children was freed from tutelage. *Id.* at 478. Presumably, this emancipation reflects an instance in which the state's sovereign interest in increasing the birthrate outweighed the family's interest in controlling the fate of its property.

64 The mechanism was a collusive *coemptio*, *id.* at 491 n.2; Thomas, *supra* note 43, at 447, 464.

65 As a technical matter, its disappearance was facilitated by the process of displacing the formal procedures of the *ius civile* (the law only available to Roman citizens) with the informal procedures of the *ius gentium* (the law applicable to aliens). *Manu* was a prerequisite of the former but not the latter. Sohm, *supra* note 20, at 456–7.

66 At first the law required formal documentation of the property transfer. Ultimately (428 AD), if the essence of the agreement for the *dos* was clear, technical wording was not prescribed. Intent transcended formality. Tony Honoré, *Law in the Crisis of Empire 379–455 AD*, at 114 (1998). Accordingly, if the parties had no express agreement but the *dos* nevertheless was provided, the transfer was presumptively valid. Code Just. 5.13.1a.

67 Thomas, *supra* note 43, at 428. The concept is captured by the phrase *onera matrimonii*. Technically, a husband had no duty to maintain his wife. Dig. 24.3.22.8 (*Ulpianus, libro trigesimo tertio ad edictum*). However, although the authority just cited dates from the late classical period, 190–235 AD, there is evidence that by 529 AD the text had been reworked to allow a court to order the husband to support an insane wife to an extent justified by the magnitude of the *dos*—at least where he allows the marriage to subsist so that he can continue to enjoy the *dos*. *See* Frier & McGinn, *supra* note 41, at 128, 145. Even here, the court might not have been enforcing a duty to support. Rather, because her insanity prevented her from procuring a divorce and thereby regaining control of her *dos*, the court order might reflect the result she would have obtained but for the incapacity.

68 *See* D'Arms, *supra* note 30, at 32.

replenishment of the state.[69] Presumably, the interest related to procreation in the context of marriages when there was *connubium* (that is, the capacity to contract a marriage), for only these marriages produced citizen children. With some exceptions, *connubium* did not exist with purported marriages between citizens and foreigners.[70] The sovereign's interest was restricted to the question of whether there was a valid marriage because it needed to know whether children were legitimate. The state also was interested in the transmission of property, and thus it was necessary to know whether a particular piece of property constituted an element of the *dos*. This, too, implicitly required one to know if there was a valid marriage. But, the state had no interest in the establishment or termination of the marriage as such. The relevant issue was what became of the property when the marriage terminated.[71] As a result, it is the Roman jurists' discussion of *dos* which is our principal source of information about Roman marriages and divorces.[72]

The purpose and effect of the *dos* contract was to effect a transfer of substantial wealth from the bride's family to that of the groom. Such a property transfer to the husband's family pursuant to a marriage might be acceptable in an environment where this arrangement was part of the glue solidly cementing political ties between socially relevant families[73]—if this relationship was enduring. But the ability of the wife to retain an identity outside of the husband's family tended to produce instability in the arrangement. Moreover, more powerful forces—death and divorce—were at work.[74] Roman law sprang into action to prevent a

69 Dig. 24.3.1 (*Pomponius, libro quinto decimo ad Sabinum*).

70 G. Inst. 1.78–80.

71 Not surprisingly, then, the phrase *tuas res tibi habeto* is encountered in Roman divorces. Treggiari *supra* note 59, at 35.

72 *Id.* at 33.

73 Thus, even allowing for the fact that after a divorce a husband no longer had to find the resources to support his wife, the loss of the revenues produced by the *dos*, or of the liquid capital made available by the *dos*, might be a significant consideration. *Id.* at 39. Indeed, not only would *dos* tend to cement families together, it also could empower the wife. *Dotata mulier virum regit* goes the old aphorism. Q. Horatius Flaccus, Carmina, Liber Tertius 24, at 21–2. However, the leverage available to the wife dissipated among families in lower economic classes, where there was a greater risk that the *dos* would have been consumed or invested in a way that precluded extraction. *Id.* The power a wife possessed sometimes included her ability to choose to limit the number of children she would bear, given that she might live in a competitive salon culture for which she would not want to spoil her figure. Hopkins, *supra* note 35, at 118. This fact, coupled with the incentive to lower birthrates to protect family wealth and high mortality rates, actually left the upper class cohorts underpopulated and hence made some places available for new arrivals. *Id.* at 118–20. But these deflationary pressures on the upper class population fostered a public policy to develop a legal regime that encouraged "suitable" marriages to produce legitimate offspring. These concerns, in turn, supported the evolution of *dos*-related legal doctrine.

74 We lack statistical information, but can glean something through historical narratives read through contemporary eyes. Treggiari, *supra* note 59, at 4–6. We do know that divorce was a datum dealt with routinely in arrangements regarding *dos*. *Id.* at 41;

possible naked transfer of wealth from one family to another without any long-term compensating political and economic advantages.

### *Controlling* Dos *by Contract*

*Basic principles* In the earliest days of *dos* the property outcome flowed from status and the change in status. As the wife moved from one power structure to another, so did the property. But this raised a problem. How could families manipulate the consequences for the property in a manner that did not subvert marriage as a mechanism for advancing the fortunes of Rome's social elites, while at the same time avoid putting the elite's wealth at needless risk? The key was to shift the control mechanism from status to contract. The traditional view of the status of marriage *in manu* stood in the way. Now Roman law seized upon the vehicle of the *dos* contract as the device which would give the contracting parties the opportunity to price the risk-rewards structure and implicitly achieve optimum efficiencies. A status-related structure might be good at bulk results, but in individual cases produce inappropriate consequences and cost inefficiencies.

Roman law accomplished this shift from regulation by status to regulation by contract in a context in which the sovereign itself had an interest in the outcome. The state wanted the marriage to produce offspring to repopulate the upper echelons of society; this process was seen as the key to maintaining the stability of the state.[75] The state's interest in the generation of legitimate children justified the principle in place by the end of the second century that a *paterfamilias* who wrongfully prevented children in his power from marrying or who refused to provide *dos* could be compelled by proconsuls or provincial governors to arrange marriages for the children and provide the *dos*.[76] The principle did not bar an objection to a particular marriage, but sought to deal with the *paterfamilias* who thought that the fruits of the assets that would fund any *dos* should remain in

Corbier, *supra* note 40, at 58. One estimate puts the divorce rate for the senatorial class as approximating the divorce rate in England in the mid-twentieth century, with the ambitious families' rates approximating American frequencies. According to one calculation, the chance was one in six that a first marriage for senators and equestrians would end in divorce within ten years, and that this rate matched the rate at which marriages terminated by death in this period. Treggiari, *supra* note 59, at 45–6. On the basis of these estimates, concerns about the reversion of *dos* would arise in one third of marriages within ten years of the marriage's inception. Because of the first-marriage age differential between husbands and wives in the upper classes, for them the first marriage more likely would end with the death of the husband. Corbier, *supra* note 40, at 55. Apart from divorce and death of the husband, it was necessary to plan for the contingency of the wife's death, in childbirth or otherwise. In seventeenth century Europe, a woman had around a 1 percent chance of dying with each birth, but that after five confinements she had around a 5 percent chance of dying in childbirth. *Id.* at 55 n.4.

75 Dig. 24. 3. 1 (*Pomponius, libro quinto decimo ad Sabinum*).

76 *Id.* 23. 2. 19 (*Marcianus, libro sexto decimo institutionum*).

his hands. Such a *paterfamilias* opposed any marriage. Although the sovereign interest was procreation, from the families' perspective the emerging principle may have served as a mechanism by which those in power could enhance the spoils of government office by effectively enforcing inter-family wealth transfers, at least as to income from the *dos*. Of course, today, we might suggest an economic public interest rationale that the inter-family wealth transfer was required because the current owner of the asset was not fully exploiting it and thus was doing Rome a disservice—in much the same way as the English economy in the nineteenth century was crippled by having so much land tied up in family trusts.

It should be borne in mind that the Roman state's primary concern was the production of children. The state did not really display an interest in the preservation of any specific marriage. The ready availability of divorce coupled with the institution of *dos* meant that the man's remarriage to another source of *dos* provided a mechanism to inject liquidity into the economy. Before the divorce the husband might deplete the *dos* from the first marriage, even if it was notionally returnable. After all, a family might be reluctant to spend its own resources, but a husband would be less inhibited about deploying the resources of others. Actually, the state wanted to get two bites at the apple. If the husband met resistance in exploiting the *dos*, he could divorce the wife and marry a more amenable financier, while the former wife with the *dos* more or less intact would be more able to find an alternative spouse[77] and thus advance the state's interests through the new marriage's offspring.

At a basic level, however, the state's sovereign interests were limited. The first concern was an appropriate marriage which produced appropriate legitimate offspring. Then the state's concern was to know to whom property belonged. This meant knowing whether there were legitimate offspring to whom the assets would pass on death, and knowing whether particular property fell inside the *dos* so that one could determine to whom it belonged once the marriage ended.[78] Beyond these matters, the state had little interest in the success or failure of any particular marriage, both as to social and economic consequences. These were issues within the domain of family "sovereignty." While they were marginally relevant to the state, they remained more important to the individuals involved.

At the private level, the availability of a substantial *dos* certainly greased the wheels for a potential marriage. Because the resources came from the family, they undoubtedly were employed to advance that family's fortune, either through the political arena by opening the door to potentially lucrative public offices or

---

77 *See* Corbier, *supra* note 40 at 52; Dig. 23.3.2 (*Paulus libro quarto decimo ad Sabinum*).

78 To this end, the phrase *tuas res tibi habeto* is encountered in Roman divorces. Treggiari, *supra* note 59, at 35.

through the economic arena by providing the inter-*familia* human framework with which to exploit economic opportunities.[79]

So how did Roman law go about making this shift from status to contract? The ready availability of divorce led the *dos* settlor by contract either to obtain a stipulated value for the *dos*, which amount was then repayable in the event of a divorce, or to obtain a stipulation from the husband as to what he would do with the *dos* if the marriage ended.[80] For our purposes, what is significant is that the individual families by agreement were able to control the outcome, presumably in their own interests.[81] In principle, too, this mechanism provided an opportunity to decouple family interests from wealth interests, overriding a rigorous *in manu* environment that moved the person and the wealth together. Put another way, in the face of a status-derived legal construct, the *dos* agreement mediated the outcome.[82] The significance of the agreement is highlighted by a conceptual shift: by about 200 AD even if formally the *dos* was the husband's, conceptually it was seen as the wife's.[83] The scope of her entitlement was defined by the agreement. Moreover, the husband's ability to subvert the agreement by neglecting or harming the *dos*' corpus became regulated by law.[84] As early as 18 BC the husband could not alienate land included in the *dos* if the wife did not consent, notwithstanding the

79 *See* D'Arms, *supra* note 30, at 58. This may resemble the nineteenth century family-based European banking alliances.

80 Thomas, *supra* note 43, at 429.

81 However, there were some practical limits to contractual freedom due to an overarching concern not to reduce the *dos* itself. *See, e.g*,. Dig. 23.4.2 (*Ulpianus libro nono decimo ad Sabinum*); *id.* 23.4.5.2 (*Paulus libro septimo ad Sabinum*); *id.* 23.4.6 (*Ulpianus libro quarto ad edictum*).

82 Because the *dos* agreement impacted the sovereign's interests reflected in the status rules, it was important to know *which* sovereign's interests the agreement impacted. To this end Roman law provided a choice of law rule applicable to the *dos* contract. Dig. V.1.65. (*Ulpian, Ad Edictum* 34). The original Latin version is ambiguous. It unequivocally states that a *dos* contract is not like a conventional contract, which is governed by the law of the place of execution. Rather, the applicable law is either the law of the place where the woman would reside with her husband, or, in an alternative translation, it is the law of him with whom she would reside. Technically, the ambiguity makes little difference for our purposes. The significant point is that it is necessary to identify which sovereign's rule-based structure is impacted. A fourteenth century commentator on Roman law, Bartolus de Saxoferrato, *Bartolus on the Conflict of Laws* (reprint 1979) (J.H. Beale trans., 1914), uses the example of a *dos* contract executed in Assisi where, if a wife dies without children, statute law allows the husband to keep a third of the *dos*. But in Perugia, where the husband comes from, a statute says the husband will take half. Bartolus takes the position that the latter statute will control. *Id.* §§ 19, 20. The contract controls the content of the *dos*, but the Perugia statute defines the extent of the husband's entitlement, that is, it implicitly limits the husband's power because notionally all the *dos* had become his.

83 Dig. 23.3.75 (*Tryfoninus, libro sexto disputationum*).

84 *Id.* 23.3.17 pr. (*Paulus, libro septimo ad Sabinum*); *id.* 24.3.24.5 (*Ulpianus, libro trigesimo tertio ad edictum*).

fact that he had taken formal title. By Justinian's time, indeed, he could not use the land as security for debt, even with her consent.[85]

*Death and* dos On death, any agreement governing *dos* operated in a more restricted zone. With one of the principals dead, the family link became more fragile. If the wife died first, the so-called *profectitious dos* (that is, *dos* deriving from her father or grandfather) returned to the source, less a retention of a fifth for each child.[86] *Dos* from another source, called *adventitious*, remained with the husband unless, at the time of its creation, the grantor stipulated for its return.[87]

This structure seems designed to encourage *dos* giving, while advancing the interests of the respective families. Post-mortem, the family ties no longer so effectively bound, so the assets potentially were returnable,[88] while taking into account that the presence of children left ties, and responsibilities, for the father's family in whose power they would reside.[89] Correspondingly, where the *dos* was adventitious (that is, not from the wife's direct power line), the structural preference shifted to the husband's line unless the source of the *dos* had sufficient leverage to negotiate for its return on the wife's death.

If the husband died first, his power line had little to offer for the future. In principle, the *dos* returns to the wife, who, as the law evolved, was not married *in*

85 G. Inst. 2.62–63; J. Inst. 2. 8 pr.

86 This fits into the bigger vision that until 178 AD (*Senatus consultum Orfitianum)* children did not succeed their mother if she died intestate. Her heirs were her agnates. But she could name her children in her will, and ultimately seems to have been under considerable pressure to do so. So much so, that an appeal to a magistrate became possible on the basis that the failure to devise to the child was negligent. Corbier, *supra* note 40, at 54.

87 *Tituli ex Corpore Ulpiani* (*Ulpiani Regularum Epitome*) 6. 4–5.

88 When the daughter died, the law "assisted the father by returning the *dos* to him, lest he suffer the loss of both a daughter and his wealth." Dig. 23.3.6 pr. (*Pomponius libro quarto decimo ad Sabinum*). Stated more realistically, the father recaptured the funds because he should not have to provide a financial subsidy for an inter-family association that no longer existed.

89 When a marriage produced children, unless there was an agreement to the contrary, the husband retained a portion of the *dos* under a variety of different scenarios. Apart from the superficial justification that there were children to support, it is obvious that family ties remained at some level, even if the children were now in the father's family's power structure. The importance of locating children in families is illustrated by the *pontifices*, the original sources of Roman jurisprudence who were legal advisors to the court. Their profession was restricted to members of the patrician class and practiced in secret. Sohm, *supra* note 20, at 88–9. The secretive class monopoly started to erode about 300 BC, and around 254 BC. Tiberius Coruncanius became the first plebeian *pontifex maximus*. *Id.* at 89–90. In a formal sense, the power of birth notionally succumbed to the power of merit when Augustus allowed a person not a *pontifex* to give a legal opinion. Thereafter, Emperor Tiberius and those succeeding him made it a practice to identify who had the privilege to give authoritative opinions. *Id.* at 92–3.

*manu* and thus would have to rely on her own family relationships. It is noteworthy that these rules applied even if the parties attempted to agree to the contrary.[90] Arguably, the sovereign interest sought to advance the appropriate family power interests over the parties' personal interests. The temptations of the flesh of the immediate participants to the marriage could not be allowed to subvert the wife's family's interest in protecting its wealth after the link to the husband's family was lost.[91] The wife's family members' interests were deeply entrenched. This is not too surprising, given the impact that the transfer of the *dos* often had on the family's residual wealth. Accordingly, we find a rule which required a wife, who had a right to recover her *dos* on the dissolution of her marriage, to include the value of that *dos*, if it came from her father or grandfather, in that person's deceased estate hotchpot, called a *collatio,* for the purpose of determining the successors' distributable shares.[92]

When no agreement regulated the return of the *dos*, with time, a *praetor* (magistrate) was authorized to order the return of a fair and equitable portion of the *dos* when a husband unjustly divorced a wife or when the marriage ended on his death.[93] In this context, the *praetor*'s zone of operations for the most part was confined to dealing with the *dos* as the parties by agreement had constituted it. Moreover, at this stage there was no sovereign interest to protect taxpayers from being called upon to support a destitute former spouse. This may be little simplistic because the structure undoubtedly was in place to protect the interests of Rome's powerful families, and the welfare of the state was inextricably interwoven with the well-being of these families. In this regard, what the *praetor* perceived as being *in bonum et aequum* might well have been influenced by broader political considerations, rather than issues of inter-family justice. After all, the *praetor* was an elected political creature (during the Empire exclusively by the Senate).[94] Parenthetically, it might be noted that the *praetors* probably were

90 Dig. 24.3.15.1 (*Paulus, libro septimo ad Sabinum*); *id.* 23.4.2 (*Ulpianus, libro nono decimo ad Sabinum*); *id.* 33.4.1.1 (*Ulpianus, libro nono decimo ad Sabinum*).

91 On a related theme, if a parent remarried after the death of the other parent, any property which the remarrying parent had received from the deceased spouse, by whatever legal vehicle, became the property of the children of the first marriage, immediately on the remarriage. Sohm, *supra* note 20, at 477. The "source family" interests were protected against potential threats from interlopers.

92 *Id.* at 564–5. Originally, the object of this requirement was to redress inequalities among the deceased's survivors that stemmed from a lack of capacity to acquire property on the part of those not *sui juris*. Later on, the rule served to override advantages conferred by the deceased during his lifetime, but the deceased could dictate that he wished the preference to remain. *Id.* at 565.

93 Thomas, *supra* note 43, at 429.

94 *Id.* at 15, 17.

"money sensitive" because at least some of them had to finance their operations out of their own resources.[95]

*Preserving the* dos *corpus* The rules regulating *dos* protected the families' interests ahead of the interests of the individual spouses. This proposition is supported by the limitations on *retentiones*, which were deductions the husband legitimately could make prior to return of the *dos*. The aim was to ensure the financial integrity of the *dos* itself. The system desired not only that the *dos* end up in the right place, but to the extent possible that the source recovered as much of the *dos* as possible. The husband's interests, as such, were subordinated to those of the financing family or its surrogate.[96]

The regulatory infrastructure covering the use and return of the *dos* became quite sophisticated in dealing with those situations not controlled by any underlying agreement.[97] As the law evolved, it became highly likely that an identifiable individual would hold a contingent reversionary interest in the *dos*. Thus, it became necessary to ensure that there was an interest to revert. When the marriage ended and the disposition of the *dos* was not regulated by agreement, a wife *sui juris*, or her paterfamilias with her consent, became entitled to recover the *dos* subject to "adjustments" reflecting administrative expenses[98] and fault, either economic in misappropriating assets or with respect to the marriage.[99] Although the husband was entitled to administrative expenses and the profits of the *dos*, his ability to alienate the assets was restricted. Italian land could not be alienated or charged without the wife's consent,[100] and by the time of Justinian, the wife generally was incapable of consenting to any such action with respect to any land.[101] During these times land, whether urban or rural, provided the foundation of family power.

---

95 As one author has put it "Men were returned to office occasionally for personal merits ...., more often by reason of their munificence and lavish bribes, in general because of their family and connections." P.A. Brunt, *The Roman Mob, in* Studies in Ancient Society 74, 76 (M.I. Finley ed., 1974). The "great houses" could afford to provide rent-free lodgings, and magistrates might distribute grain or oil at low prices, subsidizing the distribution out of their own pocket. *Id.* at 90. Such subsidies were pervasive. By the first century, the number of recipients of free grain in the city, limited to males over the age of fourteen, had risen to 320,000. *Id.* at 80, 102 n.84. The population of the Empire as a whole at this time was around fifty million. Hopkins, *supra* note 35, at 108.

96 Dig. 23.3.17 pr. (*Paulus, libro septimo ad Sabinum*); *id.* 24.3.24.5 (*Ulpianus, libro trigesimo tertio ad edictum*).

97 Thomas, *supra* note 43, at 429.

98 The husband could recover expenses incurred to prevent the *dos* from losing value, but not luxury expenses. *See* Frier & McGinn, *supra* note 53, at 177, 181–2, 185.

99 Thomas, *supra* note 43, at 429–30.

100 In time, "Italian" assets were seen as part of one's permanent holdings as distinct from one's "provincial" holdings. *See* Dig. 28.5.35.

101 G. Inst. 2.62–3; J. Inst. 2.8 pr.

Allowing fault to be considered suggests a concern to advance personal interests—but only one suspects up to a point. When the marriage ended because of the husband's fault, the *dos* in its entirety reverted. After all, why tempt a husband to both precipitate the end of the marriage and walk away with some of the *dos*? The wife's family would lose both the political benefits of the union and the assets! When the wife was at fault, the consequences differed according to whether the parents had children. If the marriage ended because of the wife's or her *paterfamilias*' fault, depending upon the number of children, up to half the *dos* could be retained by the husband.[102]

Fault primarily involved activities which brought discredit on the family or perhaps families, such as treason or kidnapping, or acts which represented a betrayal of the marriage, such as adultery or attempted murder.[103] When there were children, the fact that the children would remain in the father's power, and a burden to his family, would justify the wrongdoing wife's *dos* sharing that burden. Where fault was that of the wife's *paterfamilias*, the destruction of the inter-family symbiosis would justify the retention.

Interestingly, when there were no children, the wife's serious immorality justified the loss of a one-child equivalent of the *dos*, that is, one sixth.[104] One explanation is the injection of a sovereign interest into the equation; namely, the advancement of morality, a likely enough goal given the hold Christianity took on the Empire. But equally supportive of the penalty was that the cuckolding of the husband devalued his family. The state's sovereign interests might lie in protecting the reputation of that family.[105] Gaius, writing as early as 160 AD, described the details of actions arising from a wife's immorality.[106] About 50 years later, the Digest attributes to Paulus the proposition that the parties could not by agreement contract away the ability to sue for misconduct or vary the penalty "*ne publica coercitio priuata pactione tollatur.*"[107] We now have a sovereign interest in public moral standards, although perhaps the public interest was to deter conduct that adversely impacted important private families, independently of the moral values themselves. The potential forfeiture of part of the *dos* provided the incentive to maintain important social relationships and thus had broader political objectives beyond those of morality.

---

102 *Tituli ex corpore Ulpiani* (*Ulpiani Regularum Epitome*) 6.9.

103 *See* Frier & McGinn, *supra* note 53, at 175.

104 *Tituli ex corpore Ulpiani* (*Ulpiani Regularum Epitome*) 6.12. Thomas, *supra* note 43, at 430.

105 Thus, Augustus sent a notice of divorce to Vipsania (Augustus' daughter) on behalf of Tiberius, her husband (who was "out of town" in Rhodes at the time), divorcing her on account of her "misbehavior." The object seems to have been to protect Tiberius' reputation; otherwise it would seem that Augustus might have been able to act in his own right as *paterfamilias*. *See* Treggiari, *supra* note 59, at 34.

106 G. Inst. 4.102.

107 "Otherwise private pacts would remove the right to public punishment." Dig. 23.4.5 (*Paulus libro septimo ad Sabinum*) (Mommsen trans.).

The concept of *dos* called upon the "bride's side" to transfer wealth to the groom's side. As time passed, the necessary mechanisms developed to protect the bride's side property interests, at least within limits. But, what if the bride's family power was truly significant? We might assume that mechanisms would develop which made possible a wealth transfer from the husband's side to that of the wife. And, indeed, this is precisely what occurred. While gifts between spouses were prohibited, gifts in anticipation of the marriage were not. What emerged in the later Empire was known as a *donatio ante nuptias*. This was a gift that lay beyond those flowing from mere affection. Rather, the gift was intended to lay the financial foundation for the married household, using resources from the husband's family. It became a wealth transfer to the wife's side because in the event of divorce, not arising from her fault, the wife was entitled to demand that the *donatio* actually be paid over to her. Operationally, the arrangement was regulated by agreement. Thus, the husband could enter into a covenant to pay the *donatio*. This covenant was then used to fund the wife's *dos*.[108] This process led to the husband's premarital "gift" being subject to the contractual rules and the overarching regulatory laws relating to the *dos*. This, in turn, made it possible for the wife's side to extract from the marriage, when it ended, those assets flowing from the husband. Again, we have a situation where the families' contractual arrangement mediates the legal outcome to advance the interests of the family, within limits imposed by a regulatory umbrella.[109]

*Justinian reforms* With Justinian in the sixth century the evolution of the law regulating *dos* came to an end. What was apparently agreed to was presumptively valid.[110] But if nothing was agreed to, and the wife's family nevertheless provided *dos*, a stipulation would be implied. And, not just any stipulation, but a stipulation such as might be drafted by the leading jurists.[111] Additionally, and this would be the ultimate refinement, a stipulation governing *dos* was recharacterized. No longer was an action adjudicating *dos* rights regulated by strict law. Henceforth, the action was cloaked in equity.[112] This imported the centuries of experience gained identifying just results when adjusting the power interests at stake where the person, the family, and the sovereign crossed paths.

The Justinian reforms abolished the traditional rule that forced a widow to choose between taking under her husband's will and recovering her *dos*.[113] Other shifts also advanced the interests of a wife's family. They might buy their way into

108 A *donatio ante nuptias in dotem redacta*. Sohm, *supra* note 20, at 473–4.

109 A choice of law rule developed to provide some protection to the husband's family who transferred wealth to the wife. The husband's legal regime controlled the legal terrain. Dig. V.1 65 (*Ulpian, ad Edictum*); *see supra* note 82.

110 Code Just. 5.13.1a.

111 *Id.* 5.13.1d, c.

112 *Id.* 5.13.2.

113 *Id.* 5.13.3.

the husband's family with a *dos*, and from the match extract it and an inheritance to boot. If the husband had appointed his wife as an heir, the *dos* was deducted from the estate, and *then* her quarter share of the estate as demanded by the *lex Falcidia* was calculated.[114] Indeed, Justinian expedited the recovery of the *dos* in favor of the wife's heirs.[115] If the wife predeceased her husband, the heirs recovered the *dos* unless there was an agreement to the contrary.[116] The role of retentions against the *dos* was restricted, most notably by abolishing the portion to be withheld on account of children. Instead, the duty to support children arose by "nature," not as a consequence of resources generated by the *dos*.[117] This more expansive vision of the wife's family manifested itself in another requirement in place by 449 AD When the *dos* was forfeited due to the husband obtaining a divorce on the limited grounds recognized by the law, the husband was bound to preserve that *dos* for the benefit of the couple's children on the husband's death.[118]

Reforms also recognized the realities of family function. Previously, the husband could retain funds against the *dos* principal only when he incurred necessary expenses, but now he could recover both for useful expenses and for expenses incurred just for the wife's benefit.[119] Formalistic rigor gave way to relational reality, accomplished by equity's supplementing of the law.

A paradigmatic manifestation of Justinian's relational approach is the softening of a husband's obligation to return the *dos* on dissolution of the marriage. In the absence of an agreement to the contrary, as long as the husband did not act fraudulently, he was required to repay only as much as he was able, subject to his giving a further undertaking that if his financial condition did improve, he would pay the balance.[120]

Justinian also comprehended that over time the wife's legal identity had evolved to the point where her property claims were entitled to greater protection[121] to the potential disadvantage of both her own family members and outsiders.[122] So her entitlement to the *dos* was recognized at the expense of the grantor's other

114 *Id.* 5.13.8.

115 *Id.* 5.13.4.

116 *Id.* 5.13.6.

117 *Id.* 5.13.5c.

118 *Id.* 5.17.8, 4, 7.

119 *Id.* 5.13.5e. He could retain mere "ornamentation" made on his initiative if he could do so without injuring the property. *Id.* 5f.

120 *Id.* 5. 13. 7.

121 Indeed, an earlier law (450 AD), motivated by gender equity, held that a husband should not meddle with his wife's separate property that was not part of the *dos*, even if it was a good idea for a wife to entrust the management of her affairs to her husband. Honoré, *supra* note 66, at 174.

122 The vision of the wife's marriageability as an asset of her family (that is, her lack of autonomy) was significantly eroded in 380 AD when it was recognized that a wife with sufficient resources had not only the right to buy herself out of a forced engagement, but also an action in equity against those who had forced her into the engagement. *See id.* at 42.

heirs.[123] Indeed, in the absence of express stipulation to the contrary, where the *dos* came from outside her male agnatic line, she was presumed to be the ultimate beneficiary of the *dos*.[124]

Nevertheless, there were limits to the extent that Justinian would trust a woman's autonomy, at least vis-a-vis her husband. She could waive her rights to his assets,[125] but she could not consent to the alienation or hypothecation of her *dos*.[126] Presumably, the bright line was drawn to protect the contingent interests of *dos* providers, siblings, and heirs. Moreover, relational autonomy had limits. Relative family interests were not to be neglected. Thus, a widow who remarried "prematurely" could only recover social standing if she turned over half of what she received from the deceased to their children.[127] And the children, of course, remained in the deceased father's family. One could not engage in personal gratification or opportunism while reaping "excessive" rewards to the detriment of the former husband's family in the face of his fortuitous (or otherwise) death. Also, a post-marriage blended family as a collective was vulnerable to the misdeeds of a *dos* contributor. A *dos* from a traitor was void from the moment he entered the conspiracy. The result was that the property reverted to the estate of the traitor and thus was amenable to forfeiture to the imperial treasury.[128] Talk about using material incentives for families to keep each other on the straight and narrow, in the sovereign's interests, if not necessarily those of the polity.

## Conclusion

*Dos* was a key element of the social, political, and economic structure of Rome. Accordingly, it is not surprising to find a considerable body of legal material describing its foundations. What is interesting, and perhaps surprising, is the

123 Code Just. 5.13.11, 14, 14.

124 *Id.* 5.13.13b.

125 *Id.* 5.13.15c

126 *Id.* 5.13.15, 15a, 15b. But a balance was struck between the sexes. After 381 AD the husband no longer had to provide security for the return of the *dos*, HONORÉ, *supra* note 66, at 49, perhaps because the corpus was increasingly protected, and expenditures from *dos* resources were increasingly permitted. The risk of inter-family exploitation, however, was always present. A widow who remarried was restricted in her ability to petition for the right to administer the affairs of the children of the first marriage. *Id.* at 62. About fifty years later, the motivations of a remarrying father also became suspect. *Id.* at 160. This perhaps reflects the emergence of the child, at least in some measure, from under the umbrella of the "family."

127 Honoré, *supra* note 66, at 43.

128 *Id.* at 88–9. Justinian abated the harshness of the forfeiture rules to the extent that property of freedmen determined to be traitors would only be forfeited to the treasury if there were no surviving children of the condemned man. Dig. 48.5.9 (*Hermogenianus, libro quinto iuris epitomarum*).

manner in which Roman jurisprudence worked and reworked the concept of *dos* in a difficult environment in which the universes of personal, familial, and sovereign power intersected. Although the role of *dos* was precipitated by a social event—a marriage—that social event originally triggered a legal status change, the shift of the wife from her family's power structure to the husband's family's power structure. Intuitively and wisely, reflecting a combination of attributes which Roman jurisprudence seems to display with regularity, Roman law recognized that the sovereign's interests lay in the creation of children of the appropriate social classes. The existence of a facilitative legal environment for the regulation of *dos* advanced that goal. But equally intuitively and wisely, Roman law recognized that the content of the *dos* arrangement was something in which the state had little interest. Indeed, given the fact that the efficiency of any arrangement was not something that the state could readily determine, Roman law stayed its hand. The situation was to be regulated by agreement. The true parties in interest, the respective families, were best situated to develop the roadmap for dealing with the contingencies of life.

At most, the state's jurisprudence provided default settings for the families' roadmap. As Roman law evolved through the centuries, it increasingly recognized that suitable default settings could not be described in absolute terms. Rather, the premise was equity, fairness in the circumstances, as reasonable and honest people might understand that to be. Even here, Roman law was quick to recognize that the concept of fairness could not encompass a sovereign interest, for if it did, the over-weighting of that interest might destroy the utility and social function of *dos*. Of course the subtext of political influence must have been omnipresent, but it was a subtext with which the citizenry were at least familiar, if not totally comfortable. *Dos* remained viable only because Roman citizens became secure in the notion that they had autonomy to define the parameters of their complex financial arrangements, and were equally secure in the notion that sovereign-supplied elements would conform to their parameters. The *dos* contract could not provide a platform for the introduction of a status, especially a status reflecting the state's interests.

So much for history. As indicated at the outset, domestic American jurisprudence views wealth as personal. In the context of divorce, the state imposes outcomes, or evaluates outcomes called for by prenuptial agreements, on the basis of the state's perception of the relative priority of its own claims and the equitable interests of the divorcing spouses. In the ordinary course the spouse's family members' interests are not weighed in the analysis. Traditionally, to merit protection family interests have to be decoupled from the spouses before the marriage. If not decoupled, the family resources can be used to subsidize an ex-spouse, because the inter-spousal equities justify doing so. This outcome may seem appropriate to an extended family long exposed to the American vision of the family that prioritizes the nuclear family and assigns post-divorce financial responsibility on the basis of this prioritization. The legal regime seeks to provide adequate resources to the *individuals* surviving the divorce, and at very least to keep these individuals from the taxpayers' door. The American law has no sense, as did the Romans, that the relevant post-divorce burden to consider was that of the family of origin of the resources.

This scheme of things is highly problematic to families, nuclear or otherwise, newly arrived at "Liberty's" feet. For many foreign communities the vision of burdens and benefits flowing from a marriage is little removed from that of the Romans. Marriages represent alliances, for a multitude of purposes, between families. Financial and social burdens and benefits, both within and beyond the marriage, often link to the family, not the individual. And, as a result, any effort by the jurisprudence of an American state to adjust these burdens and benefits, or even indeed just to evaluate their merits, is an effort that potentially is deeply flawed—at least from the families' perspectives, and similarly so from the perspective of the individual spouses who may be little removed culturally from their source families. Nor need the analysis be warped by a vision of spouses recently emerging from a semi-feudal society. The French system of community of acquests excludes from the community's grasp property acquired before the marriage and that obtained through inheritance, a structure that reflects a residual "clan embrace" that surely is rooted in Rome, if not earlier.

Roman jurisprudence's pragmatism was highly deferential to the risk/reward structure developed in negotiations between the families. True, in some respects the sovereign's interests then, looked at through our eyes, may appear less urgent and less complex than the sovereign's interests today. But we probably cannot say the same of the perceptions of a Roman observer. Turning the analysis around, to a newly Americanized family today, the interests and needs of the marriage participants' families might be seen as more urgent and compelling than those of the participants, never mind those of the state.

What is to be done? Given the obvious intrinsic efficiencies of individualized judgments made by the specific families involved, the law should afford a high degree of deference to their arrangements. Even the Romans acknowledged that families might be short sighted, or employ no sight at all, and that circumstances might change. But the solution they imposed was to interject solutions that the families might have provided, had they consulted the best available jurists. Today, a conceptually possible, although sometimes technically difficult approach, is to defer to the original families' vision of the interests affected by the marriage after accommodating the state's essential needs. In this regard, the debate over public finances in the current economic climate suggests that the state's sovereign interests might be shifting back to a model that more resembles that of the Romans.

In the contemporary world, we have become comfortable with drawing a distinction between creating an obligation for a social entity to satisfy, and the separate issue of who or what is to provision that obligation. In reality, the public sector tends to provision many of the obligations, but the price for provisioning routinely is imposed on the private sector. This structure tends to be a source of friction, both because of the potential for a divergence of opinion between the public and private as to the marginal utility of those resources used to provision the state-imposed obligation, and because the private sector perceives its resource acquisition costs to be greater than those of the public sector.

Certainly, as current doctrine holds, the state cannot tolerate parties to a marriage (whether the spouses or their extended families) by their agreement burdening the taxpayers, at least in the absence of a coherent framework for allocating the public and private costs of family breakdowns in the light of the benefits to both sectors. That topic is for another day. But beyond this, as the well of the public purse runs dry, the debate is turning to the question whether public policy should permit or encourage the aggregation of wealth in a social class of limited membership. The Romans accepted such a purpose because they perceived that a social/wealth based class structure was essential for the continuity of the state. The contemporary American debate seems to lie along the lines of whether large aggregations of wealth are critically necessary for the economic viability of the state—independently of the issue of who are the holders of that wealth. If such an accumulation of wealth is desirable, the sovereign interest of the state might lie in reinforcing a legal platform that resembles that of the Romans. This platform would leave it to the agreement of the families, nuclear or extended, to optimize the economic benefits and hence wealth aggregation or protection associated with marriage. In a society notionally devoid of senatorial classes and the like, the elements of any such contractual exchanges should provide interesting grist for sociologists' mills. Is it possible that in such an environment a Capitol Hill might just morph into a Capitoline Hill?

# Index

For Product Safety Concerns and Information please contact our EU
representative GPSR@taylorandfrancis.com
Taylor & Francis Verlag GmbH, Kaufingerstraße 24, 80331 München, Germany

www.ingramcontent.com/pod-product-compliance
Ingram Content Group UK Ltd.
Pitfield, Milton Keynes, MK11 3LW, UK
UKHW022010180926
475701UK00003B/283
*9780367601096*